Essentials of Cognitive Grammar

Essentials of Cognitive Grammar

Ronald W. Langacker

OXFORD
UNIVERSITY PRESS

OXFORD
UNIVERSITY PRESS

Oxford University Press is a department of the
University of Oxford. It furthers the University's objective
of excellence in research, scholarship, and education
by publishing worldwide.

Oxford   New York

Auckland   Cape Town   Dar es Salaam   Hong Kong   Karachi
Kuala Lumpur   Madrid   Melbourne   Mexico City   Nairobi
New Delhi   Shanghai   Taipei   Toronto

With offices in

Argentina   Austria   Brazil   Chile   Czech Republic   France   Greece
Guatemala   Hungary   Italy   Japan   Poland   Portugal   Singapore
South Korea   Switzerland   Thailand   Turkey   Ukraine   Vietnam

Oxford is a registered trade mark of Oxford University Press
in the UK and in certain other countries

Published in the United States of America by
Oxford University Press
198 Madison Avenue, New York, NY 10016,
United States of America

© Oxford University Press 2013

Library of Congress Cataloging-in-Publication Data
Langacker, Ronald W.
Essentials of cognitive grammar / Ronald W. Langacker.
p. cm.
Includes bibliographical references and index.
ISBN 978-0-19-993735-6 (alk. paper)
1. Cognitive grammar.   I. Title.
P165.L355 2013
415--dc23   2012020305

INTRODUCTION

Cognitive Grammar is a theoretical framework for describing language structure as a product of cognition and social interaction. It is central to the broad and growing movement known as cognitive linguistics, which in turn is part of the "functionalist" tradition. The essential notion is that grammar is meaningful (not an independent formal system) and can only be revealingly characterized in relation to its conceptual import and communicative function. When first introduced over three decades ago, Cognitive Grammar represented a fundamental challenge to the reigning theoretical orthodoxy. To some extent this is still the case, but the field has evolved to the point that many basic ideas are now either widely accepted or at least deemed worthy of consideration. The linguistic scene today is crowded with theories, methods, and approaches no one of which has any real claim to primacy. Increasingly, however, the insights and findings of cognitive-functional approaches are exerting their influence on the view of language entertained by linguists, other scholars, and the general populace.

This book responds to the need for an introduction to Cognitive Grammar that is reasonably comprehensive, up-to-date, and accessible. The need was first addressed by the publication in 2008 of *Cognitive Grammar: A Basic Introduction* (CGBI). The present volume can be thought of as CGBI-lite. It is not a new work, consisting rather in the first half of CGBI (parts I and II), reprinted with only minimal adjustments for sake of consistency. Being intended for a wide audience and to serve a number of purposes, CGBI is too long, and in places a bit too technical, for many potential readers. Its organization does however accommodate different backgrounds and levels of interest: parts I and II are somewhat less demanding and were written to stand alone as a presentation of the theory's nature and essential descriptive notions. The result is the book you are holding: *Essentials of Cognitive Grammar* (ECG).

Suitable for a one-semester course, ECG provides a less daunting introduction to Cognitive Grammar for students at the graduate or advanced undergraduate level. It is relevant and accessible for a wide range of language professionals, while for linguists it offers a presentation of the theory that is relatively brief yet reasonably comprehensive. For readers inspired to explore the framework in greater depth, there is no lack of further material, including a number of general treatments: the two volumes of *Foundations of Cognitive Grammar* (1987, 1991); *Concept, Image, and Symbol* (1990); *Grammar and Conceptualization* (1999); and *Investigations in Cognitive Grammar* (2009). For convenience, these are referenced in the text as FCG1, FCG2, CIS, GC, and ICG.

Also available, of course, are parts III and IV of CGBI, which show the framework's descriptive adequacy by applying it to a broad range of basic grammatical phenomena. Chapter 9 discusses "grounding": grammatical indications of how entities described linguistically relate to the speaker, the hearer, and the speech event. Nominals are grounded by elements like articles and demonstratives, clauses by tense and modality. Other aspects of nominal and clausal structure are dealt with in chapters 10 and 11. The former deals with modifiers, classifiers, number, gender, inflection, and derivation. Considered in the latter are the semantic characterization of subject and object, their semantic roles in the clausal event, voice alternations (pertaining to their choice), and the incorporation of clausal elements as part of the verb. Chapter 12 examines complex sentences: coordination and the various kinds of subordination. Of special interest are expressions invoking multiple conceptualizers, each apprehending some portion of the overall content from their own perspective. The topic of chapter 13 is discourse: how it relates to grammar; its dependence on a shared "conceptual substrate"; discourse "genres"; and the building through discourse of complex conceptual structures. Finally, chapter 14 explores two general aspects of cognition essential for understanding grammar. The first is dynamicity: linguistic structures, residing as they do in processing activity, are neither static nor instantaneous—they occur through time, and their temporal manifestation is critical to their import. The second is disengagement: while cognition is grounded in sensory and motor interactions, much of the mental world we construct goes far beyond such experience. The capacities leading to this disengagement also give rise to grammar, which is thus a key to conceptual analysis.

The content of these "missing" chapters is necessary for a full understanding and proper assessment of Cognitive Grammar. At the same time, these chapters presuppose the content of the present volume, which is more readily apprehended when first presented independently. As its title implies, ECG covers the essentials. Part I gives an overview of the framework and presents a conceptual view of linguistic meaning. Part II shows how a conceptual semantics makes possible a symbolic account of grammar: like lexicon (with which it forms a continuum), grammar consists in symbolic relationships between semantic and phonological structures, and is therefore inherently meaningful. Despite being extracted from a larger work, these two parts constitute a coherent, self-contained introduction affording a good initial appreciation of the theory, its viability, and the unification it achieves.

CONTENTS

PART I

MEANING AND SYMBOLIZATION

Orientation

$\mathbf{O}$ur topic is the linguistic theory known as **Cognitive Grammar**. This framework offers a comprehensive yet coherent view of language structure, with the further advantages (I would argue) of being intuitively natural, psychologically plausible, and empirically viable. It is nonetheless a decidedly nonstandard view for which orthodox training in linguistics gives little preparation. A presentation of Cognitive Grammar must therefore start by articulating its general nature and basic vision.

1.1 Grammar and Life

Having spent most of my life investigating grammar, I am quite aware that this passion is not shared by the general populace. Let's face it—grammar has a bad reputation. For most people, it represents the danger of being criticized for breaking arcane rules they can never quite keep straight. In foreign-language instruction, grammar is often presented through mechanical exercises, the learning of irregularities, and the memorization of seemingly endless paradigms. Even in linguistics, it is commonly portrayed in a manner hardly designed to inspire general interest: as a system of arbitrary forms based on abstract principles unrelated to other aspects of cognition or human endeavor.

It doesn't have to be that way. Grammar is actually quite engaging when properly understood. Linguists, of course, are concerned with describing language, not prescribing how to talk. They are not responsible for the artificial strictures enforced by would-be grammar police. While grammar does require the learning of many forms, the same is true of lexicon, which inspires much less dread and is often a source of wonder and amusement. Furthermore, portraying grammar as a purely formal system is not just wrong but wrong-headed. I will argue, instead, that **grammar is meaningful**. This is so in two respects. For one thing, the elements of grammar—like vocabulary items—have meanings in their own right. Additionally, grammar allows us to construct and symbolize the more elaborate meanings of complex expressions (like phrases, clauses, and sentences). It is thus an essential aspect of the conceptual apparatus through which we apprehend and engage the world. And instead of being a distinct and self-contained cognitive system, grammar is not only an integral part of cognition but also a key to understanding it.

The meaningfulness of grammar becomes apparent only with an appropriate view of linguistic meaning. In cognitive semantics, meaning is identified as the conceptualization associated with linguistic expressions. This may seem obvious, but in fact it runs counter to standard doctrine. A conceptual view of meaning is usually rejected either as being insular—entailing isolation from the world as well as from other minds—or else as being nonempirical and unscientific. These objections are unfounded. Though it is a mental phenomenon, conceptualization is grounded in physical reality: it consists in activity of the brain, which functions as an integral part of the body, which functions as an integral part of the world. Linguistic meanings are also grounded in social interaction, being negotiated by interlocutors based on mutual assessment of their knowledge, thoughts, and intentions. As a target of analysis, conceptualization is elusive and challenging, but it is not mysterious or beyond the scope of scientific inquiry. Cognitive semantics provides an array of tools allowing precise, explicit descriptions for essential aspects of conceptual structure. These descriptions are based on linguistic evidence and potentially subject to empirical verification.

Analyzing language from this perspective leads to remarkable conclusions about linguistic meaning and human cognition. Remarkable, first, is the extent to which an expression's meaning depends on factors other than the situation described. On the one hand, it presupposes an elaborate **conceptual substrate**, including such matters as background knowledge and apprehension of the physical, social, and linguistic context. On the other hand, an expression imposes a particular **construal**, reflecting just one of the countless ways of conceiving and portraying the situation in question. Also remarkable is the extent to which **imaginative** abilities come into play. Phenomena like metaphor (e.g. *vacant stare*) and reference to "virtual" entities (e.g. *any cat*) are pervasive, even in prosaic discussions of actual circumstances. Finally, these phenomena exemplify the diverse array of **mental constructions** that help us deal with—and in large measure constitute—the world we live in and talk about. It is a world of extraordinary richness, extending far beyond the physical reality it is grounded in.

Conceptual semantic description is thus a major source of insight about our mental world and its construction. Grammatical meanings prove especially revealing in this respect. Since they tend to be abstract, their essential import residing in construal, they offer a direct avenue of approach to this fundamental aspect of semantic organization. Perhaps surprisingly—given its stereotype as being dry, dull, and purely formal—grammar relies extensively on imaginative phenomena and mental constructions. Also, the historical evolution of grammatical elements yields important clues about the meanings of their lexical sources and semantic structure more generally. The picture that emerges belies the prevailing view of grammar as an autonomous formal system. Not only is it meaningful, it also reflects our basic experience of moving, perceiving, and acting on the world. At the core of grammatical meanings are mental operations inherent in these elemental components of moment-to-moment living. When properly analyzed, therefore, grammar has much to tell us about both meaning and cognition.

1.2 The Nature of the Beast

The beast is Cognitive Grammar—CG for short. Some linguists view it with disdain, as it challenges fundamental dogmas and requires alternative modes of thought and analysis. Of course, others like it for just that reason. But whether they are positive, negative, or in-between, most opinions of CG appear to be formed on the basis of a strikingly limited (and often quite erroneous) understanding of it. Even its central claims and basic character are commonly misportrayed. So we need to get a few things straight at the outset.

1.2.1 An Outrageous Proposal

As its name implies, Cognitive Grammar is first and foremost a theory of **grammar**. Rather surprising, therefore, are statements to the effect that "Langacker doesn't believe in grammar—everything is semantics." Rest assured that CG neither threatens nor denies the existence of grammar. Grammar exists. The issue is rather the **nature** of grammar and its relation to other dimensions of linguistic structure.

CG's most fundamental claim is that grammar is **symbolic** in nature. What does this mean, exactly? Let us first define a **symbol** as the pairing between a semantic structure and a phonological structure, such that one is able to evoke the other. A simple lexical item, such as *skunk*, is thus symbolic because it resides in the pairing between a meaning and a phonological shape. Grammar, of course, is concerned with how such elements combine to form complex expressions. The basic tenet of CG is that nothing beyond symbolic structures need be invoked for the proper characterization of complex expressions and the patterns they instantiate. More specifically: **lexicon and grammar form a gradation consisting solely in assemblies of symbolic structures.** An immediate consequence of this position is that all constructs validly posited for grammatical description (e.g. notions like "noun", "subject", or "past participle") must in some way be meaningful.

This is not at all how grammar is viewed in modern linguistic theory. Received wisdom—repeated in every linguistics textbook—holds that notions like noun and subject are purely grammatical constructs not susceptible to any general semantic characterization. Moreover, the reigning theoretical orthodoxy claims that syntax is **autonomous**: that it constitutes a separate linguistic "module" or "component", distinct from both lexicon and semantics, whose description requires a special set of syntactic "primitives". Against this background, the CG position stands out as radical if not heretical. In the words of one distinguished critic: "Many readers will no doubt feel the same sense of outrage at this claim that I did, and I still believe that it is wrong" (Hudson 1992: 507–508).[1]

---

[1] This critic does admit that I make "a surprisingly good case for it" (Hudson 1992: 508).

I have no doubt that this reviewer really did feel a sense of outrage and that other linguists share it. And to the extent that it causes outrage, the position is indeed outrageous. That does not make it wrong, however. It may only indicate that the distorting lenses of contemporary linguistic theory and professional training are able to disguise the very real sense in which the position is both natural and intrinsically desirable. If language serves a symbolic function, establishing systematic connections between conceptualizations and observable phenomena like sounds and gestures, it would seem both natural and desirable to seek an account such that grammar is itself symbolic. If notions like "noun" and "subject" are universal and fundamental to grammar, it would seem both dubious and implausible to deny them a conceptual raison d'être. From a naive perspective (i.e. for those who lack linguistic training), it is hard to fathom why our species would have evolved an autonomous grammatical system independent of conceptual and phonological content. Is it not more reasonable to suppose that grammar, rather than being separate and distinct, is merely the abstract commonality inherent in sets of symbolically complex expressions?

Assessments of CG's central claim have been clouded by confusion on several points. One source of confusion is chronic ambivalence concerning what is meant by "autonomy". A strong version of the autonomy thesis holds that syntactic description requires a special set of purely grammatical primitives, which are not reducible to anything more fundamental. CG denies this by claiming that all valid grammatical constructs are symbolic, hence reducible to form-meaning pairings. A weaker version of autonomy merely asserts that grammar cannot be fully predicted from independent factors (notably meaning and communicative constraints). This weak formulation is fully compatible with CG, and indeed, with virtually every brand of cognitive and functional linguistics. Few would disagree that semantic and functional considerations constrain and motivate grammatical structure but do not completely determine it—speakers still have to learn the specific patterns of their language, and linguists have to describe these explicitly. It should be evident that the weaker version of autonomy does not entail the stronger one: whether grammar is **predictable**, and the **types** of elements needed to describe it, are very different issues. Linguistic theorists sometimes confound them, however, by taking the nonpredictability of grammar as establishing autonomy in the broader sense.[2] This overlooks the possibility of grammar being unpredictable yet fully describable as assemblies of symbolic structures.

Although the reduction of grammar to symbolic assemblies achieves an important conceptual unification, some theorists worry about the fate of syntax. One critic complains that CG "denies it even the status of a definable area within the larger whole of language" (Harder 1996: 260). This erroneous statement betrays a double confusion. First, it confuses the definability of syntax with the existence of a clear and definite boundary. Overlap among lexicon, morphology, and syntax does not prevent us from defining them and drawing useful distinctions, any more than the absence of a precise boundary between green and blue condemns

---

[2] I call this the **type/predictability fallacy**. A prime example is Newmeyer 1983.

us to seeing only grue—a gradation does not imply undifferentiated homogeneity. Second, the statement confuses reduction with elimination. Reducing grammar to symbolic assemblies serves to characterize it, not to deny its status as a definable level of organization. One does not deny the existence of water molecules by analyzing them as consisting in a particular configuration of hydrogen and oxygen atoms.

1.2.2 What Is CG Really Like?

Language is shaped and constrained by the functions it serves. These include the **semiological function** of allowing conceptualizations to be symbolized by means of sounds and gestures, as well as a multifaceted **interactive function** involving communication, manipulation, expressiveness, and social communion. **Functional** approaches to linguistic investigation are most basically distinguished from **formal** ones (notably generative grammar) in terms of whether functional considerations are taken as being **foundational** or merely **subsidiary** to the problem of describing language form. In practice, this matter of emphasis translates into very different substantive claims about the nature of linguistic structure and how to describe it.[3]

Cognitive Grammar belongs to the wider movement known as **cognitive linguistics**, which in turn is part of the functional tradition. Besides CG, important strands of cognitive linguistics include **construction grammar**, **metaphor theory**, the study of **blends and mental spaces**, and various efforts to develop a **conceptualist semantics**. Among other major components of functionalism are **discourse-pragmatic** analyses, the study of **grammaticalization**, and **universal-typological** investigation via cross-linguistic surveys.[4] Naturally, terms like "cognitive linguistics" and "functionalism" are fluid in reference and subsume a diverse array of views. There is at best a broad compatibility of outlook among the scholars concerned, certainly not theoretical uniformity.

A question commonly asked is: "What is **cognitive** about Cognitive Grammar? Or about cognitive linguistics in general?" These do not merit the label merely by proclaiming that language is part of cognition and that linguistic investigation contributes to understanding the human mind—that much is shared by many approaches, both formal and functional. Then what links to cognition do distinguish cognitive linguistics from either formal linguistics or other strains of functionalism? Within functionalism, cognitive linguistics stands out by emphasizing the semiological function

---

[3] See Langacker 1999b. The difference is not a matter of rigor, precision, degree of formalization, or scientific merit. Formal and functional approaches both vary widely along these parameters.

[4] I can do no more than cite a few basic references. For construction grammar, see Fillmore 1988; Goldberg 1995; Croft 2001. For metaphor theory, see Lakoff and Johnson 1980; Lakoff and Turner 1989; Grady, Taub, and Morgan 1996; Kövecses 2000, 2005. For blends and mental spaces, see Fauconnier 1985, 1997; Fauconnier and Sweetser 1996; Fauconnier and Turner 2002. For conceptualist semantics, see Vandeloise 1991; Wierzbicka 1996; Talmy 2000a, 2000b; Tyler and Evans 2003; Hampe 2005. For discourse-pragmatics, see Hopper and Thompson 1980; Givón 1983; Du Bois 1987; Chafe 1994; Lambrecht 1994; Verhagen 2005. For grammaticalization, see Traugott 1982, 1988; Heine, Claudi, and Hünnemeyer 1991; Heine 1997; Hopper and Traugott 2003. For universals-typology, see Givón 1984; Bybee 1985; Croft 1990; Talmy 1991; Kemmer 1993; Haspelmath 1997.

of language. It fully acknowledges the grounding of language in social interaction, but insists that even its interactive function is critically dependent on conceptualization. Compared with formal approaches, cognitive linguistics stands out by resisting the imposition of boundaries between language and other psychological phenomena. Insofar as possible, linguistic structure is seen as drawing on other, more basic systems and abilities (e.g. perception, memory, categorization) from which it cannot be segregated. Rather than constituting a distinct, self-contained entity (a separate "module" or "mental faculty"), language is viewed as an integral facet of cognition.

As for CG in particular, care is taken to invoke only well-established or easily demonstrated mental abilities that are not exclusive to language. We are able, for example, to focus and shift attention, to track a moving object, to form and manipulate images, to compare two experiences, to establish correspondences, to combine simple elements into complex structures, to view a scene from different perspectives, to conceptualize a situation at varying levels of abstraction, and so on. Can general abilities like these fully account for the acquisition and the universal properties of language? Or are specific blueprints for language wired in and genetically transmitted? CG does not prejudge this issue. We are evidently born to speak, so it is not precluded that language might emerge owing to substantial innate specification peculiar to it. But if our genetic endowment does make special provisions for language, they are likely to reside in adaptations of more basic cognitive phenomena, rather than being separate and sui generis. They would be analogous in this respect to the physical organs of speech.

Despite its functional nature, CG shares with formal approaches the commitment to seeking explicit characterizations of language structure.[5] For various reasons our capacity to achieve them is subject to strong inherent limitations. Nevertheless, a functional account of language has little chance of proving revealing and empirically adequate unless it is based on reasonably precise and detailed linguistic descriptions. At the same time, I believe that optimal description requires a functional perspective.

The components of a comprehensive functional theory can be conceptualized as a three-level pyramid. The first and lowest level specifies the resources available for describing linguistic structures. Ideally, this inventory of descriptive constructs would enable one to properly characterize any structure encountered in any language. Research in CG has aimed primarily at justifying particular constructs by examining diverse phenomena in numerous languages. If the descriptive inventory is adequate for all structures in all languages, it will necessarily define a very large space of possibilities, many reaches of which are sparsely populated. The second level of the pyramid deals with the "warping" of this space, such that linguistic structures tend to cluster in certain areas while generally avoiding others. A major goal of functional theory is to specify the "attractors" in this space, i.e. the range of structures that are **prototypical** in language, as well as their degree of prototypicality. Cross-linguistic research on typology and language universals is clearly essential for producing a reliable enumeration. Finally, the third and top level of the pyramid

---

[5] CG is thus considered by some functionalists to be a formal model. Formalists tend not to make that mistake.

consists of functional explanations for empirical findings at the second level. Proposing such explanations (e.g. by offering discourse motivation for aspects of clause structure) has been a basic occupation of functional investigation.

While each higher level in the pyramid logically presupposes the lower ones, in practice research at the three levels must proceed simultaneously. By emphasizing the foundational level, CG has been more concerned with structural description than with prototypicality and functional explanation. The theoretical proposals and specific descriptions of CG are, however, envisaged as being embedded in an overall account that encompasses all three levels. Descriptions of particular constructions are not meant to be freestanding, for in themselves they offer no indication of how or to what extent the constructions are functionally motivated. It is only by combining the functional and the descriptive dimensions that we arrive at a full understanding of grammatical phenomena.

Expositions of CG have perhaps not sufficiently emphasized its place within an overall functional account. This has no doubt abetted the common misconception that CG is unconstrained and makes no predictions. If anything, just the opposite is true. This may not be evident given the focus on basic descriptive apparatus: a set of constructs sufficiently flexible to describe the full range of linguistic structures (even the most atypical ones) is unlikely, in and of itself, to be highly constraining. CG's restrictiveness has other sources. A primary source is the information provided at higher levels of the pyramid—that is, enumerations of what is prototypical in language, and why. In my view, positive specifications of this sort offer the proper means of imposing restrictions (since explicit prohibitions are endless and often porous). By stating what **does** tend to occur in language, we implicitly indicate what tends **not** to occur. More precisely, by specifying the location and strength of attractors in the space of structural possibilities, we inherently make predictions about the relative likelihood of particular kinds of structures being encountered in a given language, hence about their cross-linguistic prevalence.

It is not true, then, that CG is unconstrained. I likewise reject the related misconception that I and others misled by me are given to positing wild and fanciful things limited only by the scope of our imagination. The theory and the research are actually notable for their down-to-earth nature, and in §1.3.4 I elucidate the severe restrictions imposed on what can be postulated. For some reason CG appears especially prone to being misapprehended. Competent scholars have confidently but gratuitously asserted, for example, that CG cannot handle metaphor (it can), that it does not account for ungrammaticality (it does), that it is solipsistic (it is not), that it portrays language as a static entity (it does not), and that everything is claimed to be iconic (no such claim is made). As we proceed, the incorrectness of these views will become apparent. For now let us turn to the most fecund source of misconceptions about CG, namely the notations it employs.

1.2.3 Those Diagrams

On occasion I resort to diagrams. Of course, those occasions are rather frequent, and critics will no doubt aver that I use them excessively. It is certainly true that works in CG (including this one) are often replete with diagrams, ranging from simple, cartoon-like sketches to elaborate technical displays of great complexity. There is, I suppose, no reason to be apologetic about it. After all, the pages of staid linguistics journals are often splashed with tree-like diagrams drawn by formal syntacticians (not to mention phonologists). The use of diagrams is equally prevalent in the "hard" sciences admired by linguistic theorists. Indeed, we are witnessing the emergence of "scientific visualization" and the growing recognition of its importance to theory and research. Still, since the diagrams used in CG have so commonly been misconstrued, their nature and status need to be clarified.

Among the misconceptions concerning the diagrams of CG are (i) that they are offered as precise and rigorous formal representations and (ii) that they are merely ad hoc, informal "pictures". There is actually a germ of truth in both positions. Some diagrams are just picture-like sketches casually devised to help make a point. Others are meticulously assembled from an inventory of specific notations systematically used with precisely defined values. In all cases, though, I regard the diagrams as being **heuristic** in nature. While even the most carefully drafted fall considerably short of mathematical rigor, the process of producing them forces the analyst to examine myriad details that are commonly ignored in semantic and grammatical descriptions. In my view they provide a level of precision and explicitness sufficient for most purposes, together with a kind of usability that facilitates discovery.

The notations and representational formats developed in later chapters thus do not amount to a mathematically respectable formalization. Many theorists would consider this unfortunate, taking it for granted both that language is amenable to discrete formalization and that scientific progress requires it. Reinforcing this prevalent attitude are such powerful icons as formal logic, computer programming, and Chomsky's archetypal conception of a "generative" grammar (a precise and explicit set of symbol-manipulating rules that enumerate all and only the well-formed sentences of a language). Collectively these engender and sustain certain expectations concerning what linguistic descriptions ought to look like and the level of mathematical rigor to be striven for. I believe, however, that these expectations are inappropriate for natural language, which is not a self-contained or well-defined formal system. I likewise reject the metaphor that likens mind to a digital computer and language to a program that it runs. CG is more at home in the "connectionist" ("neural network") world of dynamic systems, parallel processing, distributed representations, and computation by simultaneous constraint satisfaction.[6]

Since language (for reasons developed later) is neither self-contained nor well defined, a complete formal description (a "generative grammar" in the classical sense) is held to be impossible in principle. The same is true when any particular dimension or facet of linguistic structure is examined individually. Language does not resemble a collection of computer programs. Rather, it inheres in the dynamic processing of **real** neural networks, and while the patterns that emerge are certainly

---

[6] With the emergence of this psychologically more plausible alternative, algorithmic computation over discrete symbolic representations is becoming progressively less important in linguistics. (In this context, "symbolic" refers to the symbols used in a computation, usually considered contentless. This is quite different from "symbolic" as understood in CG, where a symbolic structure is meaningful by definition.)

amenable to analysis, the discrete notations and static representations devised by linguists can at best only approximate them. But to recognize these limitations is not to see everything as dissolving into a homogeneous mush. CG acknowledges the existence of highly elaborate linguistic structures, as well as the need to describe them as precisely and explicitly as possible—both to understand language in its own terms and to make evident what an adequate model of cognitive processing will have to deal with. If CG diagrams remain heuristic, notations can nonetheless be developed to characterize particular phenomena in as much explicit detail as present knowledge allows. Asking or claiming any more would in my estimation be premature, pointless, and pretentious. Unless and until we have a clear conceptual understanding of what is going on, there is no point in seeking mathematical precision.

The diagrams used for grammatical constructions come closest to being formal representations. When worked out in careful detail, they might be considered "quasi-formal", though I will describe them merely as **systematic**. Certain limitations have to be noted. The diagrams are necessarily selective; even the more systematic ones abstract away from many features not presently in focus. If drawn with any specificity, the diagrams representing expressions of even modest size prove quite complex and unwieldy (e.g. fig. 7.13). Moreover, reading such a diagram takes some time and effort, especially when the notational conventions have not yet been fully mastered. I recognize these points but do not accept them as valid criticisms. After all, the same limitations hold for both formulaic representations and the diagrams used in other frameworks.

The diagrams used for grammar seem not to raise many eyebrows (tree-like representations being traditional in that domain). When it comes to semantics, however, misconceptions abound and credulity is ceded more grudgingly. This is not surprising, since meaning is far more complex than grammar, and far more difficult to study and describe. CG attempts at representing it have consequently been sketchier, more informal, more preliminary, and less systematic than in the case of grammar.[7] Fair minds will recognize that, in having an account of semantics which is neither exhaustive nor definitive, CG hardly stands alone. Yet, because it accepts the centrality of meaning and tries to say something both substantive and psychologically plausible about it, the deficiencies are especially apparent. Let me then correct a first misconception by stating unambiguously that no semantic representation proposed in CG is ever considered exhaustive. For reasons outlined in chapter 2, complete semantic descriptions cannot realistically be envisaged. Any actual description must limit itself to facets of the total meaning that are either central or relevant for a specific immediate purpose. If they are principled, linguistically revealing, and empirically supported, even partial characterizations are valid and useful.

What should they look like? With syntax and formal logic as their models, linguists are accustomed to describing semantic structure by means of formulaic representations comprising strings of discrete symbols. Hence the use in CG of semipictorial diagrams (and even crude pictures on occasion) does, I think, raise eyebrows. This is not the place to debate the very real issue of whether meaning, as an actual cognitive phenomenon,

---

[7] Because grammar is claimed to be symbolic, there is no sharp distinction between semantic and grammatical diagrams. The latter incorporate representations of meaning.

(a)

(b)

FIGURE 1.1

is better approximated by discrete symbolic representations or by something more analogical in nature. I would only argue that the kinds of diagrams employed in CG are heuristically effective and not inappropriate, given our present level of understanding. One could choose, for example, to represent the concept TRIANGLE in either a propositional or a diagrammatic format, as shown in figure 1.1. Although I certainly appreciate the virtues of the formulaic description, its imagic counterpart is understandably the one I would work with for most quotidian purposes.

From the frequent use of quasi-pictorial diagrams, some critics of CG have leaped to the incorrect conclusion that semantic structure is claimed to be entirely visual or spatial in nature. A related misconception is that CG can only deal with visuospatial notions. On the contrary, the essential constructs proposed for semantic description (e.g. various kinds of **prominence**) are applicable to any cognitive domain and independent of any particular mode of presentation. Another misapprehension is that the diagrams have a consistently analog character; yet another is that the schematic images they employ purport to be direct depictions of conceptual structure. The actual intent of these diagrams is rather more modest: to allow certain facets of conceptual organization to be represented in a format that is both user-friendly and explicit enough to serve as a basis for semantic and grammatical analysis.

I believe the diagrams serve this intended heuristic function reasonably well. While less than fully systematic, they can be made quite precise and force a kind of explicitness that facilitates discovery. The diagrams must, however, be used with caution, for they can be misleading as well as informative: like any other notation, they omit as much as they reveal, and they are biasing if not distorting. Constant awareness of their limitations is well advised.

1.2.4 The Spirit of the Enterprise

From a limited exposure to CG, many people receive the impression that it is "easy", apparently basing their assessment on its intuitive naturalness, its focus on meaning, the liberal use of diagrams, and the seeming absence of constraints. I agree at least in part: it is quite easy to do CG badly, and not so hard to do it indifferently. To do it well is obviously much harder. For various intrinsic reasons, arriving at analyses that will readily be accepted as sound and convincing is arguably more difficult than in other frameworks.

By and large, linguistic theory and training foster a basic expectation of discreteness in language and thus a strong inclination to posit it. This preference is evident in all domains and in every facet of investigation. Although its liabilities are now widely recognized, the following have all been prevalent features of modern linguistic thought and practice: (1) the virtually exclusive reliance on "digital" representations composed of discrete symbols; (2) the presumed adequacy of simple yes/no judgments of well-formedness; (3) the common neglect of linguistic **variation**; (4) the sharp distinction drawn between the **synchronic** study of language structure and the **diachronic** study of how it changes and evolves; (5) the assumption that language is clearly delimited and self-contained (with respect to other mental faculties, as well as associated phenomena like gesture); (6) the division of language into separate **components**, such as phonetics, phonology, lexicon, morphology, syntax, semantics, and pragmatics; (7) the focus on regular patterns permitting crisp generalizations (with the attendant difficulty in handling irregularity and generalizations of limited scope); (8) the default assumption of **classical** categories with strict boundaries, as opposed to **prototype** categories with degrees of membership; (9) the notion that **absolute predictability** ought to be the norm, so that anything which fails to achieve it is held to be of little interest; (10) the usual practice of formulating questions in terms of mutually exclusive alternatives.[8]

This world of discrete units and sharp boundaries is definitely attractive. Dividing makes it easier to conquer. In particular, if meaning can safely be ignored, the description of grammar is greatly simplified (at least superficially). Discrete structures are more readily analyzed and more amenable to perspicuous formalization. Also, the categorical statements and strong predictability afforded by discreteness are highly valued in science. Yet language was not necessarily designed for the convenience or predilections of the analyst. We must therefore ask whether the basic discreteness commonly assumed by linguistic theorists has been **discovered in** language or **imposed on** it. Since my own experience has led me to challenge all of points (1) to (10), I reluctantly conclude that it has largely been imposed.[9] This is not to say, however, that everything in language is continuous—far from it—or to deny the utility of discrete representations, provided that we recognize their possible limitations.

To the extent that language deviates from the expectations embodied in points (1) to (10), accurate descriptions are more difficult to achieve and less likely to satisfy orthodox theorists. Consider just one central issue: the putative autonomy of syntax vis-à-vis semantics. If syntax is separate and self-contained, so that meaning can be ignored, describing it becomes much easier in certain respects. It is easier, for example, to claim that the noun category represents an irreducible syntactic primitive, lacking intrinsic semantic content, than to propose a conceptual characterization that is both linguistically revealing and psychologically plausible (see ch. 4). It is easier just to list grammatical markers and state where they occur than to also determine and represent their meanings. An autonomous form of grammatical description

---

[8] I call this the **exclusionary fallacy** (FCG1: §1.1.6). It is exemplified by the commonly asked question (pointless in CG) of whether something is "in the lexicon" or "in the syntax".

[9] By virtue of training and inclination, I personally favor discreteness, but language has chosen not to cooperate.

is more easily extended to a new language or a new structural domain than is a symbolic account requiring semantic analysis.

Adding to the difficulty are the stringent constraints imposed on CG descriptions. A strong limitation on what kinds of elements can be posited is presented in §1.3.4. Further restrictions follow from the requirement of psychological plausibility. CG's nonmodular view of language—approaching it as an integral facet of cognition dependent on more general systems and abilities—implies an ultimate responsibility to the findings of other cognitive sciences. An important additional source of control is the nonautonomy of grammar. If grammar is truly independent of meaning, the analyst is free to describe it paying no heed to semantic considerations. By contrast, the symbolic view of grammar obliges the analyst to accommodate both form and meaning. When properly conducted, their investigation is mutually informing and mutually constraining. Grammatical markings and patterns call attention to subtle aspects of meaning and pose descriptive problems requiring semantic solutions. In doing semantic analysis, a linguist can use these as both a stimulus and a check: besides being psychologically plausible and internally well motivated, semantic descriptions must articulate well with grammar. Basic constructs of CG have in fact been developed through such a dialectic, which can be offered as an optimal working method.

This illustrates the first of several philosophical principles that have guided work in CG: the principle of **integration** favors inclusiveness and unification. It emphasizes the importance of considering and reconciling information from multiple sources (within a language, across languages, and across disciplines). Moreover, it encourages a unified treatment of the various dimensions of language structure (which have much in common at an abstract level) and urges that one avoid imposing dichotomous organization where there is actually a gradation. The principle of **naturalness** maintains that language—when properly analyzed—is by and large reasonable and understandable in view of its semiological and interactive functions, as well as its biological, cognitive, and sociocultural grounding. Cognitive and functional linguists find that virtually everything in language is **motivated** in such terms (even if very little is strictly **predictable**). A third principle, **patience**, amounts to the admonition that one should not put the cart before the horse. An example of patience is the withholding of judgment on questions that are probably premature (e.g. the extent to which language is innately specified). Another is the practice of delaying efforts at formalization until we have a basic conceptual understanding of what is going on. This principle does not imply a reluctance to make strong claims and working hypotheses, however.

1.3 Grammar as Symbolization

Enough preliminaries. It is time to offer an initial sketch of Cognitive Grammar, to be fleshed out in later chapters. The central matters to be addressed are the global organization of a linguistic system and what it means to say that grammar is symbolic in nature.

If it proves empirically adequate, CG represents the kind of theory linguists ought to be seeking. First, it is **natural** in several respects. Moreover, it offers both

conceptual unification and **theoretical austerity**, properties considered desirable in other sciences. CG is natural by virtue of its psychological plausibility, as well as the central place accorded meaning. It is further natural in that its global organization directly reflects the basic semiological function of language—namely, permitting meanings to be symbolized phonologically. To serve this function, a language needs at least three kinds of structures: **semantic, phonological**, and **symbolic**. The pivotal and most distinctive claim of CG is that **only** these are needed. This is one aspect of its theoretical austerity. What makes it possible is the notion that lexicon, morphology, and syntax form a continuum fully reducible to assemblies of symbolic structures. If valid, this notion represents a fundamental conceptual unification.

1.3.1 Symbolic Complexity

Semantic structures are conceptualizations exploited for linguistic purposes, notably as the meanings of expressions. Under the rubric **phonological structure**, I include not only sounds but also gestures and orthographic representations. Their essential feature is that of being overtly manifested, hence able to fulfill a symbolizing role.[10] **Symbolic structures** are not distinct from semantic and phonological structures, but rather incorporate them. As shown in figure 1.2(a), a symbolic structure (Σ) resides in a link between a semantic structure (S) and a phonological structure (P), such that either is able to evoke the other. I describe a symbolic structure as being **bipolar**: S is its **semantic pole**, and P its **phonological pole**. In formulaic representations, a slash is used to indicate a symbolic relationship. The morpheme *cat* can thus be given as [[CAT]/[cat]], where [CAT] stands for the complex conceptualization comprising its semantic pole, and the phonological pole is rendered orthographically in lowercase.

A defining property of human language is the formation of complex structures out of simpler ones. In figure 1.2(b), we see two symbolic structures combining to produce a higher-level symbolic structure, represented by the outer box.[11] These

FIGURE 1.2

[10] For most linguistic purposes, we are more concerned with the cognitive representation of phonological structures than with their actual physical implementation. It is thus coherent to posit abstract ("schematic") phonological structures which, per se, cannot be overtly manifested.

[11] To simplify these initial diagrams, the semantic and phonological poles of higher-level structures are not separately depicted. Their semantic and phonological values are based on those of the component elements, though they are not strictly reducible to them.

lower-level and higher-level structures constitute a **symbolic assembly**. Of course, a higher-level symbolic structure is itself capable of entering into a combinatory relationship, producing a more elaborate symbolic assembly, as shown in diagram (c). We can say that a series of structures like (a), (b), and (c) exhibit progressively greater **symbolic complexity**. Through repeated combination, at successively higher levels of organization, assemblies having any degree of symbolic complexity can be formed. A **morpheme** is definable as an expression whose symbolic complexity is zero, i.e. it is not at all **analyzable** into smaller symbolic components. A morpheme can also be thought of as a **degenerate symbolic assembly** comprising just a single symbolic relationship, as in (a).

Corresponding to diagrams (a), (b), and (c) would be a series of expressions such as *moon*, *moonless*, and *moonless night*. Using hyphens for combinatory relationships, we can represent these formulaically as in (1):

(1) (a) [[MOON]/[moon]]

  (b) [[[MOON]/[moon]] - [[LESS]/[less]]]

  (c) [[[[MOON]/[moon]] - [[LESS]/[less]]] - [[NIGHT]/[night]]]

All of these happen to be fixed, familiar expressions conventionally used in English. Hence they are all **lexical items**, granted CG's definition of **lexicon** as the set of **fixed expressions** in a language. This definition is useful, straightforward, and more or less consonant with an everyday understanding of the term. It is not, however, equivalent to other characterizations proposed by linguists, e.g. lexicon as the set of **words** in a language. Observe that there are fixed expressions larger than words (like *moonless night*), and there are possible words—such as *dollarless*—that are **novel** rather than familiar and conventionally established. Note further that the CG definition suggests the absence of any strict boundary between lexicon and nonlexical expressions, since familiarity and conventionality are matters of degree. The dictionary lists *ireless*, for example, and this word does seem vaguely familiar to me, but for most speakers it is no doubt novel and unfamiliar.

Clearly apparent in lexicon are several very basic phenomena that are quite evident in many other facets of cognition. The central role accorded to them is one aspect of CG's psychological plausibility. They also illustrate the general notion that language recruits, and thus intrinsically manifests in its own organization, a broad array of independently existing cognitive processes. The phenomena in question are association, automatization, schematization, and categorization.

1. Stated most generally, **association** is simply the establishing of psychological connections with the potential to influence subsequent processing. It has numerous manifestations in CG. Here we need only recall the association between a semantic and a phonological structure that defines a symbolic relationship.

2. **Automatization** is the process observed in learning to tie a shoe or recite the alphabet: through repetition or rehearsal, a complex structure is thoroughly mastered, to the point that using it is virtually automatic and requires little conscious monitoring. In CG parlance, a structure undergoes progressive **entrenchment** and eventually becomes established as a **unit**. Lexical items are expressions that have achieved the

status of units for representative members of a speech community. When it is relevant to draw the distinction, units are enclosed in boxes or square brackets; nonunits are in closed curves, boxes with rounded corners, or parentheses. *Dollarless* can thus be given as in (2), since the components *dollar* and *-less* have each achieved **unit status**, whereas the overall expression has not.

(2)   ([[DOLLAR]/[dollar]] - [[LESS]/[less]])

It is important to realize that unit status does not entail the absence or unimportance of components, merely the routinized nature of their execution (which does however tend to diminish their individual salience).[12] Though a unit, *moonless night* is clearly analyzable into *moonless* and *night*, and *moonless* into *moon* and *-less*.

3. By **schematization**, I mean the process of extracting the commonality inherent in multiple experiences to arrive at a conception representing a higher level of abstraction. Schematization plays a role in the acquisition of lexical units, if only because their conventional forms and meanings are less specific than the **usage events** (i.e. the actual pronunciations and contextual understandings) on the basis of which they are learned. For example, the basic sense of *ring*—roughly 'circular piece of jewelry worn on the finger'—is schematic relative to the conception of specific rings in specific contexts, which vary in such details as size, material, identity of the wearer, and so on. Schematization can be carried to different degrees, depending on the diversity of the elements it is based on. Since *ring* is also used for adornments worn in other places than on the finger, we can posit for it the more schematic value 'circular adornment worn on the body', with respect to which 'circular piece of jewelry worn on the finger' constitutes an **elaboration** or specific **instantiation**. Still more abstractly, *ring* can mean 'circular object' (consider the *rings* in gymnastics) or even just 'circular entity' (e.g. the *ring* of dirt left around a bathtub).

4. **Categorization** is most broadly describable as the interpretation of experience with respect to previously existing structures. A **category** is a set of elements judged equivalent for some purpose; for example, the alternate senses of a lexical item constitute a category, equivalent in having the same phonological realization. If structure A belongs to a category, it can be used to **categorize** another structure, B, which may then become a category member. Categorization is most straightforward when A is **schematic** for B, so that B **elaborates** or **instantiates** A. For this I use a solid arrow: A → B. The arrow indicates that B is fully compatible with A's specifications but is characterized with greater precision and detail. For instance, (3)(a) might represent the categorization responsible for *ring* being applied to circular arenas, as used in circuses and bullfighting.

(3)   (a) CIRCULAR ENTITY → CIRCULAR ARENA

         (b) CIRCULAR ARENA ---> RECTANGULAR ARENA

---

[12] Likewise, when reciting the alphabet in automatized fashion we still have to say all the letters.

However, it can also happen that B conflicts with A's specifications but is nonetheless assimilated to the category on the basis of an association or perceived similarity. A is then a **prototype** (at least locally), and B an **extension** from it. For this I use a dashed arrow: A ---> B. A possible example is (3)(b), the extension applying *ring* to rectangular arenas, as used in boxing.

1.3.2 Lexicon and Grammar

If lexicon resides in assemblies of symbolic structures, can we say the same for grammar? Not according to the current orthodoxy, where grammar is sharply distinguished from lexicon and described using a special set of primitives with no intrinsic meaning. Here I argue that a clear demarcation between lexicon and grammar is far from evident. I also indicate how grammar can be described with symbolic assemblies that vary along the same parameters as those describing lexicon, and within the same ranges of values.

In the standard conception, lexical items are essentially syntactic atoms. They are "inserted" into particular slots at the bottom of syntactic tree structures, as sketched in figure 1.3(a). The individual lexical items are continuous, self-contained, and nonoverlapping. While they may be complex, their internal structure is morphological rather than syntactic. *Healthy*, for example, is analyzable into the component morphemes *health* and *-y* (or, more tenuously, into *heal*, *-th*, and *-y*). Yet it functions syntactically as a simple adjective analogous to *big*.

This neat partitioning between lexicon and syntax can only be maintained by imposing artificial boundaries, however—in particular, by ignoring lexical items larger than words. Consider **idioms**. As fixed expressions whose meanings are not predictable from their parts, idioms satisfy both the CG definition of lexicon and a

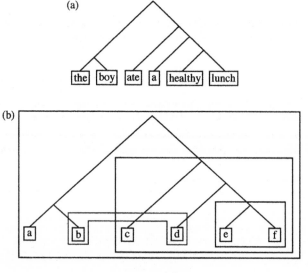

FIGURE 1.3

more restrictive one requiring semantic idiosyncrasy. They can nonetheless be of any size and exhibit internal structure that is clearly syntactic. For instance, *tall tale* represents an adjective + noun combination, *bury the hatchet* consists of a verb and its noun phrase object, while *A bird in the hand is worth two in the bush* is a full sentence. Rather than being syntactic atoms confined to particular slots in syntactic tree structures, idiomatic expressions subsume various portions of such trees, as is shown abstractly in figure 1.3(b) by the different-size boxes. The diagram also indicates that idioms can be manifested discontinuously (note the box enclosing [b] and [d]). A stock example is *keep tabs on*:

(4)   (a)   *The police **kept tabs on** all the leading activists.*

    (b)   ***Tabs** were **kept** by the police **on** all the leading activists.*

The point is still more evident if we discard the requirement of semantic irregularity (which, in any case, is a matter of degree) and simply define lexicon as the set of fixed expressions in a language. Becoming a fluent speaker involves learning an enormous inventory of expressions larger than words, representing usual ways of conveying certain notions. These conventional expressions can be of any size and undeniably subsume varying portions of syntactic tree structures, in the manner of figure 1.3(b). Numerous examples can be found in any text. Conventional among linguists, for instance, are the following expressions, all culled from the previous paragraph: *neat partitioning, lexicon and syntax, artificial boundaries, impose artificial boundaries, in particular, larger than, satisfy...definition, more restrictive, any size, of any size, internal structure, tree structures, syntactic tree structures, idiomatic expressions, various portions of, stock example, a stock example.* According to standard linguistic doctrine, many of these are excluded from the linguistic system on grounds of being semantically and grammatically regular (hence derivable by rules). Their exclusion is arbitrary, however, if a language is characterized as the set of internalized structures (conventional units) that enable its users to speak and understand. Without a substantial inventory of prefabricated expressions, fluent real-time speech would hardly be possible. Theorists have grossly exaggerated the novelty of "novel sentences".

We have seen that lexical units can be ordered in terms of their degree of symbolic complexity (e.g. *moon* < *moonless* < *moonless night* < *a moonless night* < *on a moonless night*). A second parameter along which they vary is **schematicity,** or its converse **specificity**, pertaining to the precision and detail of their characterization. From taxonomic hierarchies like those in (5), it is evident that lexical items run the full gamut semantically from highly schematic, coarse-grained descriptions to those of a specific, fine-grained nature:

(5)   (a)   *thing → creature → animal → dog → poodle*

    (b)   *do → act → propel → throw → fling*

It is less commonly appreciated that their phonological characterizations also vary along this parameter. For example, the English past-tense morpheme has the regular allomorphs [d], [t], and [əd] (as in *failed, rocked*, and *heeded*). Since the choice is phonologically predictable, linguists often posit a schematic representation that specifies only the presence of an alveolar stop (leaving voicing and the possible occurrence of [ə] to be filled in by rules). Many languages have morphemes manifested phonologically by reduplication. Thus a plural morpheme might have the schematic form CV-, i.e. a prefix consisting of a consonant plus a vowel, whose specific instantiations match the initial CV of the stem. In the Semitic languages, roots are traditionally described as comprising just a sequence of consonants (typically three), although in any actual form these occur with vowels contributing other lexical and grammatical information. In CG terms, the roots are phonologically schematic in regard to the placement and identity of the supporting vowels.

Many multiword lexical units contain schematic elements. A well-known example is *X crane X+POSS neck*, where *X* refers schematically to the agent and neck possessor. It represents the commonality inherent in an open-ended set of expressions in which *X* is instantiated by a specific nominal element: *I craned my neck, She was craning her neck, Phil always cranes his neck*, and so on. Another partially schematic unit is $V_s X$ *in the* N_b, where V_s is a verb of striking like *hit, kick, strike*, or *poke* and N_b is a body-part noun like *shin, back, face, eye*, or *knee*. Certain partial instantiations of this schema are themselves established units ("collocations"), e.g. *hit X in the back, kick X in the shin, poke X in the eye*. Even more schematic is the template *a* N_1+*less* N_2, instantiated by specific unit expressions such as *a moonless night, a childless couple, a hopeless situation, a treeless plain, a fruitless search, a cordless phone*, and so on.

It should be apparent that this list of partially schematic unit expressions could be extended indefinitely. They constitute an essential—perhaps even the preponderant—component of a fluent speaker's conventional linguistic knowledge. Yet standard linguistic theory hardly recognizes their existence, let alone accommodate them in any straightforward manner. The problem is that they conform to the stereotype of neither lexicon nor grammar, and by combining features of each, they subvert the claim that these are sharply distinct. Units like *X crane X+POSS neck*, $V_s X$ *in the* N_b, and *a* N_1+*less* N_2 are nonstereotypical for grammar by virtue of containing specific lexical elements. They are nonstereotypical for lexicon because of their partial schematicity. They are not themselves full-fledged expressions but patterns abstracted from them and potentially used in forming new ones. To this extent they are grammar-like, since grammar by definition comprises the patterns used in forming complex expressions. In an effort to preserve the standard dichotomy, *X crane X+POSS neck* could be assigned to the lexicon, as it contains the indisputably "lexical" elements *crane* and *neck*, whereas *a* N_1+*less* N_2 might be considered grammatical because its only specific components (*a* and *-less*) are "grammatical markers". This will not solve the problem, however. Apart from being aprioristic, it leaves us with an arbitrary choice in cases like $V_s X$ *in the* N_b, where V_s and N_b are intermediate in specificity (V_s designating a certain type of action, and N_b a body part). What the linguistic data seem to be trying to tell us is that lexicon and grammar form a gradation instead of being sharply dichotomous. That, of course, is a central claim of CG, which further contends that the full gradation reduces to assemblies of symbolic structures.

1.3.3 Grammar as Symbolic Assemblies

We have seen that symbolic assemblies range widely along three main parameters. First, they vary in symbolic complexity, as sketched in figure 1.2 and exemplified by a series of lexical units like *sharp* < *sharpen* < *sharpener* < *pencil sharpener* < *electric pencil sharpener*. Second, they vary in their degree of specificity (or conversely, schematicity), as seen in (5), and also in a series like (6), where the initial structure is wholly schematic, the next partially instantiated, and the last fully specific:

(6) $V_s\, X$ *in the* N_b → *kick X in the shin* → *kick my pet giraffe in the shin*

Third, symbolic assemblies vary in the extent to which they achieve the status of units and become conventional within a speech community.[13] The first two structures in (6) are plausibly ascribed the status of conventional units in English, whereas the last one—taken as a whole—is surely novel. The different facets of lexicon and grammar can all be characterized as symbolic assemblies occupying various regions in the abstract space defined by these three parameters. Bear in mind, though, that we are dealing with graded phenomena. The regions corresponding to particular traditional notions are expected to overlap, and specific lines of demarcation are held to be arbitrary.

Full-fledged **expressions**—those we could actually use—are specific at the phonological pole, for they have to be capable of being spoken, signed, or written down.[14] At the semantic pole there is more flexibility, though actual expressions tend to be rather specific. Since expressions can obviously be of any size, they range freely along the dimension of symbolic complexity. They can also have any degree of conventionality. To the extent that expressions become entrenched and attain the

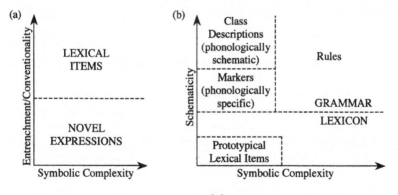

FIGURE 1.4

---

[13] For ease of discussion, I am conflating two parameters that eventually have to be distinguished: **entrenchment** or **unit status** (pertaining to a particular speaker) and **conventionality** (pertaining to a speech community).

[14] This is basically what the term **expression** is meant to convey. The notion involves many subtleties, but they will not concern us (FCG1: §11.2.1).

status of conventional units, they constitute **lexical items**. To the extent that they do not, they are **novel**. This is sketched in figure 1.4(a), where the dashed line indicates the absence of any sharp boundary.

The lexicon and grammar of a language consist of symbolic assemblies that in substantial measure have achieved the status of conventional units. Figure 1.4(b) shows their arrangement with respect to the parameters of schematicity and symbolic complexity. The elements traditionally recognized as (prototypical) lexical items are phonologically and semantically specific expressions with only limited symbolic complexity: *dog, moonless, carefully, toothbrush*. I suggest, however, that drawing any particular line of demarcation along either parameter would be arbitrary. A broader array of structures are therefore accepted in CG as lexical items, including symbolic units that are schematic either phonologically (like Semitic roots) or semantically (e.g. *do, a, -less*), as well as assemblies of indefinite symbolic complexity (such as idioms and proverbs). Also subsumed under lexicon are symbolically complex assemblies that are both semantically and phonologically schematic in certain positions, like *X crane X+POSS neck* or *X take Y over X+POSS knee and spank Y*.

Where does lexicon stop and grammar begin? The point, of course, is that there is no particular place. But this is not to say that no distinction can be drawn. The key parameter is specificity. To the extent that symbolic assemblies are specific, they would tend to be regarded as lexical, both traditionally and in CG. To the extent that they are schematic, they would generally be considered grammatical. Thus **lexicon** can be characterized as residing in fairly specific symbolic assemblies, and **grammar** in more schematic ones. Toward the two extremes are clear cases unequivocally identifiable as lexical or grammatical (e.g. *dog* vs. a pattern for forming relative clauses). In between lie many structures (such as V_s X *in the* N_b) validly thought of either way, depending on one's purpose.

The claim, then, is that grammar reduces to schematic symbolic assemblies. But what exactly does this mean? How does symbolic grammar work? Later sections and chapters answer these questions in some detail. For now, let us focus on three basic matters: grammatical markers, grammatical classes, and grammatical rules. These are all describable by means of symbolic assemblies. What distinguishes them are the regions they occupy in the abstract space defined by the parameters of schematicity and symbolic complexity.

1. As parts of expressions, **grammatical markers** are specific at the phonological pole, since they have to be capable of overt realization.[15] Even those reasonably ascribed a schematic phonological value, like a reduplicative morpheme or the regular English past tense, acquire specific segmental content in a given expression. On the other hand, grammatical markers tend to be quite schematic at the semantic pole—otherwise they would simply be lexical items. There is little agreement among linguists concerning which elements to identify as "grammatical" rather than "lexical". Examples commonly treated both ways include prepositions (e.g. *for, to, at, like*), modals (*may, can, will, shall, must*), and indefinite pronouns (*someone, anywhere, everybody, whatever, who*). These all resemble canonical lexical items

---

[15] Alternate terms for grammatical markers include "grammatical morpheme", "function word", "empty word", "formative", and "closed-class element".

in having clearly discernible meanings. At the same time, their meanings resemble those of classic grammatical markers in being tenuous, abstract, and hard to elucidate. From the standpoint of CG, which posits a gradation, such uncertainty is unproblematic; because schematicity is a matter of degree, it is actually expected that certain elements should be ambivalent as to their lexical or grammatical status. The essential point, though, is that even the most "grammatical" of grammatical markers—forms like *be*, *do*, *of*, the infinitival *to*, agreement markers, case inflections, and derivational affixes—are viewed in CG as being meaningful.

2. Grammatical markers are closely related to **grammatical classes**, which they often serve to derive or signal. A class per se, however, is not overtly manifested but resides in a set of symbolic structures that function alike in certain respects. CG maintains that grammatical classes are definable in symbolic terms and, more controversially, that basic classes like noun, verb, adjective, and adverb can be given uniform semantic characterizations (see ch. 4). Hence the members of a class all instantiate a schematic description representing their abstract commonality. For instance, the bipolar schema defining the noun class can be written as [[THING]/[...]], where [THING] specifies that a noun refers to a **thing** (in the most general sense of that term), and [...] indicates that no particular phonological properties are specified. What it means for an expression to be a noun is that it instantiates this schema:

(7)   (a)   [[THING]/[...]] → [[MOON]/[moon]]

       (b)   [[THING]/[...]] → [[[TOOTH]/[tooth]] - [[BRUSH]/[brush]]]

       (c)   [[THING]/[...]] → [[[[MOON]/[moon]] - [[LESS]/[less]]] - [[NIGHT]/[night]]]

Moon, toothbrush, and *moonless night* are all nouns because each is a symbolic structure that designates a thing.[16] Most nouns elaborate the schema both semantically and phonologically. Arguably, though, the grammatical element *thing*—the one appearing in forms like *something, nothing,* and *anything*—is more specific only at the phonological pole: [[THING]/[thing]]. Thus, in accordance with figure 1.4(b), the noun class description is schematic at both poles, the grammatical formative *thing* is schematic semantically but phonologically specific, and a typical lexical item like *moon* is also semantically specific.

3. **Grammatical rules** occupy the remaining portion of the abstract space depicted in figure 1.4(b). By **rule** I simply mean the characterization of some pattern.[17] In CG, rules take the form of schemas: they are abstract templates obtained by reinforcing the commonality inherent in a set of instances. Since grammatical rules are patterns in the formation of symbolically complex expressions, they are themselves symbolically complex as well as schematic. Complex expressions consist of specific

---

[16] This semantically based characterization is not limited to traditionally recognized lexical items, or even to fixed expressions. In this broad sense, even a full noun phrase (fixed or novel) is classed as a special kind of noun.

[17] The term "rule" is often used more narrowly, e.g. for "constructive" statements (like the rewriting rules of generative grammar) as opposed to templates.

symbolic assemblies, and the rules describing them are schematic assemblies that embody their common features.

Schematization can be carried to any degree. If particular expressions give rise to low-level schemas like *hit X in the back*, *kick X in the shin*, and *poke X in the eye*, these in turn support the extraction of the higher-level schema $V_s X$ *in the* N_b. This may then instantiate a still more abstract schema based on a wider array of data. For instance, $V_c X P$ *the* N_b (where V_c is a verb of contact) would also subsume such patterns as *kiss X on the cheek*, *grasp X by the wrist*, *chuck X under the chin*, and *grab X around the waist*. These examples further show that the different components of a complex symbolic assembly can be schematic to varying degrees.

The schematic assemblies describing grammatical patterns can also exhibit any degree of symbolic complexity. Simpler schemas are often incorporated as components of more complex ones. For instance, adjectives like *moonless*, *childless*, *hopeless*, *treeless*, *fruitless*, and *cordless* instantiate a derivational pattern that we can write as *N+less*.[18] This schematic symbolic assembly is one component of $N_1+less N_2$ (as in *moonless night*, *childless couple*, *hopeless situation*, *treeless plain*, *fruitless search*, *cordless phone*), which in turn is part of *a* $N_1+less N_2$.

A speaker's knowledge of grammatical patterns resides in a vast inventory of symbolic assemblies ranging widely along the parameters of schematicity and symbolic complexity. It is a highly structured inventory, in that the assemblies bear a variety of relations to one another, such as instantiation, overlap, and inclusion. These schemas are abstracted from occurring expressions, and once established as units they can serve as templates guiding the formation of new expressions on the same pattern. For example, once abstracted to represent the commonality of fixed expressions like *moonless night*, *childless couple*, *hopeless situation*, etc., the schematic assembly $N_1+less N_2$ is subsequently available to **sanction** the occurrence of novel expressions like *moonless world*, *dollarless surgeon*, and *ireless dwarf*.[19] All of this holds for both morphological and syntactic patterns. If we wish to make a distinction, we can do no better than follow the tradition of drawing the line at the level of the word. **Morphology** is then described by schematic assemblies (like *N+less*) whose instantiations are no larger than words, and **syntax** by assemblies (like $N_1+less N_2$) with multiword instantiations. Even so the boundary is fuzzy, if only due to expressions (such as compounds) that are intermediate between single words and multiword sequences.

1.3.4 The Content Requirement

Compared with the descriptive machinery routinely invoked in other frameworks, CG is quite conservative and highly restrictive in what it allows the analyst to posit. Any flights of fancy cognitive grammarians might be prone to are seriously

---

[18] Formulaic representations like *N+less*, $N_1+less N_2$, and $V_s X$ *in the* N_b are merely abbreviatory. Actual CG descriptions of such assemblies have to specify in some detail both the internal structure of the symbolic elements and the relations they bear to one another.

[19] The extraction of a schema need not require fixed expressions. Schematization is just the reinforcing of recurring commonalities, which can perfectly well inhere in novel expressions, none of which ever coalesces as a unit.

constrained by the **content requirement**. Adopted as a strong working hypothesis, this requirement states that **the only elements ascribable to a linguistic system are (i) semantic, phonological, and symbolic structures that actually occur as parts of expressions; (ii) schematizations of permitted structures; and (iii) categorizing relationships between permitted structures**. The thrust of the content requirement is that the linguistic knowledge we ascribe to speakers should be limited to elements of form and meaning found in actually occurring expressions, or which derive from such elements via the basic psychological phenomena listed in §1.3.1: association, automatization, schematization, and categorization. By keeping our feet on the ground, this restriction assures both naturalness and theoretical austerity.

Provision (i) of the content requirement imposes the symbolic view of grammar and grounds linguistic descriptions in the sounds and meanings that occur in actual usage. These are **directly apprehended**, in the sense that we hear or produce the sounds of a usage event and understand it in a certain way. They also have intrinsic **content** related to broader realms of experience—the sounds of speech represent a particular class of auditory phenomena, and linguistic meanings are special cases of conceptualization. By contrast, grammar is not per se something that untrained speakers are aware of. It is not directly apprehended in the same way that sounds and meanings are, nor does it manifest any broader experiential realm. Having no independently discernible content, grammar is reasonably seen as residing in the abstracted commonality of sound-meaning pairings—that is, as being symbolic in nature.

Let us see how the content requirement applies, starting with phonological structures. Provision (i) allows us to posit specific elements such as segments, syllables, and any larger sequences sufficiently frequent to become entrenched as units. As speakers of English, for example, we master particular sound segments ([a], [t], [m], [s], etc.) and a substantial number of recurring syllables (e.g. [hap], [liv], [mɛk]).[20] Provision (ii) permits schematized segments and syllables. At different levels of abstraction, for instance, schemas can be posited representing what is common to the high front vowels of a language, the front vowels, or the vowels in general. Each schema characterizes a **natural class** of segments. Similarly, the schematic template [CVC] embodies the abstract commonality of [hap], [liv], [mɛk], and many other syllables. Provision (iii) lets us posit categorizing relationships, such as those between schemas and their instantiations. Thus [[CVC] → [hap]] indicates that [hap] is categorized as an instance of the [CVC] syllable type.

Analogously, the content requirement allows the postulation of specific and schematic semantic structures, as well as relationships of semantic categorization. Conceptual units are most clearly linguistically relevant—and thus qualify as semantic units—by virtue of being individually symbolized.[21] Permitted under provision (i) of the content requirement are conceptions functioning as the conventional meanings of

---

[20] Considering them as purely phonological units, it is irrelevant whether these segments and syllables can function as morphemes. Prosodic elements naturally have to be posited as well.

[21] Semantic units need not be individually symbolized (any more than phonological units need be individually meaningful). For instance, there is no everyday term for the maximal extension of a category, i.e. the union of all instances. Yet this notion is one conceptual component of *all, most,* and *some,* which refer to various proportions of the full extension.

lexical items. Given an array of similar semantic units, such as [ROSE], [DAISY], and [TULIP], provision (ii) sanctions a more schematic structure representing their abstract commonality, in this case [FLOWER]. While [FLOWER] is itself a lexical meaning, hence directly available under (i), we can readily imagine schemas that are not. It is plausible, for example, that from notions like [HORSE], [DONKEY], and [ZEBRA] many speakers extract a schematic conception, [HORSE-LIKE CREATURE], that they have no lexical means of expressing (*equine* being a learnèd form). In either circumstance, relationships of semantic categorization are ascribable to the linguistic system in accordance with provision (iii): [[FLOWER] → [TULIP]], [[HORSE-LIKE CREATURE] → [DONKEY]]. Also permitted are relationships of semantic extension, such as [[HORSE] ---> [DONKEY]], where a donkey is categorized as an atypical kind of horse.

Examples of symbolic units allowed by clause (i) of the content requirement are specific nouns like [[MOON]/[moon]], [[TULIP]/tulip]], and [[HOPE]/[hope]]. Clause (ii) permits the class schema [[THING]/[...]], describing what nouns have in common, and (iii) lets us classify particular elements as nouns, e.g. [[[THING]/ [...]] → [[MOON]/[moon]]]. We must also consider symbolically complex expressions, for instance *moonless*, *cordless*, and *toothless*. These are permitted by clause (i), the *N+less* pattern by (ii), and their categorization as instances of the pattern by (iii). For *moonless*, we see this formulaically in (8)(a)–(c), respectively:

(8) (a) [[[MOON]/[moon]] - [[LESS]/[less]]]

   (b) [[[THING/[...]] - [[LESS]/[less]]]

   (c) [[[[THING/[...]] - [[LESS]/[less]]] → [[[MOON]/[moon]] - [[LESS]/[less]]]]

It is claimed that grammar resides in vast networks of symbolic assemblies such as these, with varying degrees of abstraction and symbolic complexity.

The content requirement keeps the analyst from resorting to several kinds of devices commonly used in formalist theories. Since patterns can only arise by the schematization of occurring expressions, this requirement rules out derivations from underlying structures with divergent properties.[22] Also ruled out are formless, meaningless elements (e.g. "traces") posited solely to drive the machinery of autonomous syntax. Last but not least, the content requirement proscribes the use of "filters", rules specifically stating what **cannot** occur in well-formed expressions. CG assumes that languages are learned and that they are learned primarily by reinforcement of the commonality inherent in what actually **does** occur. I cannot yet claim to have demonstrated that negative statements are avoidable altogether, that descriptions using only positive specifications prove optimal for all linguistic structures and strictures. This is nonetheless quite natural and desirable as a working hypothesis, if only because it offers the most straightforward account of language learning.

---

[22] Provision (iii) is intended to permit extensions (and chains of extensions) from a prototype, however. (For discussion of the difference, see FCG1: §11.3.3.)

2

Conceptual Semantics

In a rare instance of consensus, linguists agree that grammar is extremely complex and hard to properly describe. Why should it be so difficult? The reason, I suggest, is precisely the fact that grammar is meaningful. Rather than being autonomous, it resides in schematized patterns of conceptual structuring and symbolization. For this reason we need a conceptual semantics. We cannot describe grammar revealingly without a principled and reasonably explicit characterization of the conceptual structures it incorporates.

2.1 Meaning and Semantic Representations

How we think about grammar depends on our view of linguistic meaning. Unfortunately, there is no general agreement on this score. Even the most basic issues—for example, the role of cognition in semantics—are points of chronic and continued contention. Let me then outline the rationale for certain positions adopted in CG.

2.1.1 Are Meanings in the Head?

Our concern is with the meanings of linguistic expressions. Where are these meanings to be found? From a cognitive linguistic perspective, the answer is evident: meanings are in the minds of the speakers who produce and understand the expressions. It is hard to imagine where else they might be. Yet there are many scholars who resist or reject that answer.[1] A conceptualist view of meaning is not as self-evident as it might first seem and has to be properly interpreted.

What are the alternatives? The first two options, in their extreme form, leave the human mind and body out of the picture altogether. The **platonic** view treats

---

[1] In fact, semantics textbooks often specifically argue against the identification of meanings with concepts (e.g. Palmer 1981: 24–29).

language as an abstract, disembodied entity that cannot be localized. Like the objects and laws of mathematics (e.g. the geometric ideal of a circle), linguistic meanings are seen as transcendent, existing independently of minds and human endeavor. More traditional is the **objectivist** position—still prevalent in philosophy, logic, and formal semantics—identifying the meaning of a sentence with the set of conditions under which it is true. These "truth conditions" pertain to what the world is like objectively, irrespective of how it might be conceptualized. Both options stand in sharp contrast to the cognitive semantic view that meaning derives from embodied human experience. Cognitive linguistics has amply demonstrated the critical role of mental processes in semantics and grammar.

More reasonable is the **interactive** alternative, which does take people into account but claims that an individual mind is not the right place to look for meanings. Instead, meanings are seen as emerging dynamically in discourse and social interaction. Rather than being fixed and predetermined, they are actively negotiated by interlocutors on the basis of the physical, linguistic, social, and cultural context. Meaning is not localized but distributed, aspects of it inhering in the speech community, in the pragmatic circumstances of the speech event, and in the surrounding world. In particular, it is not inside a single speaker's head. The static, insular view ascribed to cognitive semantics is deemed incapable of handling the dynamic, intersubjective, context-dependent nature of meaning construction in actual discourse.

In and of itself, the interactive alternative is certainly correct. It is not however an alternative—its essential ideas are in fact accepted as basic tenets of cognitive semantics. Though common, the portrayal of cognitive semantics as being static and insular is simply wrong. Conversely, a revealing account of communicative interaction needs to acknowledge and characterize the conceptualizations employed in discourse. The cognitive and interactive approaches are therefore quite compatible, provided that the former is correctly portrayed and the latter adequately formulated. It is only with an extremist formulation of interactionism—one which denies cognition a central role—that any conflict arises.

The CG position on these issues accommodates both the cognitive and the interactive perspectives. We can best appreciate it by contrasting it with certain extreme positions standing in polar opposition to one another. Consider the opposing positions that **everything** of consequence is inside the head, and that **nothing** of consequence is inside the head. According to the former (a kind of solipsism), cognition takes place within a hermetically sealed skull affording no input from or access to the exterior; it is thus asocial and acontextual, contemplation being limited to what goes on inside. According to the latter, meaning is created through communicative interaction between people whose heads—for all intents and purposes—are totally empty. To state these positions explicitly is to see how silly they are. Even so, cognitive linguists are not infrequently charged with solipsism, and interactionist rhetoric sometimes gives the impression that anything inside the head is irrelevant.

The cognition envisaged by cognitive linguists is noninsular, being grounded in perception and bodily experience. Since mental development is stimulated and guided by social interaction, the skills and knowledge acquired are very much attuned to the sociocultural surroundings. The conceptualizations we entertain are undeniably internal, in the sense of taking place in the brain, yet reach beyond it in the sense of being conceptualizations **of** some facet of the world.[2] In speaking, we conceptualize not only what we are talking about but also the context in all its dimensions, including our assessment of the knowledge and intentions of our interlocutor. Rather than being insular, therefore, conceptualization should be seen as a primary means of engaging the world. And empty heads cannot talk, interact, or negotiate meanings.

Closely related is the issue of localization. Can meanings be **localized**, contained in the minds of individual speakers, or are they **distributed** over a speech community, the immediate context of speech, as well as the physical and sociocultural world? I take it as evident that the extreme version of distributionism, where nothing at all is ascribed to individual minds, is simply untenable. Its polar opposite—the extreme version of localism, putting everything of relevance inside a single mind—is likewise untenable. But provided that some subtle but crucial distinctions are made, I find it reasonable to say that a single speaker grasps an expression's meaning.

We must first distinguish between, on the one hand, the various circumstances that create the potential for meaningful interaction and, on the other hand, the actual mental experience of an individual engaging in such an interaction. Countless aspects of our surroundings do carry meaning potential: the fact of facing a particular interlocutor in a particular social situation, an artifact clearly designed for a certain function, an action conforming to a familiar cultural practice, and so on. Thus, if a doctor extends a tongue depressor toward my mouth and says *Open wide*, my understanding of what the doctor intends and what I am supposed to do is far more comprehensive than anything derivable from the linguistic expression alone. (I know, for example, that I will not satisfy the request by approaching a cabinet and pulling a drawer out all the way.) It would not be unreasonable to describe the relevant circumstances as being "imbued with meaning" or as "part of the meaning" an expression has in context. Yet I think we gain in clarity and analytical precision by reserving the term "meaning" for how a speaker understands an expression (in either a speaking or a listening capacity). It thus incorporates a speaker's apprehension of the circumstances, and exploits the meaning potential they carry, but cannot be identified with those circumstances. So defined, an expression's meaning resides in the conceptualizing activity of individual speakers.

But does a single individual really ever know an expression's meaning? One objection is that linguistic meanings are conventional and thus reside at the social rather than the individual level. Another is that many expressions have meanings that are only partially known by any particular speaker. The term *electron*, for instance, is understood very differently by a theoretical physicist, by an electrical engineer, and by someone like myself with only a vague, partial, and metaphorical idea of its import. It is thus concluded that meanings are distributed over the entire speech community and cannot be found in any single person's head.

While these observations are true enough, the conclusion depends on the simplistic assumption that just one kind of entity counts as "the meaning" of an expression.

---

[2] Of course, the "world" includes both the real world and the mental worlds we construct, as well as the body and even our mental experience itself (to the extent that we can reflect on it, as opposed to merely undergoing it).

We can validly distinguish, however, between what a single speaker knows and the collective knowledge of a whole society. The former is arguably more basic, since collective knowledge consists in (or at least derives from) the knowledge of individuals.[3] For purposes of studying language as part of cognition, an expression's meaning is first and foremost its meaning **for** a single (representative) speaker. This is not to deny or diminish the social aspect of linguistic meaning. An individual's notion of what an expression means develops through communicative interaction and includes an assessment of its degree of conventionality in the speech community. By their nature, moreover, certain questions have to be studied at the population level (e.g. how norms are established and maintained, the extent to which consensus is achieved, and the range of variation actually encountered). Still, these questions cannot be fully answered unless the knowledge of individual speakers is taken into account.

Lastly, consider the accusation that cognitive semantics—owing to the fixed, static nature of concepts—cannot accommodate the dynamicity of actual language use: rather than being fixed, the values of linguistic elements are actively negotiated; and rather than being static, the meanings of complex expressions emerge and develop in discourse. Though frequently made, this accusation is groundless. In the first place, meaning is not identified with concepts but with **conceptualization**, the term being chosen precisely to highlight its dynamic nature. Conceptualization is broadly defined to encompass any facet of mental experience. It is understood as subsuming (1) both novel and established conceptions; (2) not just "intellectual" notions, but sensory, motor, and emotive experience as well; (3) apprehension of the physical, linguistic, social, and cultural context; and (4) conceptions that develop and unfold through processing time (rather than being simultaneously manifested). So even if "concepts" are taken as being static, conceptualization is not.

The remaining issue is whether linguistic meanings are fixed and predetermined or whether they are actively negotiated by interlocutors. It ought to be evident that the latter is quite compatible with a conceptualist semantics—why would anyone assume that conceptualization has to be rigid and inflexible? Once more we can usefully consider two extreme positions, neither of which is tenable. At one extreme is the notion that there is no flexibility whatever: a lexical item has a fixed, invariant meaning, and the meaning of a sentence is completely predicted by rules of semantic composition. Cognitive semantics explicitly rejects this option. At the opposite extreme is the view that nothing at all is conventionally established: an element's meaning is negotiated from scratch every time it is used, with no prior expectation whatever about its possible value. I doubt that anyone actually believes this (though interactionist rhetoric sometimes suggests it). Clearly, there must be something inside the head. Speakers must have some preconception of what the words they use are normally expected to mean. Otherwise the meanings negotiated would be completely random, and *cat* would have no greater likelihood of meaning 'feline' than 'walnut', 'book', or 'through'. While everything may be negotiable, something has to be learned and conventionalized as a basis for negotiation.

---

[3] Societal knowledge is also stored in books, databases, the design of artifacts, and so on, but ultimately these reduce to the activity of individual minds in creating or using them.

2.1.2 What Are Meanings Made Of?

Admitting that meaning resides in conceptualization does not itself solve anything but merely lets us formulate the problem. What do we actually mean by "conceptualization"? What are its general nature and specific properties? How do we go about investigating it? How can we describe it? At present there are no definitive answers to such questions. Considerable progress is, however, being made in cognitive linguistics, in the broader context of cognitive science. I would argue that CG embodies a coherent and plausible view of conceptualization, allowing a principled basis for characterizing many facets of semantic and grammatical structure.

Ultimately, conceptualization resides in cognitive processing. Having a certain mental experience resides in the occurrence of a certain kind of neurological activity. Conceptualization can thus be approached from either a **phenomenological** or a **processing** standpoint: we can attempt to characterize either our mental experience per se or the processing activity that constitutes it. Cognitive semantics has focused on the former, which is obviously more accessible and amenable to investigation via linguistic evidence. As for processing, it can be studied at different levels (both functional and neurological) and by such varied means as psycholinguistic experiment, clinical research (notably on aphasia), neurological imaging, and now even computer modeling (Holmqvist 1993; Regier 1996; Lakoff and Johnson 1999: appendix). Still, these approaches rely on phenomenological characterizations for guidance and as the basis for interpreting results. And despite the rapid progress being made, a secure and detailed understanding of how specific linguistic structures are neurologically implemented remains a long-term goal.

Yet even at this early stage, speculative but plausible connections can be posited between the phenomenological and processing levels. What we experience as the prominence of conceived entities is reasonably ascribed to a high level of neural activation.[4] The spreading of activation is the evident basis for association and can thus be implicated in many linguistic phenomena (Deane 1992). I further suggest that any conceptual ordering or sequenced mental access implies a corresponding seriality in the processing that constitutes it. In mentally reciting the alphabet, for instance, we run through the letters in sequence, each prompting the next. It seems evident that this ordered conception resides in the ordered occurrence of the neural operations representing each letter, and that our knowledge of the proper sequencing resides in processing routines where the operations representing one letter precede and activate those representing its successor.

As neurological activity, conceptualization has a temporal dimension. Even the simplest conception requires some span of time for its occurrence, and with a more elaborate conception its temporal progression is subject to awareness. The meaning of a complex sentence (like this one) can hardly be apprehended instantaneously; more likely it unfolds on a clause-by-clause basis, there being no instant when all facets of it are simultaneously active and accessible. Conceptualization is **dynamic**

---

[4] Chafe characterizes discourse status in terms of activation levels: for "given", "accessible", and "new" information, he posits the respective levels "active", "semiactive", and "inactive" (1994: ch. 6).

in the sense that it unfolds through processing time, and also because the specific course of development is a significant aspect of our mental experience. Thus a pair of sentences like (1)(a)–(b) are not semantically equivalent, despite using the same words to characterize the same objective situation:

(1)   (a) *A line of trees extends from the highway to the river.*

      (b) *A line of trees extends from the river to the highway.*

Although the situation described is static, the sentences evoke dynamic conceptualizations in which we mentally scan along the line of trees in one direction or the other. These opposing ways of building up to the full conception, through processing time, result in subtly different mental experiences and different linguistic meanings.

Dynamicity bears on the fundamental issue of whether conceptual structure is basically **propositional** in nature or whether it has an **imagistic** character. What kind of format should we ascribe to thoughts and concepts, especially at lower levels of organization? Should they be formulaic in nature, comprising strings of discrete symbols? Or should they be more analogical, more directly depictive of the structure represented?[5] The propositional view, still prevalent if not predominant, treats concepts as expressions formulated in a "language of thought" (Fodor 1979), consisting of conceptual "primitives" (the "vocabulary") and principles for their combination (the "syntax"). The meaning of *enter*, for example, might be mentally represented by something comparable to the following formula (Jackendoff 1983):

(2) $[_{Event}$ GO $([_{Thing}$ X$], [_{Path}$ TO $([_{Place}$ IN $([_{Thing}$ Y$])])])]$

Cognitive linguists incline more to imagistic accounts. The best-known proposal posits a set of **image schemas**, described as schematized patterns of activity abstracted from everyday bodily experience, especially pertaining to vision, space, motion, and force. Image schemas are seen as basic, "preconceptual" structures that give rise to more elaborate and more abstract conceptions (or at least provide their skeletal organization) through combination and metaphorical projection.[6] As shown in figure 2.1, for instance, the concept ENTER can be analyzed as a combination of the image schemas object, source-path-goal, and container-content.

An imagistic approach is no less capable than a propositional one of precisely describing complex structures in terms of simpler conceptual components. It is arguably

---

[5] The issue is whether conceptualization per se is discrete and propositional in nature, independently of the discrete, propositional format imposed by linguistic encoding. Is thought itself "language-like" at all levels? Does the concept of a triangle, for example, decompose into propositions in the manner of fig. 1.1(a)?

[6] Johnson 1987; Lakoff 1987, 1990; Hampe 2005. Examples cited by Johnson are container, blockage, enablement, path, cycle, part-whole, full-empty, iteration, surface, balance, counterforce, attraction, link, near-far, merging, matching, contact, object, compulsion, restraint removal, mass-count, center-periphery, scale, splitting, superimposition, process, and collection. Note that diagrams like those in fig. 2.1 are not to be identified per se as image schemas (which are patterns of mental activity) but are merely intended to evoke them and suggest their nature.

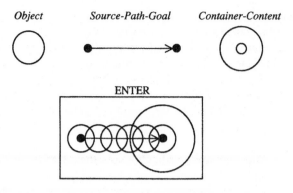

Object   *Source-Path-Goal*   *Container-Content*

ENTER

FIGURE 2.1

advantageous because—as seen by comparing (2) with figure 2.1—the nature of a mental experience is reflected more directly in a complex image than in a complex formula. Also, images seem particularly well suited (and formulas unsuited) for certain aspects of conception. Central to the concept of a trumpet, for instance, is a visual image of its shape, as well as an auditory image of its sound. Furthermore, the characterization of image schemas as patterns of activity dovetails quite nicely with the intrinsic dynamicity of conceptualization. I thus look with favor on an image-schematic approach to conceptual structure. Certainly I assume that the notions cited as image schemas function as components of more elaborate conceptual configurations.

Still, there has been some vagueness about the notion of image schemas, their inventory, and the criteria for identifying them. I am not at all sure that the examples commonly cited (n. 6) form a coherent or naturally delimited class. While adopting an imagistic orientation, for my own purposes I prefer to distinguish several kinds of fundamental notions, each "basic" in its own way and useful for the characterization of more complex structures:

1. Basic in one sense are **minimal concepts** in particular domains of experience. I have in mind such notions as line, angle, and curvature, in the spatial domain; brightness and focal colors, in vision; precedence, in time; and the kinesthetic sensation of exerting muscular force.
2. Also minimal, but independent of any particular experiential domain, are highly schematic **configurational concepts**, e.g. contrast, boundary, change, continuity, contact, inclusion, separation, proximity, multiplicity, group, and point vs. extension. Being abstract and applicable to most any domain, these come closest to the apparent spirit of image schemas.
3. Some notions commonly cited as image schemas fall instead in my third class, **conceptual archetypes**. These are experientially grounded concepts so frequent and fundamental in our everyday life that the label archetype does not seem inappropriate. Here are some examples: a physical object, an object in a location, an object moving through space, the human body, the human face, a whole and its parts, a

physical container and its contents, seeing something, holding something, handing something to someone, exerting force to effect a desired change, a face-to-face social encounter. These notions are fairly schematic, but considerably less so than the configurational concepts. Some are incorporated as components of others. While they can be quite complex and hard to describe explicitly (try explaining what a physical object is!), they are basic in the sense that they are readily apprehended as coherent conceptual gestalts at an early developmental stage.

I do not regard this three-way distinction as either clear-cut or the only useful classification. Certainly connections can be established among elements of the different groups. The minimal concept of a line, for example, bears an obvious affinity to the configurational notion of extension, as well as to the conceptual archetype of an object moving along a spatial path. Moreover, since all conceptions are dynamic (residing in processing activity), there is no sharp boundary between simple concepts and certain basic **cognitive abilities**. We can describe focal red as either a minimal concept or else the ability to perceive this color. Instead of describing contrast, group, and extension as configurational concepts, we can equally well speak of the ability to detect a contrast, to group a set of constitutive entities, and to mentally scan through a domain.

The essential point is that conceptions can be "basic" in very different ways. This makes possible a general CG proposal about certain grammatical notions that are fundamental and possibly universal. Minimally, these notions include noun, verb, subject, object, and possessive.[7] The proposal has several parts:

1. Each such notion can be characterized semantically in terms of both a **prototype**, valid for central instances, and a **schema** instantiated by all instances.
2. The prototypical meaning consists of an experientially grounded conceptual archetype.
3. The schematic meaning resides in a domain-independent cognitive ability.
4. The basic abilities are initially manifested in the corresponding archetypes. Presumably innate, the abilities make it possible for structured experience, based on these archetypes, to occur in the first place.
5. At a later developmental stage, these same abilities are extended to other domains of experience, where their application is less automatic (hence more apparent).

Let us see how this works in the case of nouns.

1. The noun category has both a semantic prototype and a semantic schema.
2. The prototype is the conception of a physical object.

---

[7] Nouns and verbs are discussed in ch. 4, subject and object in §7.4.3, and possessives (briefly) on p. 84.

3. Providing the schematic characterization is our capacity for conceptual grouping.
4. Developmentally, conceptual grouping is first manifested in the apprehension of physical objects, the noun category prototype.
5. It figures subsequently in the apprehension of the many other kinds of entities also coded by nouns.

I view the ability to perceive a discrete physical object, like a ball, as a low-level, essentially automatic manifestation of the same capacity more transparently involved in mentally forming a single entity by grouping the constitutive elements of an orchard, team, stack, alphabet, or archipelago. For most linguistic purposes, a noun like *ball* and a noun like *orchard* function alike (as singular, common, count nouns). Although the constitutive elements and their conceptual grouping are more evident with *orchard*, in each case the conception of a unitary entity emerges through cognitive processing at some level. The world does not present itself to us as a finished, predetermined structure, nor is apprehending the world like xeroxing a document. Even in the realm of concrete reality, its apprehension resides in dynamic, interactive processing activity. This is not to deny that the world is highly structured, so that certain ways of apprehending it are most likely to prove successful for both individuals and species. Because our own species has evolved to cope with the world successfully, we all comprehend it in largely commensurate ways that are grounded in common bodily experience. We all perceive physical objects and employ the same grouping capacity to recognize collective entities like an orchard or an archipelago.

Our apprehension of the world is thus active, dynamic, and constructive in nature. A fundamentally important consequence is that the conceptions evoked as linguistic meanings are **nontransparent**: they do not simply reflect or correspond to the world in a wholly straightforward manner, nor are they derivable in any direct or automatic way from objective circumstances. Instead, a conceptualist semantics must start by recognizing the prevalence—indeed, the utter pervasiveness—of imaginative devices and mental constructions. It is not merely that we frequently talk about imaginary worlds (like those of movies, fairy tales, soap operas, mythology, and linguistic theories). We further demonstrate our imaginative capacity in constructing and manipulating an extraordinary variety of **mental spaces** (Fauconnier 1985, 1997). Some types of mental spaces, respectively exemplified in (3), are those representing a hypothetical situation, a particular person's beliefs, the situation obtaining at a certain time or place, and the content of reported speech.

(3)   (a) *If we were rich, we could fly first class.* hypothetical

(b) *My lawyer thinks that the judge is incompetent.* opinion

(c) *Meanwhile, back at the ranch, a heated discussion was going on.* place

(d) *She indicated that they were having trouble with termites.*

Various other imaginative phenomena prove essential to conceptualization and linguistic meaning. A primary means of enhancing and even constructing our mental world is **metaphor**, where basic organizational features of one conceptual domain—usually more directly grounded in bodily experience—are projected onto another (Lakoff and Johnson 1980, 1999; Turner 1987). In (4), aspects of the **source domain**, pertaining to the manipulation of physical objects, are projected metaphorically onto the **target domain** of understanding and communicating ideas.

(4) (a) *I couldn't grasp what she was saying.*

    (b) *We were tossing some ideas around.*

    (c) *The message went right over his head.*

    (d) *He didn't catch my drift.*

Metaphor is one source of **blending**, in which selected features of two conceptions are combined to form a third (Fauconnier and Turner 1998, 2002). As hybrid mental constructions, blends are often quite fanciful but nonetheless are genuine objects of conception and linguistic expression. The entities portrayed in (4) as being grasped, thrown, and caught—combining as they do the abstract nature of ideas with certain physical properties of balls or other projectiles—cannot exist in reality. Neither do such blended creatures as mermaids and werewolves (let alone beagles who think in English sentences and imagine themselves as World War I pilots), but that does not stop us from thinking and talking about them. Even for the kinds of entities that do exist, what we refer to linguistically is often a **virtual** (or **fictive**) instance, i.e. an imaginary instance "conjured up" for some purpose. Cars exist, for example, but the car referred to in (5)(a) does not (it makes no sense to ask *Which car doesn't your brother have?*). It is rather an imagined instance invoked for the purpose of specifying the circumstance that is being negated.

(5) (a) *My brother doesn't have a car.*

    (b) *A kitten likes to chase a piece of string.*

Likewise, the kitten and the piece of string mentioned in (5)(b) are virtual entities conjured up to make a global generalization. The statement does not pertain to any particular kitten or piece of string, nor to any actual chasing event.

2.1.3 Where Does Meaning Stop?

At any given moment, we engage in conceptualizing activity at different levels of awareness and in varied domains of mental experience. It draws on many types of abilities (perceptual, motor, intellectual) and vast stores of knowledge (particular and general; physical, social, and cultural; individual, conventional, and contextual). The problems we now address pertain to the boundary between "linguistic" and "extralinguistic" concerns. What in all this counts as **language**? Which particular skills and bits of knowledge can we specifically characterize as being **linguistic**? Accompanying the production or understanding of any linguistic expression is a complex and multifaceted stream of conceptualization. How much of this should we identify as its **linguistic meaning**?

Standard doctrine holds that discrete boundaries ought to be expected. Language is commonly viewed as an autonomous mental "faculty" (Fodor 1983), so that knowledge of a language is fully describable by a large but limited set of statements. Linguists who reject this modular outlook still tend to posit a definite boundary between linguistic and extralinguistic knowledge, dividing the global understanding of expressions into linguistic meaning per se versus what can be pragmatically inferred. Nevertheless, received wisdom often proves erroneous. We need to ask whether these discrete boundaries are **discovered** by linguists or **imposed** on the basis of theoretical preconception. The answer, I believe, is clearly the latter: the linguistic and the extralinguistic form a gradation rather than being sharply distinct. While there are limits to linguistic meaning, and valid distinctions can be drawn, imposing specific boundaries is both arbitrary and misleading.

These issues arise for any aspect of language (FCG1: §2.1.2), but here the focus is meaning. We can start with lexical items, where two basic questions need to be considered. First, how many distinguishable meanings—often called **senses**—should be attributed to a given lexeme? Second, how much information do these senses include?

A lexical item used with any frequency is almost invariably **polysemous**: it has multiple, related meanings that have all been conventionalized to some degree. Among these related senses, some are more central, or **prototypical**, than others, and some are **schemas** that are elaborated (or instantiated) by others. To some extent the senses are linked by **categorizing relationships** to form a network.[8] Figure 2.2 is a partial network plausibly suggested for the noun *ring* (briefly discussed in §1.3.1). The boxes drawn with heavy lines indicate the most proto-typical senses. The arrows represent categorizing relationships: solid arrows for the elaboration of a schema, and dashed arrows for extension from a more central meaning.

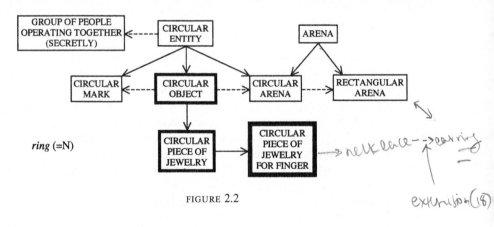

FIGURE 2.2

[8] For examples and discussion, see the following: Geeraerts 1993; Tuggy 1993, 2003a, 2003b; Tyler and Evans 2003; Riemer 2005. This network model is useful up to a point, but it may imply greater discreteness and specificity than is psychologically realistic. An alternative metaphor for complex categories is proposed at the end of §8.1.3.

An alternative is to claim that lexical items are **monosemous**, each having a single abstract meaning from which all its uses can be predicted (Ruhl 1989; Huffman 1997). Positing more specific senses, it is argued, leads to an uncontrolled proliferation of putative "meanings" that are better regarded as contextual interpretations of an item's abstract semantic value. I would counter by denying that a single abstract meaning enables one to predict, in full and precise detail, the actual range of specific senses in which a lexical item is conventionally employed. I can imagine a highly schematic meaning for *ring*—perhaps some abstract notion of enclosure—that would subsume all the more specific values depicted in figure 2.2. From this alone, however, one could hardly predict that *ring* would have exactly the set of particular uses that it manifests, to the exclusion of countless others (equally motivated by cognitive and communicative factors) that it lacks. Why should the term be used for arenas and groups of smugglers but not, say, for rubber bands?

Thus a single abstract meaning does not fully describe a lexical item's established semantic value. Such a meaning should always be sought, and—if found—incorporated in the polysemy network. By itself, though, it fails to represent a speaker's knowledge of how the expression is conventionally used and understood. This knowledge (surely part of knowing a language) resides in the entire network. To allay any fears, positing such networks does not result in an uncontrolled proliferation of senses. Meanings (like other linguistic structures) are recognized as part of a language only to the extent that they are (i) entrenched in the minds of individual speakers and (ii) conventional for members of a speech community. Only a limited array of senses satisfy these criteria and qualify as established **linguistic units**. But since entrenchment and conventionalization are inherently matters of degree, there is no discrete boundary between senses which have and which lack the status of established units. We find instead a gradation leading from novel interpretations, through incipient senses, to established linguistic meanings.

What does a particular lexical meaning include? If a lexical item (in one of its senses) refers to a certain type of entity, how much of our total knowledge of such entities constitutes its linguistic semantic value? Is there some portion of this knowledge that one possesses just by virtue of speaking a language?

Traditionally, this last question is answered in the affirmative. A lexical meaning is thought to consist of relatively few semantic features or descriptive statements, specifically linguistic in character, that are clearly distinguished from general knowledge concerning the type of entity referred to. The basic sense of *bull*, for example, is often represented by the semantic features [MALE], [ADULT], and [BOVINE], to the exclusion of anything else we might know about these creatures (e.g. their role in bullfights and rodeos). In this respect a lexical meaning would be more like a dictionary entry than an article in an encyclopedia. This approach is thus described metaphorically as the **dictionary view** of linguistic semantics, diagrammed in figure 2.3(a). The circle represents the total body of knowledge speakers have about the type of entity in question. Indicated by the heavy-line box is the small, discrete set of specifications constituting the lexical item's meaning.

These "purely linguistic" meanings have proved elusive. It has not been shown that precise boundaries can be drawn in a principled manner (Bolinger 1965; Haiman 1980), nor can descriptions like [MALE ADULT BOVINE] be considered

(a) *Dictionary Semantics*   (b) *Encyclopedic Semantics*

FIGURE 2.3

linguistically adequate. An alternative view, metaphorically referred to as **encyclopedic semantics**, is generally adopted in cognitive linguistics (FCG1: §4.2; cf. Wierzbicka 1995). In this approach, a lexical meaning resides in a particular way of **accessing** an open-ended body of knowledge pertaining to a certain type of entity. This knowledge is represented in figure 2.3(b) by a series of concentric circles, indicating that the knowledge components have varying degrees of **centrality**. This ranking for centrality is one facet of a lexical item's conventionally established value. For a given lexical meaning, certain specifications are so central that they are virtually always activated whenever the expression is used, while others are activated less consistently, and others are so peripheral that they are accessed only in special contexts. In figure 2.3(b), each heavy-line ellipse stands for the set of specifications activated on a single occasion. There need be no specification activated on every occasion, and every use may well involve a unique pattern of activation.

On the encyclopedic view, a lexical meaning is neither totally free nor totally fixed. It is not totally free because the expression evokes a certain range of knowledge and specifies a particular way of accessing it. It is not totally fixed because centrality (preferential access) is a matter of degree and subject to being overridden by contextual factors. This conception (developed further in §2.2) is both linguistically and psychologically realistic. While it does have the consequence that no discrete boundary can be drawn between linguistic and extralinguistic knowledge, any such boundary ought to be drawn on empirical grounds, not imposed a priori.

A comparable issue arises with respect to the meanings of complex expressions, such as sentences. When uttered in context, a sentence may invoke or convey considerably more than what it actually says. Owing to the previous discourse, to interpretive abilities, as well as to general and contextual knowledge, its full understanding may be far more elaborate than anything derivable from the meanings of overt elements. How much of this global understanding is properly identified as the expression's linguistic meaning? Or as the question is usually posed, which facets of it belong to **semantics** (reflecting the language per se) and which are better left for **pragmatics**?

The traditional position, that there is a definite boundary, reflects a **modular** view of language. This supposed modularity starts at the lexical level. Lexical items are thought of as building blocks, discrete units that are stacked in various arrangements to form complex expressions fully determined by the units and the patterns followed in arranging them. In semantics, this is known as the principle of **full compositionality** (an expression's meaning is predictably derivable from the meanings of its parts). The assumption of full compositionality implies a clear and definite distinction between semantics (compositionally determined meaning) and pragmatics (contextual interpretation). This is crucial for the claim of modularity made at a higher level, with respect to a language overall: that it is a well-delimited, self-contained system sharply distinct from other facets of cognition.[9]

Though standard, this modular conception is gratuitous and (I would argue) erroneous. I do not believe that a fixed boundary between semantics and pragmatics can be drawn on a principled basis in a way that makes linguistic sense.

A distinction can indeed be made between semantics and pragmatics. An expression's full contextual understanding goes beyond what can be determined from established linguistic units. Suppose we are looking at a cat, and I say *The bird is safe*. With this statement I may **implicate** that the cat is lazy or incompetent (relying on the context, encyclopedic knowledge of cats, and a general presumption of relevance), but I would not consider this to be part of its linguistic meaning. I therefore object when Levinson (1997: 19) characterizes me as a "stubborn ostrich" who "refuse[s] to countenance the existence of pragmatics."[10] He misinterprets my statement that "the distinction between semantics and pragmatics...is largely artifactual" by ignoring the further clarification that a viable linguistic semantics needs to avoid "such false dichotomies" (FCG1: 154). What is being denied is the strictly dichotomous view depicted in figure 2.4(a), with a fixed and definite boundary between two separate components. This denial does not entail either the nonexistence of pragmatics, as sketched in diagram (b), or the absence of any differentiation, as in (c). The claim, instead, is that semantics and pragmatics form a gradation, as shown in (d), with no precise boundary between the two. But toward either extreme of the scale lie phenomena that are indisputably either semantic or pragmatic.

At issue, then, is whether a discrete boundary can be found (not just arbitrarily imposed). Can we justifiably ascribe to complex expressions a level of "purely

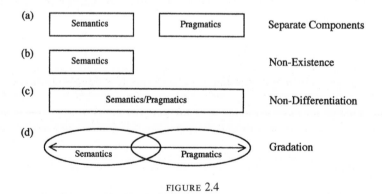

FIGURE 2.4

<hr />

[9] It is further assumed that a linguistic system is divisible into discrete "components" (such as lexicon, morphology, and syntax). I argue against this in §1.3.

[10] If I am a stubborn ostrich, it is for other reasons.

linguistic" meaning that is strictly predictable from the meanings of their parts? A variety of considerations suggests that the answer is negative. For one thing, the very question presupposes that the parts have clearly delimited linguistic meanings. That is, it presupposes the dictionary view of lexical semantics, which we have seen to be problematic. The alternative, encyclopedic approach entails that even the putative "building blocks" are flexibly construed. Rather than being fully pre-formed modules, with fixed and limited content, lexical items reside in conventional paths of access to domains of knowledge—not exclusively linguistic—that are evoked both variably and probabilistically. Even at this level we find a gradation between linguistic and extralinguistic knowledge.

When we consider semantic composition, the inappropriateness of the classic building block metaphor is even more evident. This is not to deny the existence of compositional patterns (in CG they constitute the semantic poles of schematic symbolic assemblies). The question is whether, starting from lexical meanings, these patterns alone give rise to semantic representations that are sufficiently coherent and self-contained to have any kind of independent cognitive status, or approximate anything recognizable as the meanings of complex expressions. Instead (ironically), I agree with Levinson (1997: 18–19) that indisputably "semantic" representations of this sort—compositionally derived from lexical building blocks—are "deeply inadequate mental orphans, which serve so effectively in human communication only through the rich interpretive principles we bring to bear on their development."

Among these interpretive principles are those discussed in the previous section: metaphor, blending, mental space construction, and the invocation of fictive entities. Calling me a *stubborn ostrich* was presumably not an attempt at biological classification but rather an instance of metaphor. By projecting selected features of the source domain (ostriches) onto the target domain (people), this metaphor creates the blended conception of a person who exhibits the fancied ostrich behavior of burying its head in the sand. This hybrid creature is only fictive; nobody believes that it actually exists. Yet, without describing it explicitly, the expression was specifically intended to evoke it metaphorically. Furthermore, the statement that this fictive ostrich/person *refuses to countenance the existence of pragmatics* induces the construction of mental spaces representing a belief and an attitude. It ascribes to the blended creature the belief that pragmatics does not exist, with the aim of imputing this belief (incorrectly) to its correspondent in the target domain (me). The attitude consists of being unwilling to even entertain the possibility that pragmatics exists. Since unwillingness implies that an option must at least be considered, the expression sets up a mental space that contains it, but only as an imagined potential occurrence. The creature's contemplating the possible existence of pragmatics is thus invoked as a virtual entity, conjured up just for purposes of indicating what might have been the case but actually is not.

The example is not at all unusual. When producing or understanding linguistic expressions, we engage in elaborate, highly sophisticated processes of **conceptual construction**, drawing on many and varied resources. Among these are lexical meanings and compositional patterns, as traditionally recognized. Another resource is our impressively rich imaginative capacity, featuring such devices as metaphor, blending, fictivity, and mental spaces. Moreover, the mental constructions evident in normal language use are critically reliant on general and contextual knowledge. For instance, my characterization as a *stubborn ostrich* exploited the folk conception, prevalent in our culture, that an ostrich buries its head in the sand to avoid facing up to problems. It is this notion (hardly part of a dictionary definition) that makes the full expression coherent, by providing a link between *ostrich* and *refuses to countenance the existence of pragmatics*.

Or consider once more *The bird is safe*, uttered while looking at a cat. The word *safe* implies potential danger, which in this context the speaker and hearer understand as residing in the feline. *Safe* might then be analyzed as an abbreviated way of saying *safe from the cat*, the context permitting elliptic expression. Though tacit, reference to the cat is not unreasonably viewed as part of the expression's linguistic meaning; after all, it corresponds to something (a source of danger) inherent in the meaning of *safe*.[11] Furthermore, in the same context it would also be felicitous to say the following: *The bird is safe, because it's smarter*. Here the cat is invoked not only as a source of danger but also, more saliently, as a standard of comparison. I doubt that a conceptualization excluding it would actually occur or be recognizable as what the utterance means.

An expression's meaning presupposes an extensive, multifaceted **conceptual substrate** that supports it, shapes it, and renders it coherent. Among the facets of this substrate are (i) the conceptions evoked or created through the previous discourse; (ii) engagement in the speech event itself, as part of the interlocutors' social interaction; (iii) apprehension of the physical, social, and cultural context; and (iv) any domains of knowledge that might prove relevant. Contributing in no small measure to both the substrate and its subsequent elaboration are imaginative and interpretive phenomena (such as metaphor, blending, fictivity, and mental space construction). All of this provides the setting for lexical interpretation and semantic composition. Contrary to the traditional modular view, these do not proceed autonomously or in a vacuum. A lexical item does not have a fully determinate meaning. Instead, its semantic value resides in conventional paths of access (some well-trodden, others less so) to open-ended domains of knowledge. Precisely what it means on a given occasion—which portions of this encyclopedic knowledge are activated, and to what degree—depends on all the factors cited. Likewise, patterns of semantic composition are only one of the resources exploited in the process of conceptual construction producing the meanings of complex expressions. This overall process results in highly elaborate conceptualizations whose construction is merely **prompted** by lexical meanings and compositional patterns, which are usually not themselves sufficient to **derive** them. I thus describe language as exhibiting only **partial compositionality**.

What should then be recognized as an expression's **linguistic meaning**? I suggest the following, nontechnical definition: besides elements that are indisputably semantic, an expression's meaning includes as much additional structure as is needed to render the conceptualization coherent and reflect what speakers would naively regard as being meant and said, while excluding factors that are indisputably pragmatic and not necessary to make sense of what is linguistically encoded. Admittedly, this is vague and

---

[11] This is not so for the possible implication that the cat is lazy or incompetent, cited previously as a case of pragmatic inference beyond the scope of linguistic meaning.

does not allow one to draw a line in any particular place, even for specific examples. But I also consider it appropriate. I prefer a realistic notion of linguistic meaning that is only fuzzily delimited and partially compositional, as opposed to one that (by definition) is precisely delimited and fully compositional, but whose cognitive status is quite dubious. My feeling is that focusing on the latter represents an artificial exercise, directed at something that may not exist at all, has no autonomous status if it does, and in any case represents only a small portion of the overall problem.

2.2 Conceptual Content

Linguistic meaning resides in conceptualization, which I have so far characterized as being dynamic, interactive, imagistic (as opposed to propositional), and imaginative (involving metaphor, blending, fictivity, and mental space construction). Important though they are, these general properties are not themselves adequate for describing conceptual structure in explicit detail. As the basis for semantic and grammatical description, we must now consider more specific proposals.

Most broadly, a meaning consists of both conceptual **content** and a particular way of **construing** that content. The term **construal** refers to our manifest ability to conceive and portray the same situation in alternate ways.[12] An initial example is sketched in figure 2.5. The content in question is the conception of a glass containing water occupying just half of its volume. At the conceptual level, we are presumably able to evoke this content in a fairly neutral manner. But as soon as we encode it linguistically, we necessarily impose a certain construal. Four such options are shown in the diagram, each corresponding to a distinct expression. The semantic contrast depicted (by means of heavy lines) lies in what the expressions designate (or refer to) within the conceived situation:[13] (1) *the glass with water in it* designates the container; (2) *the water in the glass* designates the liquid it contains; (3) *the glass is half-full* designates the relationship wherein the volume occupied by the liquid is just half of its potential volume; and (4) *the glass is half-empty* designates the relationship wherein the volume occupied by the void is just half of its potential volume.

The distinction between content and construal is not at all a sharp one. For instance, **level of specificity**—an aspect of construal—has a direct bearing on the content evoked: precisely because they differ in specificity, *the glass with water in it* has more content than *the container with liquid in it* (another way of coding the situation in figure 2.5). The distinction is nonetheless useful for expository purposes, as it highlights the essential point that conceptual meaning involves more than just truth conditions or the objective circumstances being described. Indeed, the meaning of many linguistic elements— especially those considered "grammatical"—consists primarily in the construal they impose, rather than any specific content. Yet every element evokes some content (however schematic it might be), and conversely, any content evoked is construed in some fashion. Content is the topic of this section. Construal is addressed in chapter 3.

[12] The term **construal** is preferable to **imagery**, used in certain earlier works, since the latter lends itself to confusion with more familiar applications (FCG1: 110).

[13] Called **profiling**, this aspect of construal is discussed in §3.3.1.

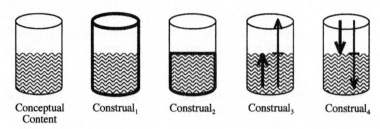

| Conceptual Content | Construual$_1$ | Construal$_2$ | Construal$_3$ | Construal$_4$ |

FIGURE 2.5

domain as content = expression ≠ construal

2.2.1 Domains

set of domains = matrix

Linguistic meaning involves both conceptual content and the construal imposed on that content. To have a uniform way of referring to content, the term **domain** is adopted in CG. An expression is said to invoke a set of cognitive domains as the basis for its meaning (i.e. as the content to be construed).[14] Collectively, this set of domains is called a **matrix**. For most expressions the matrix is **complex** in the sense of comprising multiple domains.

What is a domain, exactly? To serve its purpose, the term is broadly interpreted as indicating any kind of conception or realm of experience. Among the domains figuring in the content of figure 2.5, for example, are space, the sensation of wetness, the specific concept WATER (partly defined in terms of wetness), the more schematic concept LIQUID (immanent in WATER), the conception of a container and its contents, the more elaborate conception of filling a container with liquid, notions of volume and equality (hence equality of volume), as well as our knowledge of the cultural practice of filling a glass with water for the purpose of drinking it. We should not expect to arrive at any exhaustive list of the domains in a matrix or any unique way to divide an expression's content among them—how many domains we recognize, and which ones, depends on our purpose and to some extent is arbitrary. The important thing is to recognize the diverse and multifaceted nature of the conceptual content an expression evokes.

Obviously, many conceptions incorporate others or are in some sense reducible to more fundamental notions. Domains for which this is not the case are said to be **basic**. A basic domain is therefore cognitively irreducible, neither derivable from nor analyzable into other conceptions. Though I cannot give a definite inventory, some prime examples are space, time, and the ranges of unanalyzed experience associated with the various senses: color space (the range of colors we are capable of experiencing), pitch (the range of pitches we can perceive), temperature, taste and smell, and so on. In and of themselves, basic domains are not concepts or conceptualizations. They are better thought of as realms of experiential

---

[14] The selection of domains is itself an aspect of construal, reinforcing the point that the distinction between content and construal is not absolute.

potential, within which conceptualization can occur and specific concepts can emerge. For instance, color space—as the range of possible color sensations—is not the same as any particular color experience on a particular occasion (a kind of conceptualization), nor is it a color concept (e.g. RED). Likewise, space supports the conception of spatial configurations and time the conception of change. As basic domains, however, these are not themselves concepts but simply the spatial and temporal extensionality in which configurations are manifested and change unfolds.[15]

Most domains are **nonbasic**.[16] Of the ones listed above for figure 2.5, all are nonbasic except for space. Any kind of conceptualization counts as a nonbasic domain capable of being exploited for semantic purposes. Conceptions fall under this rubric whether they are sensory or intellectual, static or dynamic, fixed or novel, simple or complex. Included as nonbasic domains are instances of immediate sensory, emotive, and motor/kinesthetic experience (e.g. the sensation of wetness, of being afraid, or of blowing up a balloon), as well as the abstracted products of intellectual operations (e.g. concepts like JUSTICE, VERTEBRATE, and BATTING AVERAGE). Also included are conceptions manifested instantaneously at the level of conscious awareness (e.g. the image of a circle), as well as elaborate scenarios that we can only conceptualize stage by stage through processing time (like the successive steps in a complicated recipe). There is no requirement that a nonbasic domain be fixed, established, or conventionally recognized. Apprehension of the situational context thus qualifies as a cognitive domain, as does the previous discourse.

Nonbasic domains vary greatly in their degree of conceptual complexity. They range from minimal concepts (e.g. RED), to more elaborate conceptions (like the configuration of the human body), to entire systems of knowledge (such as everything we know about baseball). To some extent they arrange themselves in hierarchies, such that a conception at a given level presupposes and incorporates one or more lower-level conceptions. For instance, the concept APPLE incorporates RED; NECK invokes the overall shape of a body; and BATTING AVERAGE presupposes some knowledge of both arithmetic and baseball. In cases of this sort, where one conception—asymmetrically—presupposes another as part of its own characterization, they are said to occupy higher and lower **levels of conceptual organization**. Numerous levels of conceptual organization can often be discerned even in simple examples. In the case of ENTER (fig. 2.1), the concept of a physical object is one component of the higher-level conception of an object moving from source to goal along a spatial path. Along with the container-content schema, this is then incorporated as part of

---

[15] These basic domains are not per se the meanings of the words *space* and *time*. Their meanings are higher-order conceptions in which the dimensions function in their own right as objects of contemplation, rather than merely supporting spatial and temporal conceptualization. Similarly, the metaphorical construal of basic domains (e.g. *in a moment, bright sound, sharp taste*) results in conceptions that are not irreducible and are hence nonbasic.

[16] The term **abstract domain**, used in previous works, is infelicitous because many nonbasic conceptions pertain to physical circumstances.

ENTER, at the next higher level. In turn, ENTER is invoked for the character-ization of ENTRANCE, and so on indefinitely.

Such hierarchies are a fundamental aspect of conceptual structure and thus essential to semantics. Few linguistic meanings lend themselves to being directly and solely described in terms of basic domains or a putative set of primitive concepts.[17] Most expressions are best characterized with respect to higher-level notions whose relation to basic ones can be mediated by any number of intervening levels. As the basis for their meaning and hence the starting point for semantic description, expressions invoke conceptualizations at any level of organization and with any degree of complexity.

Consider the word *sophomore*. Among the elements that figure in its meaning are the basic domains of time and space, as well as such lower-level concepts as PERSON, KNOW, YEAR, and TWO, and higher-level notions such as LEARN, STUDY, STU-DENT, and SCHOOL. Clearly, though, the meaning of *sophomore* further—and cru-cially—invokes a still higher-level conception of the sort that Fillmore (1982) calls a **frame** and Lakoff (1987) refers to as an **idealized cognitive model** (or ICM). This is the idealized conception, quite familiar in our culture, of a nonelementary educational institution offering a course of study lasting precisely four years. While it incorporates the lower-level concepts, this ICM taken as a whole is the natural starting point for semantic description: with respect to it, we need only specify that *sophomore* desig-nates a person in the second year of study. We can say that the ICM provides the expression's conceptual content, the basis for its meaning, which results from constru-ing this content in a certain manner. In particular, *sophomore* is construed as designat-ing (profiling) a student in the second year (as opposed to *freshman*, *junior*, and *senior*, which have the same basic content but designate students in other years).

At this point some terminological clarification may be helpful. We seem to have a lot of terms that might all be applied to the same conceptual phenomenon: *concept*, *conception*, *conceptualization*, *(nonbasic) domain*, *frame*, and *idealized cognitive model*. Although usage varies and the contrasts are subtle, I should at least indicate how I myself tend to understand the terms.

The distinction between the first three terms and the second three is basically a matter of perspective: the former pertain to a notion considered in its own right, whereas the latter highlight its role in describing linguistic meanings. Within the first group of words, *conception* neutralizes the distinction between *concept*, which suggests a fixed or static notion, and *conceptualization*, which suggests dynamicity. However, since every conception is dynamic if viewed on a small enough time scale, *conceptualization* is also employed as a fully general term. The terms in the second group are often interchangeable. We can say, for instance, that *sophomore* derives its meaning by imposing a particular construal on the content supplied by a *domain*, a *frame*, or an *ICM*.[18] Yet these terms are not quite equivalent. *Domain* has the greatest

---

[17] This is clearly recognized by Wierzbicka (1996), who does base her descriptions on a set of irreducible semantic primitives (identified as lexical universals), but also posits hierarchies where a concept at any level incorporates simpler concepts previously assembled.

[18] Naturally, the resulting *concept((ualizat)ion)* may function in turn as a *domain/frame/ICM* for another expression (e.g. *sophomore yearbook*).

generality, since neither *frame* nor *ICM* applies very well to basic domains (e.g. time or color space). A *frame* may be roughly comparable to a *nonbasic domain*. If the words *idealized* and *model* are taken seriously, *idealized cognitive model* has the narrowest range of application. It would not, for example, apply to the ongoing discourse or the physical circumstances of the speech event.[19]

2.2.2 Accessing Domains

The set of domains an expression invokes is called its conceptual **matrix**. Usually there are multiple domains, in which case the matrix is said to be **complex**. In describing an expression's matrix, it is not sufficient merely to list the constitutive domains. How they relate to one another, and how they are mentally accessed, are an important dimension of linguistic meaning.

An instructive way to start is by considering one example in fair detail. The expression chosen is *glass*, in the ordinary sense whereby it designates a container used for drinking. Here are some of the domains that evidently figure in its conceptual characterization:

1. Space [a basic domain].
2. Shape [roughly that of a cylinder, closed at one end]. This nonbasic domain presupposes space, as the domain in which a shape conception is manifested.
3. Typical orientation in space [long dimension aligned along the vertical axis, with the closed end at the bottom]. Among the other domains this incorporates are space, verticality, and the shape conception.
4. Function$_1$ [container for liquid]. This presupposes the typical orientation, the concept of a liquid, and that of a container (which in turn incorporates such notions as spatial inclusion, potential motion, force, and constancy through time).
5. Function$_2$ [role in the process of drinking]. This incorporates function$_1$, as well as the conception of the human body, of grasping, motion with the arm, ingestion, etc.
6. Material [usually the substance glass].
7. Size [easily held in one hand].
8. Others [domains pertaining to cost, washing, storage, dropping and breaking, position on a table at mealtime, matching sets, method of manufacture, and so on].

According to the encyclopedic view of linguistic semantics (§2.1.3), the potentially relevant domains are an open-ended set. The example clearly indicates that, rather than being disjoint, the domains of a complex matrix overlap with one another, often to the extent of full inclusion. An attempt to convey this diagrammatically is made in figure 2.6, where domains are shown as ellipses. The heavy-line circle

---

[19] Of course, there are still more terms. For instance, *script* refers to an idealized sequence of actions. *Domain* and *mental space* are compared in §2.2.3.

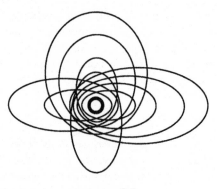

FIGURE 2.6

represents the entity designated by the expression (its profile), which has some role in all the domains of the matrix.

Not captured in figure 2.6 are the varying degrees of centrality ascribable to the domains of a complex matrix.[20] Centrality (FCG1: §4.2.2) is the likelihood of a particular domain being activated when an expression is used on a given occasion. Certain domains are so central that we can hardly use the expression without evoking them, some are activated less consistently, and others are so peripheral that we invoke them only in special circumstances, when they happen to be relevant. In our example (*glass*), domains 1 to 7 are clearly quite central, those listed under 8 more peripheral. A ranking for degree of centrality is depicted in figure 2.7. In this "exploded" diagram, the domains of a matrix are separately shown (ignoring their extensive overlap). The dotted lines, used for **correspondence**, indicate that the heavy-line circles all represent the same entity (namely the expression's designatum, represented just once in figure 2.6).

The relative centrality of constitutive domains is one facet of linguistic meaning, important for the characterization of lexical items. As part of its conventional semantic value, a lexeme not only gives access to a set of domains, but does so preferentially, making some especially likely to be activated. Occasionally a semantic contrast

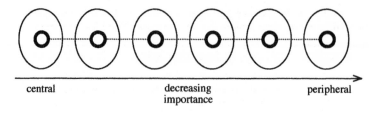

central   decreasing   peripheral
                          importance

FIGURE 2.7

---

[20] In fig. 2.3, degrees of centrality are indicated by concentric circles. The ellipses in fig. 2.6 represent domains (not individually shown in the former diagram).

resides less in the inventory of accessible domains than in their degree of accessibility. Although the same object might be referred to as either a *knife* or a *dagger*, and either can be used for stabbing someone, this possible function is far more central to the meaning of *dagger*. Or consider the contrast between *snail* and *escargot* (accepting that the latter is now an English word). Encyclopedic semantics implies that the two expressions afford potential access to the same domain inventory: it is part of our encyclopedic knowledge of snails that they are sometimes cooked and eaten (especially in French restaurants), and we know that escargots are the same creatures that infest our gardens. Yet *snail* and *escargot* clearly have different meanings, the contrast residing in how the domains are ranked (i.e. degree of centrality). With *escargot*, the domain of fancy cuisine is ranked very high; it is primarily this domain that is accessed, others—like the domain of garden pests—being activated only if there is special motivation. With *snail*, on the other hand, the domain of fancy cuisine is peripheral but fairly accessible. It is therefore natural (at least linguistically) to say *The snails were delicious*, but hardly **My garden is crawling with escargots.*[21]

Ranking for centrality implies that a lexical meaning, even if open-ended, is not totally free or unconstrained. A lexical item is partly defined by the likelihood (sometimes approaching categorical status) of particular domains being activated. It thus incorporates conventional ways of accessing a certain range of encyclopedic knowledge. At the same time, a lexical meaning is never totally fixed or invariable, for several reasons. First, the inclination for a given domain to be activated is probabilistic rather than absolute. A second reason is that the probabilities are subject to contextual modulation. Finally, they vary through time depending on the vicissitudes of usage.

These points seem fairly evident. That domains are activated with a certain probability is precisely what is meant by degree of centrality. Nor is there any doubt that the probabilities are altered by context and use. Contextual factors can obviously focus attention on a domain that might otherwise not be accessed at all or only at a lower level of activation. This in turn might lessen the activation of an otherwise salient specification. If (6)(a) induces a canonical construal of *glass*, with domains 1 to 7 all being accessed, examples (6)(b)–(d) skew the pattern by highlighting various domains of lesser centrality: breaking, matching, placement, and washing.

(6)   (a) *He took another sip from his glass.*

    (b) *This antique glass is quite fragile.*

    (c) *The glasses on that table don't match.*

    (d) *Plastic wine glasses are hard to wash.*

Directing attention to such notions tends to push more central specifications (like the role of a glass in drinking) into the background. They can even be suppressed

---

[21] Following standard linguistic practice, asterisks (and sometimes question marks) indicate that an expression is in some respect deviant or "ungrammatical". The basis for these assessments is discussed in ch. 8.

FIGURE 2.8

or overridden. In (6)(d), *wine* and *plastic* override the default specifications of *glass* with respect to shape and material. Moreover, their collocation with *glass* occurs so commonly these days that the default status of these specifications may well be diminished. Usage has a constant impact by either reinforcing the probabilities or adjusting them.

A ranking of domains for centrality measures their likelihood of being accessed and strongly activated, other things being equal. Yet other things are never really equal, since language use is never truly acontextual; an expression's manifestation is always subject to influence from the physical, linguistic, social, and psychological circumstances. Given a particular ranking, as depicted in figure 2.7, such influence results in specific patterns of activation representing a lexical item's contextual implementation in actual usage events. This is shown in figure 2.8, where the thickness of a line indicates the degree to which a domain is activated. From one usage event to the next, the domains accessed are likely to vary, as well as their level of activation. This variable activation is one reason why an expression appears to have different values on different occasions. It may be that, strictly speaking, a lexeme is never used twice with exactly the same meaning.

Followed to their logical conclusion, these observations have certain theoretical consequences that I consider quite natural (though some would regard them as unfortunate). They imply the absence of any specific line of demarcation that strictly separates linguistic meaning from either general knowledge or contextual interpretation. Since the conceptualizations that function as linguistic meanings are neither distinct from these nor well delimited, semantic structure cannot be exhaustively described. Nor is semantics fully compositional, if only because the putative building blocks—lexical meanings—do not have constant values. Moreover, since language necessarily incorporates semantics, it does not constitute an autonomous, self-contained "module" or "mental faculty".[22]

2.2.3 Domains and Mental Spaces

A cognitive **domain** was defined as any kind of conception or mental experience. The definition is very broad, intended to provide a uniform way of referring to anything exploited as the conceptual basis of linguistic meaning. Equally broad, and for a similar reason, is Fauconnier's definition of a **mental space** (1997: 11): "Mental spaces…are partial structures that proliferate when we think and talk, allowing a

---

[22] Cf. Fodor 1983. CG posits only semantic, phonological, and symbolic structures, the latter consisting in the pairings of semantic and phonological structures. Without semantics, therefore, only phonology is left.

fine-grained partitioning of our discourse and knowledge structures." It is not obvious that any conceptual structure is strictly excluded by either definition, and in practice the terms have overlapping ranges of application. What, then, is the relation between these notions? Are both terms really necessary?

As I see it, anything called a *domain* could also be referred to as a *mental space*, and conversely. From a purely referential standpoint, therefore, a single term would be sufficient. Yet referential coverage is not the only measure of a term's utility; even in the technical sphere, the same entity is often describable by means of alternate expressions that highlight different facets of it.[23] The terms *domain* and *mental space* represent nonequivalent ways of viewing conceptual structure, each reflecting a certain range of analytical concerns. *Domain* focuses on a conception's unity and internal coherence. As a way of referring to conceptual content, it tends to be used for established conceptions in relation to lexical meanings. By contrast, *mental space* emphasizes conceptual discontinuities, the partitioning of conceptual structure into semiautonomous regions. It tends to be employed for the products of imaginative operations and the structures created dynamically in discourse. These are only tendencies, however, and both terms are vague enough for general application.

The phenomena generally dealt with in mental space theory, and the analyses proposed, are readily accommodated in CG. This is actually quite evident, since any kind of conception counts as a domain, and no restrictions are imposed on how the domains of a matrix are related to one another. Thus any mental space configuration—including both the spaces and the connections linking them—can simply be incorporated as part of a matrix.

By way of illustration, consider the following metaphorical expression:

(7)   *The thought just flew right out of my head.*

Metaphor resides in a set of **connections** among a **source space**, a **target space**, and a **blended space**.[24] The target space is the one being structured metaphorically. In (7), it is the common experience of entertaining a thought but subsequently—when wanting to express it—being unable to access it. The source space is the (usually less abstract) notion serving as the basis for metaphorical projection. On one interpretation of (7), the source is identified as the conception of a bird flying out of a cage, with the consequence that the bird is no longer available for viewing. The blended space is the result of projecting the source onto the target. It is a hybrid conception, fictive in nature, combining selected features of each input space.

The spaces and connections evoked in (7) are roughly depicted in figure 2.9. The elements of the source space are a bird (B), a cage (C), and a viewer (V). The bird is in the cage, where the viewer can see it (as indicated by a dashed arrow), but then

[23] Referring to the same entity, for instance, a developer speaks of a *unit*, a contractor talks about a *structure*, and a realtor calls it a *home* (while the buyer just wants a *house*).

[24] This is the terminology used in blending theory, based on mental spaces (Fauconnier 1997; Fauconnier and Turner 1998, 2002). Previously (starting with Lakoff and Johnson 1980), cognitive linguists working on metaphor spoke (equivalently) of **mappings** between a **source domain** and a **target domain**, without positing a blend.

flies away (solid arrow) and becomes inaccessible. The elements of the target space are a thought (T), a person's head (H), and that person's "subject" (S)—that is, the subjective center of consciousness (Lakoff 1996). The dashed arrow represents the experience of having a thought, which subjectively occurs inside the head. Though not shown, the target scenario also includes a subsequent phase in which that thought is absent. Connections between spaces are given as dotted lines. Observe that connections are established between the bird and the thought, between the cage and the head, and between the viewer and the subject of consciousness. Further connections (not indicated, to simplify the diagram) hold between relationships in the two spaces: viewing a bird is likened to having a thought; and the bird flying away is likened to the thought becoming inaccessible. These connections are the basis for the metaphorical construal.

The blended space is formed from the other two by merging connected elements into new, hybrid entities retaining some, but not all, of their properties. The fictive, even fanciful nature of these imaginative creations does not make them mysterious or insignificant—on the contrary, they are crucial both conceptually and linguistically. The entity labeled T' blends the abstract nature of a thought with physical attributes of a bird, which enable it to fly through space. H' is a head, but more specifically it is a head conceived as a container that can hold an object (the way a cage holds a bird). And while S' is still a "subject" (or center of consciousness), it combines with this the properties of a viewer able to look inside a container (H') and examine its contents. This blended space provides the essential content of (7): despite its fictive character, the event that takes place there is precisely what the sentence directly describes.

In CG terms, each space in figure 2.9 qualifies as a domain, as does the entire space configuration. These spaces are part of the complex matrix comprising the expression's conceptual content. The connections between spaces conform to the general observation that the domains of a matrix are related to one another in various ways, rather than being separate or disjoint. Connections are a special case of

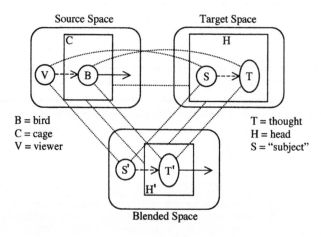

FIGURE 2.9

correspondences (represented as dotted lines), which have multiple applications in CG (FCG1: §2.3.2).

The example raises the broader issue of how domains are related to particular linguistic expressions. The kind of relationship discussed in the previous section—where a fixed expression provides a conventional way of accessing a certain set of domains—is by no means the only possibility. Besides simple lexical items (like *glass*), the overall picture must accommodate both novel and complex expressions, as well as their contextual and discourse interpretations.

For the most part, domains exist independently of any particular expression. They are not specifically linguistic, but conceptual resources that can be exploited for linguistic purposes. A given domain can thus be recruited for any number of different expressions. This is obviously true for basic domains such as time and space, which figure in the meanings of innumerable expressions without depending on any for their cognitive status. It is also true for many basic concepts (e.g. person, motion, physical object) and, on a lesser scale, for higher-order conceptions. For example, the practice of keeping a bird in a cage is easily accessible as part of the encyclopedic characterization of both *bird* and *cage* and is central to the meaning of *birdcage*. Moreover, this practice is commonly exploited in metaphorical expressions, even when there is no explicit reference to it, as seen in (7) and figure 2.9.

What happens when simpler expressions combine to form a more complex one? In principle, the matrix for the overall expression incorporates all the domains of the components. But it is not just the union of the component matrices. For one thing, as shown by *birdcage*, the composite expression provides its own way of accessing the constitutive domains. While the notion of keeping birds in cages is not peripheral with either *bird* or *cage*, taken individually, it is absolutely central to the meaning of the compound as a whole.[25] By the same token, *birdcage* affords only indirect access to certain domains that are fairly central to its components (e.g. hatching from eggs for *bird*, zoo for *cage*). Moreover, it is possible for a composite expression to invoke a domain that does not figure saliently in the meaning of any component. For instance, the compound *lipstick* pertains to the cultural practice of females coating their lips with a colored substance, typically packaged in small cylinders encased in metal or plastic and carried in purses. This cultural model cannot be ascribed to the matrix of *stick*, and for *lip* it is quite peripheral (*lip* would seldom evoke it in a neutral context). More clearly, the conception of a British soldier is central to the meaning of *redcoat* but absent from the matrices of *red* and *coat*. Nor does any word in (7) evoke by itself the idea of someone looking in an empty birdcage—this only emerges through a process of conceptual construction triggered by the entire expression.

Among the domains evoked as the basis for meaning, but not conventionally associated with component elements, are those consisting in a speaker's apprehension of the current discourse context. Suppose you are helping me put away the groceries. I see you there in the pantry holding several cans of tomatoes, with a quizzical

---

[25] By itself, neither *bird* nor *cage* necessarily evokes the practice, but *birdcage* is virtually certain to do so. Each component reinforces this aspect of the other's encyclopedic semantics.

look on your face. In this context, I might use any of the expressions in (8) to convey what is effectively the same message:

(8)   (a) *I want you to put the canned tomatoes on the top shelf of the pantry.*

    (b) *Put the tomatoes on the top shelf of the pantry.*

    (c) *Put them on the top shelf.*

    (d) *Tomatoes, top shelf.*

    (e) *On the top shelf.*

    (f) *On top.*

Our shared apprehension of the situational context provides a conceptual substrate, various facets of which are overtly expressed. By virtue of this substrate, even the most fragmentary expressions are coherent and meaningful (indeed, the first two seem needlessly verbose). I have defined an expression's meaning as including not only the content directly coded by overt elements but whatever additional structure is needed to render a conceptualization coherent and reflect what speakers would naively regard as being meant and said (§2.1.3). By this criterion, the meanings of all the expressions in (8) include at least the content expressed in (8)(a).[26]

This runs counter to conventional wisdom, which insists on a clear distinction between linguistic meaning and contextual interpretation. An expression's meaning would be limited to what is strictly derivable from the (nonencyclopedic) meanings of its parts, and as such would be well delimited, self-contained, acontextual, and fully compositional. It is thus no accident that sentence "fragments" like (8)(d)–(f) are traditionally ignored, for it is only the context that renders them coherent or supplies enough content to make them conceptually or communicatively useful. Such fragments are both normal and highly frequent in everyday language use, however. As seen in (8)(a)–(f), moreover, expressions cover the full spectrum in terms of what proportion of their essential content is contextually induced and what proportion is explicitly encoded. Insofar as possible, the entire spectrum of cases should be treated analogously. An expression is always understood with respect to some actual or imagined context. Only by avoiding an artificial dichotomy between linguistic meaning and contextual interpretation can we handle the full range of data in a unified manner.

---

[26] If all the expressions in (8) should have the same content, they are nevertheless semantically nonequivalent owing to construal. In particular, they contrast in regard to which facets of the overall content are explicitly mentioned and thereby rendered prominent in relation to tacit elements.

3

Construal

An expression's meaning is not just the conceptual content it evokes—equally important is how that content is construed. As part of its conventional semantic value, every symbolic structure construes its content in a certain fashion. It is hard to resist the visual metaphor, where content is likened to a scene and construal to a particular way of viewing it. Importantly, CG does **not** claim that all meanings are based on space or visual perception,[1] but the visual metaphor does suggest a way to classify the many facets of construal, if only for expository purposes. In viewing a scene, what we actually see depends on how closely we examine it, what we choose to look at, which elements we pay most attention to, and where we view it from. The corresponding labels I will use, for broad classes of construal phenomena, are **specificity**, **focusing**, **prominence**, and **perspective**. They apply to conceptions in any domain.

3.1 Specificity

One dimension of construal is the level of precision and detail at which a situation is characterized. I can describe the temperature by saying that it is *hot*, but also—with progressively greater specificity—by saying that it is *in the 90s*, *about 95 degrees*, or *exactly 95.2 degrees*. Similarly, *aunt* is more specific than *relative*, and *large brown rat* is more specific than *rodent*. Alternate terms are **granularity** and **resolution**. A highly specific expression describes a situation in fine-grained detail, with high resolution. With expressions of lesser specificity, we are limited to coarse-grained descriptions whose low resolution reveals only gross features and global organization.

The converse of specificity is **schematicity**. Thus *relative* is schematic with respect to *aunt*, and *rodent* with respect to *large brown rat*. A schematic characterization is **instantiated** by any number of more specific ones, each serving to **elaborate**

---

[1] This fact has not prevented uninformed commentators from claiming that it does. To the extent that **conception** and visual **perception** are analogous, I use the term **viewing** for both (GC: ch. 7). Talmy (1996) refers to them both as "ception".

its coarse-grained specifications. Elaborating *rodent*, in different ways and to different degrees, are *rat, large brown rat, vole, curious mouse, ground squirrel, ferocious porcupine with sharp quills*, and so on indefinitely. An elaborative relationship is represented by a solid arrow: A → B. Expressions can often be arranged in elaborative hierarchies, as in (1), where each expression is schematic with respect to those that follow.

(1)　(a)　*rodent → rat → large brown rat → large brown rat with halitosis*

　　　(b)　*hot → in the 90s → about 95 degrees → exactly 95.2 degrees*

Participating in elaborative relations are both lexical items and novel expressions of any size. In lexicon, such relations constitute **taxonomies**, i.e. hierarchies of conventionally recognized **types**, like the one in (2)(a). An elaborative hierarchy containing novel expressions, in this case full sentences, is given in (2)(b).

(2)　(a)　*thing → object → tool → hammer → claw hammer*

　　　(b)　*Something happened. → A person perceived a rodent. → A girl saw a porcupine. → An alert little girl wearing glasses caught a brief glimpse of a ferocious porcupine with sharp quills.*

We can make an expression as specific as we like, for it can be of any length. By making it longer, we can always describe a situation more precisely and in greater detail. There are practical limits, however. Being of finite length, a particular expression can only be specific to a certain extent, and only with respect to certain facets of the overall situation. The sentences in (2)(b) are actually rather unnatural because in each case the major elements are all presented at a comparable level of specificity. More typical are expressions like (3), exhibiting a mixture of schematic and specific description:[2]

(3)　*Somebody saw a ferocious porcupine with sharp quills.*

Lexical meanings are likewise specific in only some respects, schematic in others. For instance, *carnivorous* and *nocturnal* are each specific concerning one aspect of an animal's behavior but otherwise are quite schematic. The verb *crush* designates a fairly specific type of interaction, yet the participants it invokes are only vaguely characterized: as an agent (or energy source) and a deformable object.

　　Schematization is fundamental to cognition, constantly occurring in every realm of experience. The extraction of a schema is simply the reinforcing of something inherent in multiple experiences, at whatever level of granularity their commonality emerges. A schema should therefore be seen as **immanent** in its varied instantiations, not as separate and distinct (even if shown individually for analytical purposes). By its very nature, a schema serves a **categorizing** function: capturing what is common

---

[2] In spontaneous speech, there is a strong tendency for a single clause or a single "intonation unit" to contain just one element introducing a substantial amount of new and important information (Du Bois 1987; Chafe 1994: ch. 5).

to certain previous experiences, it can be applied to any new experience exhibiting the same configuration.

Schemas and elaborative relationships are essential in every aspect of language structure. CG claims that all linguistic generalizations arise via schematization from more specific structures. In semantics, schemas and categorizing relationships (based on either elaboration or extension) constitute the network representing the senses of a polysemous lexical item (fig. 2.2). In phonology, schemas characterize "natural classes" (like [VOICELESS STOP]) as well as phonotactic patterns (e.g. [CCVC], specifying a permissible type of syllable). The schemas expressing grammatical regularities are symbolic, each consisting of a semantic and a phonological pole. Here too schemas characterize both natural classes (such as verbs) and combinatory patterns (e.g. a passive construction). Finally, as representations of conventional patterns, schemas provide the basis for assessing linguistic well-formedness. An expression is judged well-formed to the extent that it bears relationships of elaboration (rather than extension) to the schemas invoked to categorize it.

3.2 Focusing

Through linguistic expressions, we access particular portions of our conceptual universe. The dimension of construal referred to here as focusing includes the **selection** of conceptual content for linguistic presentation, as well as its arrangement into what can broadly be described (metaphorically) as **foreground** vs. **background**.[3]

The encyclopedic view of lexical meaning illustrates both aspects of focusing. As part of its conventional value, a lexical item provides direct access to a set of cognitive domains (its matrix) ranked for centrality (likelihood of activation). The domain inventory represents a selection of conceptual content. Also, central domains are foregrounded (in the sense of being more accessible) vis-à-vis peripheral ones. Focusing is further evident in how a lexical item is actually understood in the context of a usage event. Of all the domains in the matrix, only a limited number can be activated on a given occasion (fig. 2.3(b)). This is a kind of selection. Moreover, the domains selected are activated to varying degrees (fig. 2.8). A high level of activation is a kind of foregrounding.

Focusing is thus a matter of degree. It is also relative to particular purposes, dimensions of structure, and levels of organization. In a complex matrix, a domain in the foreground—by virtue of being central (highly susceptible to activation)—may nonetheless remain in the background (being only weakly activated) on a certain occasion. We saw previously, for the compound *lipstick*, that the cultural practice of painting lips has a different status at the two levels of structural organization. At the lower level, this domain is not selected at all by *stick* and is rather peripheral to *lip*. Yet it is very much in the foreground at the higher level, being strongly evoked by *lipstick* as a whole.

---

[3] To unify these aspects of focusing, observe that selected content is foregrounded relative to unselected content. Also, certain kinds of prominence (e.g. profiling) can be thought of as extreme cases of focusing/foregrounding.

3.2.1 Foreground vs. Background

Many kinds of asymmetries lend themselves to metaphoric description as foreground vs. background. Though distinguishable, they can all be seen as manifesting a very general feature of cognition. Most broadly, they all involve departure from a baseline, the exploitation of previous experience (what has already been established) for the interpretation of subsequent experience.[4] A manifestation in perception is the phenomenon known as **figure** vs. **ground**. For instance, a sudden noise stands out as figure against the ground of silence, or a small, moving cursor against the more stable background on a computer screen. Another manifestation is categorization, which succeeds to the extent that the categorizing structure is recognized within the experience being categorized. The categorizing structure lies in the background, taken for granted as a preestablished basis for assessment, while the target is in the foreground of awareness as the structure being observed and assessed.

We can reasonably speak of background and foreground for any case where one conception precedes and in some way facilitates the emergence of another. In this broad sense, we can say that expressions invoke background knowledge as the basis for their understanding. Such knowledge is presupposed even by a detailed sentence like *I want you to put the canned tomatoes on the top shelf of the pantry*. Though seemingly explicit, its default interpretation relies, inter alia, on cultural knowledge pertaining to food storage and pantry organization. Without this background knowledge, we might interpret the sentence as indicating that the tomatoes should be removed from the cans before being placed on the shelf, or that the cans should be glued to the face of the shelf instead of being placed on its upper surface. Further in the background, but equally essential, is basic knowledge of our physical world as we experience it (e.g. the experience of reaching upward, or the knowledge that objects will fall to the ground unless supported).

In similar fashion, the source domain of a metaphor has a kind of precedence vis-à-vis the target domain. Usually more concrete or more directly anchored in bodily experience, the source domain provides a conceptual background in terms of which the target domain is viewed and understood. Viewing the target against this background results in a hybrid domain, or blended space (fig. 2.9). We can also say, with equal validity, that the source and target domains jointly constitute the background from which the blended conception emerges. Not only does the blend inherit selected features of both the source and the target but it is also foregrounded in the sense of being most directly coded linguistically. In *The thought just flew right out of my head*, it is only a hybrid, bird-like thought that is capable of flight.

Foreground and background have numerous manifestations in discourse (Langacker 2001b). In a narration, for example, static descriptions of the characters and situation serve as the background against which the "story line"—a series of bounded events—stands out as a kind of figure (Hopper and Thompson 1980). Along another axis, we can distinguish the important content a speaker foregrounds as the actual target of

---

[4] Although terms like "foreground", "background", and "baseline" are visual and spatial in origin, the asymmetries in question most likely have some temporal basis in cognitive processing. Even in vision, to perceive something as standing out against a background is to register a contrast presupposing the background as a basis for comparison (FCG1: §3.1).

discussion from subsidiary comments pertaining to its status or assessment. I have in mind examples like (4)(a)–(b), where smaller print represents this communicative backgrounding. Phonologically, it corresponds to the phrases in question being unaccented and lower in pitch.

(4) (a) *Victoria would, I think, make a good candidate.*

    (b) *Victoria would make a good candidate, I believe.*

    (c) *I think Victoria would make a good candidate.*

    (d) *I definitely anticipate that Victoria would make a good candidate.*

    (e) *Jason stated that Victoria would make a good candidate.*

In sentence (c) we observe that even a "main clause" (i.e. one foregrounded in a structural sense) can be backgrounded in this manner. The main-clause situation stays in the foreground when described in fuller detail, as in (d), or when the opinion is attributed to someone other than the speaker, as in (e).

As discourse unfolds, at each step the current expression is constructed and interpreted against the background of those that have gone before. The prior discourse is a major determinant (along with context, background knowledge, etc.) of what I call the **current discourse space** (CDS). The CDS is a mental space comprising everything presumed to be shared by the speaker and hearer as the basis for discourse at a given moment. Starting from that basis, each successive utterance updates the CDS in some fashion. In (5), for example, speaker A's question updates the CDS by introducing a proposition to be considered ('Victoria will agree to be a candidate'), as well as the expectation that an interlocutor will answer concerning its possible validity. This forms the basis for speaker B's response, which in turn creates the updated CDS presupposed by C's continuation.

(5) **A:** *Will Victoria agree to be a candidate?* **B:** *She may not.* **C:** *But Stephanie will.*

As this discourse fragment shows, reference to the CDS is inherent in the meanings of many linguistic elements. A personal pronoun, like *she*, carries the supposition that its intended referent is established, salient, and uniquely identifiable in the CDS (van Hoek 1997). Negation evokes as background the positive conception of what is being denied.[5] Speaker B's use of *not* is thus interpreted as applying to the previously introduced notion of Victoria agreeing to be a candidate. *But* indicates a contrast with what has gone before. In using it, speaker C is contrasting Stephanie's agreement to be a candidate with Victoria's possible nonagreement, just invoked by B.

The CDS also figures in various phenomena collectively referred to as **information structure**. Information is said to be **given** or **new**, depending on whether it has already been presented; if given, it can sometimes be left implicit. While *agree to be a candidate* is new for speaker A, its occurrence in A's question makes it given

---

[5] I would have no reason to say *My car isn't purple* unless the possibility of it being purple had already been mentioned or somehow brought up for consideration.

for B and C, whose responses can therefore be elliptic. When a new proposition is expressed, the portion departing from what was previously established is called the **focus**. In C's utterance, *Stephanie* is the focus, since that is the point of difference between the proposition 'someone will agree to be a candidate' (already in the CDS) and 'Stephanie will agree to be a candidate' (the contextual interpretation of C's elliptic statement). Finally, the entire sequence in (5) is construed as pertaining to a particular discourse **topic**, which—once established as such—need not be explicitly mentioned. From earlier statements, for instance, it might be clear that the entire discourse fragment relates to the next president of the local chapter of the ACLU.

3.2.2 Composition

Let us now turn to focusing that is inherent in the meanings of individual expressions. Most expressions are **symbolically complex**, being assembled out of smaller symbolic elements (§1.3.1). For example, *lipstick* has *lip* and *stick* as symbolic components. These are **component** symbolic structures, *lipstick* as an integrated whole being the **composite** symbolic structure. Likewise, *make* and *-er* are symbolic components of the composite expression *maker*. A composite structure can itself function as a component structure in an expression of greater symbolic complexity. *Lipstick* and *maker* are thus components of the higher-level composite structure *lipstick maker*. Linguists refer to this hierarchical arrangement as **constituency** and represent it in tree-like diagrams (e.g. fig. 1.3). One version of such a diagram is given for *lipstick maker* in figure 3.1.

As the diagram indicates, the relation between component and composite structures is an instance of background vs. foreground. The relative degree of foregrounding is represented here by the thickness of lines.[6] When we use the composite expression *lipstick maker*, we certainly access the individual meanings of *lipstick* and *maker*. We do not evoke them for their own sake, however, but only as a way of "reaching" the novel composite conception, LIPSTICK MAKER. Because the

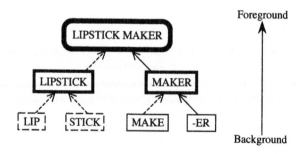

FIGURE 3.1

---

[6] Also, since LIPSTICK MAKER is a novel conception, the box enclosing it has rounded corners. The dashed and solid arrows connecting the boxes indicate relationships of categorization (extension and elaboration, respectively). Their rationale is discussed in ch. 6.

notions LIPSTICK and MAKER are individually symbolized, and thus facilitate the emergence of the composite conception, they exhibit the conceptual precedence characteristic of background status. Analogously, the conceptual components LIP and STICK are backgrounded in relation to LIPSTICK, as are MAKE and -ER in relation to MAKER. Of course, when there are multiple levels of composition, the highest-level composite structure (in this case LIPSTICK MAKER) is foregrounded with respect to the structures at all lower levels.

Composite expressions exhibit varying degrees of **analyzability**; that is, they vary in how salient the component structures are in relation to the composite conception, and how strongly they contribute to its emergence. A novel expression, such as *lipstick maker*, is fully analyzable precisely because it is novel. Since LIPSTICK MAKER is not a prepackaged conceptual unit, it has to be actively constructed on the basis of the individually symbolized notions LIPSTICK and MAKER, which are therefore highly activated and salient within the whole. With a fixed expression, on the other hand, the composite conception does constitute a prepackaged unit, so instead of being newly constructed it need only be activated. No longer is it essential that the symbolic components be recognized and their individual meanings accessed. For fixed expressions, consequently, we can posit degrees of analyzability, depending on how consistently and saliently the component conceptions are accessed along with the composite conception. *Maker*, for instance, seems more analyzable than *lipstick* (as shown by the dashed-line boxes in fig. 3.1). The discrepancy is quite evident in cases like *complainer*, *computer*, and *propeller*. We immediately understand *complainer* as 'someone who complains', but *computer* is not necessarily apprehended as 'something that computes', and *propel* may not be recognized at all in *propeller*.

How an expression's composite meaning relates to those of its components (at successive levels of organization) is called its **compositional path**. Figure 3.1 sketches the compositional path of *lipstick maker*. An important claim of CG is that an expression's meaning does not consist of its composite semantic structure alone, but further includes its compositional path, the two standing in a foreground/background relationship. While the composite conception is primary, it is viewed against the background of the component semantic structures at all lower levels. How strongly a particular component contributes to this secondary dimension of meaning depends on its proximity to the composite structure along the compositional path, as well as the expression's degree of analyzability at the various levels. LIPSTICK and MAKER are thus quite salient by virtue of proximity—*lipstick* and *maker* being **immediate** constituents of *lipstick maker*—and also because the composite expression is fully analyzable at that level. MAKE and -ER are less salient within the overall expression since they are backgrounded relative to MAKER, while LIP and STICK are less salient still since *lipstick* has a lower degree of analyzability.

Why should we define an expression's meaning as including its compositional path? For one thing, it just seems right—this is a very real dimension of conceptual organization, and to ignore it is simply pointless. More significantly, it helps explain the commonplace observation that no two expressions are exactly the same in meaning. A classic example is *pork* vs. *pig meat*. Suppose, for sake of argument, that their composite semantic structures are taken as being identical. They are nevertheless semantically nonequivalent, since they arrive at this composite conception via different compositional paths: a **degenerate** path in the case of *pork* (consisting of just the composite structure, since there are no individually symbolized components); and for *pig meat*, a path incorporating both PIG and MEAT. The semantic difference, then, is that *pig meat* evokes the component notions PIG and MEAT more saliently than does *pork*. Similar examples abound. The word *cousin*, being unanalyzable, directly invokes a particular kinship configuration, viewed holistically, whereas *parent's sibling's child* arrives at the same configuration step by step, in effect taking us on a tour of the family tree. By the same token, *triangle* does not have the same meaning as *three-angled polygon*, irrespective of whether their composite semantic structures are identical. The notions THREE and ANGLE figure in both expressions but are less salient in *triangle*, which has a low degree of analyzability. Being individually symbolized, the schematic concept POLYGON is necessarily accessed in *three-angled polygon* but remains implicit with *triangle*. It should further be evident that *three-angled polygon* and *three-sided polygon* are semantically distinct, despite their referential identity.

By acknowledging the semantic contribution of compositional paths, we can also explain why expressions that are **semantically anomalous**—having no coherent composite structure—nonetheless seem meaningful. Consider **four-sided triangle*. It is semantically anomalous because the component conceptions FOUR-SIDED and TRIANGLE are inconsistent with one another; when we attempt to combine them in the manner specified by the grammatical construction, the composite semantic structure is either defective or vacuous (depending on how we choose to look at it). The expression is not semantically empty, however: its semantic pole consists of a compositional path with meaningful components arranged in a particular configuration. By virtue of their distinct compositional paths, different anomalous expressions are nonsynonymous. While both **four-sided triangle* and **four-angled triangle* are incoherent at the composite-structure level, they contrast in meaning because their compositional paths incorporate different elements (SIDE, SIDED, and FOUR-SIDED vs. ANGLE, ANGLED, and FOUR-ANGLED).

3.2.3 Scope

In addition to foregrounding, focusing includes the initial selection of conceptual content for linguistic presentation. One facet of selection is the access an expression affords to a particular set of cognitive domains, in general or on a given occasion. A second facet is the extent of an expression's "coverage" in the domains accessed: which portions of these domains it actually evokes and utilizes as the basis for its meaning. For each domain in its matrix, an expression has a **scope** consisting of its coverage in that domain.[7]

Scope has an evident cognitive basis: there is only so much that we can mentally encompass at any one moment. For example, our visual apparatus limits what we can see at any one time. Experientially, we have a restricted "viewing frame"—the visual field—delimiting what we can visually encompass when "looking out" at the world. At any one instant, only a limited portion of our spatial surroundings falls within the

---

[7] Full coverage (where scope and domain are coextensive) is allowed as a special case.

scope of vision. We can recognize an analogous delimitation for other domains of experience. For each domain it evokes, an expression's scope is the conceptual content appearing in the subjective viewing frame inherent in its apprehension.

A scope is always **bounded**, in the abstract sense of having only limited expanse. Consider a word like *glass*, which evokes the domain of space for the specification of its characteristic shape. Entertaining this shape conception requires a certain spatial expanse, extensive enough to support its manifestation, but this spatial scope does not subsume the entire universe. Similarly, conceptualizing an event—e.g. *stumble*—requires that we mentally access a span of time long enough to encompass its occurrence, but this temporal scope does not include all of eternity. A term like *cousin* evokes a nonbasic domain comprising a network of kinship relations. While a kinship network can be extended indefinitely far in any direction, a mere fragment is sufficient to conceptualize the *cousin* relationship.

Bounding (in this abstract sense) does not imply that a scope's boundary is objectively discernible. It may only be implicit, imposed by the subjective viewing frame, and not necessarily with any great precision. Indeed, a viewing frame subjectively constant in size may subtend a region of virtually any (objective) size in the domain being viewed. Subjectively, our visual field is fixed in size (try expanding it!), yet by adjusting for distance we can greatly modify how much of the surrounding world it delimits; when viewing a distant mountain range, our visual scope is vastly greater than when looking at a painting from close up. This subjective constancy despite variation in scope is quite significant linguistically. Because of it, the same expression is often applicable to situations observable at any **scale**. The description *X is close to Y* is equally felicitous when applied to the distance between two neurons, two cities, or two galaxies. We can use the word *horse* not only for a real equine of normal stature but also for a small toy or an enormous sculpture carved from a mountain. It is not just a matter of perceiving their common shape and ignoring the gross disparity in their sizes; in relation to the subjective viewing frame (either the visual field or its conceptual analog), they may in fact be of comparable size.

One reason for grouping selection and foregrounding under a common rubric (focusing) is that scope—a matter of selection—can itself be arranged in terms of foreground vs. background. We sometimes need to distinguish between an expression's **maximal scope** in some domain, i.e. the full extent of its coverage, and a limited **immediate scope**, the portion directly relevant for a particular purpose. The immediate scope is thus foregrounded vis-à-vis the maximal scope. Metaphorically, we can describe it as the "onstage region", the general region of viewing attention.

Consider a word like *elbow*. Clearly, one domain it selects—quite central in its matrix—is the conception of the human body.[8] But it is equally clear that *elbow* is not characterized directly with respect to the human body as an undifferentiated whole. A body has major parts, including arms, and an elbow is first and foremost part of an arm. In conceptualizing an elbow, the conception of an arm in particular is most directly relevant ("onstage"). There is a conceptual hierarchy, such that BODY

---

[8] Linguists thus refer to such expressions as "body-part terms".

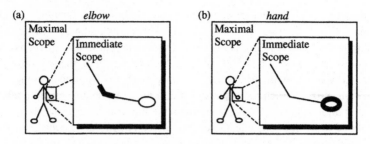

FIGURE 3.2

figures directly in ARM, which in turn figures directly in ELBOW, but BODY figures only indirectly in ELBOW (via ARM). For *elbow*, then, we can say that BODY functions as maximal scope and ARM as immediate scope. This is shown diagrammatically in figure 3.2(a).

Distinctions between maximal and immediate scope are quite significant in hierarchies consisting of successive whole-part relations. While body-part terms afford the clearest examples, there are similar hierarchies in other domains of experience:

(6) (a) *body > arm > hand > finger > knuckle*

  (b) *body > head > face > eye > pupil*

  (c) *house > door > hinge > screw*

  (d) *car > motor > piston > ring*

A striking feature of such hierarchies is that each part functions as immediate scope for the next term in the sequence. The conception of an arm is thus the immediate scope for *hand* (fig. 3.2(b)), a hand for *finger*, and a finger for *knuckle*. This type of arrangement is depicted abstractly in figure 3.3(a), where MS and IS indicate maximal and immediate scope, and a heavy-line box represents the entity designated by each successive expression (its profile). The dotted correspondence lines equate the entity designated by each expression with the immediate scope for the next. As a consequence, each term incorporates in its matrix the essential content of all the terms that precede it in the hierarchy. The result, as shown for Part$_3$ in figure 3.3(b),

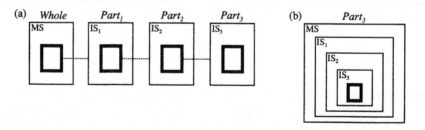

FIGURE 3.3

is a layered arrangement of successively embedded scopes. For a given expression, degree of embedding correlates with degree of foregrounding and directness of mental access. *Knuckle*, for instance, provides direct mental access to FINGER (its immediate scope), which in turn evokes HAND, and so on. The conception of a finger, a hand, an arm, and the body as a whole all figure in the meaning of *knuckle* but lie progressively farther in the background.

This layering has various linguistic manifestations. To take just one, a part can often be labeled by a compound: *fingertip, ear lobe, eyeball, toenail, bellybutton, kneecap, thigh bone, door knob, window pane, toilet seat, piston ring,* and so on. A noteworthy feature of these compounds is that the component nouns represent adjacent levels in a whole-part hierarchy. More specifically, the entity designated by the first element of the compound functions as immediate scope for the second element, as well as for the composite expression; the referent of *toilet*, for instance, constitutes the immediate scope for interpreting both *seat* and *toilet seat*. Skipping levels usually results in an infelicitous expression. We can therefore speak of a *door hinge* or a *hinge screw*, but the same entities could hardly be referred to as a *house hinge or *door screw. And as alternatives to *fingernail, eyelash,* and *shoulder blade*, compounds like *armnail, *facelash, and *body blade would simply not work.

The distinction between maximal and immediate scope is not confined to whole-part hierarchies. A rather different example is found in the contrast between a verb designating a bounded event (e.g. *examine*) and the corresponding progressive (*be examining*), formed by adding *be...-ing*. The domain of interest is time, indicated in figure 3.4 by the arrow labeled t.

For the verb itself (*V*), there is no reason to distinguish maximal and immediate scope, so the box delimiting the temporal scope in diagram (a) is labeled MS/IS. The heavy line represents the event designated by the verb, viewed in its evolution through time. The entire bounded event, including its endpoints, appears "onstage" within the temporal scope. Diagram (b) shows the effect of adding the progressive *be...-ing*. Its meaning resides in the construal it imposes on the content supplied by the verb. Specifically, it "zooms in" and imposes a limited immediate scope that excludes the endpoints of the bounded event. The composite expression *be Ving* therefore has both a maximal and an immediate scope in the temporal domain: its maximal scope encompasses the entire bounded event, of which only some internal portion falls within the immediate scope. Because the immediate scope is foregrounded, only this onstage portion of the overall event stands out as the composite expression's referent. So in contrast to *She examined it*, which designates a complete act of examination and specifies its past occurrence, *She was examining it* merely indicates that such an act was under way.

FIGURE 3.4

3.3 Prominence

Language structure displays numerous kinds of asymmetries that are reasonably considered matters of prominence. The terms **prominence** and **salience** (used here interchangeably) are not self-explanatory. Because something can be salient in many different ways, describing it as such is not an adequate characterization but only a starting point for analysis.

What are some dimensions of prominence? Focusing fits comfortably under this rubric, since anything selected is rendered prominent relative to what is unselected, and a foreground is salient relative to its background. Within a category, the prototype has greater prominence than its various extensions.[9] Space and vision have a privileged cognitive status vis-à-vis other realms of experience. More generally, an intrinsic disparity in salience seems clearly evident between the members of various oppositions: concrete vs. abstract, real vs. imaginary, explicit vs. implicit, and so on. Whether such asymmetries can all be grouped under a single label is less important than properly distinguishing them and determining which ones figure in particular phenomena.

Here I concentrate on two particular sorts of prominence: **profiling** and **trajector/landmark alignment**. Though not equivalent, they are similar in that each involves the focusing of attention (a strong kind of foregrounding). Both constructs are strongly justified on semantic grounds. They also prove essential in grammatical description.

3.3.1 Profiling

As the basis for its meaning, an expression selects a certain body of conceptual content. Let us call this its conceptual **base**. Construed broadly, an expression's conceptual base is identified as its maximal scope in all domains of its matrix (or all domains accessed on a given occasion). Construed more narrowly, its base is identified as the immediate scope in active domains—that is, the portion put "onstage" and foregrounded as the general locus of viewing attention. Within this onstage region, attention is directed to a particular substructure, called the **profile**. Thus an expression's profile stands out as the specific **focus** of attention within its immediate scope.[10] The profile can also be characterized as what the expression is conceived as designating or referring to within its base (its conceptual referent).

Consider *elbow*, diagrammed in figure 3.2(a). With respect to spatial configuration, its maximal scope is the overall shape of the human body.[11] Within this, the conception of an arm is put onstage as the immediate scope, or general locus of attention. Within the immediate scope, the expression singles out a certain substructure as

---

[9] Also, in taxonomies a **basic level category** (e.g. *hammer*) has greater cognitive salience than either a **subordinate** category (*claw hammer*) or a **superordinate** one (*tool*) (Taylor 2004: §3.3).

[10] The immediate and maximal scopes are not necessarily distinct (see fig. 3.4).

[11] Space and spatial configuration are not the only domains in the matrix of *elbow*, but they are obviously highly central. I emphasize that the semantic descriptions offered here do not purport to be exhaustive but are merely illustrative of the phenomena being discussed.

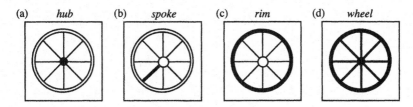

FIGURE 3.5

its profile, or referent. The profile—drawn with heavy lines—is the specific focus of attention within the onstage region.

If we now compare *elbow* with *hand*, sketched in figure 3.2(b), we see that *hand* has the same maximal and immediate scopes as *elbow* but a different profile. In fact, it is quite common that two or more expressions evoke the same conceptual content yet differ in meaning by virtue of profiling different substructures within this common base. For instance, *Monday*, *Tuesday*, *Wednesday*, etc. all evoke as their base the conception of a seven-day cycle constituting a week, within which they profile different segments. Similarly, as shown in figure 3.5, the conception of a wheel functions as the base for *hub*, *spoke*, and *rim*, which contrast semantically because they designate different parts. *Wheel*, of course, profiles the whole.

An expression can profile either a **thing** or a **relationship**.[12] The ones considered so far profile things despite incorporating relationships in their base (notably whole-part relations). Indeed, it is common for an expression to invoke a relationship for its essential conceptual content even though it profiles a thing. A good example is a kin term, such as *aunt*, diagrammed in figure 3.6. The essential content of this lexeme is the kinship relation between a female and a reference individual, R (the one with respect to whom the person is an aunt). It is this relationship that is critical for characterizing the female in question. *Aunt*, however, does not profile the relationship but rather the female it serves to identify—its referent is a person, albeit one characterized as a female relative. Note that the profile is not defined as the most important or distinctive content, but rather as the entity an expression designates, i.e. its referent within the content evoked.

FIGURE 3.6

---

[12] This fundamentally important conceptual distinction is discussed in ch. 4. For now I simply note that these terms are defined abstractly (hence things are not limited to physical objects, nor does a relationship necessarily involve multiple participants).

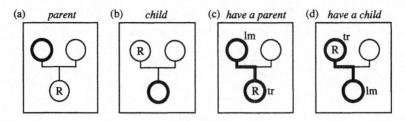

FIGURE 3.7

This distinction—between crucially invoking a relationship and actually profiling it—is exemplified in figure 3.7. All four expressions invoke the conception of a nuclear kin relation (involving one instance of reproduction). Their semantic nonequivalence derives from the different profiles they impose on this common base. *Parent* and *child* (in the 'offspring' sense) are like *aunt*, in that each profiles a thing characterized by its role in the relation; the latter remains unprofiled, since the referent of *parent* or *child* is a person, not a relationship. This relationship is, however, profiled by the composite expressions *have a parent* and *have a child*. These designate the relationship itself, viewed as a stable situation continuing through time. The semantic contrast between *have a parent* and *have a child* resides in their opposite directionality: each portrays the relationship as proceeding from the reference individual (R) of the kin term it incorporates.[13]

Although *have a parent* and *have a child* contrast in directionality, they do not have different profiles. An expression's profile is its referent, and the relationship designated is the same referentially with either direction of mental access. It is, however, common for expressions that profile relationships (like those which profile things) to have the same conceptual base and yet be semantically distinct because they profile different facets of it. For a grammatical example, consider any verb and its corresponding progressive (e.g. *examine* vs. *be examining*), diagrammed in figure 3.4. The verb designates an entire bounded event, while the progressive, without altering the overall content, singles out just an arbitrary internal portion of that event for profiling. A lexical example is *come* vs. *arrive*, diagrammed in figure 3.8. As their base, both verbs evoke the conception of a thing (represented as a circle) moving along a spatial path (arrow) to an end location (LOC). Each verb invokes a relationship in which the mover, through time, successively occupies all the positions defining the path. The difference in their meanings is that *come* profiles the full motion event, in which the mover traverses the entire path, whereas *arrive* designates only the segment in which the mover finally reaches the goal.

---

[13] The labels tr and lm indicate **trajector** and **landmark**, to be discussed shortly. The choice of trajector is responsible for the difference in directionality.

FIGURE 3.8

Profiling figures crucially in the pervasive phenomenon known as **metonymy**. In a narrow sense, we can characterize metonymy as a shift in profile. For example, a customer who says (7)(a) to a waiter is not claiming to be an Italian dessert. While this would be the usual referent of *tiramisu*, in the restaurant context its profile shifts from the dessert to the person who ordered it. Similarly, in (7)(b) the entity absent from the phone book is not the famous golfer per se but rather his name, address, and telephone number. The profile of *Tiger Woods* shifts from the person to the associated information (or its printed representation).

(7)   (a) *I'm the tiramisu.*

    (b) *She couldn't find Tiger Woods in the phone book.*

Mediating the shift in profile is a cognitive domain establishing some connection between the two entities: the restaurant scenario of customers placing orders, or else the knowledge of what a phone book is for. More precisely, then, we speak of metonymy when an expression that ordinarily profiles one entity is used instead to profile another entity associated with it in some domain. A single expression is susceptible to any number of metonymic extensions, reflecting different associations.[14] For instance, *Miró* would ordinarily be understood as referring to a person, as in (8)(a). Since Miró was a famous artist, reference to this person tends to evoke the conception of his works, as well as the more elaborate conceptions of exhibits or books featuring a single artist's works. Mediated by these domains, *Miró* is interpreted metonymically in (8)(b)–(d) as designating a work of art, a collection of works, and a book, respectively.

(8)   (a) *Miró died in 1983.*

    (b) *She bought an original Miró.*

    (c) *Miró is in Gallery B, at the end of this corridor.*

    (d) *Miró is at the bottom of the stack, right under Tamayo.*

There are many conventional patterns of metonymy, like the extension from artist to artistic creation. These can be applied productively. If Tiger Woods should give

---

[14] Being based on association in a single domain, metonymy is distinct from metaphor; instead, metaphor involves an abstract similarity between two domains (source and target).

up golf for sculpture, we can immediately refer to one of his creations by saying *This is a Tiger Woods*. Metonymy is a regular source of polysemy, which results when a particular metonymic usage becomes entrenched and conventionalized. Thus *church* can profile either a building used for religious meetings or a religious organization that meets in such buildings:

(9)   (a) *They built a new church just out of town.*

    (b) *The church he belongs to has very odd beliefs.*

And while the usual examples of metonymy pertain to things, we can also observe it in expressions that profile relationships. Consider these two uses of *come*:

(10)   (a) *They came all the way from Los Angeles.*

    (b) *He came at precisely 7:45 PM.*

In (10)(a), *come* profiles the full event of moving along an extended spatial path, as shown in figure 3.8(a). In (10)(b), however, it designates only the final stage of arriving at the goal (making it comparable to *arrive* in figure 3.8(b)). Because they profile different substructures within a common base, the two senses are related metonymically, and since they are both conventionally established, *come* is polysemous.

We have now seen numerous cases where a difference in meaning stems from alternate choices of profile within the same conceptual base. Since the content is effectively equivalent, these semantic contrasts are matters of construal—in particular, the directing of attention to a thing or relationship thereby singled out as an expression's conceptual referent. Profiling is not the only descriptive construct needed pertaining to focus of attention, however. One can easily find expressions that are semantically distinct despite having the same conceptual base and profiling the same relationship within it. An additional construct is therefore required to properly distinguish the meanings of relational expressions. This is **trajector/landmark alignment**, another kind of prominence.

3.3.2 Trajector/Landmark Alignment

When a relationship is profiled, varying degrees of prominence are conferred on its participants. The most prominent participant, called the **trajector** (tr), is the entity construed as being located, evaluated, or described. Impressionistically, it can be characterized as the **primary focus** within the profiled relationship. Often some other participant is made prominent as a **secondary focus**. If so, this is called a **landmark** (lm). Expressions can have the same content, and profile the same relationship, but differ in meaning because they make different choices of trajector and landmark.[15]

---

[15] In earlier works, every relational expression was said to have a trajector and a landmark, defined as the entities between which the profiled relationship holds (FCG1: §6.3). Under that definition, the trajector and landmark are not necessarily distinct or individually salient. I now reserve the terms for entities with focal prominence.

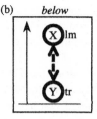

FIGURE 3.9

The prepositions *above* and *below* differ in this manner. They are clearly not synonymous. Where, however, does their contrast in meaning lie? They have the same content: each indicates the relative spatial location of two things, primarily with respect to the vertical axis. Moreover, as shown in figure 3.9, they also profile the same relationship: referentially, *X above Y* is the same relationship as *Y below X*. The semantic contrast can only reside in the degree of prominence conferred on the relational participants. We use *X above Y* to specify the location of X (the higher participant), and *Y below X* to locate Y (the lower participant). This makes X and Y their respective trajectors. In each case the other participant functions as a spatial landmark for that purpose. This difference in trajector/landmark alignment, a matter of construal, is solely responsible for *above* and *below* being semantically distinct.

If *above* and *below* contrast in their choice of trajector, characterized as the participant being located or assessed, the discourse context should sometimes determine which preposition will be used. This prediction is borne out by data like the following:

(11)　(a)　*Where is the lamp?*

　　　　(i)　*The lamp (tr) is above the table (lm).*

　　　　(ii)　**The table (tr) is below the lamp (lm).*

　　　(b)　*Where is the table?*

　　　　(i)　*The table (tr) is below the lamp (lm).*

　　　　(ii)　**The lamp (tr) is above the table (lm).*

The question in (11)(a) makes it clear that the lamp is interpreted as the thing being located. In this context, the answer is felicitous only when *the lamp* specifies the trajector, as in response (i), not the landmark, as in (ii). In (11)(b), where the table is the entity being located, these judgments are naturally reversed.

Many relational expressions have only a single focal participant. By default, the sole focal participant must be the primary focal participant, which makes it the trajector. With verbs like *come* and *arrive*, the mover has this status (fig. 3.8). The relationship they profile is the mover's translation through space, which clearly involves a series of locations that the mover successively occupies. But while these successive locations support the conception of spatial movement, they remain in the background rather than stand out as focused elements.[16] These verbs thus have a trajector but no landmark.

It is important to realize that a trajector does not have to be a mover (nor is a mover necessarily a trajector). Instead, trajector and landmark are defined in terms of primary and secondary **focal prominence**, not in terms of any specific semantic role or conceptual content. The notions are therefore applicable to any kind of cognitive domain. We can see this with the non-motion expressions *have a parent* and *have a child*, diagrammed in figure 3.7. Although they profile the same relationship, which is static and abstract, they are semantically distinct due to their opposite trajector/landmark alignments: *have a parent* is the description of a child, while *have a child* describes a parent. Note further that focal prominence is not restricted to things—a relationship can also be put in focus as trajector or landmark. In (12), for instance, *before* and *after* profile a relationship of temporal precedence between two events, which are thus the relational participants; but since these events are expressed as finite clauses, they are themselves relational expressions:

(12)   (a) *The other guests all left before we arrived.*

        (b) *We arrived after the other guests all left.*

Once again, as shown in figure 3.10, *before* and *after* designate what is referentially the same relationship. The semantic contrast between them resides in their choice of trajector and landmark, not in content or profiling.

As a final word on prominence, let us ponder the issue of where to look for it. If a certain element is salient, as either a profile or a focal participant, where exactly does its salience lie? It does not lie in the outside world. If we look at our surroundings, we do not see objects bordered with heavy lines to mark them as profiles, nor is something intrinsically a trajector or a landmark. Like other aspects of construal, prominence is a conceptual phenomenon, inhering in our apprehension of the world,

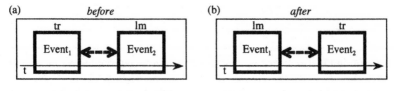

FIGURE 3.10

[16] That is, the locations are viewed merely as part of the spatial medium in which the motion occurs. Even the end location, which (as goal) has a certain amount of salience, lacks the focal prominence of a landmark and is often not expressed (*They finally came*; *We just arrived*).

not in the world per se.[17] However, merely acknowledging its conceptual nature is insufficient. Even at the conceptual level, the objects of our mental universe have no inherent status as profile, trajector, or landmark. These pertain specifically to the conceptualizations evoked as the meanings of linguistic expressions. How prominent a particular entity is—whether it functions as profile, trajector, landmark, or none of the above—depends on the construal imposed by the linguistic elements employed, in accordance with their conventional semantic values.

Consider *The lamp is above the table*. The lamp has trajector status only by virtue of how the situation is linguistically expressed. It reflects the speaker's decision to say where the lamp is, and thus to use *above*, which puts primary focus on the vertically higher participant. Yet nothing forces the speaker to construe and describe the scene this way. In another discourse context (e.g. when discussing a certain table), the speaker might say instead *The table is below the lamp*. Here the same lamp is only a landmark.

Crucially, these kinds of prominence hold for particular levels of structural organization. As we combine elements to form progressively larger expressions, the composite structure at each level has its own profile; and if that expression profiles a relationship, it has its own trajector/landmark alignment. By itself, for instance, *table* profiles a thing, as does *the table*. But at a higher structural level, *above the table* profiles a spatial relationship. It is only when we reach this level that *the table* functions as landmark. At a still higher level, where the prepositional phrase modifies a noun, the latter imposes its own profile on the composite expression: *the lamp above the table* profiles the lamp, not the table or the *above* relationship. This entire nominal can then be used as a subject or object, as in the sentence *She detests the lamp above the table*. At the sentence level, the profiled relationship is *detest* (not *above*), the trajector is *she*, and the landmark is the lamp (not the table). In sum, each structure in a symbolic assembly makes its own assignments of focus, so an entity focused in one structure need not have comparable salience in another.

3.4 Perspective

If conceptualization (metaphorically) is the viewing of a scene, perspective is the **viewing arrangement**, the most obvious aspect of which is the vantage point assumed. Under the rubric of perspective I also consider **dynamicity**, pertaining to how a conceptualization unfolds through processing time.

3.4.1 Viewing Arrangement

A **viewing arrangement** is the overall relationship between the "viewers" and the situation being "viewed". For our purposes, the viewers are conceptualizers who apprehend the meanings of linguistic expressions: the speaker and the hearer.

---

[17] This is not to deny that the world imposes itself in particular ways, thereby constraining and biasing our apprehension of it. Likewise, normal patterns of conceptualization constrain and bias the conceptualizations invoked for linguistic purposes. We nevertheless have enormous conceptual flexibility, and the biases at each level are easily overridden.

One particular viewing arrangement, common in everyday conversational interactions, arguably has default-case status, being presupposed unless there is reason to assume the contrary. In the default arrangement, the interlocutors are together in a fixed location, from which they observe and describe actual occurrences in the world around them. This default arrangement is tacitly invoked for the kinds of example sentences invented by linguists for basic illustrative purposes, e.g. *The lamp is above the table* or *John kissed Mary*.

Precisely because of its default-case status, this arrangement tends to be invisible to us. But though we take it for granted, the default arrangement is an essential part of the conceptual substrate that supports an expression's meaning and shapes its form. The default arrangement becomes more visible when we consider various departures from it, noting the changes in form and meaning that ensue. Most apparent are expressions that perform an action other than mere description, such as questions and commands:

(13)   (a) *Is the lamp above the table?*

       (b) *Kiss her!*

Semantically, these do not report on what is happening but actually comprise a particular kind of speaker-hearer interaction, traditionally called a **speech act**. This special meaning is signaled by distinct forms (involving word order, intonation, and/or absence of an overt subject). However it is not just the meanings of "special" sentence types like interrogatives and imperatives that incorporate speech acts signaled by their forms. Simple description also represents a kind of speaker-hearer interaction, and basic declarative form (i.e. the absence of special marking) can be seen as a way of indicating it.[18] We tend to ignore this specification only because it reflects the default viewing arrangement, for which zero marking is both natural and iconic (Haiman 1985).

A glance at some other noncanonical viewing circumstances reveals how much of a special case the default arrangement really is. First, a large proportion of what we describe fails to qualify as actual occurrences observed or known to be real. We often say what did not happen, as well as what may or may not occur in the future. We readily invoke hypothetical situations, even some known to be false, and trace their nonfactual development (e.g. *If you had asked for directions we wouldn't have gotten lost*). Moreover, we refer to all manner of entities that are virtual, imaginary, blended, abstract, and/or internally contradictory (*every flea*, *Santa Claus*, *pet rock*, *compassionate conservative*, *four-sided triangle*, *the square root of minus one*, *the last digit in the decimal expansion of pi*).

Rather different are departures from the default arrangement involving the relative position of the viewers. For example, instead of occupying a fixed location, the viewer is often conceived as being in motion. In (14)(a), *through this valley* describes the path of the viewer's motion, which otherwise remains implicit. In (14)(b), it is

---

[18] Simple description is usually (but misleadingly) called **assertion**. Note that questioning, ordering, and assertion are only the prototypical values of the interrogative, imperative, and declarative sentence types (viewed as forms). The same forms can be used for other speech acts, and the same speech acts can be expressed in other ways.

only the presupposed journey that makes it coherent to characterize the length of a nap by means of a spatial distance.

(14) (a) *It's pretty through this valley.*

  (b) *She's been asleep for 30 miles.*

  (c) *The trees are rushing past at 90 miles per hour.*

  (d) *The forest is getting thicker.*

Movement by the viewer can also engender a perception of change which, though virtual in nature, is described as if it were actual. While it is possible in (14)(c) that the trees actually are in motion, the more likely interpretation is that a moving viewer (perhaps riding in a train) is describing the visual impression obtained by imagining the default arrangement where the viewer is static. Similarly, the more likely interpretation of (14)(d) does not involve any actual change in the forest. Rather, movement through the forest brings the viewer into contact with different portions of it, which—when fictively construed as the same entity—are seen as increasing in density. Although these expressions make no explicit reference to the viewer's motion, it is nonetheless part of their conceptual substrate, in no small measure being responsible for their conceptual coherence as well as their form.

Another possibility is for the interlocutors to be separated in space or time. Consider the banal statement *It's warm here.* In a face-to-face conversation, *here* refers to the area where both the speaker and the hearer are located. But in the context of a long-distance phone call, the proximate region it designates is defined in relation to the speaker alone: *It's warm here, but it must be cold where you are.* Illustrating displacement in time is the recorded message one hears when making a phone call and reaching an answering machine. This message might begin with the statement *I'm not here right now*, which is contradictory presuming the default viewing arrangement (by definition, where I am right now is *here*). In recording the message, however, the speaker interprets *right now* as referring to the later time when a caller will hear it, and at that time the speaker will not be at home (*here*). What makes the message coherent and easy to understand is our apprehension of the overall communicative situation, part of the tacit conceptual substrate. An extreme example of spatiotemporal displacement is a sign or warning label, e.g. *Shake well before using* (Sadock 1974). Here the expressive medium is writing rather than speech. Moreover, the writer is not a particular person but a generalized voice of authority (perhaps the manufacturer), the reader is whoever should happen to use the product, and a usage event occurs whenever and wherever the label is read. The specific time and place of writing are unknown and irrelevant.

One component of the viewing arrangement is a presupposed **vantage point**. In the default arrangement, the vantage point is the actual location of the speaker and hearer. The same objective situation can be observed and described from any number of different vantage points, resulting in different construals which may have overt consequences. Many expressions undeniably invoke a vantage point as part of their meaning (arguably, all expressions do). In one of their basic uses, for example, *in front of* and *behind* rely on vantage point to specify the trajector's location

FIGURE 3.11

vis-à-vis the landmark. This is sketched in figure 3.11, where VP labels the vantage point and a dashed arrow indicates the viewer's line of sight. In both cases, one focal participant intervenes in the line of sight leading from the vantage point to the other participant. As in previous examples, the semantic contrast resides in choice of trajector and landmark, there being no significant difference in content or profiling.

If we imagine a scene with a large rock and a tree, how we code it linguistically depends on the vantage point we assume. Let us suppose that the rock, tree, and vantage point are roughly in alignment, as indicated in (15)(a). Then, if the vantage point is such that the rock intervenes in the line of sight (VP_1), we can happily use either sentence in (15)(b). If the vantage point is such that the tree intervenes (VP_2), the sentences in (15)(c) are appropriate instead.

(15)   (a) VP_1 ---> (**rock**)————(**tree**) <--- VP_2

      (b) VP_1: *The rock (**tr**) is in front of the tree (**lm**). The tree (**tr**) is behind the rock (**lm**).*

      (c) VP_2: *The tree (**tr**) is in front of the rock (**lm**). The rock (**tr**) is behind the tree (**lm**).*

Of course, the vantage point assumed for linguistic purposes need not be the speaker's actual location. We can easily adopt a fictive vantage point and imagine what the scene would look like from there. The following would thus be appropriate and readily understood when uttered at VP_1:

(16) VP_1: *If you were standing over there* [at VP_2], *the tree would be in front of the rock.*

This capacity to fictively adopt or at least accommodate a nonactual vantage point enables us to describe a situation from the perspective of the hearer or some other individual.

While the term suggests space and vision, vantage point is a useful descriptive construct for other domains as well, notably time. As shown in figure 3.12, the phrase *next year* evokes as its base the conception of a series of years, within which it profiles the year immediately following the one containing the temporal vantage point. In the default situation, this vantage point is equated with the time of speaking, as in (17)(a).

(17)   (a) *Next year will be full of surprises.*

      (b) *Joe believed that next year would be full of surprises.*

FIGURE 3.12

But here too we can easily adopt a vantage point other than the one defined by the speech event. In (17)(b), *next year* invokes a temporal vantage point identified as the time of the main-clause occurrence: the year in question is the one immediately following the year when Joe entertained his belief (not the year when the sentence is produced).

Closely related to vantage point is a subtle but important aspect of construal known in CG as **subjectivity** vs. **objectivity**. Though quite general in application, it is best introduced with reference to visual perception. Imagine yourself in the audience of a theater, watching a gripping play. All your attention is directed at the stage, and is focused more specifically on the actor presently speaking. Being totally absorbed in the play, you have hardly any awareness of yourself or your own immediate circumstances. This viewing arrangement therefore maximizes the asymmetry between the **viewer** and what is **viewed**, also called the **subject** and **object** of perception. In this polarized arrangement, where the asymmetry in viewing role is maximized, the viewing subject is said to be construed with maximal **subjectivity** and the object with maximal **objectivity**. Subjective construal is characteristic of the viewer's role as such—as an offstage locus of perceptual experience that is not itself perceived. Conversely, objective construal characterizes the onstage focus of attention, which (at least in that capacity) does not engage in viewing. By virtue of being attended to, an entity construed objectively is clearly more prominent than it is when construed subjectively.[19]

For linguistic purposes, we are interested in the general conceptual analog of this perceptual asymmetry. The subjects of conception are the speaker and hearer, who apprehend the meanings of expressions. When they function exclusively in this capacity, as a tacit conceptualizing presence that is not itself conceived, they are construed with maximal subjectivity. At the opposite extreme, construed with maximal objectivity, is the focused object of attention: the entity an expression puts onstage and profiles. Objective construal thus correlates with profiling and explicit mention, and subjective construal with an implicit locus of consciousness. Being implicit is not the same as being absent, however. The conceptualization constituting an expression's meaning extends beyond its onstage content (which does not exist in isolation), further encompassing its mode of apprehension by the offstage conceptualizers in the context of the overall viewing arrangement.

---

[19] When I am wearing my glasses, for instance, they are essentially part of my visual system, hence subjectively construed and nonsalient. They help shape my visual experience, but barely, if at all, do I see the glasses themselves. They become salient, however, when I construe them objectively by taking them off and looking at them.

In their tacit role as subjects of conception, the speaker and hearer are always part of the conceptual substrate supporting an expression's meaning.[20] If that is their only role, they are always implicit and construed with maximal subjectivity. To varying degrees, however, they can themselves function as objects of conception, in which case they are more salient by virtue of being construed more objectively. The extreme is to put them onstage as the focus of attention: with the first- and second-person pronouns (*I*, *you*, *we*, and their variants), the speaker and hearer are profiled, explicitly mentioned, and objectively construed. There are also intermediate possibilities. In (15), the speaker and hearer are not merely the subjects of conception, they are also the viewers whose vantage point and line of sight are invoked by *in front of* and *behind* (fig. 3.11). To this extent they figure in the scene described, so their role is not wholly subjective. But neither is it fully objective, for even in this additional viewing capacity they are offstage, unprofiled, and implicit.

The term **ground** is used for the speaker and hearer, the speech event in which they participate, and their immediate circumstances (e.g. the time and place of speaking). As the "platform" for apprehending the content evoked, the ground enters into the meaning of every expression, even when construed with maximal subjectivity. Usually, though, facets of the ground are themselves evoked as part of that content, so that to some degree they function as objects of conception. Quite often they are profiled; since we are naturally concerned with ourselves and our own circumstances, words like *I*, *you*, *here*, and *now* are highly frequent. It may however be more typical for facets of the ground to be offstage and construed with only minimal objectivity. They tend to function as implicit points of reference for specifying the location of more objectively conceived entities vis-à-vis the ground. We have already seen this in (15) and (17)(a): just as the place of speaking is tacitly invoked as the spatial vantage point for *in front of* and *behind*, so the time of speaking functions implicitly as a temporal point of reference for *next year*.

The ground's role as tacit point of reference is in fact ubiquitous. Even when implicit and construed with a substantial degree of subjectivity, the ground functions in this capacity for every full nominal and every finite clause. For example, tense is usually reckoned from the ground: *was*, *is*, and *will be* are past, present, and future with respect to the time of speaking. In the nominal sphere, a comparable parameter is definiteness, as in the contrast between *a rock* (indefinite) and *the rock* (definite). Definiteness relates to the speaker and hearer, for it depends on whether the nominal referent is uniquely apparent to both interlocutors in the current discourse context. Observe that the grammaticized markers for tense and definiteness invoke some facet of the ground but do not mention it explicitly: *now* is not incorporated in the tense markers (e.g. *-ed*, *-s*, *will*), nor do markers of definiteness (like *a* and *the*) incorporate the pronouns *I* and *you*.

---

[20] If we view an expression abstractly, independent of specific usage events, the speaker's and hearer's subjective role is just that—a **role** to be instantiated by particular individuals whenever the expression is actually used.

3.4.2 The Temporal Dimension

Conceptualization is inherently dynamic—not something that statically exists, but rather something that happens. It resides in mental processing (or neurological activity) and therefore occurs through time. When time is viewed in this capacity, as the **medium** of conception, it is referred to as **processing time**. Every conceptualization requires some span of processing time for its occurrence. Even one that we experience as instantaneous (e.g. feeling the prick of a pin) has a duration and a course of development when examined on a small enough scale. As an aspect of construal, dynamicity pertains to how a conceptualization develops and unfolds through processing time, especially on larger time scales where its consequences are introspectively accessible.[21]

Processing time has to be distinguished from **conceived time**—that is, time as an **object** of conception. Time is construed most objectively when a span of time is profiled, for instance by expressions like *moment*, *period*, *week*, and *next year* (fig. 3.12). Time is also construed objectively, though not as the focus of attention, when it functions as the cognitive domain in which a profiled relationship is manifested, as with *before* and *after* (fig. 3.10). It figures as well in the conception of any event, since events occur through time. The verb *enter*, for example, designates a relationship in space (fig. 2.1), but the change in spatial configuration constituting the profiled event can only be implemented along the temporal axis. Conceived and processing time can be hard to disentangle, if only because the conceptualization **of** time necessarily occurs **through** time. Still, for semantic purposes they have to be clearly separated. In understanding a sentence like (18), we require only a brief interval of processing time (perhaps a second) to scan through a distinct and much longer interval of conceived time (perhaps an hour).

(18)   *The long procession slowly entered the city.*

There is a natural tendency for conceived time and processing time to be coaligned, such that the order in which events are conceived as occurring dovetails with the order in which they are conceptualized and described. This **temporal iconicity** is well known from examples like (19)(a), which would normally be interpreted as indicating that the resignation preceded the marriage and that the marriage preceded the birth, although the sentence does not actually say this.

(19)   (a) *I quit my job, got married, and had a baby.*

(b) *I had a baby, got married, and quit my job—in reverse order, of course.*

Such iconicity is only a tendency, however. We can mentally access events and describe them linguistically in a sequence that diverges from their order of occurrence or even runs directly counter to it. Thus a sentence like (19)(b) could perfectly

---

[21] This dynamic view of conceptualization fits well with a psychological theory of meaning based on **mental simulation** (Barsalou 1999).

well be used in the proper context (e.g. in response to the question *What are the most important things that happened to you last year?*).

Temporal iconicity of the sort observed in (19)(a) is represented in figure 3.13(a). The upper and lower arrows respectively indicate conceived time (t) and processing time (T). E_1, E_2, and E_3 are three events (e.g. quitting a job, getting married, and having a baby). A, B, and C stand for the conceptualization of each event as it occurs in constructing or understanding a linguistic expression describing it, while the corresponding lowercase letters stand for those expressions themselves (e.g. *I quit my job, [I] got married*, and *[I] had a baby*). When a sentence like (19)(a) is uttered, the component expressions are spoken in a certain order (a > b > c), which either reflects or induces an ordering of the conceptualizations they symbolize (A > B > C). Both expression and conception occur (and are coaligned) through processing time (T). Iconicity obtains when the events thus conceptualized are further conceived as occurring in that same order ($E_1 > E_2 > E_3$) through conceived time (t). There is full harmonization in the sequencing of events, event conceptions, and event descriptions.

Diagrammed in figure 3.13(b) is the noniconic alignment of a sentence like (19)(b). As always, the sequence in which the component expressions occur (a > b > c) correlates with an ordering of the conceptualizations they symbolize (A > B > C). Here, though, this coalignment at the two poles in processing time does not extend to corresponding events in conceived time. Via the linguistic expression, these events are mentally accessed in the order $E_3 > E_2 > E_1$, while they are conceived as actually occurring in the opposite order, $E_1 > E_2 > E_3$. We can certainly accomplish this, conceptually and linguistically, but it does carry a processing cost. The need for extra processing effort is signaled by the appendage in (19)(b): *in reverse order, of course*. This directs the listener to **reconceptualize** the events described, by mentally running through them again, but in a sequence directly counter to the order of their initial presentation. Only through such **backtracking** can the listener arrive at a proper apprehension of their actual temporal sequencing.

The order of presentation is conceptually and semantically consequential even when event order is not a factor. A case in point is the semantic effect of preposing a locative expression, as illustrated by the following contrast:

(20)   (a) *A dead rat lay in the middle of the kitchen floor.*

(b) *In the middle of the kitchen floor lay a dead rat.*

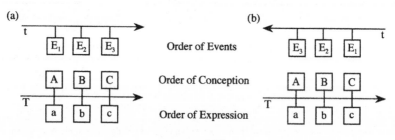

FIGURE 3.13

Despite having the same elements, the sentences have different meanings. Their semantic contrast does not reside in the objective situation described but in how it is mentally accessed. The atypical word order in (20)(b) accommodates the general discourse tendency for given information to precede new information, while also allowing the introduction of a new participant as grammatical subject (cf. Birner 1994). The sentence first directs attention to an already accessible location, and then brings a new participant (*a dead rat*) into the discourse by establishing it in that location. Evidence that the construction in (20)(b) has this special semantic value comes from the infelicity of expressions whose information structure conflicts with it.[22] For instance, (21)(b) is awkward because the subject refers to the speaker, who is always taken as given, as already established in the discourse. Conversely, (21)(c) is infelicitous because the preposed locative represents new information. Compare this with (21)(d), where the garage is mentioned in the first conjunct and is therefore given for purposes of the second.

(21) (a) *I lay in the middle of the kitchen floor.*

    (b) *?*In the middle of the kitchen floor lay I.*

    (c) *?*In a garage sat an old truck.*

    (d) *There was a garage behind the house, and in this garage sat an old truck.*

Order of presentation also has an evident semantic impact in examples like these:

(22) (a) *Your camera is upstairs, in the bedroom, in the closet, on the shelf.*

    (b) *Your camera is on the shelf, in the closet, in the bedroom, upstairs.*

Once again, the two sentences are semantically distinct, even though they contain the same elements and describe the same objective situation. They represent two variants of the "nested locative" construction (GC: 60–61), which specify the subject's location through a series of locative expressions pinning it down to successively nested spatial areas. The difference is that the first variant "zooms in" from the largest area to successively smaller ones, whereas the second variant starts from the smallest area and "zooms out". While the two sentences succeed in evoking the same overall spatial configuration, they build up to it in different ways, thereby providing very different conceptual experiences. They contrast semantically precisely because each conceptualization has its own time course, unfolding in a particular way through processing time.

The words of an expression occur in a certain temporal sequence, which linguists (unwittingly using spatial metaphor) refer to as "linear order". This temporal sequencing defines one salient path of access to the conceptions symbolized. Since

---

[22] Many scholars would say that the contrast in (20) is not one of semantics but rather of pragmatics. I would argue, however, that information structure is conceptual in nature, being special only in that the relevant cognitive domain is the apprehension of the discourse itself.

we necessarily encounter these words sequentially, in either speaking or understanding, linear order always has some effect on meaning—a difference in word order always implies a semantic contrast (though in practical terms it may be slight or even negligible). But linear order is not the only factor influencing the sequence of mental access, nor is the cognitive processing of a sentence limited to a single "left-to-right" pass through it. Processing occurs simultaneously in multiple structural dimensions, at different levels of organization, and on vastly different time scales. Even as we are attending to individual words, we must also be making more global projections at various syntactic and even discourse levels. Much of the relevant conceptual structure is not expressed at all by overt elements, which are merely prompts for the requisite meaning construction. And those notions which are expressed can be reaccessed and reconceptualized as needed, through backtracking (as in (19)(b)).

Sequencing at the conceptual level is thus not always driven by the order of overt elements in speech. We can see this from pairs of examples like (23), which describe the same spatial configuration but have contrasting meanings nonetheless:

(23) (a) *The hill gently rises from the bank of the river.*

(b) *The hill gently falls to the bank of the river.*

The difference lies in the direction of **mental scanning**. The conceptualizer, in building up to a full conception of the profiled relationship, constructs an image of the hill by tracing a mental path along it in either an upward or a downward direction. However, the direction of scanning is not determined by the order in which the words occur, but rather by their meanings: *rises from* induces upward mental scanning, and *falls to*, downward scanning. Note further that *rise* and *fall*, whose basic senses pertain to spatial motion, are used here to describe a situation that objectively is totally static. While motion is indeed involved, it is subjectively construed. In the case of objectively construed motion (e.g. *It fell*), an onstage entity moves along a spatial path through conceived time. By contrast, the mover in (23) is the offstage conceptualizer, who traces a mental path in space through processing time.

Mental scanning is not restricted to space. Directed scanning through a nonspatial domain is pivotal to the meaning of many expressions and is often reflected in their form. Commonly it consists of running through a set of conceived alternatives arranged in a certain order. Here are a few examples:

(24) (a) *Gestation period varies greatly from one species to the next.*

(b) *I'll never get into a size 8, and a size 9 is probably still too small.*

(c) *Don't mention calculus—elementary algebra is already too advanced for him.*

In (24)(a), the alternatives are an imagined set of species, the variation in gestation period being observed as we move subjectively *from one... to the next*. In (24)(b), we scan in a positive direction along a scale of possible sizes. This mental scanning is signaled by *still*, which normally indicates persistence in time (e.g. *Is she still asleep?*). It has the same value here, apart from being construed subjectively. It does not describe the insufficient size as persisting through conceived time, but through processing time, as the conceptualizer scans through a range of alternative sizes. The temporal persistence is subjectively construed by virtue of inhering in the conceptualizing activity itself. Similarly, in (24)(c) the conceptualizer moves subjectively along a scale in which mathematical subjects are ranked for difficulty. The word *already* indicates that the property of being too advanced is encountered sooner than expected (cf. *Are you done already?*). However, this imagined encounter only occurs in processing time: in scanning through the list of subjects, the conceptualizer comes upon it at the level of elementary algebra, well before reaching calculus.

Mental scanning can follow a path that is either continuous or discrete. In (23), the conceptualizer traces a continuous path along the hill's expanse in building up a conception of its overall configuration. By contrast, the scanning in (24) follows a path consisting of discrete steps (species, sizes, or mathematical subjects), but here too the sequenced mental access is a means of building up to an overall conception of some complexity. These are two forms of a general process I refer to as **summary scanning**. As we scan through a complex scene, successively attending to various facets of it, the elements apprehended at each stage are summed, or superimposed. In this way a detailed conception is progressively built up, becoming active and available as a simultaneously accessible whole for a certain span of processing time.[23]

Of considerable grammatical importance is a particular type of scanning called a **reference point relationship**. The term is best reserved for cases where the mental path is discrete, each element accessed is individually salient, and the reason for scanning along this path is primarily to find or identify the element ultimately arrived at. We can best appreciate this from a perceptual example. We often direct attention to a perceptually salient entity as a point of reference to help find some other entity, which would otherwise be hard to locate. In (25)(a), for instance, the speaker wants to direct the hearer's attention to the duck, but from a distance the boat is easier to pick out. Once the hearer has located the boat, the duck can be found by searching in its vicinity.

(25)   (a) *Do you see that boat out there in the lake? There's a duck swimming right next to it.*

(b) *Do you remember that surgeon we met at the party? His wife just filed for divorce.*

This perceptual phenomenon has a general conceptual analog, exemplified in (25)(b). The speaker first directs attention to one conceived entity (the surgeon) for the specific purpose of locating another that is mentally accessible in relation to it (the surgeon's wife).

Clearly, then, we have the ability to invoke the conception of one entity in order to establish "mental contact" with another. The entity first invoked is called a **reference point**, and one accessed via a reference point is referred to as a **target**. A particular reference point affords potential access to many different targets. Collectively, this set

---

[23] To some extent, this kind of summation is always going on as we process words in their sequence of occurrence. The examples show it to be a general conceptual phenomenon independent of word order. In ch. 4 I discuss the grammatical relevance of summary scanning.

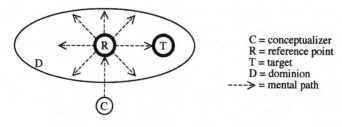

FIGURE 3.14

of potential targets constitute the reference point's **dominion**. Thus a reference point relationship comprises the elements depicted in figure 3.14. In the case of (25)(a), the reference point is the boat, the target is the duck, and the dominion is everything—including the duck—in the boat's vicinity. In (25)(b), the reference point is the surgeon, his wife is the target, and the dominion is anything readily associated with (hence mentally accessible via) the surgeon.

It is no accident that the target in (25)(b), *his wife*, contains a possessor pronoun referring to the reference point. There is good evidence that a reference point relationship represents the essential meaning of a basic possessive construction (GC: ch. 6). Here I offer just two brief observations. First, the characterization is independent of any specific conceptual content. Thus it has the abstractness and flexibility needed to accommodate the full range of possessive expressions, e.g. all those in (26)(a).[24]

(26) (a) *the boy's shoe; Jeff's uncle; the cat's paw; their lice; the baby's diaper; my train; Sally's job; our problem; her enthusiasm; its location; your candidate; the city's destruction*

    (b) **the shoe's boy; *the paw's cat; *the diaper's baby; *the destruction's city*

Second, the characterization explains why it is usually infelicitous to reverse the choice of possessor and possessed, as seen in (26)(b). This irreversibility reflects the intrinsic asymmetry of a reference point relationship, where conceiving of one entity makes it possible to mentally access another. As a schematic and fully general description, it is thus proposed that a possessor functions as a reference point, and the possessed as its target.

A reference point relationship is often conflated with specific conceptual content, such as spatial proximity in (25)(a). Still, its essential semantic import resides in the very act of mental scanning: evoking first the reference point and then a target it renders accessible. It is thus inherently and quintessentially dynamic, for how it unfolds through processing time actually constitutes its value. As shown by the arrows in figure 3.14, a reference point relation involves two phases of focused awareness, their temporal sequence defining its directionality and intrinsic asymmetry. The first phase consists of

---

[24] As a general description, the notion 'ownership' is too narrow, applying only to the first example cited. While 'ownership' (along with 'kinship' and 'whole-part') does appear to be prototypical for possessive constructions, a schematic characterization valid for all instances has to be devoid of specific content.

mentally accessing the reference point, which is thereby placed in focus. Its activation creates the conditions for accessing elements of the reference point's dominion, one of which is focused as the target. As focus shifts to the target, the reference point—having served its purpose—fades into the background. Hence the reference point and target are both salient, each at a certain stage of processing.

Once focused, of course, the target provides access to its own dominion and may then be invoked as reference point to reach another target. In this way we often scan along a **chain** of successive reference points. One such case is a chain of possessives, e.g. *Harry's cousin's lawyer's therapist.* Another is the chain of successive locations specified in the nested locative construction, as in (22)(a): *upstairs, in the bedroom, in the closet, on the shelf.* Once a particular location is singled out, it affords ready access to any smaller location within it, one of which is put in focus as the target and the next locative reference point.

3.5 Evidence for Semantic Claims

A conceptual semantics lets us make sense of how language makes sense. In and of itself, however, a conceptualist stance does not make semantic description any easier (quite the contrary). Nor does it offer any assurance that we are describing meanings in a principled and appropriate manner. How can we tell whether a proposed description has any validity?

We cannot just rely on intuition or introspection. A conceptual view of meaning does not imply that semantic structure is directly accessible to introspective awareness: engaging in conceptualization is not the same as knowing how it works, any more than seeing is knowing how vision works. We apprehend meanings (i.e. we understand the expressions we use), but this is quite different from subjecting them to explicit analysis. Indeed, at the level of conscious analysis we are generally quite oblivious to construal—both the fact that we construe the content evoked and also the specific ways in which we do so. In normal, unreflective language use our primary interest lies in what is being said, not the underlying mechanisms. These mechanisms are in any case inaccessible to conscious awareness, just as the mechanisms of vision are themselves invisible to us.

It is only through careful linguistic analysis that we can arrive at a principled and revealing characterization of semantic structure. The semantic descriptions proposed in CG utilize a particular set of theoretical constructs—notions like domain, profile, trajector, vantage point, scanning, mental space, immediate scope, and reference point relation. These constructs have all been adopted on the basis of substantial and varied empirical evidence. The general strategy employed is to seek converging evidence from each of three general sources: (i) what we know about cognition (independently of language), (ii) what is needed for viable semantic descriptions, and (iii) whether the constructs support an optimal account of grammar.

With respect to (i), the descriptive constructs proposed in CG are all based on well-known or easily demonstrated cognitive phenomena. Many have direct analogs in vision, although they clearly extend to other aspects of cognition. For example, the focusing of attention is quite apparent in both visual and auditory perception, as well as nonlinguistic thought. There is no question that we apprehend our surroundings from a particular vantage point and have the ability to mentally adopt a vantage point other than our actual one. In the same way that we can visually scan through a scene, we can mentally run through a range of options. The use of reference points is evident in perception and fundamental to conception in general. Hence the descriptive constructs adopted in CG are not in any way exotic or even problematic from the psychological standpoint. In fact, it would be peculiar to suppose that such phenomena lack an important role in linguistic meaning.

As for (ii), the primary means of justifying constructs empirically is by showing that they are needed for adequate semantic descriptions. For instance, profiling is supported by the need to distinguish expressions that differ in meaning despite evoking the same content (e.g. *parent* vs. *child, come* vs. *arrive, examine* vs. *be examining*). Likewise, trajector/landmark alignment is supported by the need to distinguish semantically nonequivalent expressions that are the same in both content and profiling (e.g. *before* vs. *after, precede* vs. *follow, have a parent* vs. *have a child*). I would argue that the constructs adopted in CG are quite successful in allowing principled representations of the similarities and differences among expressions with comparable content. Moreover, the same, limited set of constructs prove systematically applicable to an extremely broad array of diverse data.

A final source of evidence is (iii), whether the constructs adopted support an optimal account of grammar. In later chapters, I show that the constructs of CG score very highly on this count. For example, profiling turns out to be crucial for the characterization of basic grammatical classes. Subject and object are defined in terms of trajector/landmark alignment. The constructs also work well in the description of particular grammatical constructions. We have already noted the role of immediate scope in both the progressive construction (fig. 3.4) and whole-part compounding (e.g. *eyelash* vs. **facelash, shoulder blade* vs. **body blade*).

Let us now turn from general constructs to the characterization of particular expressions. How can a proposed semantic description be supported empirically? At least at this level, I suggest that native speaker intuition is not entirely irrelevant. We obviously cannot expect naive speakers to produce semantic descriptions or even to articulate the subtle differences between expressions. Still, speakers do have semantic intuitions that bear on descriptive issues and are probably no less reliable (or no more unreliable) than the grammaticality judgments traditionally employed in formal syntax. With large samples and appropriate statistical techniques, for example, speaker judgments could help determine whether *ring* 'circular piece of jewelry' and *ring* 'arena' represent alternate senses of a polysemous lexical item (as opposed to being unrelated homonyms), or whether *computer* is in fact more analyzable than *propeller*. Speaker reactions to more elaborate semantic descriptions may also be pertinent. If a proposed characterization strikes speakers as being intuitively natural and revealing, we can at least feel encouraged and prefer this to the opposite judgment.[25]

---

[25] Positive reactions of this sort are quite common in cognitive linguistics and, ironically, are one reason it tends to be underappreciated. Semantic descriptions achieved through considerable effort and ingenuity are often so natural and revelatory that they give the impression of having been obvious all along, so nothing seems to have been accomplished.

Evidence can sometimes be sought by looking at other languages (Haiman 1978). Consider the issue of whether the *if* occurring in conditional clauses (*If it rains we'll stay home*) and the *if* occurring in interrogative clauses (*I wonder if it will rain*) are semantically related. Supporting a claim of polysemy is the fact that a single form is used in both ways in numerous other languages (e.g. French). Were this merely a case of accidental homonymy, it should not be prevalent cross-linguistically. Another source of evidence is language change. It is known, for example, that particular kinds of grammatical markers evolve historically from particular kinds of lexical items. Such paths of **grammaticalization** can tell us something about the meanings of the elements involved. One common path is for a lexical verb like *have*, used for possession (*She has a cat*), to develop into an auxiliary verb marking perfect aspect (*She has finished*). This provides a measure of corroboration for the proposal that possessive constructions are based on reference point relations. It is generally accepted that perfect constructions involve a reference point in time. For instance, *He had left by 3 PM* takes 3 PM as a temporal reference point and portrays the leaving as being accomplished prior to it. This path of grammaticalization is most easily analyzed if a possessive verb is itself characterized in terms of a reference point relationship.

More consistently available as empirical evidence are the predictions a semantic description lets us make. Implicit in any such description are expectations that certain kinds of expressions ought to be semantically well-formed and others judged anomalous. Suppose it is claimed that in (27)(a) the inanimate subject is construed metaphorically in terms of the human body. The choice among *sit*, *stand*, and *lie* should thus depend on whether—by analogy to a person assuming these postures—the subject's referent is relatively compact (as in sitting) or whether it is saliently extended along the vertical or horizontal axis.[26]

(27)   (a) *The clock is {sitting/standing/lying} on the table.*

       (b) *The {vase/?pen/?football/?*watermelon/*mat/*peach} is standing on the table.*

This prediction is in fact borne out, as seen from data like (27)(b). *Stand* is unproblematic with *vase*, as such objects are commonly tall and thin. *Pen* and *football* are questionable, since the vertical orientation suggested by *stand* is hard to achieve in practice. They are acceptable, however, if we imagine that the pen is standing on end (possible with certain pens) or that the football is on a kicking tee. Because it has rounded ends, a watermelon can only *lie* on a table unless we concoct a bizarre context (e.g. it might be impaled on a spike). Neither a mat nor a peach has the right shape for a verb demanding salient vertical extension. Of course, encyclopedic knowledge tells us that mats are sometimes rolled up, and a rolled-up mat could well be stood on end; under this interpretation we can perfectly well describe it as *standing*. On the other hand, a peach is roughly spherical, with no conspicuously long dimension, so regardless of orientation it can only *sit*.

Other predictions pertain to the discourse contexts in which an expression can occur. Recall, for instance, that the characterization of trajector/landmark alignment,

---

[26] Matters are slightly more complex in that *sit* also functions as the general term, i.e. it has a schematic sense that abstracts away from the differences in posture, making it broadly applicable.

and the description of *above* and *below* as contrasting in that regard, predicted the distribution in (11): a sentence like *The lamp is above the table* is felicitous in response to the question *Where is the lamp?* and *The table is below the lamp* in response to *Where is the table?* but not conversely. Recall as well the discourse-based characterization of sentences like (20)(b), *In the middle of the kitchen floor lay a dead rat.* The description correctly predicts that such expressions will be infelicitous if the postposed subject represents given information (**In the middle of the kitchen floor lay I*), or if the preposed locative represents new information (*?*In a garage sat an old truck*).

We can sometimes make predictions to be tested experimentally. I would claim, for example, that the semantic contrast between (28)(a) and (28)(b) resides in the direction of summary scanning. The conceptualizer builds up to a full conception of the scar's configuration by scanning mentally along its extension in one direction or the other, as specified by the *from-* and *to*-phrases. Moreover, the order of words in speech induces us to access the conceptions they symbolize in the corresponding order. In (28)(a)–(b), these two conceptual orderings are in alignment: we first encounter the *from*-phrase, specifying where the mental scanning begins, and then the *to*-phrase, specifying where it ends. This coalignment of paths is optimal from the processing standpoint.

(28)   (a) *An ugly scar extends from his wrist to his elbow.*

   (b) *An ugly scar extends from his elbow to his wrist.*

   (c) *An ugly scar extends to his wrist from his elbow.*

In (28)(c), however, the two paths run counter to one another. Scanning along the scar starts at the elbow, but word order first directs attention to the wrist, at the endpoint of the scanning path. Hence a conceptual account based on dynamicity implies the need for backtracking: after initially processing the whole expression, the conceptualizer needs to back up and reconceptualize the full scanning path in the proper sequence in order to properly apprehend the overall configuration. This makes an experimental prediction: namely, that (28)(c) should take longer to process and require greater effort than the other expressions.

A frequent criticism of cognitive linguistics, that it makes no predictions, is therefore erroneous. It is, however, true that its predictions tend to be relativistic instead of absolute. For instance, one cannot predict in absolute terms precisely which nouns can occur in the construction in (27)(b). In particular, one cannot make a yes/no prediction about a noun's cooccurrence with *stand* just by examining objectively discernible properties of the nominal referent. What counts is how a situation is construed, which involves general and contextual knowledge as well as our full range of imaginative and interpretive abilities. It is not a matter of deciding categorically whether a certain combination is or is not grammatical, but rather of ascertaining the kind and degree of motivation it has in view of all relevant factors—hence the dictum in cognitive linguistics that, while virtually everything is **motivated**, very little is subject to **absolute** predictability.

A standard view, long predominant in semantic theory, is that a conceptual account of meaning is either impossible or necessarily unscientific. A scientifically respectable semantics is presumed to be objectivist in nature, subject to discrete formalization, and capable of strict predictability. However, I have tried to indicate that this approach to meaning is not the only game in town. Conceptual semantics is possible, and it is developing into a rigorous scientific enterprise. Ideally, and increasingly in practice, cognitive semantic descriptions are based on careful analysis, supported by empirical evidence, and formulated in terms of well-justified descriptive constructs. And in no small measure, conceptual semantics derives support from its efficacy as the basis for characterizing grammatical structure. This will be our focus in part II.

A SYMBOLIC ACCOUNT OF GRAMMAR

4

Grammatical Classes

We speak of a **class** (or **category**) when different elements are treated alike for certain purposes. Without categorization, we could not discern patterns or regularities, as these involve the recurrence of configurations judged to be "the same". Categories can be established for any facet of language structure. In the case of phonology, for instance, we posit such classes as consonant and high front vowel. Here we focus on classes relevant to grammar, such as noun, verb, and adjective.

A fundamental question is whether basic grammatical categories are definable in terms of meaning. After arguing that they should be (§4.1), I propose specific meanings for the noun and verb categories (§4.2) and subsequently for others (§4.3). Then, in chapter 5, I examine an important conceptual opposition dividing both nouns and verbs into two major subclasses.

4.1 Are Conceptual Characterizations Conceivable?

In elementary school, I was taught that a noun is the name of a person, place, or thing. In college, I was taught the basic linguistic doctrine that a noun can only be defined in terms of grammatical behavior, conceptual definitions of grammatical classes being impossible. Here, several decades later, I demonstrate the inexorable progress of grammatical theory by claiming that a noun is the name of a thing.[1]

4.1.1 Traditional Views and Fallacies

That grammatical classes **cannot** be defined semantically constitutes a fundamental dogma of modern linguistic theory. Statements like the following, proclaiming the impossibility of conceptual characterizations, are prominently displayed in every introductory text and every book intended for a popular audience:

---

[1] My definition of "thing" is highly abstract. It subsumes people and places as special cases and is not limited to physical entities.

No constant semantic effect is associated with the functioning of a morpheme as a noun, as a verb, or as any other part of speech. (Langacker 1968: 83)

Let's ask whether each part of speech really denotes a consistent kind of meaning.... Now it is true that any word that names an object will be a noun. But on the other hand, not every noun names an object. *Earthquake* names, if anything, an action, as does *concert*; *redness* and *size* name properties; *place* and *location* pretty obviously name locations. In fact, for just about any kind of entity we can think of, there exist nouns that name that kind of entity. So the grammatical notion of noun can't be given a definition in terms of what kind of entity it names....A particular kind of entity need not correspond to a single part of speech either....We conclude that parts of speech...are not definable in terms of meaning. (Jackendoff 1994: 68–69)

As they stand, the traditional definitions criticized in such passages are definitely unworkable. Not so clearly justified, however, is the attitude of smugness and scientific certainty often detectable in the dismissive comments of linguistic theorists. I suggest, in fact, that no persuasive case has actually been made against the semantic characterization of grammatical classes. The inadequacy of particular definitions (e.g. that a noun names an object) does not imply that notional characterizations are impossible in principle—conceivably there are others that might work. Moreover, the standard type of argument against a conceptual approach is quite simplistic and rests on very questionable assumptions.

The passage just cited from Jackendoff typifies this standard line of argument. It is simplistic because, as possible notional definitions, it considers only a limited class of concepts representing a particular level of generality: notions like 'object', 'action', 'property', and 'location'. While these are quite general, they are certainly not the most schematic conceptions we are capable of handling. Each incorporates substantial conceptual content distinguishing it from the others (e.g. a physical object comprises a continuous expanse of material substance, whereas an action per se is nonmaterial, consisting instead of a change that unfolds through time, typically involving force). These notions represent experientially grounded **conceptual archetypes** (§2.1.2) and as such are appropriate as the **prototypes** for linguistic categories. Objects and actions, for instance, are respectively prototypical for the noun and verb categories. At issue, however, is whether such classes are susceptible to **schematic** definitions satisfied by **all** members (not just central members). Characterizations appropriate for all class members will obviously have to be considerably more abstract than the archetypal notions considered. The standard argument against notional definitions fails to even contemplate the possibility of more abstract formulations.

The standard argument is further simplistic because it presupposes a common yet untenable view of linguistic meaning: an objectivist view that ignores cognition and our capacity for construing the same situation in alternate ways (ch. 3). In the passage cited, an expression's meaning is taken as being established by the objective nature of the entity designated—not by how it is conceptualized. It is assumed, for example, that the objective nature of an earthquake, as a kind of action (or event), implies that the noun *earthquake* necessarily names an action. Cognition is not seen as having any significant role in determining the expression's meaning. Ignored, for

[handwritten note: event as abstract object ↳ conceptual reification]

instance, is our conceptual capacity for construing events as abstract objects. If this capacity for **conceptual reification** is recognized, one can argue that *earthquake* does name a kind of object—namely, a conceptually reified event. An expression's meaning always incorporates a particular way of construing whatever content is evoked.

A verb like *explode* and a noun like *explosion* can both refer to the same event. According to standard doctrine, this proves that the verb and noun classes are not semantically definable: if they were, *explode* and *explosion* would belong to the same category, since they have the same meaning. This reasoning hinges on the fallacious assumption that referring to the same event makes the two expressions semantically equivalent. They are not. While invoking the same conceptual content, they differ in meaning because of how they construe it: unlike *explode*, which directly reflects the event's processual nature, *explosion* construes it as an abstract thing derived by conceptual reification. It is precisely by virtue of this conceptual contrast that the expressions belong to different grammatical categories.

On grounds of plausibility and interest, we should start with the expectation that such fundamental grammatical notions as noun and verb are definable in terms of meaning.[2] Reasons have been given for rejecting the standard argument—really the only argument—for claiming they are not. Of course, rejecting the argument does not prove that conceptual characterizations are indeed feasible. In the pages that follow, reasonably explicit semantic definitions are proposed for nouns, verbs, and other categories. They should at least demonstrate that such definitions are possible in principle.

4.1.2 The Nature of the Claim

What precisely is intended by the CG claim that basic grammatical classes are semantically definable? Several points need clarification.

First, the claim pertains to the schematic level of description rather than the prototype level.[3] By now it is widely accepted that conceptual characterizations are possible for the central or prototypical members of basic categories. Thus a prototypical noun is one that names a physical object (e.g. *spoon, car, dog, umbrella*). It is likewise prototypical for verbs to designate actions or events (*run, explode, hit*) and for adjectives to specify properties (*blue, tall, intelligent*). Far less obvious is the possibility of schematic definitions applicable to all members of a class. In the case of nouns, for instance, a schematic characterization must subsume not only physical objects but also the vast and heterogeneous array of entities designated by nouns like *air, beauty, team, integer, concert, earthquake, orbit, explosion*, and *philosophy*. Counter to standard doctrine, CG claims that characterizations of this sort can in fact be achieved.

What is the scope of this claim? For which grammatical categories are schematic conceptual definitions held to be possible? A preliminary answer is that the claim is

---

[2] For some psychological evidence bearing on this issue, see Gentner 1981, 1982 and Kellogg 1994, 1996.

[3] An integrated model of categorization, accommodating both schemas and prototypes, is presented in ch. 8 (also in FCG1: ch. 10). For prototype categorization, see Taylor 2004, Lakoff 1987, and Rosch 1978.

limited to classes reasonably considered **universal** and **fundamental** (respectively measured by how many languages and how many constructions they figure in). The most obvious cases are noun and verb. At the opposite extreme, there is no expectation that a class based on a particular grammatical idiosyncrasy in a single language should be semantically definable. It is not expected, for instance, that the verbs in English which form their past tense in *-ought/-aught* (*bring, seek, fight, buy, catch, teach*) can be specified on the basis of their meaning. Of course, limiting the claim to classes that are universal and fundamental raises a number of theoretical issues, if only because these criteria are matters of degree.

Even noun and verb are sometimes denied the status of universal categories. Such denials are based on the observation that in some languages virtually every lexical item can be used either way; it is only in the context of a higher-level grammatical construction (nominal or clausal) that a lexeme takes on noun-like or verb-like properties. This observation, however, bears only on the status of noun and verb as universal **lexical** categories—that is, whether particular lexemes are learned and stored specifically as nouns or as verbs. For CG, which views lexicon and grammar as a continuum, this is not a crucial issue. The essential claim is merely that noun and verb have a role in the grammatical description of every language. It is not precluded that a lexeme's meaning might consist of conceptual content alone, with the construal characteristic of particular categories being imposed by the grammatical configurations it appears in. (I would argue, however, that regular occurrence in a certain type of configuration leads to the entrenchment and conventionalization of the construal it induces, and that this itself amounts to the lexeme having a variant belonging to the class in question. Languages may simply differ in the proportion of lexical items for which a particular categorization is strongly established.)

CG is not at all wedded to the traditional "parts of speech" or the classes implied by standard grammatical terminology. Traditional terms lack precise definition, are inconsistent in their application, and are generally inadequate (let alone optimal) for describing grammar. Still, certain standard notions (e.g. preposition, adverb, participle) are useful enough and so frequently invoked that they can hardly be avoided. Their CG characterizations are meant to capture the conceptual basis for whatever descriptive utility they have (at least as first approximations). Nevertheless, CG draws category boundaries in different ways, based on its own fundamental notions. The classes thus defined are not precisely coextensive with traditional ones, even when standard terms are retained.

A pivotal issue concerning grammatical categories is how they relate to grammatical constructions. Based on the supposed impossibility of conceptual definitions, standard doctrine holds that all classes—even noun and verb—must be defined for each language in terms of their grammatical behavior (e.g. nouns occurring with determiners and modifying adjectives, verbs being inflected for tense). Because languages vary greatly in their specific inventories of grammatical constructions, basing definitions solely on the constructions elements occur in has the consequence that no class will be truly universal. It has in fact been proposed that constructions (rather than categories) are the basic units of linguistic structure (Croft 2001). Every construction in a language defines a category, specific to that language, consisting of just those elements that occur in it. From this perspective, there might be no need to posit any general classes analogous to the traditional parts of speech.[4]

A descriptive framework must indeed allow one to specify the range of elements that appear in a given construction. In providing a means of doing so (ch. 8), CG accommodates the classes implicitly defined by occurrence in particular constructions. For such classes it is neither required nor expected that semantic characterizations be possible (the past-tense verbs in *-ought/-aught* are a case in point). At the same time, their membership tends not to be wholly arbitrary. Unusual at best is a construction where the occurring elements have nothing more in common than the mere fact of appearing in it. On the contrary, construction-based classes show varying degrees of semantic or phonological cohesiveness. The similarity among class members may be quite tenuous (e.g. most of the *-ought/-aught* verbs involve some notion of acquisition). Or there may be a valid generalization that is nonetheless insufficient to distinguish members from nonmembers (e.g. the *-ought/-aught* verbs are monosyllabic). At the extreme, class membership—ability to occur in the construction—might be wholly predictable on the basis of meaning and/or form.

The semantic properties that figure in these regularities are not a random collection. Across languages, a certain array of notions are especially prevalent in characterizing grammatical behavior and contributing to the semantic cohesiveness of construction-based classes. Particular conceptions evidently have sufficient cognitive salience that they are often invoked for grammatical purposes, inducing classes to coalesce around them. Their degree of cognitive salience determines to what extent the corresponding classes are universal and fundamental. The most universal and fundamental categories coalesce around a highly salient conceptual archetype, as well as a basic cognitive ability (presumably inborn) that is initially manifested in the archetype and responsible for its emergence. The former functions as category prototype, while the latter provides its schematic characterization. In the case of nouns, for example, the archetype is the conception of a physical object, which emerges due to the basic ability referred to here as conceptual reification (§4.2).

Because cognitive salience is a matter of degree, CG does not posit any fixed, definite inventory of universal categories. In terms of their salience, the notions anchoring the noun and verb categories are analogous to the highest peaks in a mountain range: while they may stand out, they do not stand alone. We can further recognize categories with somewhat lesser but still substantial degrees of universality and grammatical importance, for instance adjectives (Dixon 1977). How many classes we acknowledge depends on how far down these scales we go. Any specific cutoff point would no doubt be arbitrary.

A basic category of this sort does not necessarily coincide exactly with any construction-based class. Suppose, for instance, that a particular construction applies primarily to nouns, so that reference to this category figures in any cogent description. The construction might nonetheless incorporate a semantic specification that is incompatible with the meanings of certain nouns and thus precludes their occurrence.

---

[4] If posited, such categories would constitute abstractions over a range of constructions. This is not incompatible with the CG view, which also sees lexical items as deriving their category membership from participation in grammatical constructions (ch. 8; GC: ch. 4; Langacker 2005).

nouns base archetype is object

Conversely, the construction might be extended beyond the prototype (nouns) to encompass members of another class.[5] Grammatical constructions are generally quite complex, with many factors determining the precise array of elements that appear in them. A basic category can thus be strongly motivated for its utility in describing varied constructions, regardless of whether its own conceptual characterization—taken alone—is sufficient to specify the membership of any construction-based class.

4.1.3 Initial Characterizations

If basic categories are indeed semantically definable, why has this not been evident all along? Why were viable category meanings not proposed long ago and generally accepted? We can largely blame objectivist semantics, the identification of meaning with objective features of the situation described. This long-predominant outlook eliminates just what is needed to solve the problem. It is only by recognizing the crucial role of cognition—how situations are apprehended and conceptualized—that semantic characterizations become feasible. Especially relevant are two aspects of construal: profiling and level of specificity.

I have noted the relevance of specificity, arguing that the concepts usually considered (e.g. 'object', 'event', and 'location') are too specific to serve as schematic characterizations valid for all members of basic classes. If general definitions can indeed be found, it will be at a higher level of schematicity.

Profiling is critically important for the following reason: **what determines an expression's grammatical category is not its overall conceptual content, but the nature of its profile in particular**. It stands to reason that the profile should have a determining role in categorization, for it is what an expression designates; the profile is the focus of attention within the content evoked. The content of *bat*, for example, includes the conception of someone swinging a long, thin piece of wood in order to hit a ball. This domain is central to its meaning, whether it functions as a noun (*He uses a heavy bat*) or as a verb (*It's your turn to bat*). Its categorization as a noun or as a verb depends on whether it profiles the wooden implement or the action of using it.

For defining basic categories, it is useful to have a term that is maximally general in its application. The word **entity** is adopted for this purpose. It thus applies to anything that might be conceived of or referred to in describing conceptual structure: things, relations, quantities, sensations, changes, locations, dimensions, and so on. It is specifically **not** required that an entity be discrete, separately recognized, or cognitively salient. In schematic diagrams, like figure 4.1, entities are shown as rectangles.

Preliminary definitions of some basic classes can now be presented. Each category is characterized in terms of what an expression profiles. Thus a noun is defined schematically as an expression that profiles a **thing**. It must be understood that *thing* is used here as a technical term, whose precise import will be spelled out in §4.2.2. For now we can simply note that its characterization is quite abstract (any product of conceptual reification), so things are not limited to physical objects. In diagrams, a thing is represented by a circle or an ellipse.

---

[5] As a case of the former, the unique reference of proper nouns may preclude their occurrence with determiners. A case of the latter would be the marking of plurality not just on nouns but also on adjectives.

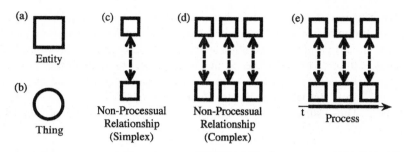

FIGURE 4.1

The members of other basic classes profile **relationships**. The term *relationship* is also used in an abstract, technical sense to be further explicated. In diagrams, relationships are often depicted by lines or arrows connecting the entities participating in them. Consistent with the characterization of entities, it is **not** required that relational participants be salient, discrete, or individually recognized.

Various kinds of relationships can be distinguished and used to characterize basic categories. Most fundamental is the distinction between a **process** and a **non-processual** relation. As the term is defined in CG, a process develops through time, represented in figure 4.1(e) by the arrow labeled t. The bar along the time arrow indicates that its evolution through time is focused rather than backgrounded. A process is further **complex**, in the sense that its manifestation at any one instant—any "time-slice" of the overall relationship—is itself a relationship.[6] A relation that lacks these properties is thereby nonprocessual. It can be nonprocessual by virtue of being **simplex**, residing in a configuration fully manifested at a single instant. While a simplex relationship may persist through time, its temporal evolution is not essential to its characterization or recognition. For example, the spatial relationship profiled by *on* in (1)(a) might endure indefinitely, but it is fully instantiated at any single moment (hence recognizable in a photo).

(1)   (a) *She is sitting **on** the roof.*

        (b) *She climbed up **onto** the roof.*

A relationship which does develop through time can be nonprocessual by virtue of being viewed holistically, so that its temporal evolution is backgrounded. In (1)(b), for instance, *onto* profiles a spatial relation that develops through time, defining the path of motion, yet the preposition itself construes it holistically, as a single gestalt (in the manner of a multiple-exposure photograph). Whether it is simplex or viewed holistically, a nonprocessual relation is **atemporal** in the sense that evolution through time is not in focus.

---

[6] Just three component relationships are depicted in fig. 4.1(e). But since a process unfolds through a continuous span of time, how many time-slices are explicitly shown is arbitrary (a matter of diagrammatic convenience).

We can now define a verb, schematically, as an expression that profiles a process. A number of other traditional categories—including adjective, adverb, preposition, and participle—are all characterized as profiling nonprocessual relationships. Although these can be distinguished on the basis of further properties (§4.3), from the CG standpoint they constitute a global category that subsumes them as special cases. Because it is not traditionally recognized, this category has no ready label. Thus I simply speak of relational expressions that are nonprocessual (or atemporal).

4.1.4 Initial Illustrations

As a preface to detailed discussion, a few examples should help clarify these characterizations and make them tangible. Let us first examine *choose* together with the derived nouns *chooser* and *choice*. Being a verb, *choose* profiles a process, sketched in figure 4.2(a). It designates the relationship between a trajector (tr), the one who chooses, and a landmark (lm), the entity chosen. For our purposes, it suffices to indicate that the trajector engages in mental activity (represented by a dashed arrow) serving to single out the landmark from a range of alternatives (given as a vertical, double-headed arrow). Clearly, the relationship profiled by *choose* unfolds through time, and is thus processual, even though time is omitted from the diagram.[7]

The nouns *chooser* and *choice* derive from *choose* and evoke the process it designates as their conceptual base. They are nouns precisely because their derivation consists in shifting the profile from the process per se to a thing characterized in relation to it. In the case of *chooser*, the profiled thing is the one who does the choosing

FIGURE 4.2

[7] For ease of representation, the time arrow is often omitted when it is not crucial for the point at issue, especially when (as here) the component relationships (time-slices) are all summarized in a single diagram. The profiled process should nevertheless be imagined as unfolding through time, as depicted in fig. 4.1(e).

(i.e. the verb's trajector).[8] *Choice* has three basic meanings. On one interpretation, exemplified in (2)(a), it designates the thing chosen (the processual landmark). Alternatively, as in (2)(b), it profiles the range of options. Finally, in (2)(c), it profiles an abstract thing obtained by conceptual reification of the base process. Shown as an ellipse in figure 4.2(e), this reified event consists of one instance of choosing.

(2) (a) *Unfortunately their top choice proved incapable of doing the job.*

    (b) *They offer a wide choice of investment options.*

    (c) *She made her choice in just seconds.*

Consider next the boldfaced expressions in (3). As their essential content, they largely share the conceptual base sketched in figure 4.3. The circle stands for a mover, the solid arrow for the path of motion, and the partial box for a container with an opening. Starting from outside the container, the mover ends up inside it. Representing this final locative relationship is a dashed, double-headed arrow. Diagrams (a)–(e) respectively indicate the profiles imposed on this content by the highlighted forms in (3)(a)–(e).

(3) (a) *The anthropologist is now **in** the tomb.*

    (b) *The **inside** of the tomb was elaborately decorated.*

    (c) *The **entrance** to the tomb is narrow.*

    (d) *He reluctantly **enter**ed the tomb.*

    (e) *His **entry** into the tomb took only a few seconds.*

FIGURE 4.3

[8] Some readers may recall the use of *chooser* in reference to a Macintosh desk accessory, where it designated a place in which choosing occurred.

In (3)(a), *in* profiles a simplex spatial relationship between a trajector and a landmark, both characterized as things. This makes it a preposition, which per se is atemporal. While the trajector presumably moved to reach the specified location, the preposition does not itself designate (or necessarily even evoke) this motion. The word *inside* can also be a preposition, roughly equivalent to *in*, but in (3)(b) it functions as a noun. In this particular use it profiles the container's interior surface. Although a container suggests the idea of something being in it, here this notion is very much in the background. *Entrance*, of course, is a noun. It has an abstract sense (like *entry* in (3)(e)), but in (3)(c) it merely designates the opening in a container through which admission is gained. In (3)(d), the verb *enter* profiles the process of the trajector moving along a spatial path to the landmark's interior. Finally, *entry* in (3)(e) is a noun designating an abstract thing, derived from the verb by conceptual reification. The profile consists of one instance of the verbal process.

As a last example, consider the various senses of *yellow* exemplified in (4), respectively diagrammed in figure 4.4.

(4) (a) **Yellow** *is a nice color.*

  (b) *This* **yellow** *would look good in our kitchen.*

  (c) *The ball is* **yellow.**

  (d) *Gradually the paper* **yellow**ed.

  (e) *There's a lot of* **yellow** *in this painting.*

In (4)(a), *yellow* functions as a kind of proper noun, for its referent is unique. Its profile is an abstract thing, consisting of a certain region (labeled Y) in the basic domain of color space. In (4)(b), *yellow* designates a bounded area within region Y, corresponding to some particular shade of yellow. Since there are many possible shades, in this use *yellow* is a common (rather than a proper) noun. Moreover, since the profiled area is bounded, it is also categorized as a count noun (rather than a mass noun).

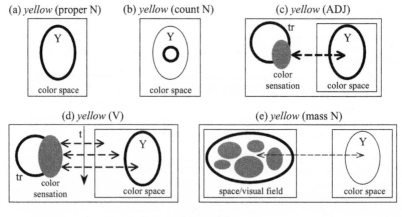

(a) *yellow* (proper N)   (b) *yellow* (count N)   (c) *yellow* (ADJ)

(d) *yellow* (V)   (e) *yellow* (mass N)

FIGURE 4.4

As an adjective, in (4)(c), *yellow* profiles an atemporal relationship whose single focal participant (its trajector) is a thing. The nature of this relationship (shown as a dashed arrow) is that a color sensation associated with the trajector falls within the yellow region of color space.[9] Suppose, now, that the color sensation changes through time, progressing from a color outside region Y to one inside it, as described in (4)(d). When classed as a verb, *yellow* profiles this entire complex relationship and foregrounds the change through time. In (4)(e), finally, *yellow* functions as a mass noun, taking the mass-noun quantifier *a lot of*. Here it refers collectively to various patches of yellow color manifested within the spatial extension of the painting. The thing profiled by a mass noun is not inherently bounded, has no intrinsic shape, and need not be spatially continuous (cf. *There's a lot of mud on this carpet*).

4.2 Nouns and Verbs

CG advances the controversial (if not outrageous) proposal that essential grammatical notions can be characterized semantically, not just at the prototype level but also at the schema level. Their prototypes consist of experientially grounded conceptual archetypes. Their schematic characterizations (valid for all instances) make reference to basic cognitive abilities initially manifested in those archetypes and later extended to other cases. Though its ultimate scope remains to be determined, the proposal is made at least for certain notions reasonably considered both fundamental and universal: noun, verb, subject, object, and possessive. Here we consider noun and verb.

4.2.1 Prototype Level

For nouns, the archetype functioning as category prototype is the conception of a physical object. For verbs, it is the conception of participants interacting energetically in a "force-dynamic" event (Talmy 1988). Both figure prominently in a more elaborate conceptual archetype which I refer to as the billiard-ball model:

> We think of our world as being populated by discrete physical objects. These objects are capable of moving about through space and making contact with one another. Motion is driven by energy, which some objects draw from internal resources and others receive from the exterior. When motion results in forceful physical contact, energy is transmitted from the mover to the impacted object, which may thereby be set in motion to participate in further interactions. (FCG2: 13)

This cognitive model represents a fundamental way in which we view the world. The featured role within it of the noun and verb archetypes is thus concomitant with their status as the most fundamental grammatical categories.

---

[9] It is not required that the color sensation coincide with the trajector, only that they be associated. For instance, the yellow portion of a *yellow croquet ball* may be limited to a stripe around its circumference. In this case, the stripe is said to be the croquet ball's **active zone** with respect to the *yellow* relationship.

It is usual in categorization for the greatest differentiation between the members of two classes to be observable in their prototypes. Accordingly, the noun and verb prototypes are polar opposites with regard to the billiard-ball model, contrasting in all their basic properties. The archetype for nouns is as follows:

1. A physical object is composed of material substance.
2. We think of an object as residing primarily in space, where it is bounded and has its own location.
3. In time, on the other hand, an object may persist indefinitely, and it is not thought of as having any particular location in this domain.
4. An object is **conceptually autonomous**, in the sense that we can conceptualize it independently of its participation in any event.

In each respect the archetype for verbs stands diametrically opposed:

1. An energetic interaction is not itself material, consisting instead of change and the transfer of energy.
2. Thus an event resides primarily in time; it is temporally bounded and has its own temporal location.
3. By contrast, an event's location in space is more diffuse and also derivative, as it depends on the locations of its participants.
4. This is so because an event is **conceptually dependent**; it cannot be conceptualized without conceptualizing the participants who interact to constitute it.

These archetypes are so elemental and pervasive in our experience that we generally take them for granted. Still, their conceptual emergence is seen here as presupposing certain basic cognitive abilities. Four in particular seem essential: our capacity for **grouping**, for **reification**, for **apprehending relationships**, and for **tracking relationships** through time. That we have these abilities can hardly be disputed. Once recognized, they allow plausible schematic characterizations of the noun and verb categories.

4.2.2 The Noun Schema

Our capacity for grouping is readily demonstrated at the level of basic perception. Let us first examine figure 4.5(a). In viewing it, we automatically perceive a group of two black dots, on the left, and another group of three, on the right. So strong is this grouping tendency that we cannot just see the five as a bunch of dots with no particular clustering. Nor, without special mental effort, can we see them as being grouped in any other way (e.g. a group of three dots on the left, and one of two on the right).

Several factors encourage grouping, the primary ones being **contiguity** and **similarity**.[10] The dots in figure 4.5(a) clearly form groups of two and three on the basis of spatial contiguity. On the other hand, the dots in figure 4.5(b) sort themselves into

---

[10] Similarity might be regarded as an abstract sort of contiguity (adjacency in **quality space**, discussed in ch. 5).

(a)   (b)

FIGURE 4.5

groups on grounds of similarity: despite their spatial admixture, we can readily perceive a group of six black dots whose color sets them apart from the larger group of white ones. We are likely as well to perceive the black dots as forming two groups of three on the basis of spatial proximity. This further clustering illustrates an essential point: namely, that grouping (like many other cognitive phenomena) occurs at multiple **levels of conceptual organization**. In this case, higher-level groups based on contiguity emerge within the lower-level group based on similarity.

A further basis for grouping is the recognition of familiar configurations. The conception of any such structure resides in mental operations that tie together—or **interconnect**—the entities interpreted as constituting it. These interconnections single out the constitutive entities and establish them as a group. In figure 4.5(b), for instance, the three black dots on the left are perceived as forming a straight line, as are the three on the right. The perception of a line functions as an interconnecting operation that in each case reinforces the grouping based on spatial contiguity. A more elaborate example of a group established in this manner is a constellation. When we look at the nighttime sky and see the Big Dipper, the stars comprising it do not stand out from the rest due to any special similarity (all stars look pretty much alike), nor even by spatial proximity (since other stars are interspersed). What causes their emergence as a group is their interpretation as points defining a familiar schematic image, whose recognition consists in mental operations through which the component stars are interconnected.

Once a group is established, it can function as a single entity at higher levels of conceptualization. For instance, the two lines that emerge by grouping in figure 4.5(b) (each consisting of three black dots) are further perceived as being parallel. They function as **unitary** entities with respect to this higher-level assessment: the judgment of parallelism does not pertain to the dots individually, but to the lines they constitute. This capacity to manipulate a group as a unitary entity for higher-order cognitive purposes is what I refer to as **reification**. Thus each emergent line in figure 4.5(b) is reified by virtue of being treated as a single element in the perception of parallelism, and in any other conception invoking them as such (e.g. in counting them, comparing their length, or observing their slope).

We can now define a **thing** as any product of grouping and reification.[11] Since these are general cognitive phenomena, not limited to space or perception, things can

---

[11] Equivalently, I have also defined a thing as a **region**, characterized abstractly as a set of interconnected entities (FCG1: §5.2). By avoiding this intermediate term (and the spatial metaphor it incorporates), the definition presented here is a bit less cumbersome.

emerge from constitutive entities in any domain or at any level of conceptual organization. Consider a *recipe*, for example. Though it may be written down, a recipe per se does not exist in space. By our abstract definition, however, a recipe is a thing whose constitutive entities are the successive steps involved in preparing some dish. These steps are interconnected and established as a group just by virtue of being conceived as occurring in a certain sequence. They are reified by being conceptualized as a single, unified procedure with the overall goal of creating the dish. Similarly, a *committee* qualifies as a thing even if its constitutive entities—the members—never assemble in one place. Their grouping and reification are effected by the very conception of their consulting and working together with a common purpose. Rather different in nature, but still a thing, is a *moment*. As a continuous span of time, its constitutive entities (points in time) are grouped on the basis of temporal contiguity. The group is reified through its conception as being a single unit of temporal experience, quite brief in overall duration.

A thing produced by grouping and reification can itself function as a constitutive entity with respect to a higher-order thing. Through successive application of these mental operations, things representing any level of conceptual organization can be arrived at. For instance, a *plate* is a thing. So is a *stack* of plates, obtained by placing such objects one on top of the other. If four such stacks are arranged in a certain configuration, they can be perceived as a *square*. A number of these squares can be put together to form a *row* of squares. Imagining several such rows being laid out in parallel gives rise to the conception of *three parallel rows*, which can further be thought of as a single *array*. And so on indefinitely. Despite its complexity, an expression like (5) poses no particular conceptual problems. (It could plausibly occur as a catalog entry describing a work of modern art.)

(5)   *an array of three parallel rows of squares each consisting of four stacks of plates*

More abstractly, a sports *league* might consist of two *conferences*, each with three *divisions*, each having several *teams*, each comprising a number of *players*.

We are ready now to consider the basic CG proposal that **a noun profiles a thing** (in the technical sense just outlined). This schematic characterization would seem to have a real chance of proving viable. Note first that it straightforwardly accommodates the many nouns whose referents clearly consist of multiple, individually recognizable elements. Here is just a small sample: *group, set, pair, collection, stack, team, orchestra, row, archipelago, trio, constellation, list, association, library, silverware, repertoire, herd, flock, colonnade, tribe, family, bunch, alphabet, chord, squadron, forest, six-pack, deck [of cards], choir, staff, [offensive] line, crew, colony, place setting, litter [of kittens], fleet, triptych, convoy, lexicon, audience*. For nouns like these, a description of the sort proposed—where constitutive entities are grouped and reified to form a unitary entity at a higher level of organization—seems not just workable but absolutely necessary.

If the definition works well for cases like these, what about the nouns considered prototypical, which designate physical objects? Here it would seem problematic, since we do not think of a *rock, board, mattress, cat,* or *potato* as a group. Nor is it obvious what their constitutive entities might be.[12] Moreover, it is problematic that the definition is problematic, for if valid it should certainly apply unproblematically to the prototype. The difficulty, though, is only apparent. There is in fact a good rationale for the grouping of constitutive entities being least evident in the prototype.

A thing is a set of interconnected entities which function as a single entity at a higher level of conceptual organization. A key point is that an entity (as defined in §4.1.3) need not be discrete, cognitively salient, or individually recognized. Thus even something continuous and homogeneous, like a *board*, can be described without inconsistency as having constitutive entities. These might be identified as the patches of wood—indefinite in number and arbitrarily delimited—which collectively occupy the full volume of its spatial extension. That a board comprises a continuous expanse of this substance is obviously central to its conception.[13] The very act of apprehending this continuity, of registering the existence of substance at every point, serves to interconnect the constitutive entities and establish them as a group. It is **not** implied that there is discretization at any level of processing, such that a board is perceived as a constellation of separate elements. Indeed, the absence of individuation is precisely what makes physical objects prototypical. They represent the special circumstance where grouping and reification are so automatic that constitutive entities are never consciously accessible. It is only when these operations are extended to other cases, where they are nonautomatic if not atypical, that we can be cognizant of their effect.

With physical objects it is thus the product of grouping and reification, the conception of a unitary entity, that predominates at the conscious level. A typical object is both continuous and has a definite spatial boundary. Yet, since neither property is specified by the abstract definition of a thing, substances lacking these properties also qualify as things. The category schema therefore accommodates mass nouns, which prototypically designate substances. Though a substance may be spatially manifested, its essential characterization is qualitative. Of course, any particular instantiation of a substance, e.g. a puddle of *water*, may be continuous and bounded, exhibiting a certain shape. These spatial properties are not crucial for identifying the substance, however, nor are they specifically implied by the mass noun's meaning. We can identify water as such even if it totally surrounds us, with no evident boundary. Likewise, separate puddles of water are construable as a single instance of the substance, as in the expression *all that water on the floor*. Despite their spatial discontinuity, the discrete patches form a group on the basis of their qualitative similarity.[14]

The schematic characterization must of course accommodate the many kinds of nouns that designate abstract entities. Some of these are treated in chapter 5 (see also

---

[12] The constitutive entities cannot be identified as parts. Many objects lack discernible parts, which in any case are best characterized in relation to the whole rather than conversely (§3.2.3).

[13] We can speculate that this aspect of its conception resides in a kind of mental scanning (below the level of conscious awareness) serving to register the continuous existence of the substance throughout the board's extension (FCG1: §3.1).

[14] Directly analogous is the mass-noun sense of *yellow*, as in *There's a lot of yellow in this painting*, diagrammed in fig. 4.4(e). The constitutive entities are an indeterminate number of patches of color, which emerge as a group on the basis of similarity (they all project to the same region in color space).

FCG2: §1.2). Here I simply note that the proposed schema makes no direct reference to physical entities, but only to cognitive abilities, so its applicability to abstract things poses no intrinsic difficulty. To be sure, this discussion in no way constitutes a proof that the noun schema is correct or adequate as it stands. Still, in view of the prevailing doctrine that grammatical categories are not semantically definable, the mere existence of a seemingly plausible candidate is rather significant. At the very least, it may demonstrate that a semantic characterization of nouns is not impossible in principle.

4.2.3 The Verb Schema

The schema for verbs presupposes two fundamental cognitive abilities: the capacity for apprehending relationships and for tracking relationships through time. These are so basic and obvious that discussion might seem superfluous. Nonetheless, they involve certain subtleties that need to be exposed.

In the most elemental terms, apprehending a relationship is a matter of conceptualizing multiple entities as part of the same mental experience. They must somehow be brought together within a single processing "window" (whether through memory, imagination, or direct observation). There must further be some mental operation that involves them both and thereby establishes a connection between them. Consider the perception of two tones. If we hear them an hour apart, they will almost certainly constitute separate and unrelated experiences.[15] But if we hear them just a second apart, we cannot avoid connecting them through some mental assessment—observing, for example, that the second tone is higher in pitch than the first, that they have the same duration, or simply that there are two of them close together. Hence they are not conceived in isolation but in relation to each other.

Entities conceived in relation to one another are **interconnected** by the mental operations that link them. Thus they implicitly form a group, i.e. a set of interconnected entities. These are, of course, the same notions used for the characterization of a thing. The question therefore arises whether the present account can properly distinguish between things and relationships. In fact it can, because additional factors come into play: focusing and reification. When entities are interconnected, we can focus either on the interconnecting operations or on the group they establish. By focusing on the interconnections, we conceptualize a relationship. We conceptualize a thing by focusing instead on the group that emerges and construing it as a single entity for higher-level purposes.

Like things, relationships can be apprehended at multiple levels of organization, with the group emerging at each level having the potential to be focused and reified. Recall figure 4.5(a), which we cannot see as merely a collection of dots. Through assessments of proximity, we automatically connect the two dots on the left, as well as the three on the right, and establish them as groups. At a higher level of organization, we might observe that these groups are unequal in size, or that they have the

---

[15] Naturally, the tones can be experienced together if the first is reactivated via memory. This would usually only happen in the context of a psychological experiment.

same location along the vertical axis. In figure 4.5(b), relationships are evident at several levels: certain dots stand out from the rest by being the same in color; within the group thus established, subgroups emerge through assessments of spatial proximity; in scanning through each subgroup, the path connecting the dots is seen as being straight; finally, the lines perceived in this manner are judged to be parallel.

Relationships like these are **simplex**, in the sense that each consists of a single configuration fully manifested at a single point in time. We can also apprehend relationships that are **complex, consisting of multiple** component relationships, typically manifested successively through a continuous span of time (fig. 4.1). Event conceptions have this character. Imagine a simple (as opposed to simplex) event, such as a ball rolling down an incline, sketched in figure 4.6. The event unfolds through time. At each instant the ball occupies some position in space, but in each case a different one; collectively these positions define its spatial path. The situation obtaining at any one moment constitutes a simplex relationship: a single configuration in which the ball occupies one particular location. The overall event comprises an indefinite number of such relationships and is therefore complex.

Experientially, apprehending an event is similar to watching a motion picture, as opposed to examining a series of still photographs. An event's conception is continuous rather than discrete, even though each time-slice consists of a simplex relationship. These component relationships—referred to as **states**—are neither individuated nor separately examined at the level of conscious awareness. Instead, we conceptualize an event as seamlessly unfolding, with each state developing organically out of its predecessor. The notation of a wedge (>) is used in figure 4.6 to represent this continuity (and counteract the discreteness suggested by static diagrams).

In their seamless continuity, an event's component states (simplex relationships) are quite analogous to the patches of substance constituting a physical object. The nonindividuation of their constitutive entities results in both objects and events being perceived as continuous.[16] This perception of continuity implies some kind of mental operation serving to register the uninterrupted occurrence of constitutive entities throughout their expanse. We can plausibly describe this as **scanning**. It is by means of scanning—through space in the case of objects, and through time for events—that

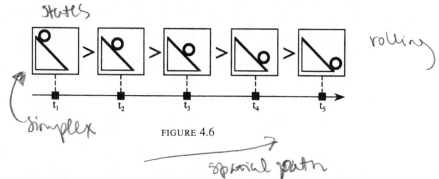

FIGURE 4.6

[16] These comments pertain to low-level processing, where the constitutive entities are elemental. It is not denied that many objects have discernible parts or that many events have recognizable phases. Presumably these emerge at higher levels of conceptual organization.

their constitutive patches or states are integrated to create the seamless conception of their spatial or temporal extensionality. The scanning that occurs with events constitutes our capacity for tracking a relationship through time.

Essential here is the distinction made earlier (§3.4.2) between **conceived time** and **processing time**. The arrow in figure 4.6 represents conceived time (t), time as an **object** of conception. We conceive **of** time whenever we conceptualize an event (which by definition is manifested temporally). Of course, since conceptualization is a mental activity, it happens **through** time and has its own temporal duration. Time functioning as the **medium** of conception is referred to as processing time (T). Every conception—even of a static situation—requires some span of processing time for its occurrence. Naturally, both sorts of time play a role in the conception of events. When we track a relationship through time, the tracking occurs in processing time and the event itself in conceived time.

Let us now elaborate the previous diagram so that both conceived time (t) and processing time (T) are represented. Depicted once more in figure 4.7 is the conceptualization of a ball rolling down an incline. The conceptualizing activity itself occurs during span T_1–T_5 of processing time. Each of the larger rectangles corresponds to the conception active at a given moment, wherein the ball occupies a particular location at a certain point in time. Collectively these points define the temporal interval t_1–t_5 during which the event is conceived as occurring.[17]

One way in which we conceptualize events is by directly observing their actual occurrence. In this circumstance, the distinction between conceived time and processing time might seem superfluous, since the temporal intervals coincide. If figure 4.7 represents the actual, real-time observation of a ball rolling down an incline, the time span during which the conceptualization occurs (T_1–T_5) is precisely the same as the time during which the event occurs (t_1–t_5). However, the direct observation of actual events is only one of the many viewing arrangements that provide the conceptual substrate for linguistic expressions (§3.4.1). Suppose, instead, that the conceptualization in figure 4.7 is one of either recalling a past event or imagining a future one.

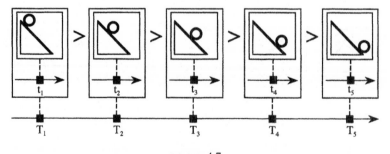

FIGURE 4.7

<hr />

[17] Once more, it is arbitrary how many component states and temporal locations are indicated diagrammatically, since the conceptualization is actually continuous.

In this case the time of conceptualization and the time of the event's occurrence are clearly distinct. Moreover, they are usually not even the same in duration: how long it takes to conceptualize an event (by mentally running through its component states) and how long it takes for it to actually occur are very different matters.

In principle, then, we need to distinguish the time of an event's conception from the time of its occurrence, even in cases where they happen to coincide. The notation in figure 4.7 is meant to be neutral as to whether the intervals T_1–T_5 and t_1–t_5 represent the same span of time or different ones, and also as to their relative duration. Its essential import is rather that the component states are mentally accessed through processing time in the order of their occurrence through conceived time, and further, that just one component state is strongly activated at a given processing moment. Stated more technically, the component states are sequentially accessed through processing time such that, at a given instant T_i, the only state in focus is the one obtaining at the corresponding instant t_i. This amounts to mentally tracking an event as it unfolds through time, that is, scanning sequentially through it along the temporal axis. Accordingly, it is referred to as **sequential scanning**.

While it may seem mysterious, sequential scanning is actually quite pedestrian. In fact, we engage in this mode of scanning whenever we directly observe an event. Suppose we actually watch a ball roll down an incline. In our real-time viewing of this occurrence, we see the ball in just one position at any moment, and we necessarily access these component states in the precise sequence of their temporal manifestation. Sequential scanning is thus inherent in this viewing arrangement (without being restricted to it). If a relationship develops through time, the most natural way of apprehending it is to track it through time in this manner. Hence sequential scanning is equally applicable whether an event is observed, remembered, or imagined.

We are nonetheless capable of viewing events in another manner, sketched in figure 4.8. In this mode of scanning, it is no longer the case that only one component state is focused at a given moment of processing time. While the states are still accessed in their natural sequence, they undergo **summation**: that is, they are mentally superimposed, resulting in their simultaneous activation. Therefore, at each moment T_i of processing time, the focused conception comprises all the configurations thus far encountered in scanning through the conceived time interval t_1–t_i. The end result is that all the component states are simultaneously active and available. They form a single gestalt comparable to a multiple-exposure photograph. Our capacity for **summary scanning** is not in doubt. It occurs, for example, whenever we watch an object move—say a golf ball rolling on a putting green—and then represent its trajectory by means of a line with a corresponding shape. Indeed, television replays sometimes make the summation explicit by successively superimposing the images of the ball in each position, just in the manner of figure 4.8, until the final picture shows the ball in all positions simultaneously.

Sequential and summary scanning should not be thought of as mutually exclusive but as two facets of the normal observation of events. Sequential scanning represents the actual nature of the real-time viewing experience, where just one component state is accessible at any given instant. As we view an event sequentially, the successive states are retained in short-term memory, producing a transient record that can

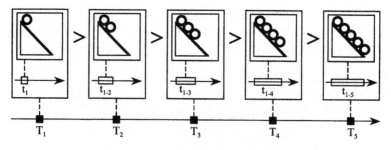

FIGURE 4.8

then be accessed in summary fashion. We thus have the option of conceptualizing an event by focusing selectively on either mode of scanning. Depending on which mode predominates, we can either highlight its inherent sequentiality or impose a holistic construal.

The term **process** is adopted for a complex relationship that develops through conceived time and is scanned sequentially along this axis. This characterization makes reference not only to schematic conceptual content (a complex relation extending through time) but also to a particular way of mentally accessing it (sequential scanning). The same content can therefore be construed as either a process or a nonprocessual relationship, depending on whether it is accessed via sequential scanning (in the manner of fig. 4.7) or summary scanning (as in fig. 4.8). A basic proposal of CG is that **a verb profiles a process**. Sequential scanning is thus implied by categorization as a verb.[18] When the same content is viewed in summary fashion, the resulting expression belongs to another grammatical category (e.g. an infinitive or a participle).

4.3 Classes of Relational Expressions

The noun and verb prototypes—physical object and energetic interaction—are maximally distinct with respect to the billiard-ball archetype (§4.2.1). A glance at figure 4.1 reveals that the noun and verb schemas are also polar opposites. These schemas are based on different cognitive abilities (grouping and reification vs. apprehending and tracking relationships). They contrast in the nature of their profile (thing vs. relationship), degree of elaboration (simplex vs. complex), and mode of scanning (summary vs. sequential). Between the two extremes lie expressions that differ from nouns because they profile relationships, and from verbs because these relations are nonprocessual. We must now consider the characterization and classification of these intermediate cases, which correspond to such traditional categories as preposition, adjective, adverb, infinitive, and participle.

---

[18] In diagrams like fig. 4.1(e), the bar along the time arrow represents sequential scanning. The span of time through which the relationship is tracked sequentially is called its **temporal profile**. (I acknowledge that this term is potentially misleading, for a verb does not profile the span of time per se, but the **relationship** scanned sequentially through it.)

4.3.1 Focal Participants

No single classificatory scheme makes all the necessary distinctions and captures all the significant similarities among linguistic elements. There are different grounds for categorization, yielding cross-cutting classes that are equally and simultaneously valid. The factors used for the characterization of nouns and verbs suggest a number of natural groupings (analogous to "natural classes" in phonology), none of which coincide with traditional categories. One such class consists of expressions that profile relationships. These relational expressions include both verbs, which profile processes, and expressions designating nonprocessual relationships. The latter are themselves a natural category. Also natural would be a category based on summary scanning (subsuming everything but verbs). We will find some evidence for each of these classifications.

For relational expressions, an additional basis for classification resides in the number and the nature of their focal participants (§3.3.2). A profiled relationship construes its participants at different levels of prominence. It is usual for one participant to be made the primary focus, as the entity being located, evaluated, or otherwise described. This is called the **trajector** (tr). Additionally, there is often a secondary focal participant, called the **landmark** (lm).[19] These constructs were initially adopted on purely semantic grounds. They are necessary to distinguish many pairs of expressions that are otherwise semantically identical, like *above* and *below* (fig. 3.9). Trajector/landmark organization is thus inherent in the meanings of relational expressions, even when the focused elements fail to be overtly manifested. The verb *swallow*, for instance, has both a trajector (the swallower) and a landmark (the swallowee) as part of its internal semantic structure. In a sentence like *He swallowed it*, these are specified by the subject and object pronouns. Yet the verb itself evokes these participants schematically and accords them focal prominence, even in the absence of a subject or object nominal (e.g. *Swallow it!*; *the pill he swallowed*).

Thus one basis for categorizing relational expressions is whether they have just a single focal participant (by definition, the trajector) or two. There is nothing contradictory about a relationship having only one participant. The abstract characterization in §4.2.3 merely specifies that a relationship consists of interconnections. Since it is not required that the interconnected entities be salient, explicit, or even individuated, the notion of a one-participant relationship is perfectly coherent. The verb *rise*, for example, designates the process of its trajector moving through space in an upward direction. The profiled relationship consists of the trajector occupying a spatial location at any given moment and how this location changes through time. In contrast to the mover, however, these locations are neither individuated nor singled out for separate focus. Similarly, an adjective like *pretty*, *tall*, or *stupid* situates its

---

[19] Since the characterization of relationships (§4.2.3) does not specify focal prominence of the interconnected entities, there may well be relational expressions best analyzed as having more than two focal elements or none at all. A possible case of the former are verbs like *give*, which occur with two object-like nominals: *She gave us a kitten*. The latter may be illustrated by certain verbs of Cora (a Mexican language of the Uto-Aztecan family) that occur in subjectless clauses: *nʸeeri'i* 'be all lit up', *suuna* '[water] pour', *tʸee* 'be long', *kun* 'be hollow' (CIS: ch. 2).

trajector vis-à-vis a scale representing the degree to which it exhibits a certain property. There is just one focal participant because the adjective itself specifies both the property and the scalar position. Neither is construed as an independently existing entity requiring separate identification.

A relational expression also has only one focused participant when the profiled interconnections hold between different facets of the trajector itself (not between the trajector and a distinct landmark). Consider the adjective *square*, which describes its trajector as having a certain shape. The conceptualization of this shape resides in a number of mental operations assessing particular subparts with respect to one another: that there are four sides, that each side is straight, that opposite sides are parallel, that adjacent sides are perpendicular, and that all sides are equal in length. Collectively these assessments constitute the profiled relationship, manifested within a single participant. This participant—the adjectival trajector—is the same element that is profiled when *square* is used as a noun. As shown in figure 4.9, the noun and the adjective have the same conceptual content, involving both a thing and a specification of its shape. They differ in what they profile within this base: the noun profiles the thing, while the adjective profiles the configurational assessments (represented diagrammatically for both by dashed arrows).

A relationship is conceptually dependent on its participants; it evokes its participants (if only schematically) as an intrinsic aspect of its own conception. Consequently, the focal participants in a profiled relationship are themselves part of the relational profile, as shown for *square* in figure 4.9(b). Bear in mind that focal prominence is one dimension of construal, a matter of how a situation is conceived and portrayed, not something objectively discernible in it. Hence the same situation can often be described by expressions that confer focal prominence on different elements, even elements at different levels of conceptual organization. The sentences in (6), for example, might all be used to describe the same event:

(6)   (a) *The bride hugged the groom.*

(b) *The groom hugged the bride.*

(c) *The couple embraced.*

FIGURE 4.9

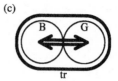

FIGURE 4.10

Even if the bride and groom participate equally, the speaker has the option of focusing either on what the bride does, resulting in (6)(a), or on what the groom does, yielding (6)(b). The contrast is sketched in figure 4.10(a)–(b), where the circles labeled B and G stand for the bride and groom, and a double arrow represents the exertion of force. Choosing either person as trajector (primary focal participant) has the effect of selecting that person's action as the profiled process (in which the other person functions as landmark). Yet the speaker need not risk charges of gender discrimination by making this arbitrary choice. A safer option is (6)(c), diagrammed in figure 4.10(c). Here the profiled process subsumes the actions of both people and portrays them as symmetrical. Accordingly, trajector status is not conferred on either one individually, but rather on the group comprising them. This group—a thing that emerges at a higher level of conceptual organization—is the only focal participant in the profiled relationship.[20]

A relationship's focused participants are thus not restricted to any particular level of conceptual organization. Nor are they limited to things: the trajector or the landmark of a relational expression can itself be a relationship. The boldfaced elements in (7) exemplify the various possibilities. In (7)(a), the trajector of *in* is a process, instantiated by the clausal expression *their baby was born*. In (7)(b), the landmark of *intend* is specified by *to complain*—an infinitival expression designating a complex nonprocessual relationship. It is even possible for both focal participants to be relationships. In (7)(c), the trajector and landmark of *before* are both processes, respectively expressed by the clauses *the guests all left* and *she got there*.

(7) (a) *Their baby was born **in** July.*

(b) *I **intend** to complain.*

(c) *The guests all left **before** she got there.*

Focal participants prove crucial for characterizing several traditional parts of speech—namely adjective, adverb, and preposition. Each profiles a nonprocessual relationship. What distinguishes them is their trajector/landmark organization, shown abstractly in figure 4.11. Adjectives and adverbs differ from prepositions in having only a single focal participant (a trajector but no focused landmark). They differ from

---

[20] This is another kind of circumstance where a profiled relationship holds between subparts of the single focused participant.

one another in the nature of their trajector: a thing in the case of adjectives, a relationship for adverbs. On the other hand, a preposition has two focal participants, its landmark being a thing. Since a preposition's trajector can either be a thing or a relationship, it is characterized schematically as an entity (represented by a rectangle).[21]

Traditionally, an adjective is said to modify a noun. Its trajector is thus a schematic thing, which the modified noun specifies in finer detail. In *square tablecloth*, for example, *tablecloth* elaborates the schematic trajector of *square*. The relationship profiled by an adjective holds between its trajector and an entity which fails for some reason to stand out as a separate, focused participant. This might be because the relation holds between subparts of the trajector, as in the case of *square* (fig. 4.9). Alternatively, the nontrajector entity may be abstract and fully specified by the adjective itself. A degree adjective like *tall* locates the trajector on a scale indicating the extent to which it exhibits a particular property. A color adjective, such as *yellow* in figure 4.4(c), connects a thing to a particular region in color space. In such cases, where the adjective itself uniquely identifies the nontrajector entity (a scalar region or a certain quality), the latter is neither independently salient nor individually focused.

An adverb is traditionally defined as modifying a verb (e.g. *work fast*), a preposition (***directly** into the fire*), an adjective (***exceedingly** handsome*), or another adverb (***almost** excessively brilliant*). These are precisely the basic categories characterized as profiling relationships (processual and nonprocessual), so they constitute a natural grouping in CG. The notation in figure 4.11(b) is meant to indicate that a relationship functions as trajector, while being neutral as to what kind of relationship it is. The minimal contrast with adjectives is apparent from pairs like *work fast* and *fast worker*. In both cases, *fast* locates some activity at the positive end of a scale assessing its rate of execution. The only difference is that the adverb confers focal prominence (trajector status) on the activity itself, whereas the adjective confers it on the actor.[22]

(a) Adjective   (b) Adverb   (c) Preposition

FIGURE 4.11

---

[21] Once more, these traditional categories are neither fundamental nor essential to CG, which can however reveal the conceptual coherence responsible for their evident utility in describing grammar. The characterizations are devised for basic lexical examples, so they will not apply without adjustment to all phenomena for which the traditional labels have been employed.

[22] To be sure, the actor can only be assessed for rapidity relative to some activity it engages in. This activity, which mediates the actor's placement on the scale, is its **active zone** with respect to the profiled relationship.

In contrast to adjectives and adverbs, prepositions are indifferent as to the nature of their trajector. The distinctive property of this class is the conferring of secondary focal prominence on a thing. This landmark is expressed by the prepositional object (e.g. *in **August**; under **the bed**; with **a screwdriver***). Normally the same preposition has both "adjectival" uses, where its trajector is a thing (***the last weekend** in August; **the dust** under the bed; **a boy** with a screwdriver*), and also "adverbial" uses, where its trajector is a relationship (***They got married** in August; **It's hot** under the bed; **She opened it** with a screwdriver*). This overlap is one reason for thinking that the traditional categorization—where adjectives, adverbs, and prepositions are viewed as mutually exclusive classes—is less than optimal.

4.3.2 Complex Relationships

The relationship profiled by a preposition can either be simplex or complex. In the case of spatial expressions, a simplex preposition specifies a single location: *in the garage; under a tree; near the exit*. In contrast, a complex preposition describes a series of locations amounting to a spatial path: *into the garage; along the river; through a tunnel*. A specific example is the difference between *in* and *into*, diagrammed in figure 4.12(a)–(b). Because *in* profiles a single spatial configuration, it has just one component state. By contrast, the profile of *into* consists of multiple configurations and thus comprises a continuous series of states (only three of which are shown). The dotted correspondence lines indicate that the trajector is the same throughout, as is the landmark. Observe that the single configuration profiled by *in* is the same as the final state of *into*.

Since the relationship profiled by a verb is also complex, we must pose the question of how a verb differs from a path preposition. It cannot just be a matter of conceptual content, for this can sometimes be the same. In some uses, for example, the verb *enter* would seem to have the same content as the preposition *into*. This is shown in figure 4.12(c), where the component states are identical to those in 4.12(b). In the CG analysis, the crucial difference resides not in content but in construal. There are two respects in which the verb construes the content **temporally** and the preposition **atemporally**. First, the verb specifically invokes conceived time (t) and portrays the complex relationship as developing along this axis. While the temporal dimension is not excluded from the preposition's meaning, neither is it focused—it

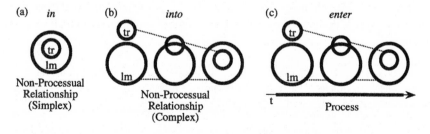

FIGURE 4.12

remains in the background and may even be absent altogether.[23] Second, the verb highlights temporality by scanning through the component states sequentially (indicated by the bar along the time arrow), whereas the preposition achieves a holistic view by scanning them in summary fashion (compare figs. 4.7 and 4.8).

The expressions that profile complex relationships are not restricted to verbs and path prepositions. Also having this character are some of the elements traditionally referred to as participles and infinitives.[24] In English, these include the kinds of expressions exemplified in (8): infinitives with *to* (e.g. *to enter*), present participles (*finding*), past participles that occur in the perfect (*[have] painted*), and those occurring in the passive (*[be] demolished*).

(8)   (a) *The firemen tried **to enter** the burning building.*

    (b) *They kept **finding** errors in the manuscript.*

    (c) *I have already **painted** the fence.*

    (d) *The building was completely **demolished** by the explosion.*

For the moment, we can limit our attention to infinitives. What is the meaning of an infinitival phrase like *to enter*? In particular, how does it contrast semantically with the verb *enter*, on the one hand, and the preposition *into*, on the other? Since there is no apparent difference in conceptual content, the component states are the same as in figure 4.12(b)–(c). The contrast must therefore reside in construal, with temporality suggesting itself as the relevant factor. Yet merely describing *to enter* as either temporal or atemporal would be insufficient, for it has to be distinguished from both *enter* (which is temporal) and *into* (atemporal). There is a ready solution, however. Since the verb differs from the preposition in two respects—by specifically and saliently invoking conceived time, and by scanning sequentially along this axis—the infinitive can be seen as intermediate, resembling the verb in one respect and the preposition in the other. Because it derives from the verb, the infinitive certainly views the component states in relation to time. Its atemporality must therefore be due to scanning—evidently, the infinitival *to* imposes summary scanning on the verbal process. Thus the infinitive *to enter* preserves the component states of *enter*, still conceived as extending through time, but scans them in summary fashion. Its diagrammatic representation would be the same as figure 4.12(c), minus the bar for sequential scanning on the time arrow.

Since the varied elements referred to as infinitives and participles all derive from verbs, the process designated by the verb stem figures prominently in their meaning.

---

[23] In expressions like *the road into the forest*, the spatially extended trajector (the road) simultaneously occupies all the specified locations vis-à-vis the landmark. Here there is no development through time, since the entire spatial configuration obtains at any one instant. (The expression does tend to evoke the idea of something moving along the road, but this is tenuous and unprofiled.)

[24] Participles and infinitives are actually quite diverse, and often the same form has uses representing different categories. Hence the present discussion does not apply to everything bearing these traditional labels.

They share the further property of imposing a summary view on the verbal process. Consequently, the derived structure—representing a higher level of conceptual organization—is nonprocessual. Despite their verbal base, infinitives and participles are not themselves verbs. Typically they profile nonprocessual relationships.

It is also quite common for the same forms to function grammatically as nouns. For instance, *to*-infinitives occur in certain environments which (at least arguably) are reserved for nominal expressions:

(9)   (a) ***To complain*** *would be futile.*

    (b) *What I really want is **to live forever**.*

As nouns, they profile a thing identifiable as a conceptual reification of the verbal process.[25]

This extension to nominal use is quite straightforward, given the CG description of basic categories. Things and nonprocessual relationships represent a natural grouping since both construe a situation in summary fashion. Consequently, the holistic view imposed by infinitival or participial marking is one of two essential factors involved in deriving a noun from a verb. The other requisite factor is a shift in profile from the relationship to a thing. Suppose, then, that an infinitive or participle should undergo such a shift. If there is no additional marking to signal it, the same form will profile a thing and thus be classed as a noun. This is neither implausible nor unlikely. An implicit shift in profile is nothing other than the ubiquitous linguistic phenomenon known as **metonymy** (§3.3.1).

These steps are shown abstractly in figure 4.13.[26] Diagram (a) represents a process. Its profile is a complex relationship, scanned sequentially. Diagram (b) shows the minimal adjustment brought about by infinitivalization or participialization: the imposition of summary scanning (indicated by the absence of a bar along the time

FIGURE 4.13

---

[25] More clearly nominal are participles marked by *-ing* that take possessives: ***Your being so stubborn*** *really complicates matters*; *The judge's leniency was attributed to **his having a clean prior record**.* These too profile an abstract thing obtained by reification. Rather than a reification of the process, nouns based on participles often profile a processual participant. English exploits this option quite sparingly (e.g. *the damned*; *his betrothed*).

[26] In these abstract representations, correspondence lines are omitted to simplify the diagrams. The relational participants are presumed to be the same in all the component states.

arrow). This does not itself imply a change in profile. As exemplified in (8), an infinitive or participle may still profile a complex relationship comprising all the component states of the verbal process. A summary view does however constitute one essential step toward nominalization. The other step is a shift in profile to a thing, which can be either a participant in the original process or else a conceptual reification of that process itself. The latter option is depicted in diagram (c).

In CG, the grammatical markers deriving infinitives and participles are necessarily considered meaningful. One facet of their meaning consists in their suspension of the verb's sequential scanning. The resulting holistic construal of the verbal process is the only property shared by all infinitival and participial expressions. They differ from one another in regard to what additional effect they have on the processual base. Elements considered infinitival usually have the least effect. Indeed, the suspension of sequential scanning may be the only change they bring about. As shown in figure 4.13(b), an infinitive profiles all the component states of the process and has the same trajector/landmark alignment. If it undergoes the further step of nominalization, depicted in 4.13(c), all the component states are included in the abstract thing it profiles. At least as a first approximation, these diagrams might serve as a characterization of the English infinitival *to*.[27]

By contrast, the elements referred to as participles have a more substantial impact on the processual base. Affected are not only the mode of scanning but additional factors like profiling and focal prominence. In one way or another, participles invoke a certain vantage point for viewing the processual content. English shows this fairly clearly. The so-called present participle, formed with *-ing*, takes an "internal perspective" on the verbal process. The so-called past participle, derived by *-ed* (and a variety of irregular inflections), adopts a "posterior" vantage point.

Among their central uses, present participles occur in the progressive, as noun modifiers, and as clausal adverbs:

(10)   (a) *A monkey is **climbing** the tree.*

    (b) *The monkey **climbing the tree** is very cute.*

    (c) ***Climbing the tree**, the monkey lost its grip.*

In these constructions the participle profiles a complex relationship, whose characteristic feature is that it represents an internal portion of some longer process. Stated in CG terms, *-ing* imposes a limited **immediate scope** (IS) in the temporal domain (§3.2.3). Since the immediate scope is the "onstage" region, the locus of viewing attention, those portions of the processual base that fall outside its confines are excluded from the profile. This is seen in figure 4.14, where the beginning and end of the verbal process lie outside the immediate temporal scope, which delimits the relationship profiled by the participle. The ellipses (...) indicate a further effect of *-ing*: to abstract away from any differences among the focused states, thus viewing

---

[27] Certainly more is involved. Most obviously, *to*-infinitives usually have a future orientation relative to the main-clause event (cf. Wierzbicka 1988: ch. 1).

FIGURE 4.14

them as effectively equivalent. Hence the profiled relationship is construed as mass-like and homogeneous.

Past participles occur in the perfect construction (with *have*), the passive (with *be*), and as adjectives formed on both intransitive and transitive verbs:

(11)   (a)   *The students **had collected** a lot of money for the trip.*

     (b)   *This building **was designed** by a famous architect.*

     (c)   *The pond is **frozen**.*

     (d)   *The **demolished** cathedral took a century to rebuild.*

The perfect indicates that the profiled relationship is prior to a time of reference, given as R in figure 4.15(a). Its apprehension from this posterior vantage point provides a connection to the meanings exhibited by *-ed* (and its morphological variants) in other constructions. They all highlight the **end** of the verbal process, focusing either the final participant or the final state. The passive *-ed* confers primary focal prominence on the final participant. The bold arrows in diagram (b) represent the direction of influence: the participant shown at the top acts on the one at the bottom or somehow initiates their interaction. The more active participant would normally be chosen as trajector. However, the participial morpheme overrides the trajector/

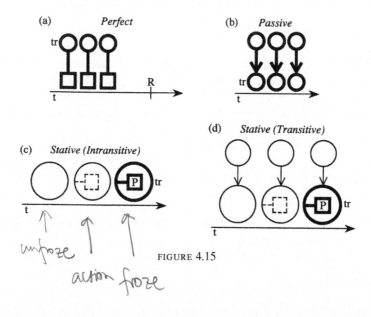

FIGURE 4.15

landmark organization of the verb stem, conferring trajector status on the more passive participant that would otherwise function as landmark.

The participial forms in (11)(c)–(d) are appropriately described as "stative-adjectival", for they restrict the profile to a single state and function grammatically as adjectives. The verb stem designates a process in which a participant undergoes a change of state (e.g. from liquid to solid, in the case of *freeze/frozen*). As a result, this participant—represented by the larger circle in diagrams (c) and (d)—exhibits a property, P, that it did not have previously. The stative-adjectival -*ed* imposes on the processual base a profile restricted to the participant's manifestation of this property. Since there is only one profiled participant, it functions as trajector. This is so even for transitive verbs (like *demolish*), where the verb's trajector acts to induce a change in its landmark (the trajector of the participle). In either case, the participle's profile is limited to the resultant situation of a single participant exhibiting a property, so the profiled relationship conforms to the CG characterization of adjectives (fig. 4.11(a)).

In all the cases examined, the formation of a participle or infinitive has the effect of **atemporalizing** the process designated by the verb it derives from. The processual base loses its temporality in various ways: by nominalization, by the restriction of its profile to a single component state, or just by imposition of summary scanning. However it happens, the resulting expression is not a verb, for it is no longer **temporal** in the sense of profiling a complex relationship scanned sequentially through conceived time.

4.3.3 Structural Motivation

If they are not pushed too far, traditional grammatical classes have considerable descriptive utility over a wide spectrum of diverse languages. It is not without reason that terms like noun, verb, adjective, adverb, preposition, infinitive, and participle are constantly and unavoidably used by linguists of all persuasions. The conceptual characterizations proposed for these categories both explain their descriptive efficacy and make them available for a symbolic account of grammar. To the extent that they are valid and useful, CG is able to exploit them.

They are not adopted uncritically, however. Their CG characterizations reveal the limitations of traditional classifications that view the parts of speech as disjoint lexical categories. For example, if one accepts that a noun profiles a thing, it can be shown that the same description applies to pronouns, demonstratives, and articles. Hence these are most reasonably seen not as disjoint from but as belonging to the class of nouns, being distinguished from "lexical" nouns by their additional, special properties. Also problematic is the traditional division among adjectives, adverbs, and prepositions (fig. 4.11). Treating them as separate and on a par fails to capture the fact that prepositions (and prepositional phrases) function either adjectivally or adverbially, depending on whether their trajector is a thing or a relationship. Rather than positing disjoint classes, it seems preferable to recognize a broader category of expressions designating nonprocessual relationships. Overlapping subclasses can then be defined (as needed) based on cross-cutting properties such as complexity, nature of the trajector, and the presence of a landmark.

The CG account of categorization meets the requirements of being flexible, allowing cross-cutting classifications, and accommodating both construction-based and meaning-based classes (ch. 8). Still, classification per se is less important than elucidating the conceptual factors that underlie it. In describing basic classes, we have focused on conceptual phenomena reasonably considered fundamental. These same phenomena allow the characterization of other categories that might well prove grammatically significant, even though they are not traditionally recognized. Three in particular seem worth considering: expressions that profile relationships (rather than things); expressions that profile nonprocessual relationships; and expressions based on summary (as opposed to sequential) scanning. At least some motivation can be found for each of these higher-level groupings.[28]

If nothing else, the first potential category—expressions that profile relationships—permits a succinct characterization of adverbs: an adverb profiles a relationship whose trajector is also relational (fig. 4.11(b)). This is admittedly rather tenuous, and there is no assurance that this grouping will prove to be strongly motivated. It may just be that, taken as a whole, the class of relational expressions is too variegated to exhibit any common behavior distinguishing them from nouns.

The other two groupings are supported by general features of nominal and clausal organization. Let us first consider nominal expressions, often referred to (infelicitously) as "noun phrases". A noun phrase profiles a thing, typically expressed by a noun called the **head**. Elements like articles (*a, the*) and demonstratives (*this, that, these, those*) serve to **ground** the profiled thing by relating it to the context of speech. Various sorts of **modifiers** may also be included. In (12), modifiers are given in bold.

(12) (a) *an expensive dress*

(b) *the box on the top shelf*

(c) *the only student to hand in her assignment*

(d) *that man complaining to the waiter*

(e) *the brand preferred by most customers*

(f) *this broken cup*

(g) **the break cup*

(h) **that man complain to the waiter*

A pattern is evident: the kinds of elements able to modify nouns are just those described as profiling nonprocessual relationships. Included are expressions headed by adjectives (*expensive*), prepositions (*on*), infinitives (*to hand in*), present participles (*complaining*), and past participles (the passive *preferred* and the stative-adjectival *broken*). However, a noun cannot be modified directly by a verb (*break*) or a complex processual expression headed by a verb (*complain to the waiter*); (12)(g)–(h) are

---

[28] I have no evidence worth mentioning for a grouping based on complexity (simplex vs. complex). This factor may be inherently nonsalient.

clearly "ungrammatical". We can therefore make a generalization concerning the structure of English nominals: namely, that **noun modifiers designate nonprocessual relationships**. Its role in capturing the regularity indicates that this class of expressions constitutes a natural grouping.[29]

The same data suggests the naturalness of a grouping based on summary scanning. This higher-level category consists of nouns together with their possible modifiers—that is, relational expressions other than verbs. If nouns can be modified by numerous kinds of relational expressions, why should verbs be excluded? Apparently nouns and their modifiers have some affinity, something in common that sets them apart from verbs. That something is their summary mode of scanning. A noun phrase profiles a thing, which—as primary focus—tends to impose its holistic perspective on the construal of other nominal elements. The overall nominal conception is thus most coherent (and easiest to process) when the other elements share that perspective to begin with. Because the sequentiality of verbs is inconsistent with a summary view, languages generally do not permit them to directly modify nouns.[30] To serve in this capacity, they must first be rendered atemporal by infinitivalization or participialization.

The relation between a noun and a full noun phrase is parallel in many respects to the relation between a verb and a full, "finite" clause. For the moment, we can characterize a finite clause (in English) as one specified for tense (present vs. past). A basic descriptive generalization of CG is that **a finite clause profiles a process**. In simple examples like (13), the lexical verb is the head, since the process it designates is also profiled by the clause as a whole. The tense marking grounds this process by relating it to the time of speaking.

(13) (a) *His new hairstyle **resembles** a porcupine.*

  (b) *My cup **broke**.*

Being processual, a verb cannot itself modify a noun, as we saw in (12)(g)–(h). Conversely, the kinds of elements that modify nouns cannot stand alone as clausal heads, since they profile nonprocessual relationships. The following sentences are therefore ungrammatical:

(14) (a) **Her dress **expensive(s)**.*

  (b) **The box **on(s)** the top shelf.*

  (c) **The students **to hand in their assignments**.*

  (d) **That man **complaining to the waiter**.*

[29] This is not just a regularity of English but represents a strong universal tendency. Bear in mind, though, that since noun modification is a complex matter involving numerous factors, no single generalization can serve as a full description of noun modifiers in any language.

[30] Why, then, can verbs and clauses be modified by relational expressions based on summary scanning? I imagine this reflects an intrinsic processing asymmetry. It is quite possible for a holistic conception to be evoked at any instant in the course of sequential scanning. In contrast, the sequentiality of a verb or clause cannot be implemented in the simultaneous view effected by summary scanning.

(e) *This brand **preferred by most customers**.

(f) *The cup already **broken** when I found it.

Observe that a well-formed clause can in each case be produced by adding the verb *be*:

(15) (a) Her dress **is expensive**.

(b) The box **is on the top shelf**.

(c) The students **are to hand in their assignments**.

(d) That man **is complaining to the waiter**.

(e) This brand **is preferred by most customers**.

(f) The cup **was** already **broken** when I found it.

Be is a verb, so it profiles a process, albeit a highly schematic one. In (15) it is *be* that functions as clausal head—the schematic process it designates is profiled by the clause as a whole. When *be* is added to an atemporal expression, it lends its processual profile to the latter's more substantial content, which can thus be presented in clausal form. The shared property of occurring in this construction further supports the higher-level category of expressions that profile nonprocessual relationships.

An additional point in favor of these CG characterizations is that they let us make sense of the English "verbal auxiliary" system. In a finite clause, the lexical verb can be accompanied by markings for the passive, the progressive, the perfect, or any combination thereof. Each marking consists of two elements: a schematic verb (either *have* or *be*) and a participial inflection (*-ing* or *-ed*) on the following verb.

(16) (a) The child **was** frightened by a loud noise.   [passive: *be* + *-ed*]

(b) My father **is** contemplat**ing** retirement.   [progressive: *be* + *-ing*]

(c) They **have** silenced all their critics.   [perfect: *have* + *-ed*]

Though long noted (e.g. in Chomsky 1957), this dual marking has generally been taken as arbitrary and unprincipled, a case of pure grammatical idiosyncrasy. Indeed, the constitutive elements (*have, be, -ing, -ed*) are often considered individually meaningless. These views are quite erroneous. The CG analysis not only posits specific, motivated meanings for each element but also provides a principled explanation for why they occur in pairs.

The meanings of *-ing* and *-ed* have already been described (Figs. 4.14 and 4.15(a)–(b)). Each views a process from a certain perspective and scans the component states in summary fashion. Their effect is thus to atemporalize a verbal process, deriving a participial expression that designates a complex nonprocessual relationship. Being nonprocessual, this expression can modify a noun, as in *a child frightened by thunder* or *a person contemplating retirement*.[31] For the same reason,

---

[31] Perfect participles are exceptional in this regard (see FCG2: 232).

however, a participle cannot stand alone as the head of a finite clause. A clause profiles a process. If it is to head a finite clause, consequently, a participial expression must first be rendered processual. The verbs *have* and *be* serve this purpose. Though quite schematic in their content, they incorporate the temporality (sequential scanning through conceived time) characteristic of verbs and clauses. When *have* or *be* combines with a participle, the former imposes its temporality on the latter's more specific content. The resulting composite expression profiles a specific process and can therefore function as a clausal head.

Why bother? Since a participle derives from a verb in the first place, why not simply use that verb alone to head a finite clause? We bother because participialization imposes a particular perspective on the verbal process. *X frightened Y* is not the same as *X was frightening Y*, which takes an internal perspective on the event, nor the same as *Y was frightened by X*, which focuses the experiencer instead of the stimulus. To adopt these special perspectives, we therefore resort to complex expressions involving multiple levels of conceptual and grammatical organization. The verb first evokes a type of process (e.g. *frighten*). At a higher level of organization, participial inflection imposes a certain perspective on that process and views it atemporally (*frightened*). Through combination with *have* or *be*, the participial expression can then be "retemporalized", yielding another process at the highest level of organization (*be frightened*). This higher-order process is not the same as the original one, however. While their content is the same, the derived process differs in either profiling or trajector/landmark alignment.

Because the perspectives they embody are compatible with one another, the passive, progressive, and perfect constructions can occur in any combination. When they all occur together, they apply in that order at successively higher levels of organization, each operating on the basic or higher-level process already assembled. Moreover, each consists of atemporalization (by the participial morpheme) and then retemporalization (by *have* or *be*). The maximal sequence is shown in (17), where boldface indicates the element added at each level.

(17) *criticize* (processual) > *criticized* (atemporal) > **be** *criticized* (processual) > **being** criticized (atemporal) > **be** *being criticized* (processual) > **been** being criticized (atemporal) > **have** *been being criticized* (processual)

The highest-level process can then be grounded (by tense), and its participants specified, to form a full finite clause:

(18) *The disgruntled employee had been being criticized by his coworkers.*

In sum, the conceptual characterizations proposed for basic grammatical categories prove instrumental in revealing, describing, and explaining important regularities of nominal and clausal structure. In particular, they allow the formulation of two broad generalizations (possibly universal): that noun modifiers designate nonprocessual relationships, and that a finite clause profiles a process. They further show the principled nature of the dual marking for the passive, progressive, and perfect in

English, and explain why infinitives and participles only combine with *be* or *have* in their clausal use (not when they modify nouns).

A final point concerns a major exception to the generalization that noun modifiers are nonprocessual. Standing in clear violation (as the generalization is currently formulated) are finite relative clauses. A relative clause is one that modifies a noun. In many languages, relative clauses can be finite, from which it follows (granted the second generalization) that they are processual. For example, the relative clauses in (19) are grounded via their inflection for past and present tense:

(19)   (a) *the documents **that I shredded***

       (b) *a woman **who loves adventure***

To accommodate this exception, the generalization can be revised as follows: **ungrounded noun modifiers designate nonprocessual relationships**. Because they are grounded, finite clauses are now excluded from the statement's scope.

Rather than being problematic, the exclusion of finite clauses turns out to have a principled basis. A noun modifier is nonprocessual because the thing profiled by the noun—the primary focus of the nominal expression—imposes its holistic view on the relationships designated by modifying elements. Finite relative clauses are exceptional in this regard precisely because they (in contrast to other modifiers) are internally grounded. Through tense marking, they incorporate their own specification of how the profiled relationship relates to the context of speech, and thus to the speaker and hearer. Since grounding provides an independent point of access to the clausal content, the profiled process is viewed primarily in its own terms, as a grounded clause, and only secondarily in relation to the modified noun. Internal grounding insulates it from the holistic view imposed by the noun, making it sufficiently autonomous to be scanned sequentially.

5

Major Subclasses

The most fundamental grammatical categories, noun and verb, are polar opposites with respect to their conceptual characterizations. At the prototype level, the spatially compact material of a physical object contrasts with the temporally extended interaction constituting a force-dynamic event. At the schema level, where thing and process are defined in terms of mental operations, the unitizing effect of grouping and reification contrasts with the expansive nature of apprehending a relationship and tracking its evolution through time.

Despite this maximal opposition, nouns and verbs have a lot in common. The higher-level grammatical structures they respectively head, nominals and finite clauses, show extensive parallels. Moreover, each category divides into two major subclasses, and these too exhibit extensive parallelism. The basic types of nouns, traditionally known as **count** and **mass**, correspond to the conceptual archetypes **object** and **substance**. The basic types of verbs, referred to here as **perfective** and **imperfective**, correspond to the archetypal notions **event** and **state**. We will see that the count/mass and perfective/imperfective distinctions are essentially the same.[1]

5.1 Count and Mass Nouns

Why are nouns divided into two basic subclasses? Grammarians make the distinction initially on the basis of their contrasting grammatical behaviors. Nonetheless, the traditional labels "count" and "mass" suggest the possibility of distinguishing them on conceptual grounds. In this section, I explore the components of a semantic characterization and the many subtleties of their application. The differing grammatical properties of count and mass nouns prove to be merely symptomatic of a fundamental conceptual opposition.

---

[1] Although the following discussion is primarily based on English, comparable distinctions are likely to be found in most (if not all) languages.

5.1.1 Grammatical Basis

Along one axis, English nouns are divisible into two broad categories, exemplified in (1).[2] Typical for count nouns are the names of physical objects (e.g. *diamond, book, cup*), and for mass nouns, the names of physical substances (*gold, meat, water*). Yet each class includes the terms for other sorts of entities. For instance, count nouns also label creatures (*cat*), parts of larger wholes (*tail*), and geographical regions (*county*), as well as entities that are either nebulous (*cloud*) or abstract (*idea*). Likewise, mass nouns designate entities whose substantial nature is rather tenuous (*air, electricity*) or which are wholly nonphysical (*nonsense, righteousness*).

(1)   (a) **Count nouns:** *diamond, book, cup, pencil, house, tree, apple, cat, tail, pancreas, edge, county, lake, cloud, question, idea, integer, complaint...*

     (b) **Mass nouns:** *gold, meat, water, wood, coal, glue, beer, skin, steel, air, moisture, electricity, nonsense, anger, righteousness, complaining...*

It is not at all obvious, therefore, that either category is susceptible to a semantic description valid for all members (i.e. a schematic characterization). The descriptive labels that readily come to mind, object and substance, are straightforwardly applicable only to **prototypical** members, not to **all** members. The conclusion generally drawn is that the count/mass distinction can only be established and characterized in terms of grammatical behavior. As a practical matter, the classes are indeed posited—and members assigned to them—on the basis of their distinctive grammatical properties.

Some of these properties are shown in (2), taking *diamond* and *gold* as representative instances of the count and mass noun categories. We see first, in (2)(a), that only a mass noun can stand alone as a complete nominal expression, without a determiner. Other contrasting properties pertain to the kinds of determiner each allows. Only a count noun permits the indefinite article. Conversely, a number of determiners—including the quantifiers *most, all,* and *a lot of*—only occur with mass nouns. The same judgments hold for all the examples in (1).

(2)   (a) *They're looking for {*diamond/gold}.*

     (b) *a {diamond/*gold}*

     (c) *most {*diamond/gold}*

     (d) *all {*diamond/gold}*

     (e) *a lot of {*diamond/gold}*

Count nouns are so called because they designate entities that can be counted: *one diamond, two diamonds, three diamonds,* etc. Countability correlates with the

---

[2] Cross-cutting this classification is the distinction between **common** and **proper** nouns. The examples in (1) are all common nouns. Proper nouns can also be categorized as either count (e.g. *Wal-Mart, Connecticut, Tiger Woods*) or mass (*Coca-Cola, Clorox, Tylenol*).

possibility of forming a plural (e.g. *diamonds*), designating multiple instances of the type specified by the singular noun (*diamond*). By contrast, mass nouns do not form plurals (**golds*), nor are their referents countable: **one gold*, **two gold(s)*, **three gold(s)*. As suggested by the term, the referent of a typical mass noun lacks the discreteness required for the recognition and counting of multiple instances.

What, then, is the status of plurals in regard to the count/mass distinction? Only a count noun can be pluralized. Strikingly, however, a plural functions grammatically as a mass noun. Going through the properties in (2), we find in every case that *gold* and *diamonds* behave alike, in opposition to *diamond*:

(3)   (a)   *They're looking for {*diamond/gold/diamonds}.*

    (b)   *a {diamond/*gold/*diamonds}*

    (c)   *most {*diamond/gold/diamonds}*

    (d)   *all {*diamond/gold/diamonds}*

    (e)   *a lot of {*diamond/gold/diamonds}*

Diamonds is further like *gold*, and unlike *diamond*, in that it cannot itself undergo pluralization: **diamondses*. Grammatical behavior thus argues for the classification in figure 5.1. The mass noun category—in a broad sense of the term—includes both plurals and mass nouns "proper" (such as *gold*).

Plurals do not behave identically to other mass nouns, however. By its very nature, a plural (e.g. *diamonds*) refers to multiple instances of the same type (*diamond*). It thus portrays the mass it designates as consisting of individual "particles" salient enough to be countable. As a consequence, plurals occur with numerals, whereas other mass nouns do not (*eight diamonds* vs. **eight gold*). Also sensitive to the contrast between a "particulate" mass and a "continuous" one are demonstratives and certain quantifiers:

(4)   (a)   *those diamonds* vs. *that gold*

    (b)   *these diamonds* vs. *this gold*

    (c)   *many diamonds* vs. *much gold*

    (d)   *few diamonds* vs. *little gold*

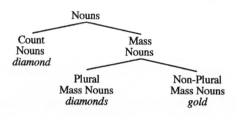

FIGURE 5.1

(e) *several diamonds* vs. **several gold*

(f) *numerous diamonds* vs. **numerous gold*

Hence there is a clear grammatical basis for distinguishing plurals from other mass nouns, as well as for their grouping in a higher-level category.

Ultimately, though, I am arguing that these grammatical properties are symptomatic of underlying conceptual differences. The discussion has already suggested the semantic characterizations roughly sketched in figure 5.2. A count noun profiles a thing construed as being discretely bounded in some fashion, whereas a mass noun referent is amorphous and not inherently limited. As a convenient notational device, I use a circle to represent the former, an ellipse for the latter. Within the mass-noun category, plurals contrast with nonplurals by highlighting the particulate nature of the profiled mass. It is not precluded that a nonplural mass might have discernible particles—we know, for instance, that *sand* consists of particles, and we even have a name for them (*grains*). The point is rather that nouns of this sort foreground the perceived continuity of the mass at the expense of constitutive entities. It does so by naming the mass directly, as an undifferentiated whole, whereas a plural is based on the term for an individual particle.

It cannot be emphasized too strongly that categorization depends on how things are conceptualized, which to some extent is independent of their objective nature. We are perfectly capable of construing the same conceived entity in alternate ways, each of which highlights certain aspects of it and downplays others. Collectively, for example, some oblong pieces of wood can be referred to as either *boards* or *lumber*. Although they are referentially identical, the plural *boards* renders salient the individual constitutive entities, whereas *lumber* suppresses their individuation in favor of their apprehension as an effectively homogeneous mass: *three boards* vs. **three lumber*, *these boards* vs. *this lumber*, etc. These different construals are incorporated as part of the established meanings of these forms, a matter of shared linguistic convention. We have the conceptual flexibility to construe the situation in either fashion and select the form whose meaning best suits our communicative intent.

A further consequence of our conceptual dexterity is the great fluidity of the count/mass distinction. It is anything but a rigid lexical opposition such that a given noun definitively belongs to one or the other category. A slight adjustment in how we construe the content evoked by a form is sufficient to change its categorization and thus its grammatical behavior. We see in (5)(a), for example, that *diamond* functions as a mass noun when we do not care whether the constitutive substance is discretely

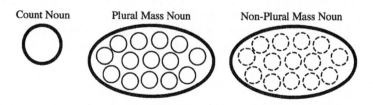

Count Noun   **Plural Mass Noun**   **Non-Plural Mass Noun**

FIGURE 5.2

instantiated, but focus exclusively on its qualitative properties. In (5)(b), on the other hand, *gold* functions as a count noun because it refers to a **kind** of gold (a discrete though abstract entity) rather than the substance per se.

(5)   (a) *Diamond is a very hard substance.*

        (b) *I'm looking for a gold that is just the right color for a ring.*

To varying degrees, particular forms are entrenched and conventionally established as either a count noun or a mass noun—or often both. Learning such conventions is part of mastering a language. Yet there is always the option of a novel construal, hence an altered grammatical potential. Indeed, general patterns for extending count nouns to mass noun use, and also the reverse, ensure that most every noun can in principle be employed in either manner.

It should not be thought that every noun fits comfortably in the classificatory scheme depicted in figure 5.1.[3] For instance, *cattle* is not a plural in form (there is no corresponding singular), yet it behaves like one grammatically: *those cattle, few cattle, several cattle,* etc. Conversely, many nouns are plural in form but diverge from typical plurals in meaning and grammatical behavior (cf. Wierzbicka 1985). A well-known example is *oats*, which appears to be the plural of *oat*, a stem that does occur (e.g. *oatmeal*). But this stem cannot be used as a singular count noun to designate one of the salient constitutive particles (**an oat, *this oat*), nor are the particles countable (**five oats, *numerous oats*). Slightly different are words like *scissors, pliers, tweezers, binoculars,* and *shorts,* which designate a single object with two prominent parts. Grammatically, they exhibit varying mixtures of singular- and plural-noun behaviors (e.g. *a scissors,* but *These scissors are broken*). Thus, while plural morphology may always indicate that the nominal referent is internally complex, the nature of this complexity is not limited to the prototypical case of multiple individuals each describable by the nonplural stem.

5.1.2 Conceptual Basis

The grammatical distinction between count and mass nouns manifests a basic conceptual distinction. I have so far described this opposition, rather vaguely, as a matter of whether the nominal referent is "discretely bounded in some fashion" or else "amorphous and not inherently limited". Obviously, this characterization needs to be refined and clarified.

A more precise definition runs as follows. A noun profiles a thing, defined as any product of grouping and reification (§4.2.2). In the case of a count noun, this thing is construed as being **bounded within the immediate scope in the domain of instantiation**. The profile of a mass noun is **not** construed as being bounded in this fashion. The key notions, then, are bounding, immediate scope, and domain of instantiation. Each term requires explanation.

---

[3] Though we must largely ignore the many idiosyncrasies of these less typical nouns, their description is not inherently problematic in CG, which accommodates both general and idiosyncratic phenomena (ch. 8).

The notion **immediate scope** was introduced in §3.2.3. For a given domain, an expression's immediate scope (IS) is the portion of its maximal scope (MS) that is directly relevant for some purpose. Metaphorically, it is the onstage region, the general **locus** of attention. An expression's profile—being the specific **focus** of attention—is confined to its immediate scope.

The count/mass distinction hinges on whether bounding occurs within the immediate scope, as shown in figure 5.3. Limiting our attention momentarily to physical entities (where the domain of instantiation is space), the shaded region in each diagram represents an expanse of material substance. For a count noun, this region is bounded, and the boundary falls within the immediate scope. The noun *board*, for example, profiles an expanse of wood which is bounded in each spatial dimension to give it a characteristic oblong shape defined by flat surfaces, straight edges, and right angles. Crucially, the existence of the boundary (and the shape it defines) is part of what needs to be apprehended in order to identify the substance as an instance of *board*. The presence of a boundary is put onstage by *board* as something that must be attended to. It is thus included in the noun's immediate scope.

But discerning a boundary is not necessary to identify something as an instance of *wood*. Suppose you remove a section of plaster from a wall and reveal a smooth surface underneath. No boundary is apparent; the material visible through the hole extends beyond it in all directions. By seeing it and feeling it, you can nonetheless determine—from the accessible portion alone—that the material is wood. A mass noun like *wood* names a kind of substance, distinguished from other substances by **qualitative** factors. The distinguishing qualities are apparent in any portion we might sample, irrespective of shape or size. The portion observable within a restricted immediate scope (like the hole in the plaster) can thus be identified as an instance of the type of substance in question.

Consequently, a mass noun has the organization shown in figure 5.3(b). While a mass can certainly be bounded, this is not required for its identification; a mass noun does not itself invoke a boundary as an onstage element to be attended to. Hence there is no bounding within its immediate scope. Moreover, it is only within the immediate scope (the general locus of attention) that focused viewing is possible. An expression's profile—its specific focus of attention—is thus confined to this region. While the substance it names may have indefinite expanse, a mass noun profiles only what is put onstage as the viewing focus. Should you look through the hole in the plaster and say *I see wood!* you would only be referring to the visible portion.

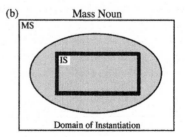

FIGURE 5.3

A noun names a **type** of thing and specifies the properties an entity must have to qualify as an **instance** of this type. Usually this **type specification** invokes a number of cognitive domains, collectively referred to as its matrix (§2.2.2). Within the matrix, a particular domain stands out as the one where instances of the type are primarily thought of as residing. It can thus be called the **domain of instantiation**. Conceptually, what distinguishes an instance from a type is that an instance is specifically thought of as occupying a particular location in this domain. Instances of the same type are distinguished from one another by virtue of occupying different locations.[4] The domain of instantiation is further characterized as the domain in which the presence or absence of bounding determines a noun's categorization as count or mass.

Let us once more consider the count noun *board*. As is usual for physical objects and substances, the domain of instantiation is space. A board has both spatial and temporal existence: it takes up space, and it endures through time. Obviously, though, we primarily think of a board as existing in space, taking for granted its persistence through time. The question *Where is the board?* is thus quite sensible, but **When is the board?* is something we would never think to ask.[5] A type like *board* has many instances, and at a given moment every instance occupies a distinct location (whereas the type itself, representing the abstracted commonality of all these instances, is a "floating" entity that cannot be localized). Even if they should be identical, two boards at different locations constitute different instances of the type—if they occupied precisely the same location, they would be the same board. By contrast, a board that occupies the same location at different times can nonetheless be recognized as the same instance (even if altered). Space being the domain of instantiation, *board* functions as a count noun because its type specification includes the notion of spatial bounding. It fails to specify temporal bounding, but since time is not the domain of instantiation, this does not make *board* a mass noun.

Domain of instantiation does however vary in the case of nouns, and time is one of the options. Among the many nouns invoking time in this capacity are *time* itself, as well as terms for spans of time of different lengths, such as *moment, minute, hour, month, year,* and *century*. In one of its senses, *time* functions as a mass noun (e.g. *We have a lot of time; Time passes slowly*). Its abstract referent is conceived as stretching endlessly in either direction—hence as being intrinsically unbounded. *Time* can also be used as a count noun, in which case it designates just a point in time (*What time is it?*) or a span of limited duration (*a short time*). The many terms for particular lengths of time are, of course, count nouns. The time span profiled by *moment* is construed as being quite short but not precisely measured. By contrast, words like *minute, hour, month, year,* and *century* presuppose elaborate conceptual frameworks in terms of which we measure the passage of time and specify temporal locations (fig. 3.12). Each of these terms designates one bounded unit in such a grid. Also invoking time as their domain of instantiation are nouns referring to events, such as *beep, flash,*

---

[4] This does not imply that we can **identify** their locations. In imagining two rocks, we imagine them as being spatially disjoint (hence in two distinct locations), regardless of where they might be.

[5] The question is perhaps conceivable if *the board* is interpreted metonymically as referring to the object's anticipated delivery.

shout, *birth*, *sneeze*, *bath*, *explosion*, and *earthquake*. These are nouns because, via conceptual reification, the events they profile are construed as abstract things. They are count nouns because the occurrences they designate are bounded in time. For instance, the continuous sound emitted by a malfunctioning car horn is quite annoying but is not *a beep*. A sound can only be identified as *a beep* if it is fairly short in duration, and if its onset and offset are observed.[6]

Despite the preponderance of nouns invoking space or time as their domain of instantiation, any number of other options are available. An example is color space, another basic domain. Recall that a color term, such as *yellow*, has two count-noun uses. As a proper noun (e.g. *Yellow is a soothing color*), it profiles a unique region in color space bounded by being distinguished from other colors (fig. 4.4(a)). As a common noun (e.g. *We need a brighter yellow for the kitchen*), it designates any limited portion of the yellow region, corresponding to a particular shade of yellow (fig. 4.4(b)).[7] Providing illustration of a different sort are terms like *chapter*, *paragraph*, *introduction*, *conclusion*, *preface*, and *preamble*, which profile restricted parts of a written work. Though writing usually has a spatial manifestation (on paper or a computer screen), this is not the essential aspect of these terms, for if a book is committed to memory and recited orally it can still have chapters and paragraphs. These words pertain primarily to functional units within a linguistic composition, and they are count nouns because they profile limited portions of the overall text. The domain of instantiation is thus the conception of the composition as an abstract textual entity, however it might be manifested.

Determining a noun's domain of instantiation raises a number of subtle issues. They stem from the fact that a noun's meaning draws on multiple cognitive domains, some incorporated as part of others, which are activated to varying degrees on different occasions (§2.2.2). Often, for example, we ignore the role of a *paragraph* as a textual unit, instead conceptualizing it as a spatially manifested entity, visually delimited by the left and right indentations of its initial and final lines. A *book* can likewise be characterized as either a physical or a textual entity (*Her book took five years to write and weighs two pounds*). We can use the term *walk* for a bounded spatial path (*It's a five-mile uphill walk*), an event (*I took a walk*), or a manner of walking distinguished from other walking styles (*His walk is peculiar*). In cases like these, each interpretation presupposes a different domain of instantiation, where instances are thought of as occupying locations that distinguish them from other instances.

Identifying a unique domain of instantiation is problematic when one domain is incorporated as part of another. Consider a body-part term, such as *arm*. One domain crucial to its meaning is a conception of the overall shape of the human body. *Arm* qualifies as a count noun because it profiles a bounded region within this whole. However, since a body exists in space, it is no less true that an arm occupies space and

---

[6] Because time is *beep*'s domain of instantiation, identical sounds heard at different times constitute different instances of this type.

[7] The region profiled by the proper noun functions in turn as immediate scope for the common noun (cf. fig. 3.3). The latter's profile is therefore bounded (limited) within the immediate scope (yellow region) in the domain of instantiation (color space)—which is precisely the definition of a count noun.

has a spatial boundary. Should space then be regarded as the domain of instantiation? If so, an arm is nonetheless characterized and delimited by its position within the overall configuration of the body. A time expression, such as *hour*, poses an analogous problem. Should its domain of instantiation be identified as the basic domain of time or, alternatively, as the conceptual framework imposed on time to effect its segmentation and measurement? The choice would seem to be arbitrary, for a measured temporal segment is bounded in both the basic domain and the conceptual framework incorporating it. Similarly, an *octave* constitutes a bounded segment with respect to both a musical scale and the basic domain of pitch. In such cases, there is no obvious basis for singling out one or the other as an exclusive domain of instantiation.

5.1.3 Bounding

Compared with immediate scope and domain of instantiation, the notion "bounding" may seem self-evident, but it too requires elucidation. For many count nouns, the profiled thing is bounded in the straightforward sense of having a discernible boundary. A *lake*, for example, is a body of water bounded in all directions by land. Moreover, its boundary—the line delimiting water and land—gives it a particular shape. It is not the case, however, that every count noun referent has a boundary or a shape in any usual sense of those terms. A general definition of bounding has to be more abstract.

We generally speak of a shape only in regard to spatially manifested entities. What is the shape of an *hour*, an *introduction*, a *beep*, an *octave*, or *yellow*? The term "boundary" is used more flexibly but is still awkward with nonspatial things. An *hour* has a beginning and an end, but does it have a boundary? Though dawn might be described (metaphorically) as the boundary between night and day, it is less natural to say that a *night* has boundaries. It is not evident that a *team*, whose members may be scattered all over a playing field, has either a boundary or a shape. What about an *alphabet*? While it may have an initial and a final letter, these hardly seem like boundaries. And what is an *alphabet* bounded **from**? The notion of a boundary is problematic even for a physical object like a *board*. By analogy to *lake*, it might plausibly be suggested that a *board* is a continuous mass of wood bounded on all sides by...by what? Not by air, since we can easily imagine a board submerged in water or floating in the vacuum of outer space. We can only say, in general, that it is bounded by the absence of wood. A bit of a reach, perhaps. We think of a *board* as having a surface and a shape, but not a boundary.

Defined more abstractly, a thing is bounded when there is **some limit to the set of constitutive entities**. What this means, in conceptual terms, is something like the following. Recall that a thing is characterized schematically as a set of interconnected entities, grouped and reified to form a unitary entity for higher-level cognitive purposes (§4.2.2). Let us then imagine the process of mentally scanning through the set of constitutive entities—accessing them in some natural sequence—in building up to the full conception of an instance of the type in question. A thing is bounded if, in carrying out this scanning operation, the requisite set of entities is eventually exhausted. The instance conception is then complete, in the sense that further scanning through constitutive entities amounts to conceptualizing another instance of the same type. In short, there is some notion of reaching the limits of a single instance, making it possible to begin the conception of another, distinct instance.

There are various ways of recognizing that the limits have been reached. The most obvious basis for bounding is **contrast with surroundings**. One aspect of conceptualizing a *board*, for example, resides in mental scanning serving to register the continuous extension of the material substance constituting it. The constitutive entities are patches of wood (indefinite in number and arbitrarily delimited). In scanning through them in any direction, we eventually reach a point at which this substance fails to be manifested. The limit (in any given direction) is defined by this point of contrast, where we detect a transition from wood to nonwood. Analogously, a *beep* is the occurrence of a certain kind of noise bounded by silence on either end. In hearing or imagining a beep, we first encounter a transition from the absence of that noise to its presence, and then from its presence to its absence. If further scanning through time reveals more of the sound, it represents the onset of another beep (not the continuation of the previous instance).

Bounding can also be effected on the basis of **internal configuration**. For example, a *bicycle* consists of a certain set of parts connected in a particular manner to form a structured whole. To recognize an instance of this type, it is sufficient to observe the requisite parts in the appropriate configuration—contrast with surroundings (transition from bicycle to nonbicycle) seems inessential. Moreover, if all the parts are present and properly configured, the instance conception is complete. Introducing further parts (a second seat, a third pedal, etc.) would hardly serve to augment or enhance its conception; more likely they would be taken as initiating the conception of another, distinct instance. The noun *alphabet* provides a more abstract example of bounding by configuration. An alphabet is constituted by a set of letters whose names we learn to recite in a well-rehearsed sequence $(A > B > C > \ldots > X > Y > Z)$. The letters are limited in number and bounded by the first and last elements in the sequence. In mentally scanning through our alphabet, we fully expect to finish: we start with A secure in the knowledge that once we reach Z we are done.

A third basis for bounding is the **function** served by a count noun referent. Consider a wooden baseball bat. Physical examination reveals no obvious boundary between the portions referred to as the *handle* and the *barrel*. The bat gets thicker as we scan from handle to barrel, but continuously, with no evident point of transition. The demarcation depends primarily on the function served: the *handle* is where we grip the bat, and the *barrel* is the part that hits the ball. Similarly, the *introduction* to an article may be visually continuous with the remainder and typographically indistinguishable. It can nonetheless be identified and delimited by the textual function it serves. What about a *team*? Its constitutive entities (the team members) are grouped on the basis of their cooperative action toward achieving a common goal. There need be nothing at all that sets them apart from nonmembers other than their participation in this endeavor.

The various means of bounding—by contrast with surroundings, internal configuration, and function—are in no way mutually exclusive. An *alphabet* is delimited not only by configuration (a fixed sequence with initial and final letters) but also by function: it comprises the full set of letters used together to represent the sounds of a certain language. Form and function are of course interdependent. The configuration of a *bicycle* is just what is needed for its function as something to ride on; if bikes were used instead for drying clothes, they would have a different form. To some extent, we can also see a bicycle as being bounded by contrast with surroundings. Its spatial expanse is limited in all directions by points of transition between the presence and absence of the substances constituting its various parts.

Conceiving of something as being bounded does not depend on being able to impose a precise line of demarcation in any specific place. Boundaries are often "fuzzy", but entities bounded fuzzily are bounded nonetheless. There is no precise boundary between the *handle* of a bat and its *barrel*, yet each is a bounded region distinguished from the other. We conceptualize an article's *introduction* as being of limited extent even when it merges imperceptibly with the main part of the text. And where, exactly, would you draw a line delimiting a *shoulder* from the rest of your body? While there is no specific place where shoulder gives way to nonshoulder, the region is clearly bounded—along the arm, for example, it does not extend as far as the elbow.

The fuzziness of many boundaries is one indication that they need not be objectively discernible. In the last analysis, bounding that "counts" for linguistic purposes is always conceptually imposed. This is not to say that we go around imposing arbitrary boundaries just for the sake of doing so. The bounding imputed to a count noun referent always has substantial motivation, for otherwise—if there were no natural basis for delimitation—we would have no reason to talk about it. The strongest grounds for delimitation are afforded by physical discontinuities that we can readily perceive, especially when the bounded entity, taken as a whole, has some culturally recognized function or significance (e.g. a *knife*, a *lake*, or a *goat*). These are matters of degree, however, with no single factor being invariant or indispensable.

Even for physical entities, bounding is commonly imposed on functional or sociocultural grounds in the absence of any perceptible discontinuity. Often, for example, territorial boundaries established by political convention (e.g. between two *nations*, *states*, *counties*, *districts*, or *precincts*) have no inherent physical basis and are thus invisible (there being no replication in nature of the lines of demarcation drawn on a map, or the contrasting colors used for different regions). This does not prevent them from being precisely defined and very real in terms of their legal and social consequences. Even more clearly imposed, yet equally real in our mental and social life, is the bounding effected by units of temporal measurement. An *hour*, for instance, can start or end at any point whatever, since time and its passing are intrinsically homogeneous. Despite this arbitrariness, an hour can be precisely measured, is rendered observable through "material anchors" (such as timers and clocks), and serves numerous functions in the organization of our daily lives.

Further indication that bounding is conceptually imposed, even when strongly motivated objectively, are the many cases where some portion of a boundary is **virtual** in nature. One such case is a container like a *tub*, *bin*, *pitcher*, *cup*, or *fish tank*, which is thought of as effecting a spatial enclosure despite being open on top. We do conceptualize the container as having an upper boundary, albeit one that is nonmaterial, hence represented by the dashed line in figure 5.4(a).[8] Not dissimilar is the

---

[8] This virtual boundary is invoked for computing the container's volume, as well as for delimiting the region where something is said to be *in* it.

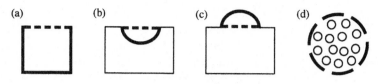

FIGURE 5.4

virtual bounding of a *hole, dent, depression, pit,* or *cavity,* sketched in figure 5.4(b). We impose a boundary on one side by mentally extrapolating the surface expected to be there were it not for the "concavity". An analogous extrapolation delimits a "convexity", such as a *bump, welt, hump, mound,* or *swelling,* as shown in diagram (c). At the extreme, a boundary can be entirely virtual. One illustration, in diagram (d), is the spatial boundary circumscribing a contiguous collection of distinct entities, e.g. a *swarm, herd, forest, mob,* or *archipelago.*

A collection virtually bounded in this manner is the product of another mental operation: conceptual grouping based on spatial contiguity (§4.2.2). This spatial contiguity may itself be virtual in nature: mentally created rather than actually observed. We can speak of a *herd of cattle,* for instance, even when its constitutive elements (individual bovines) are scattered all over the range. Indeed, we can do so even if they have never been assembled in one place and never will be, provided that there is some basis for their grouping (e.g. their collective function as the livestock of a single ranch). We nevertheless have a strong tendency to visualize them as forming a spatially contiguous, virtually bounded thing, as depicted in figure 5.4(d).[9] Our propensity for virtual grouping and bounding is quite apparent when we deal with abstract entities, such as numbers. Prime numbers, for example, are commonly described as constituting a *set,* written in a form that presents them as being spatially contiguous and bounded by brackets: { 1, 2, 3, 5, 7, 11, … }. Despite its evident utility, this visual representation is fictitious in every respect. The prime numbers have no spatial location and cannot be seen. They are not contiguous in the number sequence. And since there are infinitely many of them, in actuality they are unbounded. The bounding represented by brackets is virtual, imposed by the very fact of viewing them as a *set.* In terms of its linguistic semantics, the count noun *set* profiles a bounded entity metaphorically construed as a container for its members (Lakoff 1987). A *set* is thus bounded at this level of conceptual organization even when it is further stipulated (at another level) that its membership is infinite.[10]

5.1.4 Other Sides of the Coin

In the task of distinguishing count and mass nouns, bounding does not stand alone. It shares this burden with three additional conceptual factors: homogeneity, contractibility,

---

[9] This imagined spatial clustering might even be necessary for their conception as a unitary entity.

[10] This metaphorical bounding of infinite sets is foundational to modern mathematics (Lakoff and Núñez 2000). My description of nouns in terms of mental operations is not incompatible with one based on spatial metaphor.

and replicability. So closely related are these factors that I like to think of them as four sides of the same coin.

A mass is construed as being internally homogeneous. A typical mass noun, such as *water*, designates a substance identified by various **qualities**: a liquid of low viscosity, largely transparent, tasteless, odorless, nonalcoholic, and so on. Ideally, sampling any portion of a mass is sufficient to reveal those properties. Homogeneity thus consists of being qualitatively the same throughout. Contrast this with a typical count noun, such as *pencil*. Here there is no presumption of qualitative uniformity. Instead, it is usual for different parts (lead, shaft, eraser) to consist of different substances (graphite, wood, rubber). With respect to qualitative properties, a typical count noun referent is internally heterogeneous.

What matters linguistically, of course, is conceived rather than actual homogeneity. Objectively, no mass is truly homogeneous. Examined in fine enough detail, any two samples of water will exhibit some qualitative difference (e.g. concentrations of pesticides measured in parts per billion). We nonetheless use the word *water* every day, feeling no obligation to first engage in chemical analysis. By ignoring minor variations in quality, we construe a substance as being effectively homogeneous for purposes of identification and linguistic labeling.

How does this work for nouns such as *sand, corn, grass, gravel*, and *lumber*? The masses they designate consist of discrete, easily discernible particles, which we label with terms like *grain, kernel, blade, piece*, and *board*. Saying that a mass is homogeneous might seem problematic when it is clearly recognized as being noncontinuous, with spaces between the constitutive entities. Recall, however, that conceptualization is multifaceted and highly flexible. Inherent in the meaning of any linguistic element is a particular way of construing conceptual content, so that certain facets are focused while others remain in the background. A particulate mass can therefore be seen as either homogeneous or heterogeneous, depending on which aspects of this complex notion are put in focus. The mass-noun status of forms like *sand, corn, grass, gravel*, and *lumber* indicates that their conventional meanings emphasize aspects of homogeneity.[11]

A particulate mass exhibits several kinds of homogeneity. First, the constitutive particles are often not individually perceived or functionally important. When walking on a beach, we see what appears to be a continuous expanse of substance; we notice individual grains of sand only on closer inspection. With grass we likewise have the visual impression of continuity. If individual blades are apparent at a glance, your lawn is too sparse. A particulate mass is further homogeneous in that any portion is essentially equivalent to any other portion. Examine any patch of sand on a beach, or any patch of grass in a lawn, and what you will find is basically the same: a densely packed array of particles so numerous that you would not want to have to count them. Moreover, for all intents and purposes these particles are identical. We are quite oblivious to their individual differences, knowing them only in relation to the mass they constitute. And only collectively do they exhibit the functional and

---

[11] Homogeneity also prevails in the case of plurals (e.g. *boards, pebbles, blades of grass*), but to a lesser extent, since there is greater awareness of their particulate nature (fig. 5.2).

qualitative properties characteristic of the mass. It is hard to walk on a single grain of sand or blade of grass, and hard to build a house with a single board. Individually a pebble lacks the grainy feel of gravel, nor can a single kernel of corn give us a very good idea of its taste and texture.

The effective identity of constitutive particles is much less obvious with nouns like *silverware*, *furniture*, and *equipment*. Not only do we use their component elements individually but also we group them into different categories: for example, *silverware* consists of knives, forks, and spoons. Yet they function grammatically as mass nouns, indeed as nonplural mass nouns, where particles are not accorded any salience. We are, though, quite capable of apprehending an abstract commonality that renders them equivalent from a functional standpoint. Knives, forks, and spoons are alike in being basic implements (comparable in size and material) used in eating. Shared by chairs, tables, beds, sofas, desks, and lamps are the properties of being fairly large, hence movable only with some difficulty, and serving collectively to *furnish* a house and make it livable. And while the term *equipment* applies to a more diverse array of entities, they are generally physical devices collectively used in some endeavor. So even though the component elements belong to different categories, a noun of this sort imposes a construal of homogeneity by focusing on very general similarities, including a common function. The degree of abstraction required is no greater than for a high-level category such as *animal*. While a monkey, an elephant, and a crocodile are very different, they are nonetheless equivalent when viewed at a certain level of abstraction. The term *animal* portrays them at this level, and the plural form *animals* relies on this common schematic characterization to construe them as a homogeneous mass.

If mass nouns regularly construe their referents as homogeneous, is it also true that a count noun referent is always heterogeneous? This might at first seem doubtful. A *lake*, for example, consists of water throughout, with no imputation of any qualitative variation. But a lake is not merely an expanse of water. Another essential feature is that the water be surrounded by land—*lake* is a count noun precisely due to this bounding. The conception of a lake, one sufficient to identify it as such, must therefore include the boundary within its immediate scope. A boundary, however, is a very different kind of entity from the substance it delimits. It is, rather, a discontinuity: the point of transition between the substance and its absence. The boundary of a lake is not water but resides in the water/land interface. Thus, even though the substance may be homogeneous, the presence of a boundary introduces a measure of heterogeneity in the overall conception. A noun like *lake* represents the extreme case where the only aspect of heterogeneity is the boundary itself. There are many nouns of this sort: *lawn*, *puddle*, *meatball*, *brick*, *stain*, *beep*, *hour*, *hole*, *intermission*, etc. Each profiles a bounded entity that is otherwise homogeneous, whether the "substance" it comprises is physical or more abstract (like a sound, time, or the absence of something).

The homogeneity of a mass is thus dependent on the lack of intrinsic bounding. These two factors are in turn responsible for a third property, namely **contractibility**. What I mean by this is simply that any portion of a mass of a given type is itself a valid instance of that type. If we start with the *water* in a lake, any portion selected for individual examination can itself be described as *water*. The sample can be of any size: whether an acre-foot, a gallon, or a single drop, it is still *water*.[12] This does not hold for count nouns. Part of a lake is not itself a *lake*, for it lacks the property of being wholly circumscribed by land. By themselves, a pedal and seat are not a *bicycle*, the sequence MNOP is not an *alphabet*, and the tail of a cat is not a *cat*.

The homogeneity and lack of bounding characteristic of a mass also lead to the converse property, **expansibility**: the mass obtained by combining any two instances of a given type is also a valid instance of that type. By adding some flour to the flour already in a bowl, we obtain a larger mass that also counts as a single instance of *flour*—we can describe it as *that flour* or *the flour in the bowl*, but not as **those two flours*. On the other hand, combining two instances of a count noun type, such as *bowl*, does not result in a single larger instance, but in multiple instances: *those two bowls*. Because a count noun specifies bounding, hence some limit to the constitutive entities, it provides a way of determining when one instance ends and another begins. I refer to this property—the opposite of expansibility—as **replicability**. These opposing properties of mass and count noun referents are indicated, respectively, by *more* vs. *another*: when two instances are combined, the result is *more flour* but *another bowl*.

Since a mass is characterized qualitatively, identification of an instance does not require bounding, any particular shape, or even spatial contiguity. Consider the land of 10,000 lakes (also known as Minnesota). What counts as an instance of *water*, with respect to those lakes, is whatever we wish to single out and construe as such. As shown in (6), the instance profiled by a nominal expression may be from a single lake, from more than one, or from all of them; it may comprise all the water in a lake or just part; or any combination of these factors. The possibilities are clearly endless.

(6) (a) *the water in that lake*

    (b) *the water near the surface of that lake*

    (c) *the water in those two lakes*

    (d) *the water in the lakes in the northern part of Minnesota*

    (e) *the water in all the lakes of Minnesota*

    (f) *the water near the surface in most of the lakes in the southern part of Minnesota*

5.1.5 Variable Construal

Being conceptual in nature, the count/mass distinction reflects our capacity for conceiving and portraying a situation in alternate ways. The dexterity we exhibit in this regard has the consequence that categorization is rather fluid. In one way or another, probably every noun can be used in either manner.

---

[12] Obviously, the sample must be large enough to preserve the defining qualitative properties. Perhaps a molecule of water still counts as an instance of this type, but an oxygen atom does not. In the case of plurals, a minimum of two elements are needed to instantiate the type.

This is not to say that everything is random or solely a matter of whim. Particular categorizations are thoroughly familiar to speakers and firmly established in linguistic convention. In using *lake* as a count noun, or *water* as a mass noun, I am not doing anything inventive or unanticipated. And while many uses depart from these basic categorizations, they usually follow conventionally established patterns. Though novel, the mass-noun use of *lake* in (7)(a) manifests a general pattern for construing a bounded entity as an unbounded mass. Conversely, the count-noun use of *water* in (7)(b) follows a general pattern for construing a mass as a bounded entity. In this case, the extended meaning and the categorization it engenders are also entrenched and conventional.

(7)　(a) *You need **a lot of lake** for a speedboat race.*

　　(b) *I want two lemonades and **a water**.*

For a large number of nouns, both a count-noun variant and a mass-noun variant are well established as conventional linguistic units. Either variant can be more thoroughly entrenched and thus perceived as basic, the other then constituting a semantic extension. For *water*, the mass-noun sense is clearly primary. In contrast, *diamond* is primarily a count noun, with a secondary mass-noun use (e.g. *Diamond is one of the hardest substances known*). There are also many nouns where the two variants are roughly comparable in status: *rock, stone, brick, tile, glass, hair, fur, cloth, rope, string, cake, squash, steak, meatloaf, thought, insight, pain, rest, law, principle*, etc. As a mass noun, each names a physical or abstract "substance", whereas the count-noun variant designates a bounded entity composed of that substance.

The mass-noun use of *lake* in (7)(a) instantiates a general pattern applicable when a referent's shape and boundary are irrelevant:

(8)　(a) *In my dream I attempt the winning shot and hit nothing but **net**.*

　　(b) *You'll have to stand—there's not enough **bench** for another big person.*

　　(c) *After he dug through the wall with his knife, there was very little **blade** left.*

　　(d) *With pre-owned vehicles, you get a lot of **car** for your money.*

The effect of this pattern is to shift attention away from the overall contour of a bounded entity and focus instead on a quantifiable expanse that enables it to serve some function. Conceptually, it is a matter of "zooming in", so that the boundary recedes from focused awareness. A more technical representation is given in figure 5.5. Starting from the count-noun sense, the mass-noun sense is obtained by imposing a limited immediate scope that excludes the contours of the count-noun profile. By definition, an expression's profile is confined to its immediate scope (the onstage region). The mass-noun profile is therefore limited to some internal portion (construed as homogeneous) of the count-noun referent.

Another count-to-mass pattern reflects the everyday activity of grinding, mashing, crushing, or pulverizing one or more discrete objects, thereby converting them into a homogeneous substance. As seen in (9), a count noun that names such an

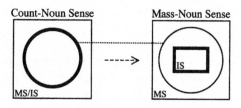

FIGURE 5.5

object comes to be used instead to designate the mass obtained by destroying its shape and structural integrity.

(9) (a) *By mashing a dozen potatoes, you get enough **potato** for this recipe.*

(b) *After a cat got in the way of our SUV, there was **cat** all over the driveway.*

(c) *Putting powdered **rhinoceros horn** on his cereal failed to enhance his virility.*

The simplest pattern for extending a mass noun to count-noun use likewise reflects an everyday activity, that of eating and drinking. Illustrated by the count-noun use of *water* in (7)(b), it is just a matter of restricting the profiled mass to a bounded quantity, typically the amount that constitutes a single serving. This extended meaning is well established for certain foods (notably desserts) and numerous beverages: *an ice cream, a crème brûlée, a tiramisu, a cherries jubilee, a clam chowder, a beer, a coke, a soda, a lemonade, an iced tea, a whiskey, a Grand Marnier, a gin and tonic,* and so on.

Another common pattern of mass-to-count conversion pertains not to quantity but to quality. If I speak of *a dry wine, a tasty beer, a hard steel,* or *a good glue,* I am not referring to any particular quantity of the substance. My concern is with the qualitative properties that differentiate one kind or brand from another. In technical terms, the shift in meaning involves a change in what is taken to be the domain of instantiation—the domain where instances primarily reside and are distinguished by their locations. For expressions like *a dry wine,* the profiled instance is not distinguished from others by its location in space (the usual domain of instantiation for physical substances) but by qualitative differences. The domain of instantiation is therefore one that we can describe metaphorically as **quality space**. Constituting this multidimensional "space" are all the qualitative properties relevant for the characterization of various substances. A particular substance is characterized by a typical range of values with respect to each of these dimensions.

These values delimit a bounded region in quality space, as shown in figure 5.6. The diagram on the left represents the basic meaning of a mass noun designating a physical substance. Although it is characterized by a bounded region in quality space (serving to distinguish it from other substances), it is in physical space—the domain of instantiation—that instances occur, and in this domain no bounding is imposed. We can thus identify an instance without it having an evident boundary, a particular shape, or even spatial continuity (recall the examples in (6)). Instead it is identified qualitatively, as shown by dashed lines, which indicate that any portion sampled projects to the defining region in quality space.

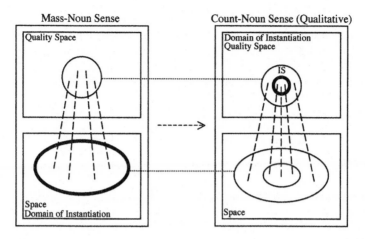

FIGURE 5.6

Depicted on the right in figure 5.6 is the extended meaning observed in expressions like *a dry wine* and *a tasty beer*. The essential change is that the domain of instantiation is shifted from physical space to quality space. It is therefore in quality space that instances occur and have distinguishing locations. Each instance represents a particular kind selected from the range of possible kinds for the substance in question, so it profiles a subpart of the region defining that substance qualitatively. Because it contains the profile, that region constitutes the immediate scope. Hence the qualitative sense of a mass noun fully satisfies the technical definition of a count noun: the thing it profiles is bounded within the immediate scope in the domain of instantiation.

The same sort of relationship between mass- and count-noun senses obtains in more abstract examples. We observed it previously for nouns naming colors:

(10) (a) *Yellow is a cheerful color.*   [proper noun; fig. 4.4(a)]

      (b) *We need a bright yellow for the baby's room.*   [common (count) noun; fig. 4.4(b)]

      (c) *There's a lot of yellow in this picture.*   [mass noun; fig. 4.4(e)]

For color terms, quality space is simply color space (the range of colors we can perceive). When used as a proper noun, *yellow* profiles a bounded region in this domain, which functions as domain of instantiation. The common noun use, corresponding to the diagram on the right in figure 5.6, takes that region as immediate scope and profiles some portion of it. *A bright yellow* thus designates a shade of yellow, just as *a dry wine* designates a kind of wine. The mass-noun sense corresponds to the lefthand diagram in figure 5.6. Here the domain of instantiation is space (or perhaps the visual field). The profile is a spatially extended mass—possibly discontinuous—consisting of an abstract substance characterized solely by the quality of the visual impression engendered.

Emotion terms like *anxiety*, *hate*, *anger*, *happiness*, and *depression* exhibit a precisely analogous trio of senses, exemplified in (11). In this case, quality space consists of whatever dimensions are taken as characterizing and distinguishing the various kinds of emotive experience. Space and time function jointly as domain of instantiation: a patch of emotive "substance" occurs wherever and whenever somebody experiences the emotion in question. Numerous discontinuous patches of this sort may constitute a single instance of this abstract type of substance.

(11)   (a) ***Anxiety*** *is one of the hardest conditions to treat.*   [proper noun]

     (b) *I feel a very intense **anxiety**.*   [common (count) noun]

     (c) *There's a lot of **anxiety** around here.*   [mass noun]

Also analogous are the respective nouns in (12), each derived from the verb *walk* by a different pattern of **nominalization**. Here quality space comprises the various parameters serving to distinguish and characterize different types of actions and, more specifically, different types of locomotion. The proper noun, which names a general means of locomotion, profiles a bounded region in this domain, a restricted portion of which is designated by the common noun indicating a particular walking style. For the mass noun, space and time function jointly once again as domain of instantiation. A patch of this *walking* "substance" occurs wherever and whenever somebody engages in this action. Any number of such patches, possibly discontinuous, may constitute a single instance of this type.

(12)   (a) ***Walking*** *is very good exercise.*   [proper noun]

     (b) *He has a peculiar **walk**.*   [common (count) noun]

     (c) *There's a lot of **walking** going on in this neighborhood.*   [mass noun]

These are but three of the numerous patterns of nominalization that a verb like *walk* can undergo. As a verb, it profiles a process unfolding through time (the domain of instantiation) in which the trajector moves along a spatial path in a normal mode of bipedal locomotion. A noun is derived by shifting the profile to a thing somehow involved in this process. The things profiled in (12) are abstract and rather tenuous (regions of different size in "quality space"; a "substance" comprising patches of activity projecting to the larger region). Generally, though, the profile shifts to something more tangible and salient. As shown in (13), it may be the actor, an instrument of walking, or the path traversed. It can also profile an event consisting of one instance of the process (see figs. 4.2 (d) and 4.13 (c)), as well as an organized social event involving multiple instances.

(13)   (a) *Tell that **walker** to keep off the grass.*

     (b) *My **walker** is broken again.*

     (c) *It's a very difficult **walk**—7 miles and uphill all the way.*

     (d) *Did you enjoy your **walk**?*

     (e) *We're organizing a 5 K run and **walk** to support cancer research.*

5.2 Perfective and Imperfective Verbs

Like nouns, verbs in English divide into two basic subclasses initially distinguished by their grammatical behavior. You will not be shocked to learn that these two subcategories are semantically definable. More surprising, perhaps, is the further claim that the semantic contrast between them is exactly the same as for nouns. The conceptual factors responsible for the count/mass distinction are applicable to processes as well as things.

5.2.1 Flexible Categorization

A verb profiles a process, schematically defined as a relationship scanned sequentially in its evolution through time. The two major subclasses are referred to in CG as **perfective** and **imperfective** verbs.[13] The terms reflect the conceptual characterization of perfectives as being bounded in time, whereas imperfectives are not specifically bounded. Moreover, perfectives construe the profiled relationship as internally heterogeneous, involving some kind of change through time, while imperfectives construe it as homogeneous, the continuation through time of a stable situation. Some typical examples are listed in (14).

(14)   (a) **Perfective verbs:** *fall, jump, kick, bite, throw, break, ask, tell, persuade, learn, decide, cook, melt, evaporate, die, kill, create, calculate...*

   (b) **Imperfective verbs:** *be, have, know, doubt, believe, suspect, like, love, detest, appreciate, hope, fear, resemble, contain, reside, exist...*

The conceptual distinction is quite apparent. The verbs in (14)(a) designate occurrences with a beginning and an end. Something happens—some change is observed in the situation described. For instance, to *fall* is to rapidly change location along the vertical axis, and to *learn* something is to change from not knowing it to knowing it. By contrast, the verbs in (14)(b) profile stable situations of indefinite duration. Nothing changes, and nothing happens. This is not to say that the profiled relationship has no beginning or end, only that the verb itself excludes them from what it puts onstage for focused viewing. To say that something *exists* does not imply that it has always existed or that it always will but does portray the situation as constant during whatever is taken to be the relevant span of time (the temporal immediate scope). And while learning something constitutes a change, to *know* it represents a steady situation with no intrinsic endpoint.

Despite its conceptual basis, the perfective/imperfective distinction first calls attention to itself through contrasting grammatical behavior. The usual diagnostics are occurrence in the simple present tense (*-s* for third-person singular) and in the progressive (marked by *be...-ing*). As shown in (15), a perfective (e.g. *learn*) does

---

[13] Other terms are often used, e.g. "active" vs. "stative". With respect to another common classification—into "accomplishment", "achievement", "activity", and "stative" verbs (Vendler 1967)—perfectives subsume the first three, while imperfectives correspond to the fourth.

not occur in the present but does take the progressive. An imperfective (such as *know*) displays the opposite behavior.[14] We will see that these grammatical properties are a consequence of how perfectives and imperfectives are characterized conceptually.

(15) (a) *He learns the poem.*   (a') *He is learning the poem.*

   (b) *He knows the poem.*   (b') *He is knowing the poem.*

Numerous verbs that appear to designate stable situations nonetheless function grammatically as perfectives. Thus, in reference to something going on right now, the verbs in (16) resist the present tense and take the progressive instead:

(16) (a) *She {sleeps/swims/dreams/perspires/meditates/wears a very expensive gown}.*

   (b) *She is {sleeping/swimming/dreaming/perspiring/meditating/wearing a very expensive gown}.*

The processes in question are readily construed as internally homogeneous. This is so even for a verb like *swim*, involving activity, force, and motion: the process is homogeneous in the sense that any stretch of swimming is comparable to any other, with repetitive movement of arms and legs resulting in steady progress through the water. It is also true, however, that we normally conceive of these processes as occurring in bounded episodes. They are therefore comparable to the things profiled by count nouns such as *lake*, *lawn*, *brick*, *beep*, and *hole*, which are likewise homogeneous yet bounded. In both cases the boundary itself provides a measure of heterogeneity. And in both cases, inclusion of the boundary within the expression's immediate scope is sufficient to effect its categorization as either a count noun or a perfective verb.

Like the count/mass distinction, the perfective/imperfective contrast is anything but a rigid lexical specification. While it is usual for a verb to have a primary classification as either perfective or imperfective, many verbs are comfortably used both ways. Categorization is flexible and subject to subtle conceptual influence from a variety of sources.

The verbs in (17) are among those well established in both perfective and imperfective use. In each case the first example profiles a bounded event, and the second a stable situation. Being imperfective, the verbs in the second column are able to occur in the simple present tense. The perfectives in the first column cannot, so the past is used for illustration. To describe the same events occurring at the present time, one would have to use the progressive (e.g. *The SWAT team is surrounding the house*).

(17) (a) *The SWAT team surrounded the house.*   (a') *A hedge surrounds the house.*

   (b) *She covered the hole with a picture.*   (b') *A picture covers the hole.*

---

[14] For this diagnostic purpose, one must only consider the "true" present tense, which indicates an occurrence of the profiled process at the time of speaking. Excluded are various "special" uses involving other conceptual factors, like its use for generics (*A cat chases birds*), habituals (*She works out every day*), and scheduled future events (*We leave next week*).

(c) *He demanded my resignation.*   (c') *That problem demands attention.*

(d) *We connected the wires.*   (d') *A tunnel connects the two buildings.*

(e) *I realized the enormity of the problem.*   (e') *I realize the enormity of the problem.*

Flexible categorization is nicely illustrated by the basic posture verbs *sit*, *stand*, and *lie*. Each can be used perfectively to profile the act of assuming the posture in question, as in (18)(a), in which case they normally occur with *down* or *up*. Each also occurs alone in another perfective sense, shown in (18)(b), where it designates a bounded episode of being in that posture. Like the verbs in (16), this use requires the progressive to describe a present situation, even though the profiled process is internally homogeneous. The posture verbs can also be used imperfectively, as in (18)(c), which suggests that the park is the statue's permanent home. Suppose, however, that the statue is placed there only temporarily, while its permanent location is being prepared. The standing would then be construed as constituting a bounded episode—hence perfective—so in (18)(d) the progressive is employed. With a human subject, like *Sam* in (18)(e), a posture verb is normally construed perfectively, for the simple reason that people are mobile, so that any particular postural configuration is bounded in duration. By contrast, a country that lies between two others does so indefinitely, so in (18)(f) *lie* behaves imperfectively.[15]

(18) (a) *Rebecca sat (down), then she stood (up) again.*

(b) *He is {sitting/standing/lying} on the couch.*

(c) *A statue of the president stands in the middle of the park.*

(d) *A statue of the president is standing in the middle of the park.*

(e) *Sam {*lies/is lying} on the beach right now.*

(f) *Belgium {lies/*is lying} between Holland and France.*

These examples illustrate the general point that a verb's **participants** (i.e. the entities participating in the profiled relationship) influence its categorization as perfective or imperfective. In (18)(e)–(f) the choice reflects the nature of the subject. A case of the object exerting influence is provided by basic verbs of perception. Note first that these can be used imperfectively: *I see light; I hear music; I feel pain.* This itself is interesting, for sensations are usually fairly brief, not your typical "stable situation of indefinite duration". Linguistically, however, stability and duration are not absolute but relative to some concern. What matters is whether a situation is construed as stable for the purpose at hand (with no requirement of absolute invariance) and whether this stability endures through the stretch of time considered relevant.

---

[15] Using the progressive would signal a perfective construal and thus suggest that Belgium could be picked up and moved somewhere else. (Of course, this is perfectly acceptable when working on a jigsaw puzzle where each piece represents a nation of Europe.)

This scope of concern constitutes a verb's immediate temporal scope—the span of time put onstage for focused viewing. Its absolute length is thus quite variable and depends on what kind of event is being talked about (e.g. the formation of the solar system, the rise and fall of an empire, or a trip to the store). Because perception is a moment-to-moment affair, for verbs like *see*, *hear*, and *feel* the time frame for assessing change or stability is very short.

Object nouns such as *light*, *music*, and *pain* imply a perceptual experience capable of enduring for a certain span of time, if only a matter of seconds. It can thus be presented as constant throughout the brief temporal interval relevant for describing immediate sensations. This allows the perception verbs to be used as imperfectives. Sometimes, however, an imperfective construal is precluded: **I see a flash*; **I hear a shot*; **I feel a twinge of pain*. Here the object nominals impose a **punctual** interpretation. Since they themselves are point-like in nature, so is the perceptual experience they engender; it essentially consists of just an onset and an offset, with nothing in between. The sensation is thus too brief to be viewed as stable, even for a limited period. It does however constitute a bounded event, resulting in a perfective interpretation: *I saw a flash*; *I heard a shot*; *I felt a twinge of pain*.[16]

Various other factors can influence a verb's construal as perfective or imperfective. Normally, for instance, the verb *like* describes a stable attitude and is therefore imperfective, as in (19)(a). But as seen in (19)(b), the adverbial *more and more* facilitates a perfective construal by introducing the notion of change.

(19) (a) *She likes her new teacher.*

      (b) *She's liking her new teacher more and more.*

Another factor is scope. Responsible for the contrast between the imperfective use of *wind* in (20)(a) and the perfective use in (20)(b) is whether the spatial configuration is apprehended in global fashion, as in looking at a map, or locally, from the perspective of someone traveling along the road. On the one hand, with a global view, the entire road-mountain configuration is simultaneously visible within the immediate spatial scope. That configuration is stable through time, so the verb describing it is imperfective and occurs in the simple present tense. On the other hand, with the local view afforded by driving along the road, only a small portion of the overall configuration is visible at any one moment. In (20)(b) that portion is construed as the immediate spatial scope for the subject nominal—what constitutes *this road* is that segment of the entire road which is visually accessible at any one time. While driving through the mountains, therefore, what counts as *this road* is perceived as moving, and indeed, as *winding* through them (much like a snake is perceived as winding through the grass). *Wind* is thus perfective, and takes the progressive, because it profiles a change unfolding through time rather than a stable configuration.

---

[16] Although these expressions are conceptually perfective (by virtue of profiling bounded events), they do not allow the progressive: **I'm seeing a flash*. Their punctual nature makes them semantically incompatible with the progressive, which profiles an ongoing situation internal to a bounded event (and excludes its endpoints).

(20)   (a) *According to the map, this road winds through the mountains.*

(b) *The way this road is winding through the mountains, we'll never get there on time.*

The choice between a perfective and an imperfective construal is not necessarily determined by anything inherent in the scene described. It often depends on general or contextual knowledge, or it may simply be a matter of how the speaker decides to portray the situation. If you came upon a statue in the park, how would you describe it? The choice between (18)(c) and (18)(d) depends on knowing the intention of whoever put it there. Or suppose your professor, obviously deep in thought, happens to strike the exact same posture as Rodin's famous statue *The Thinker*. To describe this you might very well say (21)(a). The perfective construal reflects our general knowledge that the sitting and meditating done by people occurs in bounded episodes. For the statue itself, however, (21)(b) is more appropriate.

(21)   (a) *Our prof is sitting and meditating.*

(b) *Rodin's* Thinker *sits and meditates perpetually.*

The contrast in (22) represents a case where a perfective vs. an imperfective construal is purely a matter of speaker choice. Recall that *see* allows both options, depending on the nature of its object: *I see light* vs. **I see a flash*. An imperfective construal is possible with *light* but hardly with *a flash*, since only the former has sufficient duration to allow a stable perceptual experience for even the brief period constituting the immediate temporal scope. Hence *see a flash* is normally perfective, even though its punctual nature precludes the progressive: **I'm seeing a flash*. Part of what we know about flashes, however, is that sometimes they induce an afterimage which, in contrast to the flash itself, may endure for some moments. We can thus say either (22)(a) or (22)(b), where *flash* is understood metonymically. Both options are permitted, since the afterimage has no fixed length in relation to the immediate temporal scope. The perfective construal in (22)(a) specifically portrays this visual experience as a bounded episode. In (22)(b), the speaker decides instead to focus on its constancy during the relevant span of time. Though presumably not ignorant of its temporary nature, the speaker chooses to ignore this.

(22)   (a) *I'm still seeing that blinding flash which occurred a moment ago.*

(b) *I still see that blinding flash which occurred a moment ago.*

5.2.2 The Count/Mass Analogy

A noun profiles a thing, defined abstractly as any product of grouping and reification. A verb profiles a process, defined abstractly as a relationship scanned sequentially in its evolution through time. Despite their maximal conceptual opposition, nouns and verbs show certain parallels, one being their division into two major subclasses. Remarkably, for each category this major division has the same conceptual basis: the count/mass distinction for nouns is precisely analogous to the perfective/imperfective distinction for verbs. In both cases, the distinction involves the interrelated factors of bounding, homogeneity, contractibility, and replicability.

The count/mass distinction hinges on whether the thing profiled by a noun is construed as being bounded within the immediate scope in the domain of instantiation. For physical objects (the category prototype), the domain of instantiation is space, and bounding is effected by the spatial boundary defining an object's shape. For nouns in general, however, the domain of instantiation varies, and bounding needs to be characterized more abstractly: a thing is bounded when there is some limit to the set of constitutive entities.

For verbs, the domain of instantiation is always time. The perfective/imperfective contrast therefore hinges on whether the profiled process is bounded within the immediate temporal scope, and it is bounded if there is some limit to the set of constitutive entities. But what are these entities? What aspects of a process should we identify as being analogous to the patches of substance constituting a physical object, or the discrete particles of a group (e.g. *stack*) or plural mass? The answer lurks in the characterization of a process as a **complex** relationship, one consisting of **component** relationships distributed through a continuous span of time (fig. 4.6). These time-slices—the **component states** of the process—are naturally taken as being its constitutive elements. For the most part, of course, we do not apprehend them separately but only as facets of a continuous whole, where each morphs seamlessly into the next. In this respect, they resemble the arbitrarily delimited patches of substance constituting a physical object, which are likewise perceived as continuous. Recall that, as defined, an **entity** need not be discrete, salient, or individually recognized.

The essential difference between perfectives and imperfectives is depicted in figure 5.7. In the simplified format adopted, a line represents a relationship evolving through time. Hence each point on the line corresponds to a component state— that is, the relationship obtaining at a single moment.[17] In diagram (a), for perfective verbs, vertical bars indicate that the profiled relationship is bounded in its temporal extension. These are transition points marking the beginning and end of the relationship's manifestation. Crucially, its entire manifestation falls within the immediate temporal scope. The profiled process is therefore bounded within the immediate scope in the domain of instantiation (time). Such bounding is not intrinsic to the characterization of imperfective verbs. In diagram (b), ellipses (. . .) indicate that the relationship extends indefinitely. The immediate temporal scope segments out some portion of this ongoing situation and puts it onstage for focused viewing. The verb's profile is restricted to just that portion. Though limited by the immediate scope, the profiled relationship is not bounded in the sense of there being a beginning and end to its manifestation—the relationship itself extends beyond the immediate scope in either direction. The limitation is not inherent in the situation described but extrinsic, pertaining to how it is viewed. Thus the profiled relationship is not specifically bounded within the immediate scope in the domain of instantiation.

---

[17] Compare this with the slightly less simplified format of fig. 4.13 (a), where representative component states are shown explicitly as relationships. For present purposes there is no need to portray each state's internal structure. Also omitted is the bar along the time arrow, indicating sequential scanning.

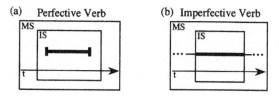

FIGURE 5.7

Comparing figure 5.3, for count vs. mass, and figure 5.7, for perfective vs. imperfective, reveals that the two distinctions are essentially the same. The only differences in the diagrams reflect the distinction's application to things in the first instance and to processes in the second. This parallelism observed with respect to bounding continues when we turn the coin over to examine its other sides: homogeneity, contractibility, and replicability.

Like a count-noun referent, a perfective process is construed as being internally heterogeneous. And like a mass-noun referent, an imperfective process is construed as being internally homogeneous. The "geneity" of a verb (hetero- vs. homo-) is a matter of whether the component states of the process are conceived as being effectively identical. Perfectives are therefore heterogeneous because the profiled relationship changes through time. Imperfectives are homogeneous because they profile the continuation through time of a stable situation. You can see the parallelism by comparing the leftmost and rightmost diagrams in figure 5.8, where a wavy line indicates heterogeneity and a straight-line homogeneity. The diagrams in the

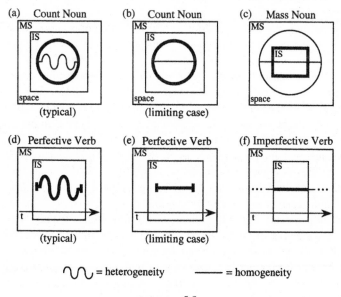

FIGURE 5.8

middle show that the noun/verb parallelism extends even further. For each category, we have noted examples construed as bounded despite being uniform throughout: count nouns such as *lake*, *lawn*, and *beep*; perfective verbs like *sleep*, *swim*, and *meditate*. These represent the limiting case of heterogeneity, where the thing or process is homogeneous apart from the measure of heterogeneity introduced by the boundary itself.

A mass is contractible in the sense that any portion of an instance is itself a valid instance of the mass-noun type. The analogous property holds for imperfective verbs. Suppose I learn a poem and manage to remember it for over a month. During this time span, the statement *I know the poem* is valid for any interval of any length (*I knew the poem last week, I know it right now, and I will still know it tomorrow*). There is no need to consider the entire month-long situation—whatever interval is selected for focused viewing (as the temporal immediate scope) is sufficient to manifest an instance of the profiled process. Contractibility is not characteristic of count nouns or perfective verbs. Part of a *lake* is not itself a lake. Analogously, if it takes me an entire month to learn a poem, the statement *I learned the poem* is inappropriate for describing the progress made during a single day or week.

In addition to being contractible, a mass is also expansible in the sense that combining two instances yields a single, larger instance. Count nouns lack this property due to bounding, which limits the extent of an instance. They instead exhibit the property called replicability, which simply means that putting instances together yields multiple instances. Hence *the water in those two lakes* invokes one instance of *water* but two instances of *lake*, despite their referential identity. It is therefore as expected that imperfectives are expansible and perfectives replicable. If I knew a poem in March and also knew it in April, it is equally valid to say that I knew the poem during the entire two-month period. But if a full instance of learning it occurred in March, and another in April, they would constitute two separate instances of learning: *I knew the poem* once, but *I learned the poem* twice.

A specific indication of replication is the adverbial phrase *again and again*. As expected, it only occurs with perfectives. While a sufficiently forgetful person might well say *I learned the poem again and again*, it is a bit strange to say *??I knew the poem again and again* for the same series of alternating periods of knowing the poem and not knowing it. *Learn* replicates because an event of learning is inherently bounded and (alas) gives no guarantee that the resulting knowledge will endure—it may have to be learned on multiple occasions. But since *know* is imperfective, it induces the expectation of indefinite continuation. For *know* to be replicable, we need to make a semantic adjustment and construe the profiled relationship as occurring in bounded episodes. We have the conceptual flexibility to do this if we can imagine a plausible scenario, and here we can, owing to the frailty of human memory. In similar fashion, *??She resembled her mother again and again* strikes us as semantically anomalous until we start to think of plausible interpretations. We need only imagine a scenario in which resembling someone constitutes a bounded episode able to recur. And indeed, since people change we can imagine a person resembling her mother for numerous periods during her life, interspersed with periods of nonresemblance. Alternatively, she might resemble her mother just in a certain respect manifested on multiple occasions, as in her tone of voice while angry.

Such examples illustrate a number of general points. First, the grammatical well-formedness of sentences ("grammaticality") cannot be judged independently of what they are interpreted as meaning. Moreover, semantic interpretation is not exclusively linguistic but depends on what we know or can imagine about the world. And finally, because it is influenced by these factors, linguistic categorization is flexible.

5.2.3 Interaction with Tense and Aspect

The usual basis for distinguishing perfective and imperfective verbs is contrasting grammatical behavior, primarily their interaction with tense and aspect: English perfectives take the progressive but resist the simple present tense; imperfectives do the opposite. From the CG perspective, the behavior of perfectives and imperfectives is merely symptomatic of their conceptual characterizations. These allow us to explain not only the basic distributional pattern but also some apparent exceptions.

For semantic explanations, we must first describe the meanings of the relevant grammatical elements: progressive aspect (marked by *be…-ing*) and tense (both present and past). As suggested by its form, the progressive combines the meanings of *-ing* and *be*. The former was briefly discussed in §4.3.2. It is one of several elements (others being participial *-ed* and infinitival *to*) that construe a process holistically, thus making the profiled relationship nonprocessual. Moreover, *-ing* takes an "internal perspective" on this relationship. What this means, in technical terms, is that *-ing* imposes an immediate temporal scope delimiting some internal portion of the overall relationship and selecting it for focused viewing. Hence only this portion is profiled, as was shown in figure 4.14, which also indicates a third property of *-ing*: namely, that the profiled relationship is construed as homogeneous. This is so even when the verb that *-ing* attaches to describes a change. While the component states may then be different, they are nonetheless equivalent when viewed at a certain level of abstraction. In particular, they all qualify as representative internal states of the same base process.[18]

Starting with a verb like *climb*, then, *-ing* derives a participial expression, *climbing*, which profiles—and construes as homogeneous—a relationship comprising some internal portion of the verbal process. The profiled relationship is nonprocessual by virtue of being scanned in summary fashion (rather than sequentially). This holistic construal enables it to modify a noun, as in *the monkey climbing that tree*. Alternatively, it combines with *be* to form a progressive, *be climbing*. Since *be* is a schematic verb, it lends its processual nature to the relationship profiled by the participle. A progressive can therefore serve as the head of a finite clause (§4.3.3): *A monkey is climbing that tree.*

The overall effect of a progressive is thus to convert a perfective process into an imperfective one, as sketched in figure 5.9. The bounded occurrence profiled by the former functions as conceptual base for the latter, which profiles an internal portion that excludes the endpoints. Two subtle matters bear emphasizing. First, while a verb

---

[18] The level of abstraction required to construe them as homogeneous is no greater than the one implied by mass nouns like *furniture, equipment,* and *silverware,* or the plural *animals* used in reference to a monkey, an elephant, and a crocodile (§5.1.4).

FIGURE 5.9

and its progressive are both processual, they profile **different processes**, one characterized in relation to the other. Second, while a progressive indicates that the verb it is formed on is perfective, the expression as a whole is imperfective.[19]

This semantic characterization explains why the progressive only occurs with perfectives. Quite simply, because its function is to imperfectivize a verb, there is no point in using it with a verb that is already imperfective. It thus makes perfect sense that the conventions of English preclude this option. While it cannot be claimed that languages are maximally efficient and always avoid redundancy, the added complexity of a progressive imperfective would serve no apparent purpose.[20]

Also explained is why the progressive does not occur with perfectives that are punctual, e.g. *I'm seeing a flash*. A punctual event is just too brief to allow an internal perspective. It essentially consists of just an onset and an offset, with nothing in between, so excluding the endpoints leaves nothing to view and profile within the immediate temporal scope. There are of course exceptions to this exception, and these too can be explained. I noted in (22)(a) that *see a flash* permits the progressive when used in reference to an afterimage. Another example is *blink*. One cannot say *He is blinking* with respect to a single blink viewed in the normal fashion. There is simply not time to say it or to observe the event's interior phase. Yet *He is blinking* is a perfectly normal, grammatical expression. It would usually be understood as referring not to one blink but to a series of blinks, construed as constituting a single overall event of bounded duration. On this **repetitive** interpretation, *blink* profiles a higher-order perfective process with sufficient length to be rendered progressive. The sentence then profiles some internal portion of this bounded series. Or imagine that a single blink has been recorded using high-speed photography and is now being projected on a screen at a normal viewing rate. We thus observe a single blink occurring over a time span of several seconds. Since *blink* is no longer punctual, *He is blinking* is quite acceptable.

The remaining question is why perfectives do not occur in the simple present tense. Indeed, out of all four combinations of tense and perfectivity, only the present perfective is problematic:

---

[19] Progressives behave like other imperfectives grammatically: they occur in the present tense (*A monkey is climbing that tree*) and do not themselves take the progressive (**A monkey is being climbing that tree*).

[20] Although the progressive as a whole is limited to perfectives, *-ing* by itself occurs with either sort of verb: *the monkey **climbing** that tree; a monkey **resembling** my uncle*. This does serve a purpose, since either a perfective or an imperfective process must be viewed holistically when it is used to modify a noun (§4.3.3).

(23) (a) *He learned the poem.*   [PAST PERFECTIVE]

(b) **He learns the poem.*   [PRESENT PERFECTIVE]

(c) *He knew the poem.*   [PAST IMPERFECTIVE]

(d) *He knows the poem.*   [PRESENT IMPERFECTIVE]

Why do we find this particular distribution rather than some other? Also needing explanation are various exceptions, where a perfective does occur in the present.

We must first examine the meanings of the English tense inflections.[21] In the traditional view (sufficient for immediate purposes), tense relates an occurrence to the moment of speaking. Translating this into CG terminology, we can say that tense imposes an immediate temporal scope, positioned with respect to the speech event, within which the profiled process must be manifested. Obviously, for past tense the immediate scope is prior to the speech event. Perhaps less obviously, for the present tense in English it precisely coincides with the time of speaking (Langacker 2001a). This is shown in figure 5.10, using a box with squiggly lines to indicate the speech event. The profiled process is represented with a simple line (without bars or ellipses) because these structures themselves are neutral in regard to the perfective/imperfective contrast. The past tense indicates that an instance of the process occurs prior to the time of speaking, and the present tense indicates that an instance exactly coincides with the time of speaking.

Consider, then, the result of applying these tense morphemes to a perfective or an imperfective verb. With the past tense, the immediate temporal scope can be of any duration—it need only occur prior to the time of speaking. Therefore, it can always be large enough to encompass a perfective process instance, including its endpoints, as shown in figure 5.11(a). Past imperfectives are also unproblematic because imperfectives are mass-like in nature, hence contractible. Suppose a stable situation endures indefinitely and thus extends beyond the immediate scope in either direction, as shown in diagram (c). Owing to contractibility, that portion which falls within the immediate scope qualifies as a valid instance of the imperfective process type. This portion, segmented out for focused viewing, satisfies the requirement of an instance occurring prior to the speech event. The same holds for

FIGURE 5.10

---

[21] Since future *will* is noninflectional (belonging instead to the modal system), English is usually analyzed as having just two grammatical tenses. We are only concerned with the "true" present, pertaining to things happening at the moment of speaking (see n. 14).

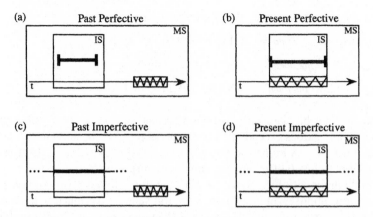

FIGURE 5.11

present imperfectives, as seen in diagram (d). The time of speaking is quite brief (the second or so it takes to utter a finite clause), so a stable present situation will normally extend beyond it in both directions. Nevertheless, the contractibility of an imperfective process ensures that the small sample coinciding with the speech event is a valid instance of the process type.

That leaves present tense perfectives, diagrammed in figure 5.11(b). There would seem to be nothing wrong with this configuration; conceptually, it is perfectly coherent for a bounded event to precisely coincide with the speech event. So why do present perfectives give the impression of being semantically anomalous? It is not because they are internally inconsistent, but rather because the configuration in diagram (b) is hard to achieve in normal language use. By "normal use", I refer to the default-case viewing arrangement where the speaker observes and describes actual events and situations (§3.4.1). Relative to this arrangement, diagram (b) represents the description of an actually observed, bounded event. This is problematic in two respects. First, it is seldom the case that an observed event is the same in duration as the utterance of its verbal description. It takes just a second to say *He learns the poem* or *She changes the tire*, but few actual occurrences of these events are so brief. The second problem can be posed as a question: What does the speaker know, and when does he know it? To describe an observed event, the speaker must first observe it, or at least enough of it to know what it is. But by the time the speaker has accomplished this, it is already too late to initiate an utterance describing the event that exactly coincides with it.

Present tense perfectives are therefore not problematic owing to any intrinsic conceptual incoherence. The reason, instead, is that the configuration in figure 5.11(b) is incompatible with the default-case viewing arrangement. Yet there are many other viewing arrangements where the same problems do not arise. It turns out, in fact, that present perfectives are very common. If they are usually considered anomalous, it is simply because the default arrangement is taken for granted as the basis for their interpretation.

In one departure from the default arrangement, the speaker not only describes an action but actually performs it by virtue of the speech event itself. The expressions in

(24) are called **performatives** (Austin 1962; Searle 1969). A verb like *order, promise*, or *sentence* names a type of **speech act** and is therefore perfective. For an utterance to count as a performance of that act, the verb must be in the present tense, with the speaker coded as subject. Moreover, the speaker must intend to perform the action profiled by the verb, and the conditions required for its successful performance must all be satisfied (e.g. the speaker in (24)(c) must have the requisite authority).

(24) (a) *I order you to leave at once.*

    (b) *I promise to stop smoking.*

    (c) *I hereby sentence you to 30 days in the county jail.*

In performative use, perfective verbs are more than happy to occur in the present tense. The problems that arise in the default viewing arrangement are absent when the speaker actually performs the action named. There is no problem of temporal duration. Indeed, the profiled event and the speech event have to be the same in length, since—as shown in figure 5.12—a performative represents the special case where the event profiled by the sentence is the speech event itself. Nor is there any problem of speaker knowledge. Since the speaker performs the action described, and necessarily intends to do so, he does not have to observe its occurrence in order to identify it. He simply performs the action he intends to perform. And because he performs it by speaking, the action coincides exactly with the time of speaking.

Present tense perfectives are extremely prevalent in the "play-by-play" mode of speech practiced by sportscasters:

(25) *He hits a high fly to left. Jones comes in a few steps... he shades his eyes... he grabs it for the final out.*

This definitely approaches the default viewing arrangement, in that the announcer observes events and describes them. Yet it is special in certain ways that eliminate (or at least mitigate) the problems of duration and speaker knowledge. For one thing, the events described have a typical duration that roughly approximates the length of their description.[22] For another, these events are highly stereotypical, so the announcer

FIGURE 5.12

[22] A home run cannot be observed in just a second or so, since the ball has to travel quite a distance, and one has to observe its entire flight to be sure it clears the fence. Hence the announcer does not say *He homers to left!* but rather something like the following: *He hits a long fly to left... it's going, going, gone!* (not *It goes!*).

FIGURE 5.13

can either anticipate them or identify them virtually at their onset. Usually, then, a play-by-play account can shadow the events described with a very small time lag. In apprehending this mode of speech, we adopt the convention of ignoring whatever time lag there may be. Equivalently, it might be said that our conception of this genre incorporates the fiction of coincident description.

There are other nondefault arrangements sanctioning present tense perfectives (Langacker 2001a; ICG ch. 7). But what about the default viewing arrangement? How do we describe an actual perfective process observed as occurring at the present moment? For this we use the progressive, e.g. *He is learning the poem*, as shown in figure 5.13(a). We start with a bounded process (*learn*) whose overall occurrence includes the time of speaking. From this perfective process, the progressive derives an imperfective (fig. 5.9). It does so by imposing an immediate temporal scope, IS_1, that excludes the endpoints of the bounded event, and by construing the onstage portion as homogeneous. Of the original perfective process, the resulting imperfective (*be learning*) profiles the segment delimited by IS_1, which likewise includes the time of speaking. It is to this imperfective process that the present tense applies. The present imposes its own immediate scope, IS_2, coincident with the speech event (cf. fig. 3.3 (b)). Hence the composite expression (*is learning*) profiles just that segment, which—owing to contractibility—is a valid instance of the imperfective process type (*be learning*).

For bounded events in the past, the progressive is not required (*He learned the poem*). We need only impose an immediate scope large enough to encompass the entire occurrence (fig. 5.11(a)). A past progressive is nonetheless possible: *He was learning the poem*. Diagrammed in figure 5.13(b), the past progressive lets us focus the portion of an overall event that was observable at some previous moment.

6

Constructions

General Characterization

$\mathbf{M}$ost of the expressions we employ are symbolically complex, to some degree analyzable into smaller symbolic elements. Grammar consists of the patterns for constructing such expressions. Accordingly, the expressions and the patterns are referred to as **constructions**. In this chapter and the next, I consider the general nature of constructions and then examine some basic aspects of their description.

6.1 Symbolic Assemblies

CG makes the fundamental and highly controversial claim that grammar is **symbolic** in nature. More specifically, it holds that grammar and lexicon form a continuum residing exclusively in **assemblies** of symbolic structures. Constructions are symbolic assemblies. The objective of grammatical analysis is to describe such assemblies in clear and precise detail.

6.1.1 Composition, Integration, and Symbolization

A symbolic structure (Σ) consists in the pairing of a semantic structure (S) and a phonological structure (P): $[[S]/[P]]_{\Sigma}$. It is thus bipolar, S being its semantic pole and P its phonological pole. As shown in figure 1.2, symbolic structures combine with one another to form more elaborate symbolic structures: $[\Sigma_1] + [\Sigma_2] = [\Sigma_3]$. These three structures constitute a symbolic assembly. At a higher level of organization, $[\Sigma_3]$ may itself combine with another symbolic structure to form one that is still more elaborate: $[\Sigma_3] + [\Sigma_4] = [\Sigma_5]$. And so on indefinitely. In this way, expressions exhibiting any degree of symbolic complexity can be progressively assembled: words, phrases, clauses, sentences, even discourses.

With respect to a particular level of organization, we can say that the **component structures** $[\Sigma_1]$ and $[\Sigma_2]$ are **integrated** to form the **composite structure** $[\Sigma_3]$. For instance, the component expressions *jar* and *lid* can be integrated to form the composite expression *jar lid*. All three structures are symbolic. The construction can thus be represented as follows, where uppercase and lowercase letters respectively indicate the semantic and phonological poles: [[JAR]/[jar]] + [[LID]/[lid]] = [[JAR LID]/[jar lid]].[1] These structures and the relationships among them constitute a symbolic assembly.

Shown abstractly in figure 6.1(a) are the structures and relationships inherent in a simple construction. The component symbolic structures, $[\Sigma_1]$ and $[\Sigma_2]$, as well as the composite structure $[\Sigma_3]$, each consist of a semantic structure and a phonological structure connected by a relationship of **symbolization** (s). At each pole, the two component structures participate in relationships of **integration** (i) with each other and relationships of **composition** (c) with respect to the composite structure. Moreover, the integration of P_1 and P_2 symbolizes the integration of S_1 and S_2. The same structures and relationships are shown in diagram (b) for the specific case of *jar lid*. Of course, this representation is still quite abstract. A serious analysis of this or any other construction requires that each structure and each relationship be described in explicit detail.

Consider first the component semantic structures [JAR] and [LID]. A full description of either component involves semantic specifications in numerous cognitive domains ranked for centrality (recall the discussion of *glass* in §2.2.2). For sake of practicality, we must therefore confine our attention to those facets of these complex meanings that play some role in the construction of concern, and even here we can hardly avoid oversimplification. In the case of [JAR], relevant specifications include the fact that it profiles a thing, further identified as a physical container open at the top. The pictorial representation at the left in figure 6.2(a) is merely an informal, mnemonic abbreviation for these and other properties—it is **not** claimed that

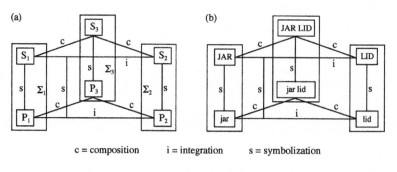

c = composition   i = integration   s = symbolization

FIGURE 6.1

---

[1] In formulaic representations, it is convenient to abbreviate by omitting the composite structure. *Jar lid* would then be given as follows: [[[JAR]/[jar]] - [[LID]/[lid]]]. Despite this simplified notation, the composite structure is a distinct entity whose presence must always be understood.

(a) Integration of Component Semantic Structures

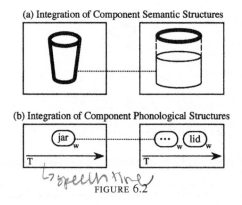

(b) Integration of Component Phonological Structures

FIGURE 6.2

the meaning of *jar* is a picture. Likewise, the sketch on the right in 6.2(a) abbreviates the relevant specifications of [LID]. It too profiles a thing, further characterized as the cover for an opening in the upper side of a container. [LID] itself does not specify any one kind of container (consider *pot lid, box lid, coffin lid*) and thus evokes it schematically. The dotted line in 6.2(a) shows how [JAR] and [LID] are integrated. It indicates that the container profiled by [JAR] **corresponds** to the schematic container evoked by [LID]: that these are two representations of the same conceived entity. Corresponding elements are superimposed, and their specifications merged, in forming the composite conception.

Analogously, figure 6.2(b) shows the integration of the component phonological structures [jar] and [lid]. Here, too, the representations are highly abbreviatory. In lieu of comprehensive phonological descriptions (cf. FCG1: §9.1), it is merely indicated that [jar] and [lid] are words (w), each occurring at a certain point in the flow of speech. The arrow labeled T is processing time—in particular, speech time. One aspect of the characterization of a word is the potential for other words to precede or follow it along this axis. This provides a basis for phonological integration. In 6.2(b), a correspondence line identifies [jar] with the word directly preceding [lid] in the temporal sequence.[2] Hence the merger of corresponding elements produces the word sequence *jar lid* at the composite-structure level.

Composition is largely a matter of combining component structures in accordance with the correspondences holding between their elements at the semantic and phonological poles. Component-structure elements that correspond to one another correspond to the same element at the composite-structure level. In this way, the structures and correspondences shown in figure 6.2 give rise to the configuration in figure 6.3, representing the construction as a whole. The composite semantic structure profiles the cover for a container identified not just schematically but as a jar in particular. The composite phonological structure is the two-word sequence *jar lid*, with the first word bearing

---

[2] [lid] itself evokes this word only potentially and in schematized form (indicated by ellipses). Its role in the construction brings it to the fore. The notation is arbitrary in the sense that one could equally well show [lid] as corresponding to the word following [jar].

FIGURE 6.3

stress: [jár lid]. These composite structures stand in a relationship of symbolization to one another, and one of composition to their respective component structures.

6.1.2 Composition as Categorization

A crucial point is that the composite structure is not merely the sum of the component structures it is based on, at either pole. The composite structure is an entity in its own right, usually with emergent properties not inherited or strictly predictable from the components and the correspondences between them. From figure 6.2(a) alone, one could not predict that the composite expression *jar lid* profiles the lid rather than the jar. Likewise, from figure 6.2(b) one could not predict that stress falls on the first word of the compound rather than the second. These are properties of the expression as a whole, emerging only at the composite-structure level. As a general matter, component structures should be thought of as resources drawn on—along with others—in arriving at the composite expression. While they motivate the composite structure to varying degrees, and may supply most of its content, they should not be thought of as building blocks that need only be stacked together to form the composite whole. As discussed in §2.1.3, the relation between them is one of partial (rather than full) compositionality.

Since the composite structure is a distinct entity, not reducible to its components, together they form an **assembly** of symbolic structures. They form an assembly (as opposed to being separate and unrelated) precisely by virtue of being linked by correspondences. "Horizontal" correspondences constitute the relationship of integration, which links the component structures. "Vertical" correspondences constitute the relationship of composition, which links the component structures to the composite structure. And as shown in figure 6.1, the phonological integration symbolizes the semantic integration. In the case of *jar lid*, the fact that *jar* directly precedes *lid* in the temporal sequence symbolizes the fact that the container evoked by *lid* is specifically the one profiled by *jar*. Though easily taken for granted, this symbolizing relationship between semantic and phonological integration is a critical aspect of constructional meaning. It ensures that integration at the two poles is coordinated, and is thus responsible for the symbolic link between [S₃] and [P₃] at the composite-structure level. Without it, nothing would ensure that in a sentence like *They found a jar lid under the coffin* the lid is interpreted as belonging to the jar rather than the coffin.

The structures in a symbolic assembly are linked not only by correspondences but also by relationships of **categorization** (§1.3.1). At the semantic pole of *jar lid*, for example, the component and composite structures exhibit the categorizing relationships shown in figure 6.4. First, as indicated by a solid arrow, [LID] is schematic with respect to [JAR LID]: while the two are consistent in their specifications, the latter is more specific. This "vertical" elaborative relationship is due to a "horizontal" one, whereby [JAR] provides a finer-grained description of the schematic container evoked by [LID]. Finally, a dashed arrow indicates that [JAR LID], taken as a whole, constitutes a semantic extension vis-à-vis [JAR]: that is, they are inconsistent in their specifications. The discrepancy resides in their profiling. Although [JAR] profiles the container, the composite structure inherits its profile from [LID], so [JAR LID] designates the cover.

In a categorizing relationship, the categorizing structure lies in the background. Occupying the foreground—as the structure of concern—is the **target** of categorization (the structure being categorized). This asymmetry can be observed in symbolic assemblies, where a composite structure is foregrounded relative to its components (fig. 3.1). It is the composite structure that we primarily attend to and employ for further composition at higher levels of organization. The component structures are not invoked for their own sake, but as "stepping-stones" for purposes of "reaching" the composite conception. Moreover, a categorizing structure is usually not exhaustive of its target but merely provides a way of apprehending it.[3] In this we find a

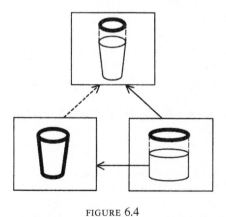

FIGURE 6.4

---

[3] While [DOG] categorizes [POODLE], for example, the latter is semantically more elaborate: [[DOG] → [POODLE]].

general basis for the point that a composite structure is more than just the sum of its components. Though standard and unavoidable, the metaphor inherent in terms like "construction" and "composition" should not be pushed too far. While component structures serve to evoke a composite structure, and provide a way of apprehending it, the latter should not be thought of—in any strict or literal sense—as being constructed out of them. Stepping-stones are not the same as building blocks.

The potential for being misled by the "construction" metaphor is one motivation for speaking of component and composite structures as forming a symbolic "assembly". Within an assembly, the composite structure stands in the foreground by virtue of being the target of categorization.[4] Thus far, of course, we have only considered simple symbolic assemblies representing a single level of composition. But assemblies can be of any size, representing multiple levels of grammatical organization. In a complex assembly, it is typical for the composite structure at a given level of organization to function as a component structure with respect to another, "higher" level of organization. If the component structures are stepping-stones for reaching the composite structure, that in turn may be a stepping-stone for reaching another composite structure, and so on indefinitely. Hence the structures in a complex symbolic assembly define a **compositional path** that can be of any length (§3.2.2).

Illustrating an assembly with just two levels of grammatical composition is the compound *jar lid factory*. At the first ("lower") level of organization, the component structures *jar* and *lid* are integrated to form the composite structure *jar lid*. At the higher level, *jar lid* functions as a component structure, combining with *factory* to form the full expression. It would be possible to continue—for example, by adding *supervisor* to derive the more complex expression *jar lid factory supervisor*. That in turn might combine with the compound *training school*, yielding the still more complex *jar lid factory supervisor training school*. And so on.

To keep things manageable, let us confine our attention to *jar lid factory*. Its semantic pole is sketched in figure 6.5, showing only correspondences (not categorizing relationships).[5] The assembly of *jar lid* is just as described in figure 6.3. Its composite structure is one of the two component structures at the higher level of organization. The other component, *factory*, profiles a building or facility used for manufacturing some product, represented as a circle. Effecting the integration of *jar lid* and *factory* is a correspondence between the profile of the former and the schematic product evoked by the latter: a *jar lid factory* is one that manufactures jar lids. The result is the structure shown at the top, the composite structure for the overall

---

[4] Given the limitations of a two-dimensional printed page, this foregrounding is normally shown by placing the composite structure above the component structures.

[5] For sake of practicality, every diagram is selective in what it portrays, being limited to what is essential for the point at hand. The labels in fig. 6.5 (*jar, lid, jar lid*, etc.) are meant to be suggestive of the phonological pole, but not to actually describe it in even the minimal fashion of fig. 6.3. Though seldom represented in explicit detail, the phonological pole must always be understood as a crucial part of symbolic assemblies.

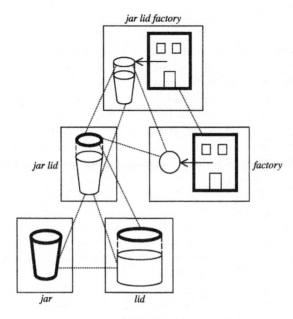

jar lid factory

jar lid   *factory*

jar   *lid*

FIGURE 6.5

expression. What it profiles is the facility, since a *jar lid factory* is a kind of factory (not a kind of lid or jar).

The five structures indicated in figure 6.5 constitute a symbolic assembly of modest complexity. Within this assembly, component structures serve as stepping-stones for arriving at composite structures, at two successive levels of organization. The ultimate target, shown at the top, comprises the composite form and meaning of the full expression. These stand in the foreground. At either pole, the other structures define a compositional path leading to the final target. Though it lies in the background, this path is not unimportant. The path followed in reaching the final composite structure is a secondary but significant aspect of an expression's form and meaning.

6.2 Constructional Schemas

Symbolic assemblies can either be specific or schematic. Specific assemblies constitute linguistic expressions (like words, phrases, clauses, and sentences). More schematic assemblies are referred to in CG as **constructional schemas**. These provide the basis for semantic and grammatical composition.

6.2.1 Role in Compositionality

An expression is said to be compositional to the extent that its composite structure derives in a regular, predictable way from its component structures. Compositionality is an essential feature of language, enabling us to create and understand an endless supply of new expressions. Thus we need to be clear about its nature, as well as its limitations.

The simplest hypothesis would merely identify an expression's composite meaning with the set of its component meanings. Composition would then be just a matter of viewing the component meanings collectively. On this account, the composite meaning of *jar lid factory* would be the unordered set {[FACTORY], [LID], [JAR]}. It is readily seen, however, that there is more to composition than mere summation. Otherwise, distinct expressions with the same components would always be semantically equivalent. But they are not. We cannot, for instance, ignore the semantic differences of *jar lid factory* (factory for making jar lids), *lid factory jar* (jar used in a lid factory), and *jar factory lid* (cover for a roofless jar factory). An expression's composite meaning is not just a pile of component meanings, but an integrated structure where elements relate to one another in very specific ways. These structural relationships are spelled out by correspondences, categorizations, and profiling at the semantic pole of symbolic assemblies, as shown for *jar lid factory* in figure 6.5. When arranged in other configurations, the same component elements give rise to other meanings.[6]

What guides us in putting assemblies together? How do we know which elements correspond, or what is profiled within the composite conception? What tells us, not only that the semantic assembly in figure 6.5 is possible but also that it represents the phonological sequence *jar lid factory* (as opposed to *lid factory jar* or *jar factory lid*)? We know such things by virtue of knowing the grammar of our language. Grammar consists of conventionally established **patterns** for putting together symbolic assemblies. As viewed in CG, these patterns are themselves symbolic assemblies, precisely analogous to the complex expressions they characterize except for being schematic rather than specific. Since they are both constructions and schematic, they are naturally called **constructional schemas**. They are acquired through a process of **schematization**, being abstracted from occurring expressions as skeletal representations of shared organizational features. Once learned, a schema serves as a template for dealing with novel expressions on the same pattern.

The examples considered so far all instantiate a basic compounding pattern of English. The constructional schema describing that pattern is sketched in figure 6.6. Apart from the greater schematicity of semantic and phonological elements, this diagram is just the same as figure 6.3. At the phonological pole, it simply refers to words (not to *jar* and *lid* in particular). Semantically, the component and composite structures are equally schematic: they merely profile things (which makes them nouns). The only further specification—general enough to be almost vacuous—is that the thing profiled by the second component is somehow associated with some other thing. A correspondence identifies this associated entity with the one profiled by the first component.

Learned by exposure to innumerable compounds of this sort (*toothbrush, alarm clock, pear tree, peanut butter, tablespoon, baby sitter, belly button, can opener, cowboy, fingernail, pie crust, ski-plane, birthday party, football,* etc.), this constructional

---

[6] Describing the semantic poles of *lid factory jar* and *jar factory lid* (by means of diagrams analogous to fig. 6.5) is left as an exercise for the reader.

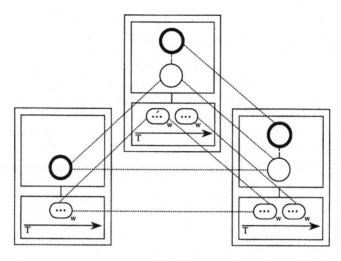

FIGURE 6.6

schema guides the formation and interpretation of new ones.[7] We noted previously that certain features of these composite expressions are not apparent from just the component structures and the correspondences connecting them: from *jar* and *lid* alone, one could not know that the compound as a whole profiles the lid rather than the jar, or that the first word bears primary stress: *jár lid*. These features are quite regular, however. Rather than being idiosyncrasies of this one expression, they are characteristic of the general compounding pattern. The pattern itself specifies that the first component bears stress (*tóothbrush, alárm clock, péar tree,* etc.) and that the second component determines profiling (thus a *toothbrush* is a kind of brush, an *alarm clock* a kind of clock, and so on). Accordingly, these specifications are incorporated in the constructional schema the expressions all instantiate.

Can we say, then, that *jar lid* is compositional? Are its composite form and meaning predictable from the components *jar* and *lid*? That depends on what is presumed available as the basis for prediction. Since composition is more than just summation, the component structures alone are insufficient; the basis for prediction also has to include a conventionally established compositional pattern. The issue of compositionality must therefore be formulated in terms of whether the composite structure derives from component structures in the manner specified by a constructional schema. By this definition, *jar lid* approximates full compositionality.[8] In CG, of course, compositionality is claimed to be a matter of degree. If *jar lid* and *tabletop* come close to being fully compositional, the same cannot be said for *laptop*, whose

[7] It is not important that certain compounds are written as single words, others as two words, and still others as words separated by hyphens. This is simply a matter of orthographic practice that does not reliably correlate with actual phonological differences.

[8] *Jar lid* is arguably not quite fully compositional because the constructional schema does not guarantee that the association between jar and lid will be the obvious one of the lid serving as cover for the jar. Conceivably, for example, *jar lid* could be interpreted as a lid decorated with the picture of a jar.

expected meaning (roughly 'top of lap') is related only metonymically to its actual meaning ('portable computer'). At the extreme, there may be no connection at all between component and composite meanings. The meanings of *under* and *stand*, for example, play no apparent role in the composite meaning of *understand*. Though morphologically complex, this verb is semantically unanalyzable (§3.2.2).

Discrepancies between an expression's expected meaning and its actual meaning arise because the component structures and constructional schema are not the only resources available in creating or understanding it. Also available for exploitation are general knowledge, apprehension of the context, and imaginative capacities like metaphor, metonymy, fictivity, and blending. Their effect can range from the minor one of merely supplementing the contributions of component structures, to more substantial adjustments like metonymic shift (§3.3.1), all the way to cases where the composite conception is drastically different from either component. As a consequence, most expressions are only partially compositional, their actual meaning diverging in some respect from anything derivable by strictly compositional means. Normally, though, the compositional meaning does have a major part in determining the actual semantic value, and for many purposes discrepancies can often be ignored. Despite their limitations, therefore, composition and compositional patterns have to be a central focus of linguistic investigation. It is thus the compositional aspects of meaning that primarily concern us in this chapter and the next.

In accordance with the standard view that syntax is autonomous (§1.2.1), linguists generally make a clear-cut distinction between patterns of grammatical composition ("rules of grammar") and patterns of semantic composition ("rules of semantic interpretation"). CG, on the other hand, views grammar as symbolic in nature and therefore meaningful. It thus proposes a fundamentally different organization, where grammar (along with lexicon) consists solely of symbolic assemblies. On this account, patterns of grammatical composition are characterized by schematic assemblies, i.e. constructional schemas (like fig. 6.6). Patterns of semantic composition are simply the semantic poles of those assemblies. Hence they are not distinct from grammar, but an inherent and indispensable facet of it.

6.2.2 Categorization of Expressions

A constructional schema invoked for producing or understanding an expression participates in a categorizing relationship with that expression. If the latter fully conforms to the schema's specifications, so that it fully **instantiates** the schema, the relationship is one of **elaboration**: [SCHEMA] → [EXPRESSION]. If there is some conflict in their specifications, the relationship is one of **extension**: [SCHEMA] ---> [EXPRESSION]. In either case, the categorization constitutes the expression's interpretation with respect to established linguistic convention, as embodied in the schema. An elaborative relationship represents a judgment of conventionality (often referred to as "grammaticality"). While an expression that conflicts with a schema is to that extent nonconventional ("ungrammatical"), this need not be grounds for stigma. The pleasures of innovation and the pressures of actual language use are such that we are always pushing the envelope of established convention. Thus a certain measure of nonconventionality is usual and readily accepted.

By way of illustration, *jar lid* conforms to the compounding pattern and therefore elaborates the constructional schema describing it. This categorizing relationship, involving the entire assemblies in figures 6.3 and 6.6, is shown in figure 6.7. Of course, this overall configuration is itself a kind of symbolic assembly, pertaining to a different dimension of linguistic organization. Internally, both schematic assemblies (constructional schemas) and specific ones (expressions) describe the combination of simpler symbolic structures to form one of greater complexity. Such relationships—those internal to constructions—are traditionally labeled **syntagmatic**. The term is used in contrast to **paradigmatic**, which pertains to relationships of categorization. Paradigmatic relationships hold between schemas and their various instantiations and are thus external to constructions.[9]

While all the details in figure 6.7 are descriptively important, we can often get by with less cumbersome representations. In one abbreviatory format, the same

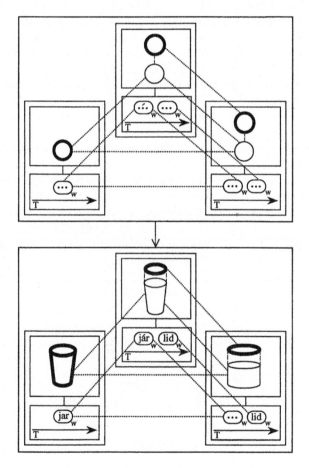

FIGURE 6.7

[9] Hence all constructions are symbolic assemblies, but not conversely, since the latter include both syntagmatic and paradigmatic relationships.

assembly is sketched in figure 6.8. The constructional schema's component and composite structures are given as N_1, N_2, and N_3 (since each profiles a thing and is thus a noun). There is no indication of correspondences, as corresponding elements are not represented individually. Relationships of categorization are, however, shown, both within constructions and between them. Within both the constructional schema and the instantiating expression, the first and second component structures categorize the composite structure in relationships of extension and elaboration, respectively (cf. fig. 6.4). These relationships are syntagmatic. In the paradigmatic plane, the entire assembly constituting the constructional schema categorizes the entire assembly constituting the expression. This global categorizing relationship resolves itself into local ones, whereby the component and composite structures of the schema categorize those of *jar lid*.

If we adopt instead a formulaic representation, where the composite structure is left implicit, the global categorization can be given as follows: $[[N_1] - [N_2]] \rightarrow$ $[[[JAR]/[jar]] - [[LID]/[lid]]]$. This global relationship comprises the local categorizations $[N_1] \rightarrow [[JAR]/[jar]]$, $[N_2] \rightarrow [[LID]/[lid]]$, and $[N_3] \rightarrow [[JAR\ LID]/[jar\ lid]]$. Of course, any of these can further be resolved into categorizing relationships at the semantic and phonological poles. For instance, if N_1 is represented as $[[THING]/$ $[\ldots]]$ (the noun schema), the first local categorization decomposes into $[THING] \rightarrow$ $[JAR]$ plus $[\ldots] \rightarrow [jar]$.

When the composite structure instantiates the same grammatical category as a component structure, it may be possible for the former to function as a component structure in the same construction, at a higher level of organization. English commonly exploits this potential with respect to the first element of the basic compounding pattern: since the composite expression *jar lid* is a noun, it can function as the first component of the higher-order compound *jar lid factory*. Figure 6.9 shows that the same constructional schema categorizes the compounds at both levels of organization.[10] In principle, we can continue indefinitely, using each successive composite structure as the first element of another compound: the owner of a *jar lid factory* is a *jar lid factory owner*; a number of such owners may form a *jar lid factory owner association*; if there are many such associations, it may be necessary to assemble a *jar lid factory owner association list*; someone who does so is a *jar lid factory owner*

FIGURE 6.8

---

[10] To handle this and other cases, the constructional schema must actually be slightly more general than the version sketched in fig. 6.6. In particular, it must allow the possibility for either component structure to consist of multiple words instead of just a single word.

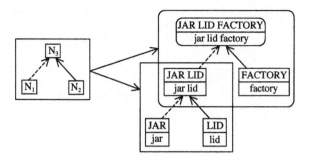

FIGURE 6.9

association list compiler; and so on for as long as imagination permits. While this is hardly the best example, it illustrates the general point that a limited set of constructional schemas (in this case just one) can sanction an open-ended set of potential instantiating expressions.

In practice, of course, there quickly comes a point where such compounds are too specialized and unwieldy to be very useful. (When is the last time you needed to refer to someone who compiles lists of associations of owners of factories making lids for jars?) English compounds of this sort seldom go beyond two levels of organization, and most of those established as lexical units exhibit just one. Thus, while *jar lid* is to some extent familiar and conventional, *jar lid factory* is certainly not. This difference in degree of entrenchment and conventionalization is represented in figure 6.9 by the boxes enclosing the two constructions. When it seems relevant to make the distinction, boxes with rounded corners are used for novel structures, regular boxes for those with the status of conventional units.

Two-level compounds are quite common in English, however, and a fair number are established as fixed expressions (e.g. *baseball bat, toothpaste tube, birthday party, pancake batter, football helmet, laptop user*). Among the conventional units of the language, we must therefore recognize a two-level compounding pattern, shown on the left in figure 6.10. The constructional schema representing this pattern incorporates two instances of the basic schema, where the composite structure of one instance functions as the first component of the other. The conventional basis for a form like *jar lid factory* is thus not limited to the individual elements and the single-level constructions bracketed in figure 6.9—in using this complex expression, a speaker follows the established precedent of embedding one compound as the first component of a higher-level compound. To the extent that complex expressions conform to patterns of composition encompassing multiple levels of organization, we can posit constructional schemas to capture these regularities. In principle, constructional schemas, like expressions, can exhibit any degree of symbolic complexity.

Let me end this section on a cautionary note. Every notation has its limitations and is bound to be misleading in some respect. One potentially misleading aspect of the present diagrams is the representation of schemas and their instantiations (and more generally, categorizing structures and the targets of categorization) as separate,

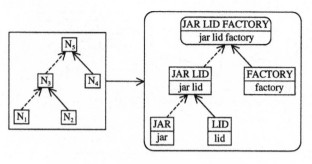

FIGURE 6.10

nonoverlapping boxes. While this is necessary for analytical purposes, such elements should not be thought of as discrete, as independent, or as bounded containers stored in different parts of the brain. Indeed, they are not "stored" as such, but reside in patterns of neural processing. It is thus implausible to suppose that schemas are either self-contained or wholly distinct from their instantiations. They are better seen as being **immanent** in their instantiations (i.e. as "lying within" them). What I mean by this is that schemas reside in certain aspects of the processing activity in which their instantiations reside.

6.3 Unipolar vs. Bipolar Organization

The conventional units posited in CG are restricted by the content requirement (§1.3.4) to semantic, phonological, and symbolic structures. A symbolic structure reduces to the pairing of a semantic and a phonological structure (its two poles). Linked together in assemblies, symbolic structures provide a seamless account of lexicon, morphology, and syntax. In this way, CG achieves a natural, restrictive, and unified conception of linguistic organization that directly reflects the semiological function of language: permitting meanings to be symbolized by sounds.

If every symbolic structure comprises a semantic structure and a phonological structure, the converse fails to hold. It is not the case that every semantic or phonological structure directly participates in a symbolic relationship. For both semantics and phonology, we have to distinguish two kinds of structures and dimensions of organization: those based on symbolic considerations (hence **bipolar**) and those whose basis is purely semantic or phonological (**unipolar**).

6.3.1 Delimitation of Structures

The phonological units of a language are not limited to those which serve as the phonological poles of symbolic structures. A large number of units must be recognized whose role is purely phonological—they contribute to the formation of phonological structures but do not themselves participate in symbolizing relationships. Examples of such units are individual sounds ([p], [ɪ], [k], [e], [n], etc.), as well as permitted sound combinations like consonant clusters ([bl], [mp], [str]) and syllables ([pɪk], [bley], [nɪks]). Also included are phonological sche-mas representing such abstract entities as classes of sounds ([VOICELESS STOP], [HIGH FRONT VOWEL]), permitted syllable types ([CV], [CCVC]), and accent patterns (e.g. [(... ɷσ)$_w$], whereby stress falls on the penultimate syllable of a word).

Consider *picnics*, for example. On purely phonological grounds, we can describe it as a word of two syllables, with accent on the first: ((pík)$_σ$ (nɪks)$_σ$)$_w$. Each syllable instantiates a syllable schema ([CVC] and [CVCC]), consists of a series of sounds, which belong to various classes, and so on. Note that a linguist could arrive at this description without knowing anything about the word's meaning or grammatical analysis. The structural elements in question are posited on a strictly phonological basis, with no reference to symbolic relationships or the semantic pole. Such ele-ments are said to be **unipolar**, since just a single pole figures in their delimitation and characterization.

The word *picnics* is thus divisible on unipolar grounds into the major parts *pic* and *nics*. But obviously, it can also be analyzed into the basic elements *picnic* and *s*. Here, though, the rationale is nonphonological. While *picnic* and *s* do comprise phonological structures, the only reason for dividing the form into these two parts pertains to meaning: these are the parts that symbolize the semantic components [PICNIC] and [PLURAL]. It is by virtue of functioning as the phonological poles of symbolic units that these portions of the word are recognized as being structurally significant. Since two poles figure in their delimitation and characterization, these elements are said to be **bipolar**.

At the phonological pole, we can thus distinguish between unipolar and bipolar organization, depending on whether structural elements are delimited on the basis of strictly phonological considerations (like *pic* and *nics*) or in terms of their symbol-izing function (*picnic* and *s*). There is a definite tendency for phonological structures with bipolar motivation to coincide with those having unipolar motivation.[11] Yet, since unipolar and bipolar phonological structures have different functions and dif-ferent rationales, this tendency is easily overridden. Also, a phonological structure that does participate in a symbolizing relationship does not necessarily do so in all its occurrences. The syllable [pɪk], for example, has bipolar motivation in *pick*, but not as part of *picnics* or *picture*. Likewise, [nɪks] has symbolizing function in *nix*, *nicks*, and *Nick's*, but not as part of *Phoenix*. In and of themselves, syllables are unipolar structures, so their exploitation for symbolic purposes is purely contingent. Thus, while [bley] occurs as a syllable in *blatant*, *blazon*, and *blazing*, it does not itself contribute to their meanings (i.e. it is not a morpheme).

The distinction between unipolar and bipolar organization has to be made at the semantic pole as well. Semantic structures with bipolar motivation are those which directly participate in symbolic relationships (functioning as the semantic poles of symbolic structures). On the other hand, semantic structures have unipolar motivation

---

[11] They coincide in the case of *toothless*, *unhelpful*, *jar lid*, and indeed, in most multiword expressions. Their coincidence no doubt facilitates language processing.

when they are conventionally exploited in constructing linguistic meanings but lack individual symbolization.[12] An example is the notion of an immediate part, i.e. the relationship between two successive levels in a whole-part hierarchy (fig. 3.3). For instance, the head is an immediate part of the body, the ears are immediate parts of the head, and so on. This relationship plays a small but significant role in the structure of English. Notably, it provides the associative link between N_1 and N_2 in many noun compounds: *fingernail*, *tabletop*, *tree branch*, *bicycle seat*, *window pane*, *weekend*, etc. When the whole-part relationship is nonimmediate, such a compound is generally infelicitous; we say *ear lobe*, *doorknob*, and *book chapter* but not **head lobe*, **house knob*, or **book paragraph*. Yet the notion of whole-part immediacy is not specifically symbolized in these expressions. It remains covert, despite its role in this and other patterns.

6.3.2 Dimensions of Composition

Being symbolic in nature, lexicon and grammar are primarily concerned with bipolar organization. Aspects of this organization include both minimal symbolic structures and their arrangement in symbolic assemblies of any degree of complexity. At either pole, it subsumes not only the ultimate component structures but also the composite structures at every level of organization. The disparity between unipolar and bipolar organization becomes most apparent when we consider the compositional path these structures define, the stepping-stones for arriving at the composite form and meaning of a symbolically complex expression.

This disparity starts with morphemes, which are symbolically minimal in the sense that they cannot be decomposed into smaller symbolic elements. Though mininal from a bipolar standpoint, by virtue of participating in an irreducible symbolic relationship, a morpheme's semantic and phonological poles are usually complex in unipolar terms. Phonologically, for example, *picnic* consists of two syllables, each comprising three sound segments, but only as a whole does this complex structure enter into a symbolic relationship. The semantic pole of *picnic* is also quite elaborate, involving numerous conceptions (of a social event, of certain kinds of food, of eating outdoors in a natural setting, etc.) none of which is symbolized individually. A major source of the great expressive power of language lies precisely in the fact that symbolizing structures are not limited to individual sounds (for this would imply a restricted inventory) and that one such structure can evoke a conceptualization of indefinite complexity.

In symbolically complex expressions, the disparity pertains to paths of semantic or phonological composition. What can we identify as a path of composition in the case of unipolar structure? The most obvious candidate is the combination of smaller elements into larger and larger ones. At the phonological pole, segments are grouped

---

[12] The distinction between unipolar and bipolar organization is not equivalent to the one drawn between phonetics and phonology or between conceptualization and semantics. Phonology and semantics represent the conventional exploitation of general phonetic and conceptual potential in accordance with the structure of a language. Unipolar and bipolar organization are two aspects of this **linguistic** structure, at each pole.

into syllables, syllables into words, and words into phrases.[13] An evident semantic analog is the conception of constitutive entities forming groups at successively higher levels of organization. In American professional football, for example, players form teams, which are grouped as divisions, which make up conferences, which constitute a league. There are other natural ways of building up progressively "larger" conceptions. We often build up the conception of a complex path by invoking its segments one at a time in proper sequence (imagine arranging flights from San Diego to Kansas City to Chicago to Milwaukee). Another natural progression leads through a whole-part hierarchy (e.g. from body to leg to knee), where each conceived entity provides the configuration required to conceptualize the next, which thus incorporates it.

At the semantic pole, the composition of bipolar elements often goes against the grain of natural, unipolar paths such as these. The description of a journey, for instance, need not reflect its inherent, chain-like sequencing. In contrast to (1)(a), which presents it iconically, (1)(b) imposes conceptual groupings on the cities that conflict with their sequence of access in the composite conception.

(1)   (a) *I traveled from San Diego to Kansas City to Chicago to Milwaukee.*

(b) *I traveled between San Diego and Milwaukee via Chicago and Kansas City.*

A second example pertains to the combination of smaller elements into larger ones. In its bipolar structure, a plural noun reflects the organization intrinsic to the conception of constitutive entities forming a group. The compositional path from *pea* to *peas* follows the natural conceptual progression from a single particle to a mass of such particles. However, this coalignment of paths is not observed in the case of *corn*. While the masses designated by *peas* and *corn* are quite analogous in unipolar terms, each comprising particles of roughly comparable size, their bipolar paths proceed in opposite directions. For *peas*, the path of composition goes from particle (*pea*) to mass (*peas*), but *corn* takes the mass as its starting point. To speak of a single particle, we resort to a composite expression with *corn* as one component—for example, *corn kernel*. The difference between unipolar and bipolar organization is also apparent from cases where different compositional paths lead to composite conceptions that—in unipolar terms—are essentially the same. The sentences in (1) are one illustration. Or consider *corn kernel* vs. *kernel of corn*. Unlike the former, the latter specifically evokes the notion 'intrinsic relationship' as one step in its compositional path. Individual symbolization by *of* serves to reinforce this facet of the composite conception (GC: ch. 3).[14]

With respect to phonological composition, the disparity between unipolar and bipolar organization was already shown with *picnics*. The unipolar compositional

---

[13] A fuller description would recognize other kinds of structures and dimensions of unipolar phonological organization (e.g. prosody). Also, the hierarchy does not imply any claims about the order in which structures emerge in language development or are accessed in linguistic processing.

[14] Providing a more elaborate example is the trio of expressions *triangle*, *three-sided polygon*, and *three-angled polygon*. Ultimately they all lead to the same composite conception (fig. 1.1(b)), but they reach it through very different paths.

path starts with segments, continues with the syllables *pic* and *nics* as intermediate stepping-stones, and terminates with the composite form, the full word *picnics*.[15] By contrast, the bipolar path arrives at the same composite form in just a single step, starting from the irreducible symbolizing structures *picnic* and *s*. The disparity is further evident from cases where two different paths of symbolic composition yield identical composite forms (indistinguishable in regard to intrinsically phonological properties like sound segments and their grouping into syllables). For example, *tolled* and *told* are pronounced exactly alike. In unipolar terms, each is a word consisting of a single syllable: $((towld)_\sigma)_w$. Yet their phonological composition is quite different in bipolar terms. Whereas *tolled* decomposes straightforwardly into *toll* plus *-ed*, the symbolic organization of *told* is more abstract. One component is *tell*, which is not directly observable as part of *told*. The other component—the symbolization of past tense—does not consist of just the ending *-d*, but of that together with the contrast between the vocalic nucleus [ow] and the vowel [ɛ] that would otherwise appear. What marks the past tense in this form is the overall discrepancy between the component structure $((t\varepsilon l)_\sigma)_w$ and the composite structure $((towld)_\sigma)_w$.

This illustrates an important general point—namely, that bipolar structures are more varied in nature and often more abstract than unipolar ones. In performing their symbolizing function, bipolar structures are not limited to providing explicit phonological "substance" of their own but may also reside in "operations" on the substance provided by another component. The modification effected on this component—the discrepancy between the composite form and what its form would otherwise be—may itself constitute a symbolizing structure.[16] The verb *sat*, for instance, does not divide naturally into a part meaning [SIT] and a part meaning [PAST] (the way *tolled* divides into *toll* plus *-ed*). We do not isolate [s...t] as the symbolization of [SIT], nor is [PAST] symbolized by the vowel [æ] per se. What we want to say, instead, is that [sæt] consists morphologically of [sɪt] plus a pattern of vowel modification: $[[... \text{ɪ} ...] ---> [... \text{ æ } ...]]$. The phonological pole of *sat* is thus as sketched in figure 6.11(a). This variant of the past-tense marker (which also occurs in *sang*, *began*, *swam*, *rang*, and *spat*) makes schematic reference to both the stem and the composite form: $[... \text{ɪ} ...]$ and $[... \text{ æ } ...]$. These schematic elements respectively categorize [sɪt] and [sæt], which elaborate them. The categorizations shown (also correspondences, which are not shown) serve to link these symbolizing structures in a phonological assembly, the phonological pole of a symbolic assembly.

An analogous assembly, for *rose* (the past tense of *rise*), is given in figure 6.11(b). Compare this to diagram (c), representing the phonological pole of the homophonous noun. As unipolar structures, their composite forms are precisely the same, but viewed

---

[15] Like any other, the path metaphor has its limitations. It should not be taken as implying that the stepping-stones are arranged in strictly linear fashion, since at any level two or more stepping-stones must be accessed simultaneously in order to reach the next. This metaphor captures the directionality of composition (from categorizing structures to successive targets of categorization) but not the notion of convergence from multiple sources.

[16] The modification may consist of altering sound segments, changing their order, deleting them, adding or changing prosodic features (like stress and tone), or any combination of these (FCG1: §9.1.3). Such modifications generally symbolize highly schematic meanings (those characteristic of "grammatical" elements).

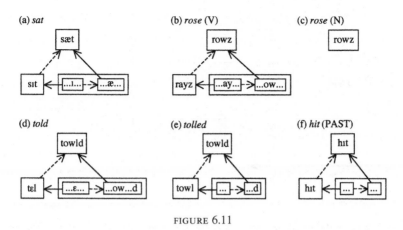

FIGURE 6.11

in bipolar terms the path to [rowz] leads through [rayz] in the case of the verb, but reaches it directly in the case of the noun.[17] Diagrams (d) and (e) show the contrasting bipolar paths of *told* and *tolled*, whose composite forms are likewise indistinguishable. The notation for *tolled* is meant to indicate that affixation can be regarded as a special case of a modifying operation, that where the only modification consists in the addition of segments at the beginning or end of a stem. Another special case is zero modification, illustrated by the past-tense form of *hit*. At the extreme, when there is no discrepancy between a component structure and the composite structure, the modification effected by the other component amounts to an identity mapping.

We can usefully think of unipolar and bipolar composition as proceeding along two different axes. This is shown for *picnics* in figure 6.12, where horizontal and vertical arrows respectively indicate these two dimensions of phonological organization. Along the vertical axis, the symbolically delimited components *picnic* and *s* categorize the composite form *picnics*. In the manner of figure 6.11(e), the plural suffix -*s* effects the modification of a schematically specified stem by adding [s] as its final segment. Each of these structures—internally—can also be analyzed in unipolar terms; this involves their segmental composition, the grouping of segments into syllables and of syllables into a word. Each structure is thus complex from the unipolar standpoint. For the component structure *picnic* and the composite structure *picnics*, this unipolar composition is partially represented along the horizontal axis: the word *picnic* decomposes into $(pik)_\sigma$ and $(nik)_\sigma$, and *picnics* into $(pik)_\sigma$ and $(niks)_\sigma$. Of course, each of these syllables further decomposes into segments.

Thus, as bipolar composition proceeds from component to composite structures at successively "higher" levels of organization, each structure along the compositional

---

[17] We can still speak of a compositional path—it is simply degenerate. In the case of a nondegenerate path, the ultimate composite structure is the one that is actually pronounced. Though tacit, other structures along the path represent a secondary aspect of the expression's phonological value. In this way, the noun *rose* and the verb *rose* are phonologically distinct, just as *pork* and *pig meat* are semantically distinct by virtue of reaching the same composite conception by alternate routes.

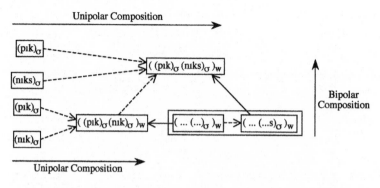

FIGURE 6.12

path is individually configured in unipolar terms in accordance with the "tactic" patterns of the language. That is, each is structured internally as specified by schemas describing conventionally permitted elements and combinations of elements (like segments, syllables, and words). This structuring need not be consistent from one level to the next, since the addition of another symbolizing element can trigger a reconfiguring of the unipolar structure. A reconfiguration of this sort is apparent in figure 6.12 from the discrepant syllabic organization of *picnic* and *picnics*. Specifically, the segment sequence [nɪk] constitutes an entire syllable in the former but not in the latter, where it is only a portion of (nɪks)$_\sigma$. The addition of final [s] to symbolize pluralization induces an alternate syllabification at the composite-structure level.

6.3.3 The Nonproblem of Mismatch

By clearly recognizing the distinction between unipolar and bipolar organization, CG reveals the straightforward nature of phenomena often considered problematic. Consider a possessive phrase like *the king of Denmark's castle*. The apparent problem it poses concerns the placement of the possessive ending *'s*, which shows up on *Denmark* even though the actual possessor of the castle is the king. Hence there seems to be a "mismatch" between the form of the expression and what it actually means. Another sort of example involves the definite article in expressions like *the big dog*. In normal speech, *the* loses its phonological independence and cliticizes (i.e. loosely attaches) to the following word: *th'big dog*. Once more, we find an evident mismatch between form and meaning: whereas *the* is phonologically associated with *big*, semantically it pertains to the dog.

There is no real problem, however. The apparent mismatches are simply a manifestation of unipolar and bipolar composition representing two different axes of phonological structure. In fact, the examples cited differ only in degree from a case like *picnics* (not usually considered problematic). We see in figure 6.12 that, in strictly phonological terms, the plural ending *-s* specifically combines with *nic* to produce the augmented syllable *nics*. This aspect of unipolar organization is quite consistent with the fact that, for purposes of semantics and grammar, plural *-s* combines with *picnic* as a whole. Delimited by symbolic considerations, these elements are integrated along the "vertical" axis of bipolar composition. In particular, *picnic* elaborates the schematic stem invoked by the plural morpheme, which modifies it by adding [s] as the final segment. The incorporation of [s] in the stem's final syllable is then a consequence of the structure at each level being configured in accordance with general unipolar patterns.

Analogously, the symbolic components of *the king of Denmark's* are unproblematically identified as *the king of Denmark* and *'s*, despite their disparity in size (a matter of unipolar structure). Their bipolar integration instantiates a pattern whereby *'s* is added to the final word of the possessor nominal. The phonological pole of this construction is sketched in figure 6.13(a).[18] For *th'big dog* we can likewise take the symbolic components to be the ones expected on semantic and syntactic grounds: *the* and *big dog*. The apparent mismatch results from the article's unipolar characterization as a clitic attaching to the immediately following word, even when the other component is a multiword expression. If only for sake of discussion, I describe a clitic as an element that combines with a word to form a larger structure also analyzed as a word. The phonological pole of *th'big dog* is then as shown in diagram (b).

The composition observed in a unipolar hierarchy (segment > syllable > word > etc.) is basically additive in nature. At each level, phonological elements of roughly comparable size combine to form a larger structure where they are still evident with only minimal distortion. Bipolar composition can also have this character. It is often effected simply by juxtaposing structures roughly equal in size and complexity, as in *jar lid* (fig. 6.2(b)). In general, though, bipolar composition is more flexible and more abstract. Simple juxtaposition is not the only kind of operation deriving composite phonological structures from component structures. The components are often quite

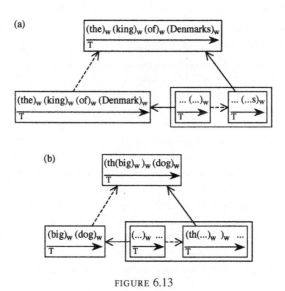

FIGURE 6.13

---

[18] For convenience, orthography is used and syllabification is omitted. To make it clear that the order of words is relevant, I have reintroduced the arrow representing speech time (T). This dimension of phonological space is always present even when not explicitly shown.

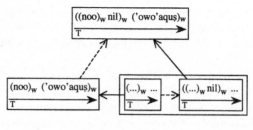

FIGURE 6.14

disparate in size, complexity, or type, and they may not be discernible in undistorted form at the composite-structure level. *Sit*, for example, is only partially evident in *sat*.

Such disparities and distortions are not confined to morphology. Consider a syntactic example from Luiseño.[19] It is typical in a Luiseño clause for a clitic to occur following the initial word or phrase. In (2), the clitic *=nil* appears following the first word of a clause that would otherwise have the form *Noo 'owo'aquș* (which is also possible). The clitic offers a basic indication of how the clausal process and its trajector relate to the speech situation. Here it specifies that the trajector is first-person singular (1s) and that the profiled process lies in the past. In this case (though not always) the information turns out to be redundant, since the same information is supplied by the subject pronoun *noo* 'I' and the past durative suffix *-quș*.

(2) *Noo=nil   'owo'a-quș.* 'I was working.'

    I=1s:PAST   work-PAST:DUR

How should we describe this construction? Semantically and grammatically, we want to say that the two component structures are the basic clause *noo 'owo'aquș* and the clitic *=nil*, which invokes a clause schematically. Phonologically, though, the clitic appears on the subject pronoun. Stated more generally, the clitic occurs **inside** the clause, following whatever happens to be the first word or phrase. There seems to be a mismatch, where the clitic combines phonologically with an element other than the one it pertains to semantically and combines with grammatically. It should now be clear, however, that this is a false impression which only arises by failing to properly distinguish unipolar and bipolar organization. The component structures are indeed *noo 'owo'aquș* and *=nil*, integrated as shown in figure 6.14. But while *=nil* combines with an entire clause in bipolar terms, the combinatory operation consists in placing it after the initial word, so it winds up inside the clause in terms of unipolar organization. With respect to their overt segmental content, the two component structures are drastically different in size, and instead of their being juxtaposed, one is incorporated in the other. As a consequence, the clausal component *noo 'owo'aquș* is not preserved without distortion at the composite-structure level, since the clitic interrupts it. The construction is nonetheless straightforwardly described in CG.

---

[19] Luiseño is a Native American language, formerly spoken in southern California, belonging to the Uto-Aztecan family.

7

Constructions

Descriptive Factors

Describing the grammar of a language consists primarily of describing its constructions. To understand grammar in any depth, we must therefore look at constructions in more detail. The following sections examine four basic factors in their description: **correspondences**, **profiling**, **elaboration**, and **constituency**. While the phonological pole will mostly be ignored (doubtless to your relief), bear in mind that the semantic structures under discussion represent just one pole of **symbolic** assemblies.

7.1 Correspondences

Of the four descriptive factors to be considered, correspondences are perhaps the most fundamental. They indicate how component and composite structures fit together in a coherent assembly (as opposed to being an arbitrary collection of unrelated elements). At the semantic pole, they specify the **conceptual overlap** between component structures, thus providing the basis for their integration. They also specify how each component structure overlaps with the composite structure, thereby indicating what it contributes to the unified conception that emerges. Viewed from the opposite perspective, these "vertical" correspondences represent the selection of certain facets of the composite conception for individual symbolization by component structures.

A word about notation. The dotted lines employed here for correspondences are at best a rather blunt descriptive instrument. Though sufficient for present purposes, they (and the diagrams containing them) lack formal precision. To properly understand their import, an intelligent user has to rely on certain tacit but natural principles of interpretation. For example, the correspondence line in figure 6.2(a) is meant to indicate that the jar as a whole is identified with the schematic container as a whole. You probably had no trouble interpreting it in this fashion, even though the line, in fact, connects just the side of the jar and the side of the container (and indeed, just particular locations on each). There is also a certain arbitrariness in how many correspondences are explicitly shown. For instance, the global correspondence in 6.2(a) could perfectly well be resolved into any number of local correspondences equating various parts of the two containers (e.g. the bottoms, the sides, the openings on top). Usually the number shown is the minimum needed for proper interpretation. When it is clear how structures are supposed to overlap, correspondences may even be omitted altogether (as they were in figs. 6.11 to 6.14).

7.1.1 Multiple Correspondences

Often it suffices to indicate a single global correspondence between component-structure elements (e.g. fig. 6.5). In other constructions multiple correspondences must be posited. A correspondence line is fairly unobtrusive from a notational standpoint, yet adding one to a construction has semantic and grammatical consequences that can be quite substantial. Let us briefly consider two examples.

The first case concerns a well-known construction in French (and other Romance languages), illustrated by the sentences in (1). They describe the causation of motion, where the thing moved is part of the body. The part moved is expressed by means of a nominal consisting of a definite article plus a body-part noun. Literally, then, the sentences translate as *I raise the hand*, *She closes the eyes*, etc. In English such sentences would usually be interpreted as indicating that the body part moved belongs to some person other than the actor.[1] But in French they are normally understood to mean that the body part in question is indeed an intrinsic part of the actor's own body. The sentences do not convey this explicitly, however. Whereas English specifies the possessor by means of a pronoun like *my* or *her*, in French one merely says the equivalent of *the hand* or *the eyes*. How do speakers know that the body part belongs to the person designated by the subject?

(1) (a) *Je lève la main.*   (I raise the hand)   'I raise my hand.'

 (b) *Elle ferme les yeux.*   (she closes the eyes)   'She closes her eyes.'

 (c) *Il ouvre la bouche.*   (he opens the mouth)   'He opens his mouth.'

It must first be acknowledged that this is not the only conceivable interpretation. In the proper context, these sentences might indeed indicate that the subject acts on a part belonging to some other body. In this event they simply instantiate the general direct object construction of French, and the object happens to be some contextually identifiable body part. As a strongly favored default, however, the sentences do imply that the actor is the possessor. We can account for this by also positing for French, as a special case of the general object construction, a more specific construction that incorporates the default interpretation. The constructional schema describing the

---

[1] For instance, a therapist might say *I raise the hand* in regard to patients too weak to raise it themselves. Alternatively, the sentence might refer to the hand of a mannequin or even a disembodied hand that for some reason needs elevation.

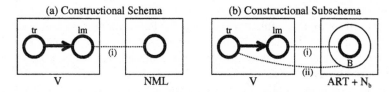

FIGURE 7.1

latter constitutes a particular, conventionally established elaboration of the schema describing the general pattern. The general schema and the more specific subschema are sketched in diagrams (a) and (b) of figure 7.1 (showing just the component structures and their integration).

The elements of the general schema are a verb (V) and an object nominal (NML). The verb profiles an interaction (represented as an arrow) between its trajector and landmark. The nominal profiles a thing. The pivotal feature of the object construction is the correspondence labeled (i), which identifies the verb's landmark with the nominal profile. All of these elements are also present in the constructional subschema, which is, however, more specific. In particular, the nominal is specifically characterized as consisting of the definite article (ART) plus a body-part noun (N_b).[2] The large circle labeled B represents the body as a whole, with respect to which the profile is a part. Another feature of this subschema—the crucial one—is correspondence (ii). This second correspondence equates the verb's trajector with the body evoked by the object nominal. It is this additional correspondence that imposes the default interpretation.

The semantic consequences of this second correspondence are seen more concretely in figure 7.2, which compares the composite structures that result from invoking the general schema and the subschema. They represent the specific expression *lever la main* 'raise the hand', which can instantiate either the general pattern or (by

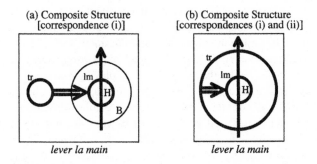

FIGURE 7.2

---

[2] This characterization takes the form of a lower level of composition (not indicated). The resulting composite structure functions as a component structure in this subschema.

default) the subpattern. The verb *lever* 'raise' profiles an event consisting of the trajector exerting force (double arrow) so that the landmark moves (single arrow) in an upward direction. The letter H abbreviates the multifaceted semantic specifications of *main* 'hand'. Though not irrelevant, the meaning of the definite article is omitted (see FCG2: §3.1.1).

Constructed in accordance with the general schema, based on correspondence (i) alone, *lever la main* merely indicates that the trajector induces the upward motion of a contextually identifiable hand. There need be no connection between the actor and the hand other than their coparticipation in this relationship. This is shown in diagram (a). Comparison with diagram (b) shows the effect of adding correspondence (ii), in accordance with the subschema. This tighter integration of verb and object yields a more compact composite conception, where the same individual serves as both actor and as host for the body part. This construction implies that the trajector induces the upward motion of his own hand.

Actually, the integration is tighter still. The default interpretation further specifies that the causal force is internally transmitted, and that the landmark moves in the manner characteristic of the body part in question. Thus (1)(a) would not be used, for instance, if the speaker were to grasp the left hand with the right and pull it upward.[3] Observe that these further specifications are not an automatic consequence of adding correspondence (ii). Strictly speaking, they represent still another correspondence, whereby the force profiled by the verb is identified with that inherent in our cognitive model of the body part in question and how we normally move it. In schematized form, all of these specifications are incorporated in the constructional subschema describing the default interpretation. They are aspects of the **constructional meaning** this schema imposes on instantiating expressions.

Also illustrating the effect of adding a correspondence are phrases like *tall giraffe*, *intelligent ape*, and *honest politician*. They consist of a noun modified by a "scalar" adjective, one attributing to its trajector a property whose presence is a matter of degree. The point at issue is that a phrase like *tall giraffe* has two very different meanings. On the one hand, it might indicate that the giraffe is tall in relation to the scale of normal human experience. At the zoo, for instance, a father might say to his child *Look at that tall giraffe!* meaning only that the giraffe is tall relative to the things usually encountered by the child. The giraffe might actually be quite small as giraffes typically go, but to the child it looms quite large. On the other hand, a *tall giraffe* may be one that is tall *for a giraffe* (the kind of giraffe that would wind up playing basketball).

The component structures of *tall giraffe* are roughly sketched in figure 7.3. Being an adjective, *tall* profiles a nonprocessual relationship whose trajector is a thing and which lacks a focused landmark. Its trajector is characterized schematically as a physical entity with a salient vertical dimension when in its canonical orientation; thus we use it with respect to vertically aligned entities like people, buildings, mountains, trees, and flagpoles (but not, say, for snakes). The arrow represents a scale measuring degree of extension along the vertical axis from a horizontal surface

---

[3] In that case one would say *Je me lève la main* (literally, 'I raise me the hand').

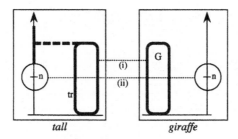

FIGURE 7.3

(usually the ground). Along this scale, the region labeled n comprises the range of values considered normal. The relationship profiled by *tall* is that of the trajector (when upright) projecting to some location beyond the scalar norm. As for the noun *giraffe*, I have basically just shown it as a thing with vertical alignment. Also shown is an arrow representing our knowledge that giraffes typically fall within a certain range (n) in regard to their height. The letter G stands for all the other specifications constituting the noun's encyclopedic meaning.

The two interpretations of *tall giraffe* do not stem from any difference in the meanings of the component structures but are, instead, a matter of how they are integrated, as seen in the diagram. Correspondence (i) represents the basic conceptual overlap defining the ADJ + N construction. If this is the only correspondence, no connection is made between the scales evoked by the adjective and by the noun. The height specified by *tall* can then be interpreted with respect to any norm that might suggest itself, the default being typical human experience. More likely, though, the adjectival norm will be identified with the characteristic height of giraffes in particular. Their identification is effected by correspondence (ii). This additional correspondence reflects a well-entrenched, conventionally established pattern for combining scalar adjectives with nouns. It is part of a constructional subschema that instantiates the schema describing the ADJ + N construction in general.

7.1.2 Redundancy and Inconsistency

Correspondence lines are a graphic indication of conceptual overlap. Component and composite structures can overlap to any extent, even completely. A case in point is the Luiseño example from the previous chapter, *Noonil 'owo'aquṣ* 'I was working'. Here the clitic =*nil* evokes no element not specified in as much or greater detail by the clausal component *noo 'owo'aquṣ*. The construction's semantic pole is roughly sketched in figure 7.4 (its phonological pole is given in figure 6.14). The clausal component profiles the specific process of working, represented as a solid arrow. Its trajector is identified by the subject pronoun *noo* as being the speaker (S), and the past durative suffix -*quṣ* places it prior to the time of speaking. The clitic =*nil* also evokes a process, but only schematically (hence the arrow representing it contains ellipses). It serves to identify the trajector as the speaker and to locate the process in the past. Thus all the basic elements of one component have counterparts in the other.

FIGURE 7.4

In particular, the specific process profiled by the clause corresponds to the schematic one profiled by the clitic.[4] This entails that the processual trajectors also correspond. The clitic, however, provides no information that is not also supplied by the clause, so when corresponding elements are superimposed to form the composite conception, the latter proves identical to the clausal component.

The clitic is thus redundant. Redundancy is not to be disparaged, for in one way or another every language makes extensive use of it. By providing the listener with extra clues, it helps ensure that a partially degraded message can still be understood. It allows the speaker to either emphasize a certain notion through repetition or to portray it from multiple perspectives. The second-position clitics of Luiseño exemplify the natural cognitive strategy of "zooming in" from general to particular. Anchored by the initial element, they "frame" the clause by introducing a schematic depiction of the profiled process, its central participant, and their relationship to the speech situation. By introducing a skeletal representation of the global situation, the clitics facilitate apprehension of the remaining clausal elements, which then flesh it out.

The redundancy afforded by grammatical elements is traditionally referred to as "agreement". The Luiseño clitics would thus be described as agreeing with the subject in person and number and with the inflected verb in tense. The traditional notion of agreement is highly problematic, however; often the "agreeing" elements have nothing to agree with or provide differing information about the entity characterized (Barlow 1992). CG takes another approach. The kinds of redundancy in question are not handled by "copying" information from one part of an expression to another, but simply as matters of multiple symbolization. That is, information about some entity is symbolized by more than one component structure within the same symbolic assembly and thus has multiple manifestations in a single complex expression. The representations of that entity (like the trajector in fig. 7.4) correspond to one another and map onto the same element in the composite conception.

---

[4] The inner boxes enclosing these processes are included just as a way of indicating that the processes participate as wholes in this correspondence.

So-called agreeing elements are therefore analyzed as making independent semantic contributions that happen to overlap with information provided elsewhere. Yet this overlap varies in extent, and sometimes the "agreeing" element is the only source of the information in question. In Luiseño, for example, a subject can be omitted, so in a sentence like (2) the clitic is the only element serving to identify the trajector. In this case each component structure evokes a highly schematic entity that the other specifies in greater detail. The clausal component *waxaam 'owo'aquṣ* evokes a schematic trajector which the clitic *=nil* identifies as the speaker. Conversely, the clitic evokes a schematic process which the clause identifies as that of working. When pieced together, the two component structures afford a full characterization of the profiled event.

(2)   *Waxaam=nil*   *'owo'a-quṣ*   'Yesterday I was working.'

yesterday=1s:PAST   work-PAST:DUR

When elements of two component structures correspond, they each correspond to the same composite-structure element, and each component structure provides some information about it. Often one characterization is schematic, the other specific. Usually the two are consistent and in some way complementary. But nothing guarantees this. Rather than complementing one another, two characterizations may be exactly equivalent, as for the trajector in the case of *noo* and *=nil* in *Noonil 'owo'aquṣ*. Nor does any divine or linguistic force prevent two characterizations from being inconsistent. For instance, a speaker of Luiseño might produce a sentence like (3), whether from inattention, some special motive, or sheer perversity. Here the subject pronoun and the clitic make contradictory specifications concerning the trajector: whereas *noo* describes it as first-person singular ('I'), the clitic *=chamil* specifies first-person plural ('we'). This is not a good sentence of Luiseño. But what exactly is the import of "good"?

(3)   **Waxaam=chamil   noo   'owo'a-quṣ*   'Yesterday {I/we} {was/were} working.'

yesterday=1p:PAST   I   work-PAST:DUR

Linguists mark such expressions with an asterisk and describe them as "ungrammatical" or "ill-formed". In most expressions so labeled, the problem turns out to be semantic inconsistency. Now inconsistency (like redundancy) has its uses. One can imagine special circumstances where a sentence like (3) might actually be employed to good effect.[5] But as they evolve through usage, the conventions of a language are shaped for communicative efficiency in typical situations, so in general they avoid the salient presentation of blatantly contradictory specifications. The conventions of Luiseño naturally reflect the usual situation of wanting to characterize the clausal trajector in a single, consistent manner. There are constructional schemas describing clauses in which a subject and a clitic are compatible in regard to the person and

---

[5] For instance, it might allow a speaker to subtly acknowledge having the psychiatric disorder of multiple personalities.

number of the trajector. There are none for cases where they are incompatible. A sentence like (3) is thus perceived as nonconventional ("ungrammatical") because it conflicts with the only schemas available to sanction it.

7.1.3 A Nonargument for Autonomy

Conformity to relevant constructional schemas does not itself guarantee that an expression is internally consistent semantically. A famous example is (4):

(4)   *Colorless green ideas sleep furiously.*

Chomsky (1957: 15) cited this sentence in arguing for the **autonomy** of syntax (§1.2.1)—that is, its independence from meaning. He claimed that (4) is perfectly well-formed grammatically despite its semantic incoherence. In terms of its grammar, (4) is precisely analogous to (5)(a). Conversely, we see from (5)(b) that a semantically impeccable expression can nonetheless be completely ungrammatical:

(5)   (a) *Friendly young dogs bark harmlessly.*

    (b) **Dogs harmlessly young bark friendly.* [with the meaning of (5)(a)]

It was thus concluded that grammar is properly described without essential reference to meaning.

Critics of the autonomy thesis have tried to deny that (4) is semantically anomalous. They correctly point out that speakers try to make sense of seemingly incoherent expressions, and that this is not impossible, even in such extreme examples. For instance, *green* could be interpreted as meaning 'new, unproven, immature' (cf. *greenhorn, green banana*), and *colorless* as 'plain, uninteresting' (cf. *colorless personality*). Likewise, *sleep furiously* might conceivably describe a person clinging so tenaciously to sleep that all attempts to wake him are futile. One could then construe the sentence metaphorically as indicating that uninteresting new ideas remain dormant and resist all efforts to make them catch on.

I believe, however, that such criticisms are beside the point. Chomsky is certainly correct that a sentence like (4) is semantically anomalous if each word is given its normal, default interpretation. And while the words do not then fit together to yield a coherent meaning, we can nonetheless recognize the sentence as being put together in accordance with regular syntactic patterns. Where Chomsky goes wrong is in claiming that this proves the autonomy of grammar. We can see this by observing that the facts are readily accommodated in CG, which—as a symbolic account of grammar—represents the antithesis of the autonomy thesis.

The semantic sins committed in (4) are violations of **selectional restrictions**. *Green*, for instance, selects for the noun it modifies some physical entity capable of exhibiting color, but *ideas* fails to satisfy this restriction. It is thus sufficient to examine a single case of this sort (rather than tackling (4) in all its complexity). Consider the phrase *tall idea*. Now certainly we can give it a coherent interpretation. It might well be taken as referring to a "big", audacious idea (cf. *tall tale*). Relevant here,

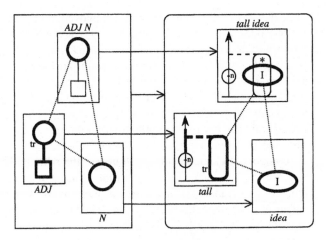

FIGURE 7.5

though, is the literal meaning, where each word is strictly understood in its most basic sense. So interpreted, *tall idea* is semantically anomalous.

In its strict, literal sense, the adjective *tall* characterizes its trajector as a physical entity that exists in space and has salient vertical extension in its canonical orientation. When *tall* modifies *idea*, a correspondence equates the adjectival trajector with the thing profiled by the noun, as shown on the right in figure 7.5. But an idea (I) is abstract, hence it does not exist in space and has no shape or spatial orientation (notationally, the ellipse is meant to indicate its amorphous, nonphysical nature). *Tall idea* is thus anomalous because the noun fails to satisfy the restrictions imposed by the adjective on its trajector. When corresponding elements are superimposed to form the composite semantic structure, their specifications clash instead of merging into a coherent conception—attempting their unification is like trying to fit an elliptical peg into a rectangular hole. An asterisk is added to the diagram to highlight this conceptual inconsistency.

Despite this semantic anomaly, *tall idea* is "grammatical". It follows the regular pattern by which adjectives modify nouns in English (e.g. *tall giraffe, good idea, green apple*). What this amounts to, in CG terms, is that *tall idea* instantiates the constructional schema describing that pattern. An adjective profiles a nonprocessual relationship with a thing as trajector but with no focused landmark. As shown on the left in figure 7.5, a correspondence identifies the adjectival trajector with the thing profiled by the noun, which is also profiled at the composite-structure level. Phonological integration consists of the adjective occurring directly before the noun. The diagram indicates that *tall idea* fully conforms to this schema. Examined individually, all the schema's specifications are satisfied: *tall* is an adjective, *idea* is a noun, the thing profiled by *idea* corresponds to *tall*'s trajector, it is also profiled by the composite structure, and *tall* directly precedes *idea*. Yet integrating an adjective and a noun in the manner specified by the schema does not itself guarantee that the lexemes chosen will be semantically compatible. As conventions for putting together complex expressions, constructional schemas are a critical resource for speaking and understanding. But they are not the only resource employed, and speakers cannot necessarily be trusted to use them in a conceptually coherent way.

Let us now return to the original examples. Sentence (5)(a) is fully grammatical and semantically coherent. It conforms to the appropriate constructional schemas, at both the semantic and phonological poles, and semantic integration in accordance with those schemas yields a consistent composite conception. The other two sentences are "ill-formed", albeit in different ways. On the one hand, sentence (4) is comparable to *tall idea*: grammatical in the sense that it conforms both semantically and phonologically to sanctioning schemas, yet conceptually incoherent when component elements are integrated in the manner they specify. On the other hand, (5)(b) is semantically well-formed, on the assumption that it employs the same constructional schemas as (5)(a) and has the same composite meaning. Its blatant ungrammaticality stems from how the component structures are integrated phonologically. Words do not occur in the order specified by constructional schemas to symbolize their semantic integration (e.g. adjectives do not precede the nouns they modify).[6]

I conclude that the possibility of distinguishing between semantic anomaly and "ungrammaticality" fails to establish the autonomy of syntax. The contrast is straightforwardly handled in a symbolic account of grammar.

7.2 Profile Determinance

It is typical in constructions for the composite semantic structure to profile the same entity as one of the component structures. As a composite whole, for instance, *jar lid* profiles the same entity as *lid*: a *jar lid* is a kind of lid, not a kind of jar (fig. 6.3). Similarly, *jar lid factory* has the same profile as *factory* (fig. 6.5), and—despite its semantic anomaly—*tall idea* designates the idea, not the relationship profiled by the adjective (fig. 7.5). Metaphorically, we can say that the composite structure generally "inherits" its profile from a component structure. The component structure that "bequeathes" its profile to the composite structure is referred to in CG as the **profile determinant**.

The profile determinant is often indicated by using heavy lines for the box enclosing it. This notation is first employed in figure 7.6, showing the integration of the preposition *in* and the nominal *the closet* to form the prepositional phrase *in the closet*. The nominal component profiles a thing depicted as a rectangle, both to indicate its status as a location and to mnemonically represent its usual shape. The letter C abbreviates all its other semantic specifications (relation to a room, approximate size, storage function, and so on). No attempt is made to include the meaning of the definite article. The preposition *in* profiles a simplex,

---

[6] For sake of completeness, we can note another kind of ill-formedness, in which an expression violates the specifications a constructional schema makes at its semantic pole. An example is **happily girl* (instead of *happy girl*). Here an adverb is used in lieu of the adjective specified by the constructional schema in fig. 7.5.

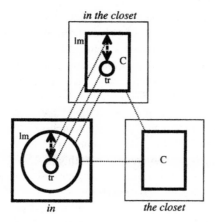

FIGURE 7.6

nonprocessual relationship between two things, typically one in which the trajector is spatially included in the landmark.[7] The nominal and the preposition are integrated through a correspondence between the profile of the former and the landmark of the latter. The heavy-line box indicates that the preposition functions as profile determinant in this construction. As a composite whole, *in the closet* designates a relationship of spatial inclusion, not the closet.

By calling attention to profile determinants, heavy-line boxes prove useful in dealing with complicated diagrams. A separate notation for this purpose is actually redundant, however. Profile determinance is based on other features of symbolic assemblies that are separately specified, namely profiling and correspondences. We can thus identify a profile determinant by examining component and composite structures, as well as the correspondences connecting them. By definition, the profile determinant is the component structure whose profile corresponds to the composite-structure profile. *Lid* is thus the profile determinant in *jar lid* because, as seen in figure 6.3, the profiles of *lid* and *jar lid* correspond (whereas neither corresponds to the profile of *jar*). From figure 7.6, we can tell that *in* functions as profile determinant because the relationship it profiles corresponds to the relationship profiled by *in the closet*.[8] Thus heavy-line boxes merely highlight an aspect of constructions which can be ascertained independently.

A construction's profile determinant is roughly equivalent to what is traditionally called a **head**. As most commonly defined, the head (at a given level of organization)

---

[7] This is at best an oversimplification, for even "spatial" prepositions have other dimensions to their semantic characterization, notably function. In the case of *in*, the landmark's function as a container for the trajector is arguably more fundamental than the purely spatial relationship (Vandeloise 1991, especially ch. 13).

[8] This is shown by correspondence lines connecting their trajectors, their landmarks, and the arrows representing the relationships. To keep diagrams simple, the latter correspondence is often omitted (e.g. in figs. 7.5 and 7.8). Corresponding participants are a consequence of a correspondence between two relationships and can thus be exploited as a shorthand way of indicating the correspondence.

is the component element that represents the same grammatical category as the composite expression.[9] The equivalence of head and profile determinant is then entailed by a basic claim of CG: that an expression's grammatical category is determined by the nature of its profile. From this it follows that a component element which bequeathes its profile to a composite expression thereby determines its grammatical category. Thus, in accordance with general CG principles, the notion head is defined conceptually with respect to the semantic pole of symbolic assemblies (rather than being an irreducible grammatical construct, as per the autonomy thesis).

Although it is usual for a single component structure to function as profile determinant, not every construction conforms to this prototype. Departures from the canonical arrangement fall into three broad categories: cases of **corresponding profiles**, **conflated profiles**, and **exocentricity**.

Illustrating the case of corresponding profiles are Luiseño clauses containing clitics, e.g. *Noonil 'owo'aquṣ* 'I was working'. In figure 7.4, we see that both the clause and the clitic profile a process—respectively, the specific process of the speaker working in the past and the schematic process evoked by the clitic. A pivotal feature of this construction is the identification of these two processes: the clause and the clitic offer specific and schematic characterizations of what, in referential terms, is precisely the same occurrence. Because the component-structure profiles correspond to each other, they each correspond to the composite-structure profile. Hence there is no basis for singling out either one as profile determinant to the exclusion of the other.

Another such example is nominal **apposition**, involving the juxtaposition of two expressions each of which profiles a thing. There are various patterns of nominal apposition. The two component structures can be simple nouns, as in *pussycat*, or full nominals, as in *Billy the Kid*, *my son the doctor*, and *our good friend Hillary Clinton*. In one such pattern, exemplified by *his strange belief that chickens are immortal*, the second nominal represents the conceptual reification of a clause. Here the reified proposition expressed by the second component (*that chickens are immortal*) constitutes the very belief profiled by the first (*his strange belief*). The details distinguishing these various constructions do not presently concern us. What matters is that they all instantiate the abstract configuration in figure 7.7: both component structures profile things, and their profiles correspond, so both correspond to the composite-structure profile. Hence the composite expression designates a single entity characterized by two sets of semantic specifications (X and Y). But since both component-structure profiles correspond to this entity, which component is the head?

The issue posed by corresponding profiles is largely terminological. Faced with the configuration of figure 7.4 or figure 7.7, we might want to say that both component structures are heads, since each of their profiles corresponds to the composite-structure profile. Alternatively, because neither component-structure profile does so exclusively, we might want to say that neither component is a head. The choice is

---

[9] Alternatively, a head is defined as a lexical element that provides an overall expression's essential semantic content. The two definitions sometimes conflict. In the progressive *be playing*, for example, *be* determines the category of the overall expression (imperfective verb), but the "lexical head" is *play* (a perfective verb).

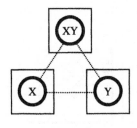

FIGURE 7.7

immaterial. Somewhat arbitrarily, I follow the second course and reserve the term "profile determinant" for instances where just a single component structure has the same profile as the composite structure.

An analogous terminological question arises in cases of conflated profiles. These are cases where the composite-structure profile is not identified with that of any single component structure, taken individually, but rather with the more complex entity obtained by conflating them. Thus, while each component-structure profile corresponds to some facet of the composite-structure profile, only collectively do they match it as a whole. Should we then say that all the components function as profile determinants, or that none of them does? Once more I take the second option.

An example of this sort is the nested locative construction (previously discussed in §3.4.2). Sentence (6) locates its trajector by successively "zooming in" to smaller and smaller areas. Each locative element places the trajector within a restricted location, which the next locative takes as the immediate scope for its interpretation. In this path of search, *upstairs* confines the trajector to the upper story of a house. The following locative, *in the bedroom*, is interpreted relative to this location—only upstairs bedrooms are relevant—and the definite article implies that there is only one. Only this bedroom is invoked for interpreting *in the closet*, and only the bedroom closet for *on the shelf*.

(6)   *Your camera is upstairs, in the bedroom, in the closet, on the shelf.*

To keep things simple, we will limit our attention to the last two locatives. We must therefore consider how *in the closet* and *on the shelf* are integrated to form a complex locative expression. This is sketched in figure 7.8, where the two component structures are the composite structures of the respective prepositional phrases. *In the closet* profiles a relationship of spatial inclusion (fig. 7.6). *On the shelf* profiles a relationship in which the trajector makes contact with the upper surface of a shelf, which supports it. In the context of an overall expression like (6), it is pertinent to represent both the immediate spatial scope (IS) and the maximal scope (MS). For each prepositional phrase, the profiled relationship is manifested within a restricted scope of attention (the "onstage" region) selected from a larger spatial setting.

Two correspondences are responsible for the integration of component structures. First, their trajectors correspond. The same entity—in (6), the camera—is located both in the (upstairs bedroom) closet and on the shelf. A second correspondence accounts for the "zooming in" effect of nested locatives. It needs to specify that the

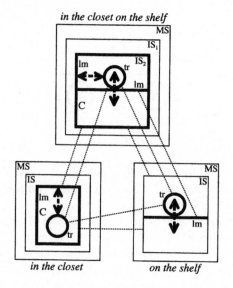

FIGURE 7.8

area to which the first component confines its trajector functions as the immediate scope for interpreting the second locative. The first locative, *in the closet*, confines the trajector to the closet's interior, which is essentially coextensive with the closet itself. This region is thus connected by a correspondence line to the box representing the immediate spatial scope of *on the shelf*. As a consequence, the composite structure shows two nested immediate scopes, reflecting the successive loci of attention for the two component structures. IS_1 is the immediate scope imposed by *in the closet*, and within it, IS_2 is the immediate scope for *on the shelf*.

In a complex locative of this sort, what does the composite structure profile? It would be both arbitrary and counterintuitive to claim that it designates either component-structure relationship to the exclusion of the other. Instead, the profiled relationship is itself complex, representing the conflation of the component relations. The trajector is located simultaneously with respect to two landmarks, the closet and the shelf.[10] By itself, then, neither component has the same profile as the composite expression. Each component-structure profile corresponds to a single facet of the conflated profile observed at the composite-structure level. Thus neither component structure is singled out as profile determinant.

There is one more type of situation where a profile determinant cannot be identified. This is the case of constructions in which neither component-structure profile corresponds to the composite-structure profile. In traditional terminology, expressions of this sort are said to be **exocentric**. The term is appropriate, for it indicates that the "center" (i.e. the composite expression's profile) is "external" (not being profiled by either component).

---

[10] In sentence (6) as a whole, the camera's position is specified by a complex locative with four component relationships and four landmarks.

A simple illustration is the compound *pickpocket*. It is one instance of a compounding pattern (some others being *scarecrow, breakwater, killjoy, cureall, turnkey,* and *spoilsport*) in which the two components are a verb and a noun corresponding to its landmark (cf. Tuggy 2003b). *Pick* has various meanings, but in this compound it profiles an action of removing something from a location (cf. *pick up*). Figure 7.9 thus shows the trajector exerting force (double arrow) to induce this motion (single arrow). Relevant here is a more specific sense, in which the original location (given as a box) is focused as the landmark.[11] A *pocket* is a kind of location. In the diagram, small and large circles respectively indicate the contents of the pocket and the article of clothing it is a part of. Correspondences identify the pocket with the landmark of *pick*, and its contents with the object removed.

It is normal in English for the second element of a compound to function as profile determinant. This is the case for the [[N$_1$] - [N$_2$]] compounds considered earlier (e.g. *jar lid*), representing the basic pattern, and also for [[ADJ] - [N]] compounds (e.g. *blueberry, happy face, Big Bird*). [[V] - [N]] compounds are exceptional in this regard: a *pickpocket* is not a pocket, and a *scarecrow* is not a crow. Nor do they designate the process profiled by the verb. So neither component structure imposes its profile at the composite-structure level. Instead, the composite expression designates the actor: a *pickpocket* is a person who picks pockets, while a *scarecrow* supposedly scares crows. Even though the composite-structure profile is not inherited from either component, its choice follows a regular pattern, consistently corresponding to the verb's trajector. Their correspondence is therefore specified in the constructional schema for [[V] - [N]] compounds. This is not to say that these expressions are fully compositional. Indeed, the composite forms derive their specific import from cognitive domains (e.g. the practice of picking pockets) not evoked by either component structure individually.

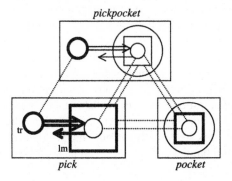

FIGURE 7.9

---

[11] This sense of *pick* is also found in expressions like the following: *Buzzards had picked the bones clean; He was picking his teeth with a knife; Don't pick your nose!; There wasn't much left on the bargain shelf—shoppers had pretty much picked it over.* The action is normally one of probing with the tip of an elongated instrument (like a beak, fingers, or tooth**pick**).

7.3 Elaboration

The structures constituting a symbolic assembly are linked by both correspondences and categorizing relationships. We have so far emphasized correspondences, and secondarily the categorizing relationships between component and composite structures. The latter define an expression's compositional path at either pole. What we have not yet considered in any detail are the categorizing relationships that link component structures to one another.

7.3.1 Elaboration Sites

It is typical in a construction for one component structure to contain a schematic substructure which the other component serves to **elaborate**, i.e. characterize in finer-grained detail. In *jar lid*, for example, *lid* evokes a schematic container specified in finer detail by *jar* (figs. 6.3 and 6.4). Similarly, *giraffe* elaborates the schematic trajector of *tall* in *tall giraffe* (fig. 7.3), and *pocket* the landmark of *pick* in *pickpocket* (fig. 7.9). A schematic element elaborated by another component is called an **elaboration site**, or **e-site** for short.

As in the case of profile determinants, it is useful to mark e-sites explicitly, even though such marking is actually redundant in fully described assemblies. The notation adopted here is hatching, as shown in figure 7.10. Diagram (a) represents the component structures in a prepositional phrase construction, such as *in the closet* (fig. 7.6). The preposition profiles a nonprocessual relationship between two things, and a correspondence equates its landmark with the profile of the following nominal. The box with hatching identifies the landmark as an e-site. Only schematic within the preposition itself, this element is specified in finer detail by the nominal component. The solid arrow indicates that this schematic substructure categorizes the other component in a relationship of elaboration.

Observe that the correspondence line in diagram (a) connects two circles, while the arrow for elaboration runs between two boxes. The reason for the difference is that correspondence pertains to conceptual **reference**, whereas elaboration is a matter of **characterization**. On the one hand, the correspondence line indicates that the prepositional landmark and the nominal profile refer to the same entity: they are two manifestations of a single entity in the composite conception. On the other hand, the boxes represent the total information provided about the corresponding entities—the conceptual **base** evoked for their characterization, within which they stand out as profiles. Referentially, it is specifically the nominal profile that is identified with the preposition's landmark, but the entire conceptual base of the nominal contributes to

FIGURE 7.10

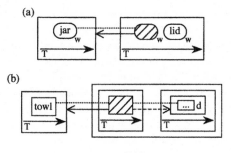

FIGURE 7.11

the landmark's description. From the standpoint of diagrammatic clarity, however, it is sometimes awkward to include a separate box representing the elaboration site. The notation in diagram (b) is thus employed for abbreviatory purposes.

Elaboration and elaboration sites can also be recognized at the phonological pole. Two examples are given in figure 7.11. Diagram (a) shows the phonological integration of *jar* and *lid* in *jar lid* (cf. fig. 6.2(b)). Part of the overall characterization of every word is its potential for preceding and following other words, which can thus be invoked as e-sites. In this construction, the word preceding *lid* functions as an e-site, which *jar* elaborates. Diagram (b) depicts the integration of *toll* and *-ed* in the past-tense form *tolled* (cf. fig. 6.11(e)). The representation of *-ed* reflects an essential feature in the characterization of an affix: it inherently makes schematic reference to a stem and specifies how that stem is modified by adding segmental material. Here the schematic stem evoked by *-ed* is an e-site elaborated by *toll*.

7.3.2 Autonomy and Dependence

Elaboration sites point to a fundamental aspect of linguistic organization. They indicate that certain structures, by their very nature, do not stand alone but require the support of others—they are **dependent** on other, more **autonomous** structures for their own manifestation. Thus dependent structures cannot be described independently, in their own terms, but only in relation to the autonomous structures that support them. As a consequence, a dependent structure refers schematically to an autonomous, supporting structure as an intrinsic aspect of its own characterization. This schematic substructure functions as an e-site when the dependent structure combines with an autonomous one.

The asymmetry between autonomous and dependent components, referred to as **A/D-alignment**, is a general feature of language design. It is found in both unipolar and bipolar organization, at both the semantic and the phonological poles. In the case of unipolar phonological organization, an obvious example is a prosodic element like tone or stress, which requires the support of segmental content for its manifestation (one cannot put high tone or primary stress on silence). At the segmental level, vowels are autonomous and consonants in the same syllable are dependent on them. The autonomous, self-contained nature of vowels allows them to occur independently as full syllables. Consonants, on the other hand, consist primarily in modulating or interrupting the sonority provided by vowels and thus require the support of vowels to be fully manifested and clearly perceived. The stem/affix distinction exemplifies A/D-alignment in the case of bipolar phonological organization. Stems and affixes both consist of sound segments, and the same segment or segment sequence can function in either capacity. What distinguishes them is that a stem is autonomous, and thus potentially stands alone, whereas an affix intrinsically makes reference to a stem, as seen in figure 7.11(b).[12] More obviously dependent are morphemes that actually change the segmental composition of a stem, e.g. the symbolization of past tense by changing *sit* to *sat* (fig. 6.11(a)). It is only in relation to the vowel that would otherwise be expected that the vowel of *sat* has symbolizing function.

At the semantic pole, a prime example of unipolar A/D-alignment is the distinction between things and relationships. For typical cases (and with certain oversimplifications), we can say that things are conceptually autonomous and relationships are dependent. It is possible for a physical entity (e.g. a rock, a table, or a cat) to be conceptualized in and of itself, without its relationship to other objects being invoked in any crucial or salient way. By contrast, a relationship is conceptually dependent on its participants. For example, we cannot conceptualize a spatial relation (like *on*, *under*, or *near*) without to some extent (if only schematically) invoking the entities that participate in it. As the term suggests, apprehending a relationship resides in conceiving entities in relation to one another. Thus it does not exist independently of those entities.

Our main interest lies with A/D-alignment in bipolar semantic organization, at the semantic pole of grammatical constructions. Here a component structure is said to elaborate whatever schematic portion of the other component its profile corresponds to. Thus in figure 7.10, representing the prepositional object construction, the nominal component elaborates the preposition's landmark. Since a landmark is salient as a matter of definition, and the object nominal specifies it in finer-grained detail, the preposition is dependent with respect to its object. This nominal is generally autonomous with respect to the preposition. It does not feel conceptually "incomplete" if used in some way other than as a prepositional object.

Thus, in a prepositional phrase like *near the door*, the component structure *near* is dependent with respect to the more autonomous component *the door*, which elaborates its schematic landmark. But can we not also say that *near* elaborates *the door*, since *near the door* represents a more detailed and elaborate conception than just *the door*? Certainly we can. Part of our encyclopedic knowledge of doors is that, as physical entities, they participate in spatial relationships with other such entities. *Near* can therefore be taken as instantiating this schematic specification. These two elaborative relationships are depicted in figure 7.12. *Near* locates its trajector somewhere in the landmark's neighborhood, given as an ellipse. Diagram (a) shows its landmark being elaborated by *the door*. Conversely, diagram (b) shows *near* elaborating a schematic locative relationship implicit in the meaning of the nominal.

---

[12] The crucial factor is whether one element makes intrinsic reference to the other, not whether it actually occurs independently. On this basis, a stem can be distinguished from an affix even when it never occurs in unaffixed form. Likewise, vowels are autonomous vis-à-vis consonants even in languages where the minimal syllabic form is CV, so that a vowel never stands alone as a syllable.

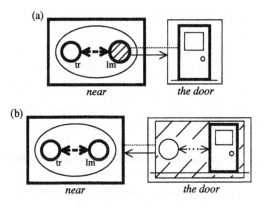

FIGURE 7.12

These two elaborative relationships are not equal in status, however. They differ in both the salience of the e-site and the extent to which the other component elaborates it. The e-site of *near* is highly salient (the landmark being a focused participant) and quite schematic relative to *the door*. By contrast, the e-site ascribed to *the door* is rather peripheral to its semantic characterization. The spatial relationships that a door bears to other objects are not part of the nominal profile and may not even come to mind in using the expression. Moreover, the degree of elaboration effected by *near* is somewhat limited. Although the *near* relationship per se is more specific than the one implicit in the nominal, the latter is more specific in regard to the landmark. The example is not untypical. Each component structure can usually be thought of as elaborating something evoked at least potentially by the other. To some extent, therefore, each component structure is dependent on the other. Yet there tends to be a marked asymmetry, such that the dependence in one direction is stronger and more clearly evident. In the case at hand, *near* is more strongly dependent on *the door* than conversely.

A/D-alignment is thus a relative matter. One structure is dependent on another to the extent that the latter elaborates a salient substructure within it. The key notions here are **salience** and **elaboration**, both of which are matters of degree. When, based on these factors, the degree of dependence is substantially greater in one direction than the other, we can reasonably simplify by focusing just on that direction. If a construction were a trial, a jury given these instructions would render the judgment "dependent" for *near* and "autonomous" for *the door*, based on the preponderance of evidence. But some trials result in hung juries. In many cases the component structures exhibit little or no A/D-asymmetry, either because each is dependent on the other to a significant extent or because both are largely autonomous.

Illustrating bidirectional dependence are Luiseño sentences like (2), *Waxaam-nil 'owo'aquṣ* 'Yesterday I was working'. In one direction, the clausal component *waxaam 'owo'aquṣ* 'yesterday... was working' depends on the clitic to specify its schematic trajector. It is identified as being the speaker by the initial segment of *=nil*. However, as shown in figure 7.4, the clitic itself invokes a schematic process elaborated by the clausal component (except in regard to its trajector). While on balance the clitic is more highly dependent, its elaboration of the clausal trajector is hardly trivial.[13]

A case where the judgment hangs in balance, there being no preponderance of evidence, is the phonological pole of a compound like *jar lid*. In figure 7.11(a), *jar* was shown as elaborating the word schematically evoked by *lid* as the one preceding it. The choice, though, is arbitrary. *Lid* could just as well have been shown as elaborating the schematic word following *jar*. Although the degree of elaboration in the two directions is equal and quite substantial, neither component is strongly dependent on the other, owing to the salience factor. A word is phonologically autonomous, capable of being pronounced in isolation as a self-contained whole. Moreover, since words like *jar* and *lid* are not limited to any particular grammatical environment, they are phonologically independent in bipolar terms as well. Thus it cannot be said that a preceding or a following word is a salient feature of their phonological description. The elaboration site shown in the diagram reflects an aspect of the "encyclopedic" characterization of words: the background information that words are strung together in sequences and can therefore precede and follow other words. The e-site's nonsalience has the consequence that the extent to which either *jar* or *lid* is dependent on the other is fairly minor. Both are largely autonomous.

7.3.3 Complement and Modifier

To appreciate the grammatical significance of A/D-alignment, we can best start by considering a typical example. Figure 7.13 depicts the semantic pole of the nominal expression *a table near the door* (still ignoring articles).[14]

At the lower level of organization, *the door* elaborates the landmark of *near* to form the prepositional phrase *near the door*. *The door* is thus autonomous, and *near* is dependent. Since the composite structure inherits its profile, *near* is the profile determinant. At the higher level of organization, *(a) table* elaborates the trajector of *near the door* to derive the full expression. The former is thus autonomous and the latter dependent. At this level *table* functions as profile determinant, since the overall expression designates the table (rather than the spatial relationship).

In traditional terminology, *near* and *table* function as **heads** at their respective levels of organization. At the lower level, *the door* is said to be a **complement** of *near*; at the higher level, *near the door* is a **modifier** with respect to *table*. The descriptive utility of these notions implies, from the CG perspective, that they must have conceptual characterizations. We have seen that a head is a profile determinant, characterized in terms of a typical feature of symbolic assemblies: that of a component-structure profile corresponding to the composite-structure profile. The notions complement and modifier are likewise definable with reference to symbolic

---

[13] The clitic is more highly dependent because the clause elaborates the schematic process to a greater extent than the clitic elaborates the schematic trajector (i.e. the clause provides far more detailed information). Also, the clausal trajector is specified only by the first element of the clitic (*n* marks first-person singular), whereas the clause combines grammatically with the clitic as a whole.

[14] I take no position on whether the indefinite article combines directly with *table* (as shown here) or with the complex expression *table near the door*.

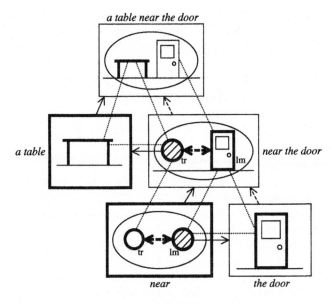

FIGURE 7.13

assemblies. Each represents a commonly observed configuration in which the head participates in an elaborative relation with the other component structure. The difference between them resides in the direction of elaboration, as shown in figure 7.14. A complement is a component structure that **elaborates** a salient substructure of the head. The head is thus dependent, and the complement is autonomous. Conversely, a modifier is a component structure that contains a salient substructure **elaborated by** the head. In this case the head is autonomous, and the modifier is dependent.

By these definitions, *the door* is a complement in figure 7.13, since *near* is the head and *the door* elaborates its landmark. At the higher level, *near the door* is a modifier because its trajector is elaborated by the head noun *table*. The definitions extend straightforwardly to other standard instances of complement and modifier constructions. In a phrase like *tall giraffe* (fig. 7.3), *tall* is said to modify *giraffe*. This is so because the noun is the head and elaborates the adjective's trajector. Like the object of a preposition, the object of a verb is a complement, since the verb functions as head and the nominal elaborates its landmark (fig. 7.1). It is unproblematic

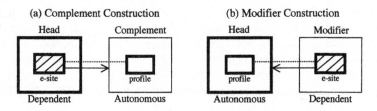

FIGURE 7.14

that the definitions extend to cases the terms are usually not applied to.[15] The CG strategy is not to adopt traditional notions uncritically, but rather to offer explicit conceptual characterizations that preserve their valid insights while avoiding their limitations.

The status of an element as a complement or a modifier plays a role in many grammatical phenomena. As a simple case, consider the following contrast:

(7)   (a) *He tried to annoy his mother.*   [complement construction]

    (b) *He cried to annoy his mother.*   [modifier construction]

While the two sentences seem quite parallel, there is one crucial difference: the infinitival clause *to annoy his mother* functions as complement with respect to *try* but as a modifier with respect to *cry*. It is a complement of *try* because it specifies a schematic activity essential to the meaning of this verb, the target toward which the subject's effort is directed. By contrast, *cry* designates a typically spontaneous emotional reaction; conscious effort to achieve a purpose is not inherent in its meaning. Sentence (7)(b) does indicate that the crying is intended to annoy the mother, but this does not reflect the meaning of the verb; rather, it manifests a grammatical construction in which an infinitival clause expresses the purpose for an action. *To annoy his mother* is thus an adverbial modifier of the clausal nucleus *he cried*, which specifies that action. One consequence of the complement/modifier distinction in such examples pertains to word order. As seen in (8), the infinitival clause can readily occur in sentence-initial position when it functions as a modifier, but hardly as a complement.

(8)   (a) **To annoy his mother he tried.*   [preposed complement]

    (b) *To annoy his mother he cried.*   [preposed modifier]

Not every construction involves a complement or a modifier. Though typical, the configurations in figure 7.14 are just two of the varied forms symbolic assemblies can assume. As defined, for example, a complement or modifier only has that status in relation to a head. The terms are thus not applicable in constructions that lack a profile determinant, such as nominal apposition (fig. 7.7) and nested locatives (fig. 7.8). They are also not applicable when neither component structure contains a salient substructure corresponding to the other's profile. One such case is *go away angry*, in which a complex verb combines with an adjective. Their integration is sketched in figure 7.15.

Go away designates an event in which the trajector moves out of an original location that serves as a point of reference (R). The bar along the time arrow indicates sequential scanning of the profiled process. *Angry* profiles an atemporal relationship in which the trajector exhibits a certain emotional state (a). Being nonprocessual, this relationship is not profiled in its evolution through time. The conceptual base for *angry* does, however, include the specification that this emotion typically occurs in episodes of limited duration. An unfilled bar represents the time span of one such episode. *Go away* and *angry* are integrated by means of two correspondences. First, their trajectors correspond: the

---

[15] In *jar lid*, for instance, *jar* is a complement to *lid* (fig. 6.3). Why? By now it should be evident.

FIGURE 7.15

person who goes away is also the person who is angry. Second, the time spans correspond: the episode of anger is coextensive with (or at least includes) the time of leaving. *Go away* is the head, since the composite expression is processual.

In this expression, *angry* is neither a complement nor a modifier with respect to *go away*, for neither elaborates a salient substructure within the other. While we know that a person who goes away may well do so while in a certain emotional state, this is quite peripheral to the meaning of the verb, which would generally not evoke it independently. Nor is spatial motion central to the meaning of *angry*, although we certainly know that a person in this state is usually capable of it. A component structure which, like *angry*, fails to either elaborate the head or be elaborated by it is sometimes called an **adjunct**.

Although CG is able to characterize traditional grammatical notions like head, adjunct, complement, and modifier, these terms are not themselves the basic units of CG description. They are more accurately thought of as convenient labels for certain kinds of configurations commonly observable at the semantic pole of symbolic assemblies. Thus it is not expected that every construction will have a head, or that every component structure combining with a head will be clearly and uniquely identifiable as a complement or a modifier. Like the factors defining them, these latter notions are matters of degree and are not mutually exclusive.

7.4 Constituency

Constituency is a fundamental construct in both traditional grammar and modern syntactic theory. It is also recognized in CG and readily accommodated. However, CG has a very different take on the nature of constituency, as well as its role in language structure.

7.4.1 Two Conceptions of Constituency

Syntacticians generally describe constituency by positing fixed hierarchical structures that are metaphorically conceived as inverted "trees". Styles change and details vary, but in one classic format the nominal *a table near the door* might have the tree representation in figure 7.16.[16]

---

[16] This is the counterpart of fig. 7.13, which however does not show the decomposition of *a table* and *the door* into article plus noun. NP stands for **noun phrase**, a standard but infelicitous term that CG replaces with **nominal**.

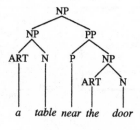

FIGURE 7.16

In theories assuming the autonomy of grammar, these tree structures are conceived as purely syntactic objects, with no intrinsic semantic or phonological content. While the trees play a role in semantic and phonological "interpretation", based on the content supplied by the lexical items "inserted" into them, syntactic structure per se is seen as a separate level of representation distinct from both semantics and phonology. CG is more highly constrained; owing to the content requirement (§1.3.4), it cannot posit autonomous syntactic objects of this sort. Nor are they necessary. An account of grammar based solely on symbolic assemblies proves not only adequate but more revealing.

Syntactic tree structures represent three kinds of information: grammatical category (through labels like N, P, NP, etc.), "linear order" (left to right on the page), and constituency (hierarchical grouping). All of these are also provided by the symbolic assemblies of CG.

Information concerning category membership is intrinsic to the semantic pole of each symbolic structure in an assembly. It inheres in the nature of the profile. Depending on the profile, a symbolic structure instantiates one or another class schema defined primarily on this basis, e.g. [[[THING]/[. . .]] → [[JAR]/[jar]]]. Recall that schemas are **immanent** in their instantiations even when, for analytical purposes, they are shown separately.

Information concerning linear order is intrinsic to the phonological pole of each symbolic structure. "Linear order" is actually temporal order, the sequencing of elements in the flow of speech. Time is a basic dimension of phonological structure and is thus inherent in its characterization, even when left implicit in diagrams. When it is shown explicitly, as in figure 6.3, time is represented by an arrow labeled T.[17]

---

[17] Observe that such arrows are placed at the phonological pole of each symbolic structure in an assembly, both component and composite structures. Time and temporal sequencing are aspects of a symbolic structure's own internal characterization at any level. It is thus at the composite-structure level that temporal ordering is specified for the elements in a complex expression. To ascertain their ordering from a diagram, one must therefore look at the composite structure's phonological pole—it is not indicated by the placement of component structures relative to one another on the page. Of course, it does facilitate the reading of diagrams if component structures are arranged left to right in a way that mirrors their phonological sequencing. But that is not essential, and sometimes diagrammatic convenience dictates otherwise. In fig. 6.13(b), for instance, a simpler diagram results from placing *big dog* on the left and *the* on the right, despite their being pronounced in the opposite order: *th'big dog*.

Constituency is observed in symbolic assemblies when a composite structure at one level of organization functions in turn as component structure with respect to a higher level. Though it plays a role in grammar, it is quite wrong to suppose that constituency is solely or even primarily a grammatical phenomenon. It is simply one manifestation of hierarchical organization, evident in virtually every realm of human functioning. It is evident, for example, in perceptual grouping (fig. 4.5), in the apprehension of whole-part hierarchies (body > arm > hand > finger > knuckle), in hierarchical categorization (thing → object → vehicle → truck → pickup truck), in planning a complex endeavor (with goals, subgoals, sub-subgoals, etc.), in dealing with collections of different sizes (army > division > brigade > batallion > company > platoon > soldier), and even in complex motor routines (decomposable into subroutines, sub-subroutines, and so on). What these share is the capacity to operate at multiple levels of organization, where a single entity at one level in some way arises from multiple entities at another level.

All the information provided by tree structures is thus inherent in symbolic assemblies. From the standpoint of CG, extracting this information and presenting it separately as an autonomous formal object is not just superfluous but a kind of gerrymandering. Of course, in their hierarchical arrangement, symbolic assemblies like figure 7.13 do resemble syntactic tree structures. Nevertheless, the two are quite different in their fundamental nature: whereas each structure in an assembly has both a semantic and a phonological pole, the "nodes" in a tree structure (NP, P, PP, etc.) are seen as purely grammatical elements with no intrinsic semantic or phonological value. A further difference is that syntactic constituency is considered a basic and invariant aspect of grammatical description, so that a particular kind of expression should always be assigned the same, definite tree structure. In CG, on the other hand, constituency is viewed as flexible, variable, and nonessential. Rather than being basic to grammatical description, "classic" constituency hierarchies like figure 7.16 emerge from other phenomena and represent just one of the configurations that symbolic assemblies can assume (GC: ch. 5).

Specifically, "classic constituents" represent the special situation where a particular kind of conceptual grouping is symbolized by a particular kind of phonological grouping. The conceptual grouping is that of two component structures being integrated through correspondences involving salient substructures (notably profile, trajector, and landmark). The phonological grouping is based on temporal contiguity, the component structures being adjacent in the flow of speech. The groups arising in this fashion—the composite semantic and phonological structures—may themselves participate in further grouping at a higher level of organization. When this occurs at multiple levels, the phonological grouping in each case symbolizing the semantic grouping, it results in configurations of the sort represented in standard syntactic tree structures like figure 7.16.

7.4.2 Limitations of the Classic View

It may be that classic constituents have a privileged status owing to their prevalence and the obvious nature of the factors invoked as the basis for grouping. If so, it must still be recognized that there are numerous dimensions of semantic and phonological organization, as well as various grounds for grouping elements and delimiting structures of different sizes. The same semantic and phonological content can thus be grouped and organized in alternate ways that are incommensurate yet simultaneously valid. Hence there are more facets to the structure of a complex expression than can be represented in any one constituency hierarchy.

We have seen, for example, that unipolar and bipolar organization present two dimensions of composition that cannot be conflated in a single hierarchical structure (fig. 6.12). Beyond this, unipolar and bipolar organization are themselves multifaceted. For unipolar structure, I will merely note in passing the need to distinguish, at the phonological pole, between prosody and segmental composition. With respect to bipolar organization, let us briefly consider two aspects of linguistic structure usually excluded from "grammar" in the narrow sense: lexical units and focus. They represent symbolically motivated groupings that often cross-cut the constituency hierarchies posited in syntactic analysis.

Lexical items are fixed expressions, familiar to speakers and conventional in the speech community. Most are symbolically complex. I point out in §1.3.2 that lexical units need not coincide with syntactic constituents, and, indeed, the elements constituting them need not even be adjacent. One example is the sequence *take it for granted that*, which is certainly an established unit with its own global meaning.[18] While this lexical unit is arguably a syntactic constituent in (9)(a), if we take it as including schematic reference to the clause introduced by *that*, it cannot be one in (9)(b), where its elements are noncontiguous:

(9) (a) *Most commentators **take it for granted** [**that** money is the primary source of political influence].*

   (b) ***It** has been **taken** more or less **for granted** by most commentators [**that** money is the primary source of political influence].*

This lexeme represents a coherent conceptual grouping whose components are linked by correspondences at the semantic pole and are individually symbolized by phonological elements. It is thus a symbolic assembly, entirely defined by semantic structures, phonological structures, and symbolic links between the two, even though—in its most general description—the phonological components do not form a group based on temporal adjacency. Though symbolic in nature, this lexical unit is delimited on the basis of entrenchment and conventionality in a way that cross-cuts classic constituency hierarchies.

Similar in this respect is focus, one aspect of information structure (§3.2.1). Very roughly speaking (and most descriptions are pretty rough), an expression's focus is that portion of it which the speaker wishes to foreground as a significant departure from what has already been established in the immediately preceding discourse.

---

[18] It is of course decomposable into smaller meaningful structures—notably *take . . . for granted* (cf. *You've been taking me for granted!*) and an independent construction involving *it* and a *that*-clause (e.g. *I resent it that he treats us so badly*). This is perfectly consistent with the entire sequence being established as a unit in its own right.

In English, nonfocused elements tend to be reduced in stress, so that the focus stands out phonologically by virtue of having full, unreduced stress (indicated here by small caps). For instance, the first sentence in (10) provides a discourse context with (a) and (b) as possible continuations. The focus in (a) is *likes*, since the other elements are merely restatements of what has just been said. In (b), the focus consists of *sister* and *coffee*, for both elements stand out as being new and significant.

(10)   *My mother puts orange juice on her cereal.*

    (a) *She LIKES it that way.*

    (b) *My SISTER puts it in her COFFEE.*

The focus in cases like (b) is not a syntactic constituent in the classic sense. It is nonetheless a symbolic structure recognized in CG as one facet of an expression's grammatical organization. At the semantic pole, its component elements form a group apprehended as such because they collectively constitute what is new and significant in the discourse. At the phonological pole, they are grouped on the basis of unreduced stress. This distinguishing phonological property (pertaining to prosody) symbolizes the distinguishing conceptual property (pertaining to information structure).[19] While structures delimited in this fashion tend to coincide with syntactic constituents of the classic sort, there is no reason to expect that they would always do so.

Hence the structures and relationships captured in a constituency hierarchy of the sort depicted in figures 7.13 and 7.16 tell only part of the story. Though central and essential, they are by no means exhaustive of the semantic, phonological, and symbolic structures that need to be described in a complete account of linguistic structure. These can all be accommodated in CG, within the limits imposed by the content requirement. Permitted by this requirement are semantic and phonological groupings of any size, effected on any basis, and delimited in any way. Semantic and phonological structures representing any level or dimension of organization can be linked to form symbolic structures. Further permitted are categorizing relationships (both syntagmatic and paradigmatic), giving rise to assemblies of structures. Out of the broad spectrum of structures and relationships thus afforded, classic constituency hierarchies emerge as a special case.

When they do emerge, such hierarchies do not themselves incorporate every semantic, phonological, and symbolic structure that figures in an expression's full characterization. They do not represent focus, for example. They also fail to accommodate semantic structures that happen not to be individually symbolized. For instance, while both sentences in (9) invoke the global meaning of the lexical unit *take it for granted that*, in (9)(b) there is no phonological structure serving to symbolize this lexical meaning as a unitary whole. Classic constituency hierarchies

---

[19] Their relationship is both iconic and symbolic, for at each pole the focused elements stand out from the background with respect to a natural dimension of prominence (loudness or informativeness). While they are often excluded or marginalized, CG considers prosody and information structure to be integral parts of phonology and semantics. Likewise, symbolic structures based on them are integral parts of grammar.

are further problematic in cases where phonological integration is not effected by juxtaposition in the temporal sequence. An example from Luiseño is the integration of a clitic with a clause, where the clitic neither precedes nor follows the clause but occurs inside it (fig. 6.14).

7.4.3 Grammatical Relationships

In theories of autonomous syntax, constituency is commonly invoked for the representation of basic grammatical relationships. Prime examples are the **subject** and **object** relations. In an early and well-known account (Chomsky 1965), these notions were defined in terms of particular tree configurations. The definitions presupposed the constituency shown in figure 7.17(a), where S = "sentence" and VP = "verb phrase". A subject was defined as a noun phrase (NP) attached as a "daughter" to S and a "sister" to VP, whereas an object NP is a daughter to VP and a sister to V. In the sentence *Alice admires Bill*, *Alice* is thus the subject and *Bill* the object. The definitions are purely grammatical, making no inherent reference to meaning.

Compare this with the CG account, where subject and object receive a conceptual characterization. They are defined in terms of several factors observable at the semantic pole of symbolic assemblies: correspondences, profiling, and trajector/landmark alignment. This is shown for *Alice admires Bill* in figure 7.17(b).[20] A subject is characterized as a nominal whose profile corresponds to the trajector of a profiled relationship, and an object as one whose profile corresponds to a landmark. Only conceptual factors are invoked in these definitions.

The diagrams in figure 7.17 show the same constituency, with *admires* and *Bill* forming a group that combines as a whole with *Alice*. Presumably this represents the default-case grouping, reflected in the most natural placement of a slight hesitation: *Alice / admires Bill*. But there is a crucial difference between the syntactic definitions of subject and object and the CG definitions: the former **rely** on this constituency,

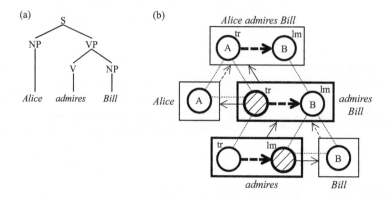

FIGURE 7.17

---

[20] Tense is ignored, and the process profiled by *admire* is represented by a dashed arrow, often used for mental relationships.

whereas the latter are **independent** of it. Reliance on syntactic tree structures for defining grammatical relationships makes it necessary to posit a definite, invariant tree structure for a given type of expression. There is no such necessity in CG, for rather than being "purely syntactic", the relationships in question are taken as being conceptual in nature. Their manifestation in a symbolic assembly does not require any particular constituency. As a consequence, CG allows variable constituency for expressions that exhibit the same grammatical relationships. While these relationships often correlate with particular constituency configurations, their characterization does not depend on them. Hence there is no need to force expressions into rigid constituency hierarchies which they appear not to manifest.

Consider an alternate pronunciation of *Alice admires Bill*, possible in slow, deliberate speech: *Alice / admires / Bill*. Intonation suggests a "flat" constituency—that is, the three components combine with one another at a single level of organization, with no internal grouping. This is shown in figure 7.18, where *Alice* and *Bill* respectively elaborate the trajector and landmark of *admires* at the same level. By virtue of correspondences, *Alice* is still identified as the subject and *Bill* as the object, despite the absence of constituency grouping. The syntactic definitions of subject and object preclude this option. Since *Alice* is the subject and *Bill* the object with either intonation, the constituency in figure 7.17(a) must be posited for both.

Provided that *Alice* elaborates the trajector and *Bill* the landmark, the former qualifies as subject and the latter as object even with the third possible constituency, where *Alice* first combines with *admires* to form *Alice admires*, which then combines with *Bill* at a higher level of organization. The grouping of subject and verb to form a constituent that excludes the object is in fact observed in English, at least in the context of certain larger constructions. We find it, for example, in clause-internal topic constructions like (11)(a), as well as certain cases of coordination, as in (11)(b). Subject and verb also form a constituent in relative clauses like the one in (11)(c).

(11) (a) *Bill Alice admires (Harvey she doesn't).*

    (b) *Alice admires, but Sharon detests, their new teacher.*

    (c) *The teacher [Alice admires] speaks fluent Arabic.*

Relative clauses further illustrate the advantages of the flexible constituency afforded by a conceptual characterization of grammatical relationships. Usually a

Alice admires Bill

FIGURE 7.18

relative clause in English directly follows the noun it modifies, as in (12)(a). In this case they clearly form a syntactic constituent of the classic sort. What, then, do we say about sentences like (12)(b), where the clause is separated from its head?

(12)   (a) *The package [that I was expecting] arrived.*

   (b) *The package arrived [that I was expecting].*

In autonomous approaches to syntax, it is commonly claimed that a sentence like (12)(b) is "derived" from an "underlying structure" like (12)(a) by a rule that "moves" the relative clause to the end. This analysis follows from the assumption that grammatical relationships are properly represented by particular configurations in syntactic tree structures. Since the relative clause bears the same grammatical relationship to its head in (12)(a) and (12)(b), the two must form a syntactic constituent in both expressions. This is overtly the case in the former, but not in the latter, where they are separated. To preserve the assumption, it must therefore be maintained that (12)(b) has the same syntactic tree structure as (12)(a) in a hypothetical underlying structure. A rule that moves the relative clause is then hypothesized to account for the fact that it does not form a constituent with its head at the "surface structure" level.

By acknowledging the conceptual basis of grammatical relationships, CG accommodates the data without resorting to the dubious theoretical constructs of underlying structures and transforming operations. Neither expression in (12) "derives" from the other. Instead, they represent two alternate ways of successively grouping the same component elements in arriving at the same composite conception. These alternate compositional paths are respectively shown in diagrams (a) and (b) of figure 7.19. As usual, irrelevant details are suppressed (namely tense, the definite article, progressive aspect, and the subordinator *that*). For the relative clause, only the composite structure is represented. It profiles a mental relationship (dashed arrow) whose trajector is identified as the speaker (S) through elaboration at a lower level of organization, but whose landmark remains schematic.

In diagram (a), this landmark is elaborated by *the package*, which serves as profile determinant. The resulting composite expression, *the package that I was expecting*, is a standard example of a head noun being modified by a relative clause. Note that *the package* functions semantically as the clausal object, because its profile corresponds to the landmark of *I was expecting*. At the higher level of organization, the complex nominal *the package that I was expecting* elaborates the trajector of *arrived* and is therefore its subject. *Arrived* is the profile determinant at this level, since (12)(a) as a whole designates an instance of arriving (not the package or the process of expecting).

In diagram (b), we find the same three components: *the package*, *arrived*, and *that I was expecting*. Observe also that the same elements correspond as in diagram (a), and their composite semantic structures are identical. The only difference resides in the order of composition, i.e. constituency. Here, in accordance with the general subject construction, *the package* combines with *arrived* to form the composite expression *the package arrived*. At the higher level of organization, *the package*

(a)   *the package that I was expecting arrived*

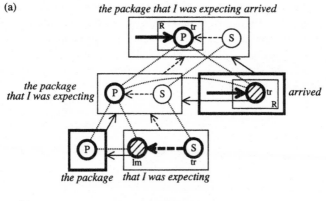

(b)   *the package arrived that I was expecting*

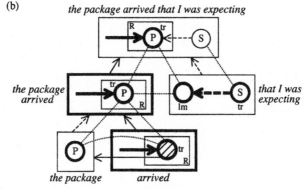

FIGURE 7.19

arrived is integrated with the relative clause by virtue of a correspondence between the former's trajector (the package) and the latter's schematic landmark. This correspondence ensures that the package is understood semantically as the object of the relative clause, even though (12)(b) is not a classic relative clause construction (since *the package* and *that I was expecting* do not combine directly to form a higher-order nominal).

Despite the difference in constituency, both assemblies in figure 7.19 provide all the essential semantic and grammatical information. Since the composite semantic structures are identical, the sentences in (12) are basically the same in meaning. The only semantic contrast resides in a secondary dimension of meaning, namely the compositional path leading to the ultimate composite structure: in (12) (a), one step along this path consists of the nominal expression *the package that I was expecting*; in (12)(b), we find instead the clausal expression *the package arrived*. Both represent natural conceptual groupings. *The package* forms a conceptual group with *that I was expecting* because they jointly offer a full characterization of the central clausal participant. By the same token, *the package* forms a conceptual group with *arrived* because they jointly specify the profiled event. Each sentence chooses one of these natural groupings for explicit symbolization by juxtaposition, thereby yielding a classic constituent. But only one can be symbolized in this manner, so whichever one is chosen, the other remains implicit. While remaining unsymbolized may lessen the salience of a grouping, this does not entail its total absence at the conceptual level. Recall a general point made earlier: there are more facets to the structure of a complex expression than can be represented in a single constituency hierarchy.

8

Rules and Restrictions

$\mathbf{A}$ language allows its speakers to construct and understand an endless supply of new expressions. We might say that it **licenses** or **sanctions** their formation. However, it does not give speakers license to do whatever they want. To be considered normal or correct, expressions have to be put together in certain ways and not others. Linguists therefore talk about the "rules" of a language and the "restrictions" on possible expressions. But what does this actually mean? Applied to language, terms like "rule" and "restriction" are metaphorical, hence potentially misleading. Thus we need to consider how they might realistically be interpreted. What is the nature of linguistic rules and restrictions? Where do they come from? How can we describe them? How do they relate to actual language use?

8.1 Networks and Schemas

In a preliminary way, the questions just posed have already been answered. The rules and restrictions of a language reside in large numbers of **schemas** arranged in **networks**. Schemas are abstracted from occurring expressions and can then be used in constructing and understanding new expressions. We must now examine these matters in greater depth and detail. A good way to start is by posing another fundamental question.

8.1.1 What Is a Language?

Actually, there is no such thing as "a language", at least as this term is commonly understood, both by linguists and by ordinary people. To a large extent this understanding is metaphorically constituted. A very general metaphor, applied to language in many ways, construes linguistic entities as physical entities. We can *pick up a language* (like our clothes pick up cat hairs) or *acquire* it (the way we might acquire an art collection). Linguists talk about *linguistic structure* and *constructing sentences*. When we speak of *empty statements, putting ideas into words*, and *getting something out of what someone says*, we are thinking of expressions as containers and meanings as their content (Reddy 1979). A language too is conceived as a container, an elaborate one with a number of compartments, each holding an array of separate objects. Thus a linguist might ask (quite pointlessly from the standpoint of CG) whether a certain rule is *in the lexicon* or *in the syntax*. Another metaphor likens knowing a language to knowing a set of facts. This engenders the common supposition that a language is fully describable with a grammar book and dictionary, hence available for inspection once these materials are prepared. Linguistic theorists subscribe to this metaphor when they talk about *linguistic knowledge* (as if knowing Finnish were comparable to knowing U.S. history) or the *internal grammar* of a language (the mental counterpart of the grammar a linguist might write to describe it).

Such metaphors reflect and support the conception of a language as a distinct, discretely bounded, clearly delimited entity that is basically stable and uniform within a community of speakers. Accordingly, linguists refer to "the linguistic system" or "the grammar of a language", view this as a separate mental "component", and often represent it diagrammatically with a box labeled L. The idealization and reification underlying these notions is unavoidable and perhaps even helpful if not taken too seriously. Indeed, I continue here to talk about "a language" or "linguistic system", sometimes using a box labeled L to represent it. But this conception is just a convenient fiction that must be recognized as such. A language does not reside in grammar books and dictionaries, and looking in a speaker's brain does not reveal a box labeled L.[1]

The basic reality is simply that people talk, in ways that are similar to varying degrees. Talking is a complex **activity**, so ultimately a language must be viewed dynamically, as something people do rather than something they have. The various facets of this activity—motor, perceptual, and mental—are either controlled or constituted by neural processing, so in a broad sense talking is **cognitive** activity. Moreover, since a language is acquired and used by way of interacting with others in a social and cultural context, the activity is **sociocultural** in nature.

Talking can thus be characterized as socioculturally grounded cognitive activity. Like any complex activity (e.g. building a house, running a business, or playing baseball), it draws on a wide array of resources and requires an elaborate set of general and specific abilities. Constituting the more specific abilities are recurring patterns of activity, which emerge with increasing robustness as we develop them and continue to refine them. Among these patterns are those we reify and identify as the units of a language. Such units thus consist in recurring aspects of processing activity. To different degrees, these patterns of neural processing have coalesced as entrenched cognitive routines that can be activated whenever needed. They might be thought of as mental or mentally directed skills employed in various combinations in the complex task of talking. Knowing a language is a matter of controlling a vast repertoire of skills collectively used for talking in certain sociocultural contexts.

Granted that linguistic units are dynamic in nature, residing in aspects of cognitive processing, we must next consider their status vis-à-vis other facets of cognition. It is important not to be misled by the metaphorical conception of a language as

---

[1] If there actually is a grammar in our head, who is in there to consult it?

a bounded container holding discrete and separate objects. Several expectations induced by this metaphor are almost surely incorrect. One property of physical containers which we cannot ascribe to the units of a language—individually or collectively—is that of occupying a definite, limited location. While certain regions in the brain are strongly implicated in language, the processing activity constituting linguistic units cannot be strictly localized to any one area. Nor are linguistic structures distinct or independent from nonlinguistic phenomena. Instead, they recruit and incorporate knowledge and abilities that are not specifically linguistic, without which they could not be manifested.[2] They can only emerge in the context of a broader processing matrix, as strands of activity intertwined with others to form a cohesive fabric. Finally, linguistic units are not separate and independent with respect to one another; some units overlap with others or include them as components. And rather than being distinct from their instantiations, schemas are best envisaged as inherent aspects of the processing activity in which they reside. They are immanent in their instantiations in much the same way that the schematic shape of a letter inheres in all the specific shapes the letter assumes in different fonts.

Everybody talks a bit differently. You will not find any two speakers, for example, who control exactly the same vocabulary and ascribe exactly the same meaning to every lexical item. If we reify the skills deployed in talking, referring to them individually as linguistic units and collectively as a linguistic system, we have to recognize that every speaker's linguistic system is different from everyone else's. When two systems are sufficiently similar, the differences do not impair communication and are usually not even noticed. Speakers simply talk and manage to understand each other fairly well. Having no conscious access to the system per se, they focus their attention on expressions and the contexts supporting their occurrence. But if everybody has a different linguistic system, what do we then identify as "a language", such as English (to choose one at random)?

Objectively, there is no single entity that can be so identified. There are simply lots of people—hundreds of millions of them—who talk in roughly similar ways (sometimes very roughly indeed). Strictly speaking, each person has a distinct linguistic system (or "idiolect"). These individual systems do exhibit a strong family resemblance, however, and like the members of an extended family, some systems resemble one other quite closely, others more distantly. On this basis we can group them into "dialects" of various sizes and degrees of cohesiveness. Yet we can only do this by abstracting away from individual differences and imposing artificial boundaries. If thought of as a clearly delimited entity with definite boundaries, neither a dialect nor a language exists in the wild, but only as a mental construction—the product of idealization, reification, and metaphor. The mental construction of a language is itself grounded in social interaction and cultural attitudes. Idealizations and metaphors commonly used in thinking and talking about language are part of socially transmitted cultural knowledge. The very notion that an element belongs

---

[2] Recall the discussions of encyclopedic semantics (§2.1.3) and conceptual archetypes functioning as linguistic category prototypes (ch. 4). Also exploited for linguistic purposes are basic mental phenomena like perception, association, abstraction, categorization, reification, rhythm, temporal sequencing, and motor control.

to "a language", in the sense of being regularly and intrinsically used in speaking it, constitutes one dimension of its conventional linguistic import.

It is pointless to ask whether language is cognitive or sociocultural in nature, for it is obviously both. A linguistic system comprises a vast array of skills employed in talking. Ultimately, those skills reside in recurrent patterns of neural and neurally guided processing activity. They do not develop in isolation, but as the product of social interaction in a cultural context (Tomasello 2003). In learning to talk, an individual's linguistic system converges on those of other individuals the learner interacts with. Acquisition is never really completed, for the system a person acquires continues to be refined, adjusted, and extended throughout linguistic life. These adaptations as well are effected through sociocultural interaction, and are thus coordinated to some extent among individuals who interact with one another.

In the sea of talking individuals, there is thus a constant inclination for structure to emerge and maintain itself. Individuals tend to be organized in self-perpetuating groups whose speech is very much alike and who think of themselves as speaking the same language or dialect. These "speech communities" vary greatly in size, social cohesiveness, and the degree to which they approximate linguistic uniformity. The key word, of course, is "approximate", since even the closest-knit community exhibits linguistic variation. The differences among individual linguistic systems may nevertheless be overshadowed by the extensive commonality enabling members of a speech community to freely communicate. To the extent that this is so, both speakers and linguists are prone to abstract away from the differences and focus on the massive similarities. It is through this process of idealization and reification that languages and dialects emerge as mental and sociocultural constructions.

8.1.2 Schemas

To ignore these factors, pretending that languages and linguistic units are wholly discrete, would have to be regarded as misguided. It would be equally misguided to embrace the opposite extreme and regard them as wholly continuous—a sea of infinite variation with no discernible structure. The fact is that structures do emerge with varying degrees of robustness, definition, and stability. Language is patterned, organized activity exhibiting extensive regularities that need to be discovered and described. Their characterization should, however, accommodate the inherent dynamicity and variability of linguistic structure.

The regularities that we reify and collectively refer to as "a language" consist of conventional linguistic units. They are "units" in the sense of being entrenched cognitive routines, and "conventional" by virtue of representing established linguistic practice in a certain speech community. These conventional units embody the rules of a language and the restrictions imposed on its expressions. As there are various forms such units might in principle assume, we must consider the basic nature of linguistic rules and the source of their restrictiveness.[3]

---

[3] I am using the term "rule" in a neutral sense, to indicate whatever is responsible for the patterns and regularities of a language. Theorists often use it more narrowly, for what are here called "constructive rules".

Linguists conceive of rules in one of three general ways: as **constructive rules**, as **filters**, or as **schemas**. Constructive rules are like instructions to be followed step-by-step in putting together expressions (giving them as "output"). Prime examples are the "phrase structure rules" and "transformations" of classic generative grammar (Chomsky 1957, 1965). Phrase structure rules are instructions for building syntactic tree structures like figures 7.16 and 7.17(a). Transformations specify how the "underlying" structures thereby constructed are successively modified—by operations like insertion, deletion, and movement—to yield an expression's "surface" form. Rules and expressions are thus conceived as being fundamentally different in nature. To make an analogy, if rules are the steps in a computer program, expressions are the images it generates on the screen. Hence there is no reason to expect individual rules to resemble the expressions they help produce. The sole requirement is that the rules function collectively to give only well-formed expressions as output.

Linguistic rules can also be cast in negative form, as statements of what is **not** permitted in well-formed expressions. Such a rule, for instance, might brand as ill-formed any clause in which a verb and its subject disagree in number (*it are*; *they is*). Theorists have occasionally entertained the notion that grammar might consist entirely in filters of this sort. Such an account would take as its starting point the set of all possible "strings" of words drawn from the lexicon of the language. Most of these are simply incoherent—only a very small proportion (but still infinitely many!) would be accepted as grammatical expressions. This determination is made by checking the candidate strings against the long list of prohibitions in which the grammar of the language resides. Most strings are filtered out by virtue of being flagged for violations. Expressions that draw no flags are judged grammatical.[4]

In contrast to constructive rules (which **need not** resemble expressions) and filters (which by definition **cannot**), schemas **must** resemble the expressions they characterize. Schemas emerge from expressions through reinforcement of the commonalities they exhibit at some level of abstraction. Or to phrase it more accurately, they arise within expressions, as recurring aspects of the processing activity that constitutes them. They differ from the expressions they characterize only in level of specificity, representing the coarse-grained similarities revealed by abstracting away from fine-grained details.

In CG, rules take the form of schemas. Patterns and regularities of any sort, at any level of specificity, reside in schematic units abstracted from occurring expressions. Even lexical items have this character. Though often regarded as idiosyncratic,[5] lexical items are better thought of as regularities of limited scope. The lexeme *cat*, for instance, embodies the generalization that creatures of a certain sort are conventionally designated by this form. There is no inconsistency in describing lexical items as specific fixed expressions, on the one hand, and as schemas, on the other. A lexical unit like *cat* is certainly specific compared with the schema describing

---

[4] This filtering approach is reminiscent of the old, lame joke about how to sculpt an elephant: you start with a huge block of marble, and then knock off anything that doesn't look like an elephant.

[5] Lexical items are so regarded by theorists who claim a sharp distinction between lexicon and syntax, the latter supposedly consisting of general rules. Because CG recognizes grammatical patterns at all levels of generality, lexicon and grammar are seen as a continuum.

count nouns or nouns as a general class. It is nonetheless schematic compared with any particular manifestation of *cat* in actual language use. A particular occurrence may be highly specific (if not unique) in terms of both its contextually determined meaning and the fine details of its pronunciation. But as an established unit—psychologically entrenched and conventional in the speech community—a lexical item neutralizes the fine-grained features that vary from one occasion to the next.

An actual instance of language use, in all its complexity and specificity, is referred to as a **usage event**. The essential aspect of a usage event is how the expression employed is apprehended by the speaker and hearer—their full contextual understanding of its import and the full detail of its phonetic manifestation. Importantly, the relevant context subsumes far more than just the immediate physical circumstances. Speech interactions unfold at all levels of the interlocutors' awareness: physical, mental, social, cultural, emotive, and evaluative. Part of an expression's contextual import is thus an assessment by each interlocutor of what the other knows and is currently attending to, as well as their attitudes, intentions, and desires. Further included is their awareness of the ongoing discourse itself and how the current expression fits into it.

CG is a **usage-based** model of language structure (Barlow and Kemmer 2000; Bybee and Hopper 2001; GC: ch. 4). One motivation for this label is the claim that usage events are the source of all linguistic units. The relationship between units and the usage events that spawn them is tightly constrained by the **content requirement** (§1.3.4). According to the content requirement, units are limited to structures that arise from usage events through two basic cognitive processes: schematization and categorization. Semantic units are abstracted from the contextual understanding of occurring expressions, phonological units from apprehension of their phonetic properties, and symbolic units from the pairing of the two. In each case, units emerge via the progressive entrenchment of configurations that recur in a sufficient number of events to be established as cognitive routines.[6] Since only recurring features are reinforced, the units that emerge are far less comprehensive and detailed than the usage events giving rise to them. A unit corresponds to just selected aspects of the source events, and the commonality it reflects is only apparent at a certain level of abstraction.

Units are thus schematic relative to both the source events and the further events in which they figure. Once established, they function as templates in constructing and interpreting new expressions. The relationship they bear to the corresponding aspects of subsequent usage events amounts to categorization. The categorizing relationship is one of elaboration if the schema is fully manifested, without distortion, in the target; otherwise it is one of extension. Moreover, either sort of categorization is itself capable of recurring and being established as a conventional linguistic unit. We will also see that categorizing relationships are themselves subject to schematization and categorization.

---

[6] Under some conditions a unit (e.g. a new lexical item) can be learned from a single exposure. Thus the sheer number of usage events may be less important than some measure of cumulative psychological impact (involving additional factors like cognitive salience).

Linguistic units are limited by the content requirement to schematized representations of configurations inherent in usage events. Since schemas are the reinforced commonalities of occurring expressions, they amount to positive characterizations of what actually occurs in language use. This direct relation between structure and use offers an account of language acquisition that in principle is quite straightforward.[7] By contrast, certain devices employed in other theories—such as filters, constructive rules, and underlying structures—are problematic from that standpoint because their connection with actual expressions is far more indirect. The content requirement precludes their adoption in CG.

Schemas have now been given two descriptions that might seem contradictory. On the one hand, they are positive characterizations of what actually occurs. On the other hand, they are said to embody the rules and restrictions of a language. The apparent difficulty is that "rule" and "restriction" are basically negative terms, referring to what **must not** be done or what **must** be done if one is **not** to face a penalty. The question, then, is whether schemas, being positive specifications, can achieve the restrictiveness imputed to linguistic systems. If only schemas are posited, how can speakers know that certain expressions are not permitted, even some that conform to general patterns (e.g. *mans* as the plural of *man*)? On what basis can an infinite set of potential expressions be ruled out as "ungrammatical"?

Detailed answers to such questions are provided in later sections. For now, we can simply observe that limitations need not come about through explicit prohibitions. In language as in life, a single positive model may be more effective in controlling and directing behavior than any number of injunctions. This is especially so given that conventionally sanctioned structures represent just small enclaves in the vast space of structural possibilities. As ready-made resources available for exploitation, schemas function as attractors within this space, thus inhibiting the exploration of other areas. In this way, the positive characterization of conventional patterns can indicate implicitly (and quite effectively) that options outside their range are nonconventional and will be judged ill-formed.

8.1.3 Networks of Schemas

A language comprises an enormous inventory of conventional linguistic units, all abstracted from usage events. This is sketched in figure 8.1, where the small squares stand for individual units, and the large box labeled L for the language as a whole. By now you should certainly be aware of the gross distortions inherent in this representation, which is nonetheless useful for limited purposes. The discreteness suggested by the diagram and the container metaphor it is based on must not be taken seriously.

In particular, the units of a language are not like ping-pong balls in a box. Even if ping-pong balls were square, linguistic units would still be quite different owing to their intrinsically dynamic nature. More directly relevant here is the further difference that ping-pong balls are separate and unconnected, whereas units are neither. We have seen,

---

[7] Tomasello 2003 provides a comprehensive (though necessarily preliminary) description of language acquisition in a usage-based perspective.

FIGURE 8.1

for example, that units combine with one another in assemblies that are themselves conventional units (fig. 6.6). Some units are schematic vis-à-vis others, and schemas, rather than being distinct, are immanent in their instantiations. More generally, units are connected by relationships of categorization, both elaboration and extension. They can thus form **networks** of any size (as shown in fig. 2.2 for the alternate senses of *ring*).

On this basis, we can describe a language as a **structured** inventory of conventional linguistic units. This structure—the organization of units into networks and assemblies—is intimately related to language use, both shaping it and being shaped by it. To see just how, we need to examine the interaction between occurring expressions and the linguistic system invoked for constructing or understanding them. Expressions do not exist independently, but only as manifestations of a language. A conceptualization and a sequence of sounds do not constitute an expression in and of themselves, but only via their interpretation with respect to some linguistic system. Expressions are linguistic objects whose structure and status depend on the conventional units used by the speaker and hearer in apprehending them. The relationship they bear to these units amounts to categorization.

Consider, then, the relation between a language (L) and a usage event (U) interpreted as an utterance in that language. Its interpretation as such is a matter of categorization: it resides in particular units of L being invoked to categorize particular facets of U. Quite a number of units may be invoked, representing elements of different sizes in the various dimensions of linguistic structure. It is precisely by virtue of these categorizations that the utterance counts as an expression of the language. Collectively, the categorizations provide the expression's **structural description**, its characterization with respect to L.

One such categorization is depicted in figure 8.2. [A] is a conventional unit of L, and (B) is the facet of U it categorizes. These can be structures of any size or any kind (e.g. sounds, lexical items, grammatical constructions). Their relationship can either be one of elaboration ($\rightarrow$) or extension (--->). [A] is enclosed in a box to indicate its status as a unit. (B) is enclosed in a circle, on the presumption that it is novel when apprehended in full detail as part of a usage event. If (B) is novel, so must be its categorization by [A]. This is shown by enclosing it in a box with rounded corners. Formulaically, using brackets and parentheses for units and nonunits, the categorizing relationship can thus be given as either ([A] $\rightarrow$ (B)) or ([A] ---> (B)).[8]

---

[8] The speaker and hearer must both effect this categorization, since both interpret U as an instance of L. The relationship between L and U is referred to in CG as **coding** because it figures in both the speaker's task of "encoding" situations and the hearer's task of "decoding" expressions.

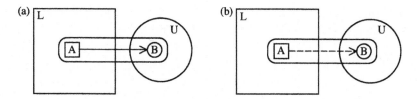

FIGURE 8.2

(B) is thus interpreted as manifesting [A] in a usage event. When (B) manifests [A] fully and without distortion, as in diagram (a), the expression is perceived as conventional ("well-formed") with respect to this particular facet of its structure. When (B)'s manifestation of [A] is only partial or distorted, as in diagram (b), the expression is perceived as nonconventional ("ill-formed") in this particular respect. The extent to which the expression as a whole is judged well-formed is thus a function of all the individual categorizations that figure in its structural description. Since we are always pushing the envelope in language use, stretching available resources to meet new linguistic challenges, a measure of non-conventionality is readily accepted if it is even noticed. Only the more blatant distortions are likely to attract attention and cause an expression to be judged "ill-formed" or "ungrammatical".

Whether it involves elaboration or extension, [A]'s categorization of (B) need not be a one-shot affair. If it is useful for [A] to be invoked and realized as (B) in the context of one usage event, the same might well prove useful in other such events. Both (B) and [A]'s categorization of (B) will then occur on multiple occasions. Should they occur sufficiently often, they will undergo entrenchment and achieve the status of units: ([A] ---> (B)) > [[A] ---> [B]].[9] Now suppose they eventually achieve unit status not just for one speaker but for most or even all members of a speech community. In this case, both [B] and the categorization [[A] ---> [B]] are nothing other than conventional linguistic units. By definition, then, they have been incorporated in the language. This overall development is summarized in figure 8.3.

Let us take some concrete examples. Imagine first that [A] is the syllable [ma], a phonological unit that occurs as part of many words. It would not be unexpected

FIGURE 8.3

---

[9] Strictly speaking, the unit [B] is schematic relative to the version of (B) that occurs in any particular usage event (since every such event is unique when examined in fine enough detail).

that a speaker might occasionally pronounce it with a nasalized vowel (a natural phonetic development, essentially just a matter of relaxing the timing of oral and velic closures). In a particular usage event, [ma] would then be manifested in slightly distorted form, as (mã). Despite this discrepancy (which will probably go unnoticed), the latter is easily interpreted as a realization of the former: ([ma] ---> (mã)). An alternate pronunciation of this sort might very well occur on many occasions, on the part of many speakers. In this way, it can eventually establish itself as a conventional unit of the language: ([ma] ---> (mã)) > [[ma] ---> [mã]]. The result of this minor linguistic change is that [mã] is now a regularly expected pronunciation of [ma].[10]

Consider next a case of semantic extension. The noun *mail*, originally referring to physically embodied messages delivered through a postal system, is now well established for what is also known as *email*—messages delivered electronically by computer. At one stage this use of *mail* was innovative. The lexical unit *mail*—at that time limited to what is now called *snail mail* or *hard mail*—was invoked to designate its electronic counterpart. This extension implies the categorization in figure 8.4(a). The occurrence of *mail* in the utterance is interpreted as manifesting the symbolic unit [MAIL/mail] even though, in the context of the usage event, it is understood as referring to electronic messages: (EMAIL/mail). This usage is now well established, so both the symbolic structure [EMAIL/mail] and its categorization by [MAIL/mail] have the status of conventional units. This is shown in diagram (b), which can be given more compactly as (c) by collapsing the two representations of [mail]. Since the original unit has not been lost, *mail* is now polysemous, having both 'hard mail' and 'email' as well-entrenched meanings. To some extent, the latter sense is still understood as an extension from the former, just as indicated in diagram (c). But this motivation is well on its way to being lost; more and more [EMAIL/mail] stands alone as an independently accessed symbolic unit.[11]

The categorization in figure 8.4 is a case of extension, rather than elaboration, because certain features of the categorizing structure are absent or distorted in the target. In lieu of messages being written down on paper is the notion of their appearing on a computer screen. Electronic transmission replaces physical delivery by postal workers. The extension is nonetheless straightforward, even obvious, as there is still a lot that [MAIL] and [EMAIL] have in common: the central role of messages, primarily expressed linguistically; the sequence of writing, sending, receiving, and reading them; their delivery via a fixed distribution network. Thus, by suspending certain specific properties of [MAIL], we obtain a more abstract conception that is fully manifested in [EMAIL]. This abstracted commonality both motivates the extension of *mail* to encompass email and ensures its ready understanding. In fact, one can plausibly argue that it now constitutes a schematic, independently accessible

---

[10] This does not necessarily imply that [ma] is no longer possible. The two pronunciations can coexist indefinitely, perhaps as casual and formal variants.

[11] The relationship between the two senses can be taken as an instance of metaphor, [MAIL] pertaining to the source domain and [EMAIL] to the target domain. The loss of motivation (the "fading" of the metaphor) is a special case of the gradual decrease in analyzability (§3.2.2) that is typical for lexical items.

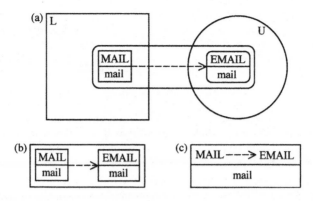

FIGURE 8.4

sense of *mail* subsuming [MAIL] and [EMAIL] as special cases. Note the following exchange:

(1)   **A:** *I got a lot of mail this morning.* **B:** *Email or hard mail?*

   As a general matter, extension relies on the implicit apprehension of something common to the source and target. Suppose we think of categorization in terms of the categorizing structure being "recognized" in the target. Its recognition is unproblematic when it is wholly immanent in the target, in which case their relationship is elaborative: ([A] → (B)). When the target conflicts in some respect with the categorizing structure, recognition engenders a certain amount of "strain". It can only come by suspending or at least overriding features of [A], to obtain an abstracted structure, (A'), observable in the target: ((A') → (B)). As shown in figure 8.5(a), (A') is thus an extension from [A] (arising as a stripped-down version of it), as well as being schematic vis-à-vis both [A] and (B). We can therefore posit an intimate relationship between extension and schematization: extension from [A] to (B) facilitates the emergence of a more schematic structure, (A'), with respect to which both [A] and (B) are elaborations. Moreover, the relationships in diagram (a) provide a general model of categorization. Elaboration represents a special case of extension, where [A] is recognizable in (B) without modification. [A] and (A') then collapse, as seen in diagram (b).

   The extent to which (A') becomes entrenched and emerges as an independently accessible unit no doubt varies. In the case of *mail*, the original, extended, and schematic senses are all well established and capable of being evoked as its meaning, depending on the context. They are thus related as shown in figure 8.5(c), where the heavy-line box indicates that the original meaning [MAIL] (i.e. 'hard mail') is prototypical and most easily elicited. This mini-network is part of a somewhat larger network representing the conventional semantic value of *mail*. In learning to use the word properly, a speaker masters the entire network (not just the schema or the prototype). A lexical item of any frequency tends to be polysemous, having multiple senses linked by relationships of categorization. Its various senses are members of a

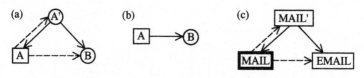

FIGURE 8.5

category that is **structured** by these relationships. It is further said to be a **complex** category because its membership and configuration are not reducible to (or predictable from) any single element.

Complex categories are characteristic of virtually every aspect of linguistic structure: the established senses of a lexical item, the phonetic realizations of a phoneme ("allophones"), the phonological realizations of a morpheme ("allomorphs"), families of grammatical constructions, and so on. They reflect the variation induced by ongoing language change and the constant challenge of adapting existing units to additional contexts and changing circumstances. Starting from a single unit, [A], repeated occurrences of the developments sketched in figures 8.2, 8.3, and 8.5 result in networks of related variants, as suggested in figure 8.6. The individual nodes in such a network can be structures of any kind or degree of complexity (up to and including multilevel constructions). Each categorizing relationship in such a network is itself a conventional linguistic unit, as indicated in figures 8.3 and 8.4. In principle, an important dimension of the network's characterization—merely hinted at by the thickness of boxes—is a measure of each unit's entrenchment and ease of activation. The most entrenched and most readily activated unit will generally be the original structure, [A], which can then be recognized as the category prototype.[12]

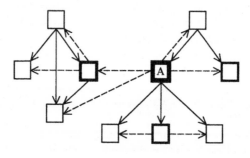

FIGURE 8.6

---

[12] The structure of a complex category at a given point in time is not necessarily a direct reflection of how it develops, either historically or in language acquisition. In the span of a couple decades, for example, the semantic network of *mail* is being reconfigured, with [MAIL] no longer a clear-cut prototype (hence the term *hard mail* to avoid confusion). We can anticipate [EMAIL] eventually taking over as the prototypical sense, with [MAIL] then being an extension from it. In some circles, this has probably already happened.

Bear in mind that the network model of complex categories is a metaphor. Like any metaphor, it is helpful in certain respects but potentially misleading in others. On the one hand, the network model is useful because it captures some essential properties of complex categories: that there are multiple variants, that these are related in certain ways, and that some are more central (or easily elicited) than others. On the other hand, the model proves misleading if the discreteness it implies is taken too seriously. It suggests that a category has an exact number of clearly distinct members, that it exhibits a unique configuration defined by a specific set of categorizing relationships, and that a target of categorization can always be assigned to a particular category member. Yet these entailments of the metaphor should not be ascribed to the actual phenomenon—if you look for a category in the brain, you will not find boxes linked by arrows. It may well be that the network metaphor has outlived its usefulness. At the very least, it should be counterbalanced with an alternative metaphor that emphasizes continuity rather than discreteness.[13]

Suppose we compare a complex category to a mountain range, with peaks corresponding to category members. Rather than being discrete and sharply distinct, the peaks in a mountain range grade into another, rising from a continuous substrate to their various elevations. The number of peaks cannot be counted with absolute precision—how many there are depends on how high we decide a prominence has to be in order to qualify as such. Moreover, many positions in the range cannot be assigned to any particular peak but are simply part of the substrate from which they all emerge. Despite this basic continuity, it would be quite wrong to insist on the total absence of discreteness. There are indeed peaks in the range, which exhibits a certain configuration (no two ranges are topographically identical). It would be pointless to deny this structure or prohibit the use of discrete terms (count nouns like *peak, valley, ridge*, etc.) in describing it. Any terms should be used judiciously, of course, and with full awareness of their limitations.

8.2 Assessing Conventionality

Linguists distinguish between expressions that are "grammatical" (or "well-formed") and those that are "ungrammatical" ("ill-formed"). In so doing, they are not **prescribing** how people ought to talk but **describing** the assessments speakers themselves supposedly make. The boundary between well- and ill-formed expressions is fuzzy at best and continually being adjusted as speakers push the limits in normal language use. Still, they can only push the limits if there are limits to push. At a given time, in a given speech community, a large body of conventions are firmly enough established that speakers invoke them as the basis for apprehending expressions. An expression is accepted as conventional to the extent that it conforms to the units invoked for this purpose. It behooves us to understand this process in a fair amount of detail. How are

[13] Originally, the network model provided an alternative to the prevalent notion that a single structure was sufficient to define a category. For a general discussion of continuity vs. discreteness, see Langacker 2006.

the units invoked? How do they give rise to judgments of nonconventionality? Can a scheme of this sort impose the proper restrictions (ruling out expressions that are not permitted)?

8.2.1 Interactive Activation

The process of assessing conventionality amounts to categorization. An expression's overall assessment resolves itself into numerous categorizing relationships, each holding between a linguistic unit, [A], and some facet, (B), of a usage event (fig. 8.2). The expression is conventional (well-formed) to the extent that these relationships are elaborative: ([A] → (B)). But now we face a basic problem. How, for a given target (B), is the categorizing unit selected? Out of the countless units comprising the linguistic system, why is unit [A], in particular, invoked to categorize (B)? The choice is critical, for the status of (B) depends on it. Consider the phrase *tall giraffe*. On the one hand, this will be judged conventional if interpreted as manifesting the constructional schema for the modification of nouns by adjectives: ([ADJ N] → (*tall giraffe*)). On the other hand, it is ill-formed if construed as a prepositional phrase, since *tall* is not a preposition and *giraffe* is a simple noun rather than a full nominal: ([P NML] ---> (*tall giraffe*)). You are no doubt objecting that one would never invoke the schema for prepositional phrases to categorize the sequence of an adjective plus noun. While that is true, it begs the question. Why is it, precisely, that [ADJ N] is invoked to categorize *tall giraffe*, and not [P NML]? After all, both schemas are established conventional units.

It would be quite legitimate to argue that linguists should not have to answer this question. Schema selection poses a problem not just with respect to language but for cognition in general. It is thus a matter for psychologists. Whatever general solution they arrive at will presumably prove valid for language as well. We can see the problem's generality by considering its manifestation in a nonlinguistic domain, namely face recognition.

I can distinguish and recognize many individuals from their faces. For each such individual, I have abstracted a schematized image constituting my knowledge of what that person looks like. When I see and recognize someone, I do so by activating the appropriate schema and using it to apprehend the current visual impression. But how do I get it right? Suppose I have just two face schemas, one for Zelda (round face, dark hair, female) and one for Quentin (long face, light hair, male). I know both people well and never fail to recognize them. So when Zelda walks into the room, presenting me with a specific visual impression of her face (Z), I succeed in activating my [ZELDA] schema and using it to effect the proper categorization: ([ZELDA] → (Z)). This is sketched in figure 8.7(a). But what prevents the alternate categorization in diagram (b)? In this case I would activate my [QUENTIN] schema and mistakenly interpret my impression of Zelda as a distorted manifestation of Quentin: ([QUENTIN] ---> (Z)). Why, then, do I respond to the sight of Zelda by saying *Hello, Zelda* rather than saying *Gee, Quentin, you sure have changed*?

Although the problem cannot be solved by linguistic methods alone, certain aspects of a general account do seem reasonably apparent. Linguistic units reside in patterns of neural activation. Since the brain is highly interconnected, the occurrence

FIGURE 8.7

of a certain pattern either facilitates or inhibits the occurrence of many others. Moreover, since neural processing takes place at various levels and unfolds through time, it is constantly influenced by what happens at other levels and earlier stages. The account envisaged is thus dynamic and interactive, with myriad factors helping to elicit the processing activity that constitutes a given mental experience.[14]

For a unit to be invoked as a categorizing structure, one such factor must be preliminary processing of the target itself. When I see a face, for instance, low-level processing of the visual impression might register such coarse-grained features as roundness and surrounding darkness (of the hair), and since these are part of my [ZELDA] schema, they will tend to elicit it. Activation of this unit provides the basis for detailed apprehension of the visual target, in which I recognize Zelda by seeing the face **as hers**. Or suppose the target is *tall giraffe* and that *tall* is recognized at the first stage of processing. Since *tall* is an adjective, and thus embodies the adjective schema, its activation tends to elicit that of the constructional schema [ADJ N]. Invoking this as the categorizing structure facilitates recognition of the following noun (for a noun is thus anticipated) and results in the entire expression being **understood as** an instance of the [ADJ N] construction.

In broad outline, then, schema selection can be described as follows. A particular target, T, tends to activate a set of units, each of which has the potential to categorize it. Initially, these units are all activated to some degree. This is sketched in figure 8.8(a), where thickness of lines indicates degree of activation. The potential

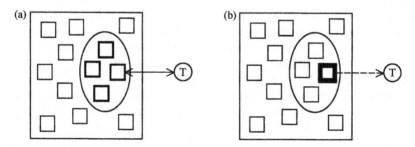

FIGURE 8.8

[14] Broadly speaking, these properties are characteristic of a "connectionist" (or "neural network") model of processing based on spreading activation and inhibition (Collins and Loftus 1975; Elman and McClelland 1984; MacWhinney 1987; Regier 1996).

categorizing structures compete for the privilege of serving in this capacity. Most likely they are mutually inhibitory, so as one becomes more highly activated it tends to suppress the others. Eventually (though it is only a matter of milliseconds) one member wins the competition, achieving a high level of activation at the expense of all its rivals. It then serves to categorize T, as shown in diagram (b).

A number of factors encourage a unit's selection as the categorizing structure. The first is degree of entrenchment, translating into inherent ease of activation. In principle (though it is hard to measure in practice), this is one dimension in the characterization of every linguistic unit. A second factor is the influence of context ("contextual priming"). If we have just been discussing Zelda, for example, my schema for her face will be slightly activated and thus more easily elicited than it would normally be. So if a person vaguely resembling Zelda should wander by, I might well mistake her for Zelda until I get a closer look. The third factor is degree of overlap with the target. The more properties a unit shares with the target (as determined by preliminary processing), the more the target tends to activate it. A significant consequence of this last factor is that more specific units have a built-in advantage over more schematic ones in the competition to be selected as categorizing structure. Being characterized in finer-grained detail, a specific unit has more properties that might overlap with the target to boost its level of activation.

There is no requirement that the unit activated to categorize a target be fully compatible with it. In fact, the unit invoked may be less compatible than other candidates, owing its selection to contextual priming or inherent ease of activation. This reflects a fundamental point: namely, that categorization is partially shaped by expectations (proceeding in "top-down" fashion) rather than being solely driven by the nature of the target (in "bottom-up" fashion). Indeed, the target itself is often largely constituted by its categorization. Once invoked by the target based on preliminary processing (which may be rudimentary), the categorizing unit imposes its own content and organization, which can reinforce, supplement, or override those inherent in the target. Supplementation occurs, for instance, when we mentally connect a set of dots to perceive a familiar shape (as in viewing constellations). Overriding the target is a common pitfall in proofreading, where we see a word as it ought to be written, not as it actually is. Whatever the details, a target is never apprehended in a neutral or wholly objective manner; there is always some **basis** for its apprehension. A categorizing unit provides this basis. Its interaction with the target results in a unified experience—not equivalent to either individually—in which the target is **apprehended as** an instance of the category. The experience of seeing Zelda's face **as** her face is not equivalent to seeing her face without recognizing it, nor to invoking the image of her face without actually seeing it. That is, ([ZELDA] → (Z)) is distinct from both (Z) and [ZELDA].

8.2.2 Restrictiveness

An utterance that occurs in a usage event constitutes a linguistic expression by virtue of a substantial number of categorizations (as depicted in fig. 8.2). These categorizations represent the structure ascribed to the expression, i.e. its interpretation with respect to the linguistic system. Of course, a target interpreted as manifesting a particular linguistic unit does not necessarily reflect it without distortion. An expression is nonconventional to the extent that targets deviate from the units invoked to categorize them.

A linguistic system's restrictiveness therefore derives not only from the conventional units it comprises but also from how they are accessed and applied in usage events. Due to these latter factors, infinitely many expressions are ruled out as ill-formed even though the units themselves are positive in nature, representations of what does occur in the language. Of course, most conceivable expressions are precluded from the outset because they bear no significant resemblance to the language in question. The units of English, for example, provide no basis for even beginning to apprehend expressions in Hopi or Tagalog; these diverge so far from the patterns of English that, except for a few accidental resemblances, they fail to elicit English units as categorizing structures. And since they do not receive a structural interpretation with respect to English, they do not even count as expressions of the language (well-formed or ill-formed). Expressions that do receive a structural interpretation, eliciting units of the language for their categorization, may be judged ill-formed nonetheless when certain categorizations are relationships of extension rather than elaboration.

This model for assessing well-formedness is flexible, dynamic, and interactive. Restrictions on permissible expressions are not stated directly (as explicit prohibitions) but emerge from factors that are matters of degree: entrenchment, extent of overlap, level of activation. A system of this sort is nevertheless able to account for the robust patterns, strict limitations, and clear-cut judgments evident at least in certain aspects of language structure. We can start by observing that, as a special case, such a system allows the emergence of fully general, essentially regular patterns. This occurs when a unit is sufficiently well entrenched and easily elicited, relative to any likely competitors, that it is virtually always invoked as categorizing structure. Internally, moreover, such a unit can be quite specific in regard to the properties a target must have to be fully sanctioned by it.

In an English nominal, for example, a simple adjective directly precedes the noun it modifies: *tall giraffe, elegant dress, sharp knife, serious misgivings*, etc.[15] This regularity is captured by a constructional schema, abbreviated here as [ADJ N], whose semantic pole is as shown in figure 7.5 and whose phonological pole specifies temporal order and adjacency. The pattern is quite general, and judgments are clear-cut: *tall giraffe* is well-formed, **giraffe tall* is not. Though it may seem evident, we need to be explicit about how such judgments are arrived at. Suppose, then, that a target nominal is determined by preliminary processing to include both the adjective *tall* and the noun *giraffe*, the former serving to characterize the latter. Given these

---

[15] This statement pertains to the internal structure of nominals, not to cases where an adjective is external to a nominal it characterizes (e.g. *The giraffe is tall*). What is meant by a "simple" adjective has to be spelled out; included, for instance, are adjectives preceded by certain adverbs (as in *very tall giraffe*) but not those followed by a prepositional phrase (**tall beyond belief giraffe*). We must also make allowance for multiple adjectives (as in *big, bad wolf*) where only one can precede the noun directly. In principle, such clarifications and qualifications should be offered for almost any example. However, practicality dictates their omission when they do not affect the basic validity of the point at hand.

specifications, how is it ascertained that *tall giraffe* is a proper way of expressing this, while **giraffe tall* is ill-formed?[16]

The constructional schema [ADJ N] provides an accessible option for making these determinations. It is well entrenched and easily elicited. Moreover, it overlaps extensively with the target, since *tall* is a simple adjective, *giraffe* is a noun, and their semantic relationship is just as the schema specifies. If [ADJ N] is indeed activated to categorize the target nominal, only *tall giraffe* will be judged conventional in regard to the placement of noun and adjective: ([ADJ N] → (*tall giraffe*)). The alternative **giraffe tall* violates the word order prescribed by the schema at its phonological pole: ([ADJ N] ---> (*giraffe tall*)). Will these judgments be consistent? That depends on what other units might be available with the potential to be selected as categorizing structure. For simple adjectives there are no serious competitors. In learning English, we are not systematically exposed to expressions like **giraffe tall* and **knife sharp*, so we do not abstract a schema that would sanction them. Should an expression of this sort be produced, it will thus be categorized by [ADJ N] and judged ill-formed.

There is nothing intrinsically wrong with expressions like **giraffe tall*—they simply happen to be nonconventional, given how the language has evolved. It might have turned out otherwise. Imagine a language just like modern English, except that a simple adjective can either precede or follow the noun it modifies: *tall giraffe* and *giraffe tall* are equally acceptable. Exposed to both patterns, learners of this fancied variety of English will abstract both [ADJ N] and [N ADJ] as conventional units. Assuming that both are well entrenched and easily activated, the one that overlaps to a greater extent with a target will win the competition to be selected as the categorizing unit. One respect in which a unit can overlap with a target is word order. On this basis, therefore, a target like *tall giraffe* will elicit the schema [ADJ N] to categorize it (all else being equal), while *giraffe tall* will activate [N ADJ]. Both are judged well-formed: ([ADJ N] → (*tall giraffe*)); ([N ADJ] → (*giraffe tall*)). We see from this example that an expression's conventionality cannot be ascertained by considering just a single unit. The full array of potentially applicable units, and their relative degrees of accessibility, must be taken into account.

When a language has alternate units performing the same basic function, they tend to specialize, so that each is used in a certain range of circumstances (instead of being freely interchangeable). It turns out that English—the real variety—does have a pattern in which an adjective follows the noun it modifies. However, this pattern is limited to adjectives exhibiting certain kinds of complexity, notably by incorporating a prepositional or infinitival phrase: *a giraffe **tall beyond belief***; *students **anxious about their grades***; *anyone **ready to confess***. We must therefore posit two constructional schemas, one in which a simple adjective (ADJ) precedes the noun it modifies,

---

[16] Both interlocutors face this problem, though in slightly different guises. The speaker intends for *tall* to modify *giraffe* and needs to find a conventional means of conveying this. The same structures and categorizations figure in the hearer's understanding of the expression and determine whether it is accepted as normal or perceived as deviant. Also, to some extent each interlocutor assumes the role of the other: the speaker imagines what the hearer faces in trying to understand the expression, and the hearer imagines what the speaker most likely intends in producing it.

FIGURE 8.9

and one in which a complex adjective (ADJ + X) follows the noun. These alternate units are depicted in figure 8.9, along with four target expressions.

Since both units are accessible, degree of overlap with the target determines the choice of categorizing structure. And since all the targets include a noun and a modifying adjective, the selection hinges on word order and whether the adjective is simple or complex. In the case of *tall giraffe*, these factors conspire to activate [ADJ N] as the categorizing unit; with *giraffe tall beyond belief*, they activate [N ADJ + X]. Hence these two expressions are judged to be well-formed. By contrast, both **giraffe tall* and **tall beyond belief giraffe* overlap with each target in one respect but conflict with it in regard to the other. Thus, while either expression might elicit either unit for its categorization, every combination results in a judgment of nonconventionality. For example, **giraffe tall* can be interpreted either as an instance of [ADJ N] with the wrong word order or as an instance of [N ADJ + X] with the wrong kind of adjective.

For many reasons, judgments are often less crisp and clear-cut. A notorious case is the past tense of "irregular" verbs in English, where speakers are often uncertain about the proper form. I myself am uncertain about the past tense of *dive*: is it *dove* or *dived*? I know that both occur, and while I was taught the former in school, the latter seems more frequent. Although I accept both options, neither feels completely right, and if forced to produce the past-tense form of *dive* I might very well hesitate. The problem arises because there are two potential categorizing units, neither of which is able to fully suppress the other and decisively win the competition to serve in that capacity. One such unit is the constructional schema representing the regular pattern of past-tense formation. Thoroughly entrenched and easily activated, this schema specifies the suffixation of *-d* to mark past tense.[17] The other unit is the symbolic structure *dove* itself, specifically learned by speakers (at least those who use it) as the past-tense form of *dive*. For me, this unit is well enough entrenched that it is activated to some degree even when I hear the form *dived* and recognize it as instantiating the regular pattern. Thus I do not entirely avoid the secondary categorization of *dived* as a distorted manifestation of *dove*. Still, *dove* is not so terribly frequent that its status is wholly secure. It does not spring quite so readily to mind as does the past-tense form of *drive*, nor is its activation strong enough to completely suppress the regular pattern.

---

[17] More precisely, it specifies the suffixation of [d], [t], or [əd] depending on phonological properties of the stem. The schema for the general pattern thus has three well-entrenched subschemas describing the individual variants.

This uncertainty regarding *dived* vs. *dove* comes about because two factors determining the choice of categorizing structure are at odds with each other. The regular pattern has a great advantage in terms of entrenchment and ease of activation. It is used so frequently, and with such a high percentage of English verbs, that it functions as the default, being activated for past-tense verbs unless there is strong motivation to override this choice. The existence of a specific, entrenched alternative—in this case *dove*—provides such motivation. Being an established unit, *dove* itself can be invoked to sanction a past-tense use of *dive*. Compared with the general pattern, it enjoys a major advantage in terms of overlap with the target: if the target is taken as being a past-tense form of *dive*, then it obviously overlaps with *dove* (which is precisely that) in far more respects than with a constructional schema that refers to the verb in only generalized fashion. In my own linguistic system, these two opposing factors are more or less in balance, hence my uncertainty.

The general point is that the factors bearing on the choice of categorizing structure vary from case to case in their relative strength and whether they tend to activate the same or different units for this purpose. The structure selected is not necessarily the most entrenched, the most specific, or the one most compatible with the target. Nor is the outcome necessarily the same from one occasion to the next. It all depends on the specific configuration of the network (for a given speaker, at a given point in time) and how the various elements and factors interact dynamically in the context of a particular usage event.

In taking *dove* as its past-tense form, *dive* follows the same pattern as a number of other monosyllabic verbs: *write/wrote*, *break/broke*, *drive/drove*, *freeze/froze*, *rise/rose*, *strive/strove*. What marks past tense in each case is the substitution $[(\dots Vy\dots)_\sigma] \dashrightarrow [(\dots ow\dots)_\sigma]$—that is, occurrence of the vocalic nucleus [ow] in lieu of either [ay], [ey], or [iy], which would otherwise be expected (cf. fig. 6.11(b)). Presumably speakers abstract a constructional schema to capture this limited regularity. If they do, the schema is too weakly established to be invoked for the sanction of novel expressions. When we coin a new verb—for instance *fease* 'make feasible'—the past tense has to be *feased*, not **fose*. The general pattern is so well entrenched that it is accessed by default for virtually all new verbs, eclipsing other alternatives. Unable to compete successfully, schemas representing other patterns are mostly inaccessible for new expressions. These "minor" patterns sustain themselves only because particular instantiations (like *wrote*, *broke*, *drove*, etc.) are specifically learned as conventional units. As such, they are able to compete with the general pattern by virtue of their far greater overlap with the target. In fact, for verbs occurring with any frequency they win the competition quite consistently. Thus we do not apprehend a form like **writed* as a well-formed instance of the regular pattern but as a distorted instance of *wrote*.

This interactive model resolves a number of well-known issues, the first of which is the problem posed by minor patterns like $[(\dots Vy\dots)_\sigma] \dashrightarrow [(\dots ow\dots)_\sigma]$. Since a pattern can be discerned, linguists feel obliged to posit a rule describing it. But if such a rule exists, why can it not be applied to other verbs, even novel ones? The model handles this by distinguishing between the mere existence of a schema (a reinforced commonality) and its capacity to win the competition for activation as a categorizing unit. Also accounted for is the clear historical tendency for minor patterns to be most persistent in words with the greatest frequency. The frequent occurrence of specific learned forms like *wrote*, *broke*, and *drove* makes them accessible enough to resist the gradual encroachment of the general pattern. Less frequent forms, like *dove*, *strove*, and the now archaic *hove*, are less readily elicited and therefore tend through time to be supplanted.[18] Finally, the model inherently explains the prevalent phenomenon known as **blocking**, observed in all domains of language structure. The term "blocking" indicates that a general pattern fails to apply in some particular situation because a more specific unit preempts it. Despite their regularity, for example, the past-tense verb **writed* is blocked from occurring by the well-entrenched alternative *wrote*, and the plural noun **mans* by *men*. Likewise, the readily available *thief*, *rapist*, *arsonist*, and *assassin* preempt the occurrence of **stealer*, **raper*, **burner*, and **assassinator* (cf. *killer*, *murderer*, *hijacker*, *embezzler*, *smuggler*, *kidnapper*). Blocking reflects the built-in advantage of more specific units over more schematic ones in competing for activation. A more specific unit is characterized by a larger number of properties, each a potential source of activation through overlap with the target.

A dynamic interactive model can therefore account for the gaps encountered in otherwise regular patterns. Consider one more case, involving a limited set of "postpositions" in Luiseño. As the term suggests, these postpositions are like prepositions, except that they follow the noun expressing their landmark (as suffixes) rather than preceding it (as separate words). The examples in (2) are representative. First, postpositions attach directly to nouns whose referents are inanimate. The constructional schema describing this pattern will be represented by the abbreviatory formula $[N_{inan}\text{-}P]$. Second, these endings occur on pronouns, whose referents are usually animate. This second pattern is given as $[N_{pron}\text{-}P]$, since in CG a pronoun is a type of noun (it profiles a thing). However, we see in (2)(c) that postpositions do not attach directly to animate nouns that are "lexical" (i.e. nonpronominal). So instead of a form like **hunwu-yk*, literally 'bear-to', we find the more elaborate expression *hunwut po-yk* 'bear it-to', where the postposition attaches to a coreferring pronoun.[19] Observe that the schema for this pattern, $[N_{an} [N_{pron}\text{-}P]]$, incorporates the one in (2)(b).

(2) (a) *ki-yk* 'to (the) house', *paa-ngay* 'from (the) water', *too-tal* 'with (a) rock' $[N_{inan}\text{-}P]$

   (b) *po-yk* 'to him', *chaamo-ngay* 'from us', *poomo-to* 'by them' $[N_{pron}\text{-}P]$

   (c) **hunwu-yk* 'to (the) bear', **nawitma-ngay* 'from (the) girl' $*[N_{an}\text{-}P]$

   (d) *hunwut po-yk* 'to (the) bear', *nawitmal po-ngay* 'from (the) girl' $[N_{an} [N_{pron}\text{-}P]]$

Since postpositions occur on both lexical nouns (if they are inanimate) and animate nouns (if they are pronominal), their nonoccurrence with animate lexical nouns is somewhat unexpected. Indeed, the more abstract constructional schema $[N\text{-}P]$,

---

[18] For this reason, blatant irregularities—like the various forms of *be* (*am*, *is*, *are*, *was*, *were*)—survive best in words with the greatest frequency.

[19] The pronoun *po-* is third-person singular, so it translates as either 'him', 'her', or 'it'. The final consonants of *hunwut* and *nawitmal* are noun endings that are omitted with postpositions, in derived forms, and when a noun is possessed.

making no distinction among the types of nouns, might well be expected to emerge as the reinforced commonality of $[N_{inan}\text{-}P]$ and $[N_{pron}\text{-}P]$. But if it does, what rules out the expressions in (2)(c), which conform to this higher-level schema? The answer depends on how rules are conceived. A theory embracing constructive rules (§8.1.2) could allow the formation of all expressions conforming to [N-P] at the level of underlying structure. An obligatory rule would then apply to those with an animate lexical noun, inserting a pronoun to bear the postposition: $[N_{an}\text{-}P] \Rightarrow [\ N_{an}\ [N_{pron}\text{-}P]]$. This transformation would account for both the absence of expressions like (2)(c) and the occurrence of those in (2)(d) to fill the gap. However, it does so at the considerable theoretical cost of permitting derivations from hypothetical underlying structures. By contrast, a theory embracing filters would posit one to screen out the nonoccurring structures: $*[N_{an}\text{-}P]$. The pattern in (2)(d) then has to be dealt with in some other manner.

Neither option is available in CG.[20] Owing to the content requirement, we can only posit schemas that are directly analogous to occurring expressions. Learners of Luiseño will therefore abstract the schemas $[N_{inan}\text{-}P]$, $[N_{pron}\text{-}P]$, and $[N_{an}\ [N_{pron}\text{-}P]]$, but not $[N_{an}\text{-}P]$, since expressions like those in (2)(c) do not occur. Let us further assume, for sake of discussion, that they also abstract the high-level schema [N-P], representing what is common to the first two patterns. We can then account for the data on the presumption that only the lower-level schemas are accessible for the sanction of new expressions. This is quite reasonable since the lower-level patterns are thoroughly entrenched, being experienced on countless occasions, and have the built-in advantage that comes with being more specific than [N-P]. The resulting inaccessibility of the higher-level pattern is indicated in figure 8.10 by enclosing it in a dashed-line box.

The diagram shows how the schemas apply to the different kinds of targets. Based on ease of activation and degree of overlap with the target, the lower-level

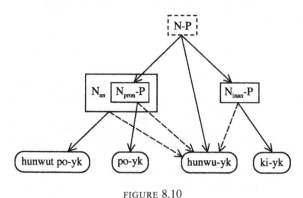

FIGURE 8.10

[20] CG's limitation to positive statements (precluding filters) is not a rigid doctrine but a working hypothesis. The framework would not be greatly changed should it be found that speakers sometimes learn specific prohibitions as well. This example shows how filters can be avoided in certain cases that might at first seem to require them.

schemas $[N_{inan}\text{-}P]$, $[N_{pron}\text{-}P]$, and $[N_{an} [N_{pron}\text{-}P]]$ are respectively activated to categorize target expressions like those in (2)(a), (2)(b), and (2)(d). These are judged well-formed. What about (2)(c)? An expression like *hunwu-yk* would indeed be found acceptable were it able to elicit [N-P] for its categorization. The high-level schema is not available, however, being eclipsed by the more specific units. We might speculate that $[N_{an} [N_{pron}\text{-}P]]$ would win the competition, since *hunwut* is fully compatible with N_{an}, but not with N_{inan} or N_{pron}. But since *hunwu-yk* conflicts with each lower-level schema in some respect, it is nonconventional whichever one is chosen.

8.3 Networks of Constructions

A general feature of linguistic organization is the existence of complex categories, in which multiple variants are linked in networks. The individual nodes in such a network can be structures of any size or any kind. As a special case, each node consists of an entire symbolic assembly. The network then defines a category whose members are related constructions. Complex categories of this sort are important in describing both lexicon and grammar, which can be seen as forming a continuum.

8.3.1 From the Grammatical Standpoint

To completely describe the grammar of a language, it is not enough to characterize general patterns. It must also be ensured that the proper elements occur in them. Out of all the elements that might be used in a given pattern, the ones conventionally exploited are often limited to a certain range or even an arbitrary subset. This is the problem of **distribution**.

For many grammatical phenomena, distribution is specified by means of constructional subschemas—structures of intermediate generality—that have to be posited in addition to a higher-level schema describing the general pattern or in lieu of such a schema. We saw this in the case of Luiseño postpositions (fig. 8.10). Even if speakers abstract the general pattern [N-P], they do not exploit all the options it potentially makes available. To specify the actual distribution, we must posit the constructional subschemas $[N_{pron}\text{-}P]$ and $[N_{inan}\text{-}P]$ but not $*[N_{an}\text{-}P]$. We must further posit the more complex schema $[N_{an} [N_{pron}\text{-}P]]$, which fills this gap in the general pattern. It is these lower-level schemas, not [N-P], that actually determine what does and does not occur.

Owing to their built-in competitive advantage, lower-level schemas are frequently invoked and thus essential to language structure. When a high-level pattern is discernible, its actual implementation in conventional usage may still be effected by more specific units. These can be quite specific, to the point of incorporating particular lexical items or grammatical markers. Alongside the schemas mentioned, we can plausibly posit for Luiseño an array of more specific units that incorporate a particular postposition or a particular noun. Here are two such units, along with instantiating expressions:

(3)   (a) [N-yk]   *ki-yk* 'to (the) house', *too-yk* 'to (the) rock', *po-yk* 'to him'

   (b) [too-P]   *too-yk* 'to (the) rock', *too-ngay* 'from (the) rock', *too-tal* 'with (a) rock'

We must further suppose that numerous specific expressions conforming to these patterns occur sufficiently often to be established as conventional units. Speakers can then invoke them as familiar, prepackaged wholes, rather than having to assemble them from component elements in accordance with constructional schemas. Instantiating expressions like *kiyk* 'to (the) house' and *tootal* 'with (a) rock' might very well be frequent enough to coalesce as units. We can certainly ascribe unit status to most every combination of a postposition and a personal pronoun, like the forms in (2)(b).

In practical terms, we cannot always know whether a particular expression is established as a unit. While this may not be of any great importance (in the grand scheme of things), in principle the degree of entrenchment can be determined empirically. Observed frequency provides one basis for estimating it. Experimentally, one can look for measurable differences in the processing of novel vs. unit expressions (Harris 1998). We have more direct evidence of unit status when an expression consistently displays some idiosyncrasy that does not follow from any regular pattern. Were it not an established unit, for example, there would be no way of knowing that 'to me' is expressed in Luiseño as *neyk*, rather than the expected **noyk* (cf. *noo* 'I'). We must also posit units in the case of a minor pattern when it cannot be predicted which elements participate in it. For instance, the past-tense verbs *wrote*, *broke*, *drove*, *froze*, *rose*, *dove*, and *strove* must all be learned as units. We cannot claim that they are simply constructed when needed by means of the constructional schema describing the pattern $[(\dots \text{Vy} \dots)_\sigma] \dashrightarrow [(\dots \text{ow} \dots)_\sigma]$. This would imply the schema's accessibility for the sanction of new expressions, but if it were accessible we could not account for its failure to apply with other verbs (e.g. **fose* as the past tense of *fease* or **sote* as the past tense of *sight* 'catch sight of').

To indicate that the past tense of *write* is *wrote*, a linguist might flag the stem with a diacritic (or "rule feature") meant to specify that it undergoes a morphological rule ablauting [Vy] to [ow]. Alternatively, one might posit a special subclass of verbs based on this morphological property, listing *write* as one of its members. Yet it seems quite unlikely that anything directly analogous to a diacritic or the symbol for a subclass would be part of the actual mental representation of linguistic structure.[21] In a CG account, the information that *write* takes *wrote* as its past-tense form is provided instead by the specific inclusion of *wrote* among the conventional units of English. The morphological rule is simply a constructional schema—a schematic assembly of symbolic structures—and the instantiating expressions (*wrote*, *broke*, *drove*, etc.) reside in specific assemblies. Thus to describe this subclass of verbs, nothing is posited other than symbolic assemblies linked by categorizing relationships.

An important aspect of the usage-based conception is that large numbers of complex expressions are learned and stored as units, including many that conform to regular patterns (Bybee 2006). The network describing an overall grammatical construction may thus incorporate specific unit expressions instantiating constructional schemas characterized at different levels of abstraction. Usually there is more to the structure of such a network than just elaborative relationships. In addition to these

---

[21] Having no intrinsic semantic or phonological content, such devices are ruled out in CG by the content requirement. Their occasional use for abbreviatory purposes carries no implication that they have any direct analog in cognition.

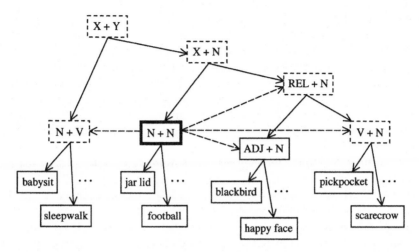

FIGURE 8.11

"vertical" connections, we can also recognize "horizontal" relationships of extension from a category prototype. A particular constructional schema can often be seen as prototypical by virtue of being frequently instantiated and easily invoked for new expressions. It thus defines the category "center", with respect to which other, less commonly exploited constructional variants constitute conventional departures.

Figure 8.11 is a partial sketch of the network for English compounds. The vast majority of examples are compounds of the form [N + N], which can thus be taken as prototypical. Other patterns, including [ADJ + N], [V + N], and [N + V], are shown as extensions vis-à-vis this basic pattern. Also part of the network are various constructional subschemas (not shown), as well as many specific expressions with unit status. Further indicated in the diagram are certain higher-level schemas that might be abstracted as the reinforced commonality of lower-level patterns, such as [REL + N] for compounds where the first element (an adjective or a verb) profiles a relationship. Of the schemas shown, only [N + N] and to a lesser extent [ADJ + N] are commonly exploited in forming new expressions. The others are enclosed in dashed-line boxes to indicate their relative inaccessibility.

Corresponding to a higher-level schema is a wide range of conceivable instantiating expressions. Usually this large space of structural possibilities is only partially, even sparsely, inhabited by expressions (either fixed or novel) that will be accepted as conventional. Moreover, the space is "warped" in the sense that new expressions are more likely to crop up in certain occupied regions than in others. Effecting these limitations are networks of schemas like figure 8.11. To the extent that a high-level schema (e.g. [X + Y]) emerges at all, it is still the overall network that specifies the details of its implementation in actual language use.

8.3.2 From the Lexical Standpoint

At first blush, a lexical item seems simple and straightforward. There is a form (e.g. [cat]), it has a meaning ([CAT]), and the two are paired symbolically:

[[CAT]/[cat]]. But at second blush, when examined more carefully, lexical items prove capable of substantial complexity in a number of dimensions. For now we can ignore the internal complexity of a semantic unit like [CAT], an elaborate conceptual structure recruiting an open-ended set of cognitive domains (§2.2.2). This internal multiplicity (characteristic of any single meaning) has to be distinguished from polysemy, in which a lexical item has not just one meaning but a family of related senses (fig. 2.2).[22] Polysemy in turn is different from symbolic complexity, the extent to which a lexical item is analyzable into smaller symbolic structures (fig. 1.2).

Yet another dimension of complexity pertains to a lexical item's occurrence in larger structural contexts. Typically a lexeme is conventionally established in a variety of contexts, which are describable in either specific or schematic terms. For instance, it is quite standard for *cat* to be directly preceded by a determiner or by an adjective, or to be followed by a complex modifier like a prepositional phrase. As conventional units, we can therefore posit the schematic configurations [DET cat], [ADJ cat], and [cat PP], as well as a considerable number of familiar expressions that instantiate them (e.g. *my cat, the cat, any cat, lazy cat, black cat, cat with kittens, cat on a hot tin roof*). A highly frequent verb, such as *give*, is well entrenched as a component of constructions that specify its various morphological realizations: *gives, gave, given, giving, to give*. Syntactically, it is well established as the lexical head in two kinds of clauses, exemplified in (4). They are distinguished by whether the verb is followed by two nominal complements, as in (a), or by a nominal and a prepositional phrase with *to*. These are commonly referred to as the "ditransitive" and "caused-motion" constructions.[23] The occurrence of *give* in these two patterns is represented by the formulas on the right.

(4)   (a) **Ditransitive:** *She gave her boyfriend a new Mercedes.*   [give NML NML]

     (b) **Caused-motion:** *She gave a new Mercedes to her boyfriend.*   [give NML [to NML]]

We can say that lexical items are conventionally used in particular **structural frames** (like [ADJ cat] and [give NML NML]) and that a set of such frames is one aspect of a lexeme's overall description. The lexeme may appear in many frames or just a few. These frames can be of different sizes (so that some incorporate others) and characterized at different levels of specificity (so that some instantiate others). They amount to constructional schemas that contain the lexical item as one component element.[24]

---

[22] A lexical item may also comprise a family of variant forms (FCG1: §10.3.3).

[23] An extensive treatment can be found in Goldberg 1995. A "ditransitive" clause is so called because it is not only transitive but has two object-like complements. The term "caused motion" indicates a relationship to sentences like *He threw the cat over the fence*, where the subject causes the object to move along the path specified by the prepositional phrase.

[24] To the extent that other components are specific rather than schematic, they constitute standard **collocations**. For example, the unit expression *burnt toast* figures in the overall characterization of both *burnt* and *toast*, representing the fact that each commonly occurs (collocates) with the other.

Knowing a large number of lexemes in structural frames is an important aspect of a speaker's mastery of a language. Representing well-rehearsed ways of deploying lexical units, they are in no small measure responsible for the fluency and facility of normal speech. This leads to a subtle but crucial point concerning the relation between a lexeme and its frames. Though standard, it is quite wrong to think of a lexeme as existing independently of its frames. Linguists are guilty of this misconception when they speak of lexical items being "inserted" into syntactic structures. What this overlooks is how lexical items are acquired in the first place: by abstraction from usage events where they occur in particular structural contexts. These contexts provide the initial basis for a lexeme's apprehension, and thus remain—in schematized form—as the learner becomes proficient in using it conventionally. Essential to knowing a lexical item is knowing how it is used. Rather than being obtained **after** a lexeme is acquired, this knowledge is an inherent aspect of its acquisition.[25]

From this usage-based perspective, the issue to be addressed is not how a lexical item comes to be used in certain frames, but to what extent it achieves any independent status vis-à-vis these frames. The abstraction of linguistic units from usage events goes hand in glove with the process of **decontextualization**. A unit is abstracted through the progressive reinforcement of commonalities that recur across a series of events. Excluded from the unit, through lack of reinforcement, are the myriad details that differ from one event to the next. To some extent, therefore, the emergence of a unit results in its detachment from the original supporting contexts. How far this decontextualization is carried depends on how varied the contexts are. Consider the morphological realizations of Luiseño *too* 'rock'. Since the forms in (3)(b) vary only in the choice of postposition, these alone support the emergence of [too-P]. If we add to this the subject form *too-ta*, we have the basis for [too-X], a more schematic frame indicating that *too* occurs with a suffix. But it also occurs with possessor prefixes (e.g. *no-too* 'my rock'), whence the alternate frame [POSSR-too]. Thus it is not the case that *too* consistently appears either with a suffix or with a prefix. Its morphological contexts are varied enough for *too* to be established independently of any particular frame.[26]

To some extent, a lexeme's meaning is shaped by the frames it occurs in. While the effect is often minor—presumably Luiseño *too* means pretty much the same in *too-ta* 'rock', *too-tal* 'with (a) rock', and *no-too* 'my rock'—it is not always quite so negligible. *Send*, for example, has subtly different senses, depending on whether

---

[25] This is especially true for verbs, which are first learned in specific structural contexts and only later generalized (Tomasello 1992, 2003). Of course, it is not denied that some lexemes might be learned in a frame-independent manner (e.g. by looking in a dictionary), or that forms learned in a certain frame can be extended to other contexts characteristic of their grammatical class. The point is simply that the problem of getting lexical items into the proper structural frames is spurious since any strict dichotomy is artificial to begin with.

[26] Still, *too* always occurs as part of a larger word, making it less autonomous morphologically than English *rock*. The suffix *-ta* occurs by default when the noun would otherwise stand alone. Like the endings *-t* of *hunwut* and *-l* of *nawitmal* (see n. 19), *-ta* can be analyzed as being semantically equivalent to the noun schema.

it is used in the ditransitive construction, as a caused-motion verb, or as part of the complex predicate *send for*:

(5) (a) *They sent me another brochure.*   [send₁ NML NML]

     (b) *We sent the new letter to all the applicants.*   [send₂ NML [to NML]]

     (c) *You can send for more information at any time.*   [[send₃ for] NML]

Send has a different kind of landmark in each construction, and since focal prominence is an important aspect of meaning, the semantic values it assumes in these contexts are distinct.

These different senses of *send* are sketched in figure 8.12. The small circles indicate event participants. An ellipse represents a participant's **dominion**, or sphere of control (fig. 3.14). A property shared by all three senses is that the trajector causes (double arrow) another entity to move (single arrow) from its own dominion into that of another participant.[27] The main distinguishing property is the degree of prominence conferred on this other participant, the "recipient", who controls the target dominion. In the case of *send₁*, the recipient is focused as landmark, with the consequence that the profiled relationship includes the recipient's subsequent access (dashed arrow) to the mover. By contrast, *send₂* confers landmark status on the mover, so that more emphasis falls on the path of motion. Not focused by the verb, the recipient is introduced only indirectly, as the landmark of the *to*-phrase serving to specify this path. With *send₃*, the recipient is not even mentioned. The complex verb *send for* deflects attention from what is sent and who receives it, focusing instead on the anticipated result of something moving in the opposite direction, into the trajector's dominion. This second mover functions as the landmark of the complex verb as a whole, not of *send₃* individually.[28] Yet some conception of this anticipated motion (dashed arrow)

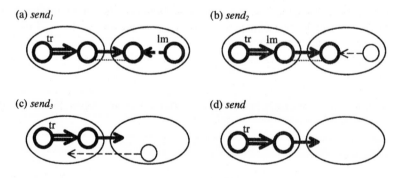

(a) *send₁*   (b) *send₂*

(c) *send₃*   (d) *send*

FIGURE 8.12

---

[27] It is convenient to show the mover in both its initial and final positions. A dotted correspondence line indicates that the entities occupying these two locations are the same.

[28] As evidence for these characterizations, the nominal identified as the verb's landmark (or object) in each case functions as subject of the corresponding passive: *I was sent another brochure*; *The new letter was sent to all the applicants*; *More information can be sent for at any time*.

colors the value of *send₃* itself. Because *send₃* is limited to this larger context, evoking it must to some extent activate the scenario as a whole.

Diagram (d) indicates what is common to *send₁*, *send₂*, and *send₃*. This more schematic sense is thus the meaning *send* has independently of any particular syntactic frame. If it emerges at all, this abstracted meaning is only secondary. From the standpoint of acquisition, it represents a further development in which the decontextualization yielding *send₁*, *send₂*, and *send₃* is carried to the extreme. From the processing standpoint, it is presumably less accessible than the more specific senses. These alternate meanings of *send* can be modeled as a network, shown on the right in figure 8.13. Given with each specific sense is the structural frame that induces it.

Shown on the left in figure 8.13 is a fragment of the network for English ditransitive constructions.[29] Central to this pattern are verbs of transfer, like *give, send, mail*, etc. We can therefore posit the constructional schema [TRANSFER NML NML], as well as subschemas like [give NML NML] and [send₁ NML NML]. An array of more specific structures, such as [give me NML], are also entrenched as units. While the transfer pattern is prototypical, ditransitives are also used in a number of other cases, e.g. with verbs of intended transfer (*promise, owe, grant, bequeath*), verbs of permission and denial (*permit, allow, deny, refuse*), and verbs of creation for someone's benefit (*make, cook, build, bake*). The higher-level schema covering all these possibilities, represented as [V NML NML], is not itself accessible for the sanction of new expressions. The conventional distribution of ditransitives is specified by the entire network, rather than any single node.

Sitting in the middle of figure 8.13, as a node in both networks, is the partially schematic structure [send₁ NML NML]. It belongs to both the lexical network representing the structural frames for *send* (and the meanings they induce) and the

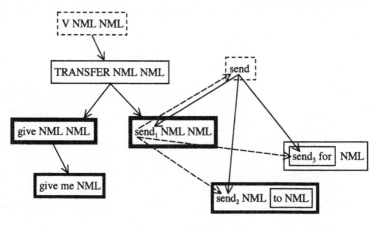

FIGURE 8.13

---

[29] Cf. Goldberg 1995. In examining such diagrams, keep in mind the limitations of the network metaphor (discussed at the end of §8.1.3).

grammatical network for ditransitive constructions. This is in no way problematic but just what we should expect. Lexical items and grammatical constructions are each abstracted from occurring expressions through the reinforcement of recurring commonalities. In either case, the typical result is a network of related variants characterized at different levels of schematicity. How far the process of schematization proceeds, and in what direction, depends on what is shared by the source expressions. From distinct but overlapping sets of expressions, there can thus emerge both constructional schemas (which abstract away from particular lexical items) and lexical variants (first induced by particular structural frames). A structure like [send$_1$ NML NML] represents an initial step with respect to both paths of abstraction. Is it lexical or is it grammatical? The answer can only be "yes", for it is both. This is one of many indications that lexicon and grammar form a gradation (§1.3.2).

8.4 Regularity

It is sometimes maintained that syntax and lexicon are sharply distinct and quite dissimilar in nature. Syntax, on this view, is characterized by regularity and is thus describable by rules, whereas lexicon is the repository of irregularity—a mass of unpredictable idiosyncrasies. CG takes a very different stand on these issues. It offers a unified account of lexicon and grammar (subsuming both syntax and morphology), in which every linguistic unit represents a reinforced pattern and thus embodies a regularity of some kind. To see this more clearly, we need to examine the very notion of regularity and consider some of its less obvious manifestations.

8.4.1 Constructional Meaning and Compositionality

Though linguists seldom bother to explain it, the notion of regularity is anything but self-explanatory. The term subsumes no less than three separate factors: **generality**, **productivity**, and **compositionality**.

1. Generality pertains to the level of schematicity at which a pattern is characterized. For instance, a pattern characterized in terms of a nominal (with no limitation as to kind) has greater generality than one referring to a pronoun in particular. Similarly, the high-level ditransitive schema [V NML NML] is more general than [TRANSFER NML NML] (limited to verbs of transfer), which in turn is more general than [give NML NML] (fig. 8.13). A fully specific fixed expression, such as *Give me that!* or *cat*, represents a pattern with the lowest degree of generality.

2. Productivity pertains to a schema's degree of accessibility for the sanction of new expressions. We have seen that the most general constructional schemas, like [V NML NML] or Luiseño [N-P], are often not available for this purpose. Conversely, a pattern of lesser generality may be fully productive within the scope of the generalization. Luiseño [N$_{inan}$-P], for example, is freely applicable to new combinations of inanimate nouns and postpositions. But a low degree of generality does not ensure productivity. We saw this for the past tense of verbs like *write*, *break*, and *freeze*. The constructional schema describing the pattern is fairly specific in regard to the verb's phonological pole: $[(\ldots Vy \ldots)_\sigma]$. Yet it cannot be activated to license

new expressions (like **fose* for the nonce-form *fease*). Despite its greater generality, the default pattern (yielding *feased*) is more entrenched and consistently wins the competition for activation. Patterns that correspond to the classic conception of syntax, being both maximally general and fully productive, are actually quite atypical. Likely candidates are schemas describing basic word order, such as [V NML] for a verb and its object.

3. *Compositionality* is the extent to which a composite structure is predictable from the component structures together with the sanctioning constructional schema. The position taken in CG is that semantics is only partially compositional (§6.2.1). While some expressions (like *jar lid*) approximate full compositionality, others (like *laptop*) diverge quite drastically from what they ought to mean. Some degree of divergence—if only in the guise of greater specificity—is usual for both fixed and novel expressions. So, as with the other two factors, compositionality fails to support the dichotomous vision of a fully regular syntax vs. a wholly irregular lexicon.

Compositionality is only partial because linguistic meanings depend on more than just component structures and constructional schemas. Many additional resources are drawn upon in arriving at composite semantic structures (§2.1.3). An expression's meaning presupposes an elaborate conceptual substrate that supports and shapes it. Furthermore, language users employ a rich array of imaginative and interpretive abilities. Strictly speaking, then, a complex expression's meaning cannot be **computed** from lexical meanings and compositional patterns (the semantic poles of constructional schemas) but is more accurately seen as being **prompted** by them.[30]

Nonetheless, constructional schemas are meaningful and make an essential semantic contribution to complex expressions. If they do not tell the whole story of how composite meanings are arrived at, such schemas at least supply essential information as to how the component conceptions fit together and how their integrated content is construed (e.g. in terms of profiling). They influence the interpretation of component lexical items and may further contribute their own conceptual content. These are all aspects of **constructional meaning**. In these various ways, grammar itself has a substantial and systematic role in determining the meanings of composite expressions.

Only in recent years have linguists come to appreciate the extent to which constructional schemas reinforce, supplement, or even override the conceptual content supplied by component lexical items (Goldberg 1995, 2006). A schema that does not incorporate any specific lexical item may nonetheless be first acquired on the basis of a small number of lexemes that share some essential content, which is therefore retained as the schema emerges (Tomasello 1992; Sethuraman 2002). This aspect of their meaning is then reinforced by the schema when the lexemes are used in the construction it defines. For example, the ditransitive construction is based initially on frequent verbs of transfer, such as *give*, *bring*, *send*, and *tell*. Thus the initial

---

[30] Sweetser 1999 demonstrates that this is so even for seemingly straightforward cases like the combination of an adjective and a noun in the [ADJ N] construction.

constructional schema, [TRANSFER NML NML], retains what is common to these verbs (roughly what is shown in fig. 8.12(a)). Subsequently, both the lexeme and the schema provide this shared content in ditransitive sentences like *She gave him an apple* or *Tell me a story*.

In adult usage, the ditransitive pattern is extended to a variety of situations involving something other than simple transfer. One class of cases is illustrated by the sentences in (6):

(6) (a) *She made him a kite.   They built us a porch.   I knitted her a sweater.*   [creation]

   (b) *He wrote me a check.   She baked them a pie.   Peel me another orange.*   [preparation]

   (c) *I bought him a clock.   Find us some old rags.   She got you a fancy car.*   [acquisition]

These differ from simple transfer in that the recipient obtains something that is not initially under the subject's control, at least in any usable form. Instead, the subject acts to make it available for the recipient's use by creating, preparing, or acquiring it. Note that all these verbs have other, more basic uses that do not invoke a recipient in any salient manner:

(7) (a) *She made a kite.   They built a porch.   I knitted a sweater.*   [creation]

   (b) *He wrote a check.   She baked a pie.   Peel another orange.*   [preparation]

   (c) *I bought a clock.   Find some old rags.   She got a fancy car.*   [acquisition]

Thus it is not a matter of these verbs originally having a transfer meaning that enables them to be used in the central ditransitive construction. Instead, they are used in this construction even though they lack this specific content, which the construction itself must therefore supply. The composite meanings in (6) combine the notion of creation, preparation, or acquisition—all of which result in an object's availability for use—with that of transfer to a recipient, contributed by the constructional schema.

This development is sketched in figure 8.14. In the upper box is a partial representation of the constructional schema [TRANSFER NML NML], showing component structures and the correspondences linking them. The box below stands for a verb of creation, preparation, or acquisition, as in (7). The notation is meant to indicate that the trajector does something which causes the landmark to become available in the trajector's dominion. The diagram represents the initial use of such a verb in the basic ditransitive construction, before the pattern in (6) has been established. At this stage, using a verb of creation, preparation, or acquisition to instantiate a schematic verb of transfer constitutes an extension vis-à-vis the sanctioning schema, not merely an elaboration. A dashed arrow is thus employed for this categorizing relationship between the verbs of the constructional schema and the target expression; this is one aspect of the expression's structural interpretation with reference to the schema. Since we are presuming that this usage is previously unfamiliar, the categorization is enclosed in a box with rounded corners.

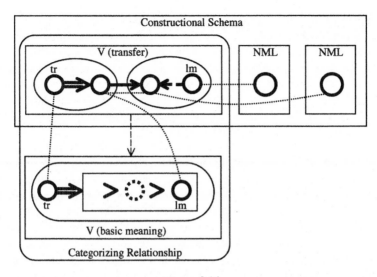

FIGURE 8.14

The result of this categorization is that the verbs in such expressions (e.g. *She made him a kite*) are **apprehended as** verbs of transfer. A categorizing judgment constitutes a unified experience not equivalent to that of apprehending the schema and the target individually (§8.2.1). In the context of this usage, therefore, the verbs in (6) are associated with the unified conception depicted in figure 8.15(a). This blended meaning subsumes the content of both schema and target, and it follows the former in its choice of landmark. When such a verb is first employed in this construction, the blended meaning—like the categorization inducing it—is a novel one. But with repeated use, the entire categorizing judgment is entrenched and established as a unit, including the blended meaning, as shown in diagram (b). At this point, we

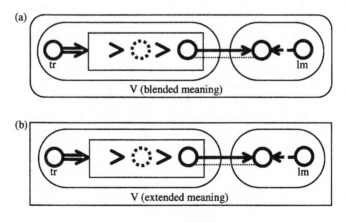

FIGURE 8.15

can reasonably say that the verb has taken on an extended meaning—one that incorporates the notion of transfer, as well as its basic content of creation, preparation, or acquisition. To be sure, it assumes this meaning only in the context of the symbolic assembly sketched in figure 8.14. It is true in general, however, that a verb's meanings are abstracted from its occurrence in particular structural frames, which are part of its characterization (fig. 8.13). To say that a verb "has" a certain meaning is merely to say that its association with this conception, in the appropriate structural context, is established as a conventional unit.

As seen in (6), this type of extension occurs not just with one verb but with many. The repeated use of such expressions leads to the entrenchment, in schematized form, of the entire configuration in figure 8.14. This amounts to a new constructional schema for ditransitives, in which a verb of creation, preparation, or acquisition is employed and apprehended as a verb of transfer. If [TRANSFER NML NML] is prototypical, this new variant is more peripheral to the category, an extension from the prototype. It is conventionally established, however, and accessible for the sanction of new expressions, including those with less frequent verbs not commonly used in this manner. On this basis we can interpret the sentences in (8) and judge them well-formed. Naturally, with repeated use in this construction, these verbs too are capable of acquiring the transfer sense this use induces. It is through such developments that complex categories are gradually built up, starting from their prototypes.[31]

(8)   (a) *She sculpted him an elephant.*   [creation]

    (b) *Skin me another cat.*   [preparation]

    (c) *I stole her a diamond ring.*   [acquisition]

8.4.2 Higher-Order Generalizations

The categorization in figure 8.14 is one aspect of the relationship between an expression and a constructional schema invoked for its structural interpretation. In expressions like (6), a verb such as *make, peel,* or *find* instantiates a schematic verb of transfer despite their semantic incompatibility. By virtue of this categorization, such a verb is **apprehended as** a verb of transfer in the context of this construction. The blended meaning that results can be established as a new, extended sense of the verb through repeated occurrence in this frame (fig. 8.15).

Because this happens not just with one verb but with many, the configuration in figure 8.14, including the blended meaning that emerges, is subject to schematization. That is, this context-induced semantic extension constitutes a recurring pattern, which can itself be established as a unit at a level of abstraction determined by the range of verbs giving rise to it. And once established, this unit can itself be invoked to sanction the semantic extension of additional verbs, like those in (8). Our concern in this final section is the nature of such a unit and its place within a linguistic system.

---

[31] I would not claim that the scenario just described necessarily represents the actual course of development for ditransitives. It is only meant to illustrate the kinds of processes that are plausibly invoked for the growth of complex categories and the interaction of lexical and constructional meanings.

It is one representative of an important but little-recognized class of regularities that I refer to as **higher-order generalizations**.

In describing a linguistic system, we are limited by the content requirement (§1.3.4) as to the kinds of units we can posit. The only units permitted are semantic, phonological, and symbolic structures that are (i) parts of occurring expressions, (ii) schematizations of permitted structures, or (iii) categorizing relationships between permitted structures. For example, symbolic structures allowed under (i) are fixed expressions such as *lazy cat, clean air*, and *valid argument*, whereas the constructional schema [ADJ N] is permitted under (ii), and the categorization [[ADJ N] → [lazy cat]] under (iii). Thus a schema like [ADJ N], representing part (ii) of the content requirement, emerges as a generalization over instantiating expressions, representing part (i), and their relationship corresponds to part (iii). This is not the only possibility, however. Because categorizing relationships are permitted as units under (iii), and (ii) allows schematizations of permitted structures, schematization can also apply to categorizations.[32] And because it captures what is common to a set of categorizations, the resulting schema constitutes a higher-order generalization.

The structure in figure 8.14 is therefore permitted under the content requirement. We can view it in several different ways, all of which are valid. For one thing, it constitutes an **augmented constructional schema**. It is a constructional schema because it specifies the integration of a verb and its nonsubject complements in sentences like (8), where the verb employed is primarily one of creation, preparation, or acquisition.[33] Moreover, in the scenario outlined above, the structure develops as an augmentation of the central schema for ditransitives based on verbs of transfer. It emerges through application of this central pattern to situations where the profiled action involves transfer only as a secondary consequence. While this usage conflicts with the basic schema, it is well within the usual range of tolerance, and as it recurs, reinforcement of its common features results in entrenchment and schematization of the entire configuration. A new constructional schema thus emerges that is based on and incorporates the original one (which is still independently accessible and prototypical for ditransitives).

This configuration can also be viewed as a partial characterization of the verbs in (6). For each such verb (*make, peel, find*, etc.), it represents the blended meaning established as one of its senses, as well as the structural frame that induces this extension from its basic semantic value. In schematized form, it represents what is common to such verbs, thus defining a particular subclass of ditransitive predicates.

Finally, the configuration in figure 8.14 can be viewed as a **pattern of semantic extension**. For each individual verb, it represents both the basic meaning (the prototypical semantic value) and the extended meaning induced in this context through its apprehension as a verb of transfer. This aspect of the configuration is separately

---

[32] Furthermore, the relationship between the schematized categorization and any particular categorization is itself a categorizing relationship permitted under (iii).

[33] Bear in mind that fig. 8.14 is simplified in various ways. It does not show constituency, composite structures, or the phonological pole. Nor does it show the blended meaning resulting from the verb's categorization by the schematic verb of transfer (this is given separately in fig. 8.15). And despite the box with rounded corners, we are considering the stage when the entire configuration has the status of a unit.

Basic Meaning   Extended Meaning

FIGURE 8.16

shown in figure 8.16. At the schematic level (as part of the augmented constructional schema), it describes an abstracted pattern by which a nontransfer verb develops a transfer sense. We saw in (8) that this pattern is applicable to additional verbs in the same constructional context. As the schematization of a categorization, it constitutes a higher-order generalization.

A generalization of this sort reflects an important aspect of our mental capacity. The abstracted regularity does not pertain to the nature of individual content structures (in this case, meanings) but rather to how such structures are related to one another. This higher-order abstractive capacity has numerous linguistic manifestations. Indeed, since component and composite structures are linked by categorizing relationships, every constructional schema represents the schematization of categorizations. Additional manifestations of this capacity are found in patterns of metonymic and phonological extension.

Although the term is used in various ways, for our purposes metonymy can be characterized as a shift in profile (§3.3.1). An expression that in its basic sense profiles some entity, A, is instead understood as designating another entity, B, which is somehow associated with A and thus mentally accessible through it. This is shown abstractly in figure 8.17.

Here the relevant point is that metonymy often follows conventionally established patterns. To take just one example, the name for a place is commonly extended to designate, instead, a noteworthy (and often tragic) event that occurred there: *Vietnam, Chernobyl, Oklahoma City, Wounded Knee, Hiroshima, Waterloo*, and so on. A given metonymic usage represents a particular place-to-event extension entrenched as a unit, e.g. [[**VIETNAM**—WAR] ---> [VIETNAM—**WAR**]].[34] Each such unit

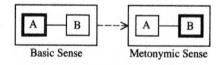

Basic Sense   Metonymic Sense

FIGURE 8.17

---

[34] The extension occurs at the semantic pole of the place expression. Note that the basic sense is not necessarily the most frequent or cognitively salient. While for most speakers *Chernobyl* evokes the nuclear disaster rather than the place where it occurred, the term is nonetheless still understood as metonymic for the place. Hence the basic sense (as determined by the direction of a metonymic pattern) and the one most easily activated need not be the same. In the case of *Vietnam*, the two senses seem equally well entrenched.

instantiates the schematized extension [[**PLACE**—EVENT] ---> [PLACE—**EVENT**]], which describes the general pattern. Moreover, this schema is commonly invoked for the sanction of new expressions. It was virtually inevitable that in the aftermath of the 2000 presidential election the word *Florida* would come to designate the vote-counting fiasco there (as in *Florida must never happen again*).

Further illustrating the schematization of categorizations is a pattern of phonological extension. Recall the imagined example (§8.1.3) of the vowel [a] being nasalized after [m]. Once established as a regular occurrence, this variant pronunciation is specified by the conventional categorizing unit [[ma] ---> [mã]]. The pattern can be extended to other vowels as well, resulting in units like [[me] ---> [mẽ]], [[mu] ---> [mũ]], etc. As this happens, reinforcement of their common properties produces the schematized extension [[mV] ---> [mṼ]], representing the generalization that any vowel can be nasalized after [m]. Of course, the pattern can also be extended to other nasal consonants, yielding units like [[na] ---> [nã]], [[ŋa] ---> [ŋã]], and the schema [[Na] ---> [Nã]] referring to nasal consonants as a class. As the variant pronunciation generalizes across both vowels and nasal consonants, the schema [[NV] ---> [NṼ]] might eventually emerge as a high-level generalization.[35]

Schematizations of categorizations are noteworthy because the generalizations they embody pertain to the relationship between content structures manifested in different expressions. The generalization expressed by the metonymic pattern [[**PLACE**—EVENT] ---> [PLACE—**EVENT**]], for example, pertains to the semantic value of a place term (like *Vietnam*) in different expressions, as part of different usage events. Likewise, the phonological pattern expressed by [[mV] ---> [mṼ]] pertains to alternate pronunciations of a given syllable on different occasions. We have the capacity, in other words, to generalize over relationships that are not evident in any single expression or usage event, in which case the schematization's scope encompasses multiple expressions. This capacity has another important linguistic manifestation in the emergence of lexical subclasses whose members pattern alike across an array of grammatical constructions. These subclasses constitute higher-order generalizations in the sense that the defining properties are distributed over multiple constructions, in each of which the subclass members behave analogously.

Although this notion has broad applicability, the kind of case I have in mind is a "conjugation class", a set of verbs that follow precisely the same pattern in their inflection for tense, person, number, and so on. It is worth going through an actual example in some detail, as the idiosyncrasies of inflectional paradigms are often considered problematic for semantically based theories of grammar. They are problematic only under the gratuitous and erroneous assumption that such a theory has to predict those idiosyncrasies on the basis of meaning. In CG, however, it is not claimed that they are **predictable**, only that they are **describable** as symbolic assemblies in accordance with the content requirement. While an entire verb paradigm is too extensive to cover here, a small fragment is enough to show the basic approach.

---

[35] Such higher-level schemas capture the sorts of regularities that classic generative phonology handled by means of rules deriving phonetic representations from underlying structures. For a comparison, see FCG1: 443–444 and GC: ch. 4.

	'love'	'sing'	'work'	
1s:PRES	amo	canto	trabajo	-o
2s:PRES	amas	cantas	trabajas	-s
3s:PRES	ama	canta	trabaja	Ø
1s:PAST	amé	canté	trabajé	-é
2s:PAST	amaste	cantaste	trabajaste	-ste
3s:PAST	amó	cantó	trabajó	-ó
	am(a)	cant(a)	trabaj(a)	

FIGURE 8.18

Chosen for illustration is the most basic conjugation class in Spanish, consisting of "regular" verbs ending in *a*. There are two other major classes, and quite a number of minor ones, but the members of the *a*-class are most numerous. This class functions as a default in that new verbs ending in *a* automatically follow this pattern. Presented with an appropriate verb stem never before encountered, a speaker immediately knows what form it assumes in all the many combinations of person, number, tense, mood, etc. At issue is the question of how this happens. What gives a speaker immediate access to all the inflected forms of any verb in this class?

The data to be considered is presented in figure 8.18. It is a partial set of forms from three common verbs, meaning 'love', 'sing', and 'work'. We will limit our attention to singular forms in the present and past indicative. This amounts to six forms for each verb stem: first-, second-, and third-person singular, in the present and past tense. The stems are given in bold for ease of identification. Observe that the final *a* fails to appear before inflectional endings consisting of a vowel: *-o* '1s:PRES', *-é* '1s:PAST', and *-ó* '3s:PAST'. Note further that the third-person singular present form is zero (Ø), i.e. the stem occurs unmodified. The component elements—stems and endings—are listed in the final row and final column.

Each individual form constitutes a grammatical construction. Two such constructions are sketched in figure 8.19. The stem, either *am* or *ama*, profiles a specific kind of process. The ending, *-o* or *-ste*, evokes a schematic process and relates it to the speech situation in two basic respects: its trajector is identified as either the speaker (1s) or the addressee (2s); and the process itself is either temporally coincident with the speech event or prior to it (cf. fig. 5.10). The two component structures are integrated both semantically and phonologically to produce the composite structure.

FIGURE 8.19

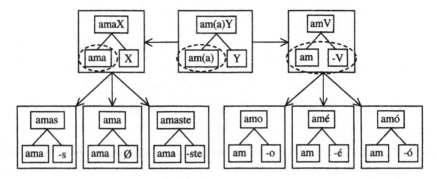

FIGURE 8.20

At the semantic pole, the specific process profiled by the stem is equated with the schematic one evoked by the ending. It is thus the specific process [LOVE] that is related to the speech situation. At the phonological pole, the specific stem *am* or *ama* is identified as the one to which the ending attaches (cf. fig. 6.11).

For a frequent verb like *am(a)*, it is quite possible that all the forms considered achieve the status of units, in which case we can posit the unit constructions in the bottom row of figure 8.20.[36] These are assemblies of symbolic structures, each with a semantic and a phonological pole, but in order to keep the diagrams simple, only the latter is shown. Analogous units can be posited for other common verbs, including *cant(a)* and *trabaj(a)*.

This array of specific assemblies is subject to schematization of different sorts, reflecting the commonalities inherent in different sets of forms. Along one axis it yields the schematic assemblies in the top row of figure 8.20. The schemas on the left and on the right show, respectively, that in certain inflected forms the stem shows up as *ama* and in others as *am*. In the middle is a higher-level schema capturing what is common to those two. The parentheses are meant to indicate that the schematized stem is neutral (unspecified) as to the presence or absence of final *a*. These higher-level schemas provide information often described by linguists in other ways using other theoretical notions. Focusing just on the stem, there is said to be an **alternation** between *ama* and *am*, with *ama* being the basic alternant. It is also said that the "thematic" vowel *a* "drops" before a suffix consisting of a vowel. Generalizing over stems, one might also posit a phonological rule that "deletes" a stem-final vowel before such a suffix. Such statements are not at all invalid from the CG standpoint. They simply correspond to particular facets of networks like figure 8.20.

Let's look at this more closely. From the top row in figure 8.20, the elements enclosed in ellipses are extracted and separately presented in figure 8.21(a). This

---

[36] Ultimately, it makes no difference whether this is actually the case. The schemas defining the conjugation class are capable of emerging regardless of whether the inflected forms of any single verb all have unit status. More generally, the abstraction of a schema requires only the occurrence of sufficiently many varied instantiations to effect the reinforcement of common features. It does not depend on any single instantiation occurring often enough to be entrenched as a unit.

FIGURE 8.21

abstracted diagram makes explicit certain factors left implicit in the previous one; in particular, it shows that the schemas define a complex category comprising variant forms of the stem. The variant *ama* occurs in the widest range of contexts and can be regarded as prototypical. With respect to this prototype, *am* constitutes an extension which only occurs in the context of a vocalic suffix. This is equivalent to stating that *ama* and *am* are alternants, that *ama* is the basic alternant, and that thematic *a* drops before another vowel. Similar complex categories emerge for other stems, such as *cant(a)* and *trabaj(a)*, based on networks analogous to figure 8.20. This array of parallel complex categories is itself subject to schematization, which yields the configuration in figure 8.21(b). This schematic network represents a general pattern of stem alternation. Moreover, the lower two structures—representing the prototype and its context-induced extension—are equivalent to a phonological rule that deletes stem-final *a* before another vowel.

An array of networks like figure 8.20, each representing inflections of a single stem, support the abstraction of other schemas reflecting the commonality of other sets of forms. To take just one example, figure 8.22 depicts a schematization based on the forms in the top row of figure 8.18 (first-person singular, present tense). It should be evident that any patterns discernible within or across inflectional paradigms can likewise be captured by schemas. A speaker's knowledge of such paradigms resides in a vast inventory of specific and schematic assemblies organized in interlocking networks. The specific assemblies represent learned forms, which run the gamut from being completely regular within the system to being wholly idiosyncratic. More schematic assemblies represent the systematicity inherent in the data at any level of abstraction.

FIGURE 8.22

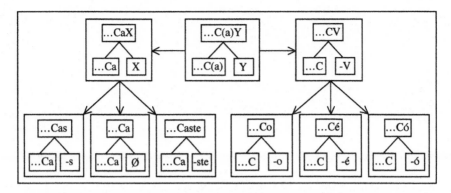

FIGURE 8.23

A schema comparable to that in figure 8.22 is abstracted for each position in a paradigm, e.g. for each row in figure 8.18. These schemas and the higher-level schemas they support constitute the network shown in figure 8.23. Collectively, they provide the characterization of a conjugation class. The entire schematic network (we have of course considered just a fragment) represents a higher-order generalization concerning verb inflection. By invoking it, a speaker presented with a new verb ending in *a* has immediate access to any inflected form and can use it with full confidence that it will be accepted as conventional.

The take-home message is that the central notions of CG are capable of handling an extremely wide range of linguistic phenomena. The few kinds of structures permitted by the content requirement, occurring in various combinations in multiple dimensions and at different levels of organization, straightforwardly accommodate seemingly disparate phenomena that are often treated separately in other frameworks. Moreover, in accordance with basic CG principles, the account they afford is unified, restrictive, and psychologically plausible.

REFERENCES

Austin, J. L. 1962. *How to Do Things with Words*. Cambridge, Mass.: Harvard University Press.

Barlow, Michael. 1992. *A Situated Theory of Agreement*. New York: Garland.

Barlow, Michael, and Suzanne Kemmer (eds.) 2000. *Usage-Based Models of Language*. Stanford: CSLI Publications.

Barsalou, Lawrence W. 1999. Perceptual Symbol Systems. *Behavioral and Brain Sciences* 22:577–660.

Birner, Betty J. 1994. Information Status and Word Order: An Analysis of English Inversion. *Language* 70:233–259.

Bolinger, Dwight. 1965. The Atomization of Meaning. *Language* 41:555–573.

Bybee, Joan. 1985. *Morphology: A Study of the Relation between Meaning and Form*. Typological Studies in Language 9. Amsterdam: John Benjamins.

———. 2006. From Usage to Grammar: The Mind's Response to Repetition. *Language* 82: 711–733.

Bybee, Joan, and Paul Hopper (eds.) 2001. *Frequency and the Emergence of Linguistic Structure*. Typological Studies in Language 45. Amsterdam: John Benjamins.

Chafe, Wallace. 1994. *Discourse, Consciousness, and Time: The Flow and Displacement of Conscious Experience in Speaking and Writing*. Chicago: University of Chicago Press.

Chomsky, Noam. 1957. *Syntactic Structures*. Janua Linguarum 4. The Hague: Mouton.

———. 1965. *Aspects of the Theory of Syntax*. Cambridge, Mass.: MIT Press.

Collins, Allan M., and Elizabeth F. Loftus. 1975. A Spreading-Activation Theory of Semantic Processing. *Psychological Review* 82:407–428.

Croft, William. 1990. *Typology and Universals*. Cambridge: Cambridge University Press.

———. 2001. *Radical Construction Grammar: Syntactic Theory in Typological Perspective*. Oxford: Oxford University Press.

Deane, Paul. 1992. *Grammar in Mind and Brain: Explorations in Cognitive Syntax*. Cognitive Linguistics Research 2. Berlin: Mouton de Gruyter.

Dixon, R. M. W. 1977. Where Have All the Adjectives Gone? *Studies in Language* 1:19–80.

Du Bois, John W. 1987. The Discourse Basis of Ergativity. *Language* 63:805–855.

Elman, Jeffrey L., and James L. McClelland. 1984. Speech Perception as a Cognitive Process: The Interactive Activation Model. In Norman Lass (ed.), *Speech and Language*, vol. 10, 337–374. New York: Academic Press.

Fauconnier, Gilles. 1985. *Mental Spaces: Aspects of Meaning Construction in Natural Language.* Cambridge, Mass.: MIT Press, and London: Bradford.

———. 1997. *Mappings in Thought and Language.* Cambridge: Cambridge University Press.

Fauconnier, Gilles, and Eve Sweetser (eds.) 1996. *Spaces, Worlds, and Grammar.* Chicago: University of Chicago Press.

Fauconnier, Gilles, and Mark Turner. 1998. Conceptual Integration Networks. *Cognitive Science* 22:133–187.

———. 2002. *The Way We Think: Conceptual Blending and the Mind's Hidden Complexities.* New York: Basic Books.

Fillmore, Charles J. 1982. Frame Semantics. In Linguistic Society of Korea (ed.), *Linguistics in the Morning Calm,* 111–137. Seoul: Hanshin.

———. 1988. The Mechanisms of "Construction Grammar." *Proceedings of the Annual Meeting of the Berkeley Linguistics Society* 14:35–55.

Fodor, Jerry A. 1979. *The Language of Thought.* Cambridge, Mass.: Harvard University Press.

———. 1983. *The Modularity of Mind.* Cambridge, Mass.: MIT Press, and London: Bradford.

Geeraerts, Dirk. 1993. Vagueness's Puzzles, Polysemy's Vagaries. *Cognitive Linguistics* 4:223–272.

Gentner, Dedre. 1981. Some Interesting Differences between Verbs and Nouns. *Cognition and Brain Theory* 4:161–178.

———. 1982. Why Nouns Are Learned before Verbs: Linguistic Relativity versus Natural Patterning. In Stan Kuczaj (ed.), *Language Development I: Syntax and Semantics,* 301–334. Hillsdale, N.J.: Erlbaum.

Givón, Talmy (ed.) 1983. *Topic Continuity in Discourse: A Quantitative Cross-Language Study.* Typological Studies in Language 3. Amsterdam: John Benjamins.

———. 1984. *Syntax: A Functional-Typological Introduction* (2 volumes). Amsterdam: John Benjamins.

Goldberg, Adele E. 1995. *Constructions: A Construction Grammar Approach to Argument Structure.* Chicago: University of Chicago Press.

———. 2006. *Constructions at Work: The Nature of Generalizations in Language.* Oxford: Oxford University Press.

Grady, Joe, Sarah Taub, and Pamela Morgan. 1996. Primitive and Compound Metaphors. In Adele E. Goldberg (ed.), *Conceptual Structure, Discourse and Language,* 177–187. Stanford: CSLI Publications.

Haiman, John. 1978. Conditionals Are Topics. *Language* 54:564–589.

———.1980. Dictionaries and Encyclopedias. *Lingua* 50:329–357.

———. 1985. *Natural Syntax: Iconicity and Erosion.* Cambridge Studies in Linguistics 44. Cambridge: Cambridge University Press.

Hampe, Beate (ed.) 2005. *From Perception to Meaning: Image Schemas in Cognitive Linguistics.* Cognitive Linguistics Research 29. Berlin: Mouton de Gruyter.

Harder, Peter. 1996. *Functional Semantics: A Theory of Meaning, Structure and Tense in English.* Trends in Linguistics Studies and Monographs 87. Berlin: Mouton de Gruyter.

Harris, Catherine L. 1998. Psycholinguistic Studies of Entrenchment. In Jean-Pierre Koenig (ed.), *Discourse and Cognition: Bridging the Gap,* 55–70. Stanford: CSLI Publications.

Haspelmath, Martin. 1997. *Indefinite Pronouns.* Oxford Studies in Typology and Linguistic Theory. Oxford: Oxford University Press.

Heine, Bernd. 1997. *Cognitive Foundations of Grammar.* New York: Oxford University Press.

Heine, Bernd, Ulrike Claudi, and Friederike Hünnemeyer. 1991. *Grammaticalization: A Conceptual Framework.* Chicago: University of Chicago Press.

Holmqvist, Kenneth. 1993. *Implementing Cognitive Semantics.* Lund: Department of Cognitive Science, Lund University.

Hopper, Paul J., and Sandra A. Thompson. 1980. Transitivity in Grammar and Discourse. *Language* 56:251–299.

Hopper, Paul J., and Elizabeth Traugott. 2003. *Grammaticalization*. 2nd ed. Cambridge Textbooks in Linguistics. Cambridge: Cambridge University Press.

Hudson, Richard A. 1992. Review of Ronald W. Langacker, *Concept, Image, and Symbol: The Cognitive Basis of Grammar. Journal of Linguistics* 28:506–509.

Huffman, Alan. 1997. *The Categories of Grammar: French* lui *and* le. Studies in Language Companion Series 30. Amsterdam: John Benjamins.

Jackendoff, Ray. 1983. *Semantics and Cognition*. Current Studies in Linguistics 8. Cambridge, Mass.: MIT Press.

———. 1994. *Patterns in the Mind: Language and Human Nature*. New York: Basic Books.

Johnson, Mark. 1987. *The Body in the Mind: The Bodily Basis of Meaning, Imagination, and Reason*. Chicago: University of Chicago Press.

Kellogg, Margaret Kimberly. 1994. Conceptual Mechanisms Underlying Noun and Verb Categorization: Evidence from Paraphasia. *Proceedings of the Annual Meeting of the Berkeley Linguistics Society* 20:300–309.

———. 1996. Neurolinguistic Evidence of Some Conceptual Properties of Nouns and Verbs. Ph.D. dissertation, University of California, San Diego.

Kemmer, Suzanne. 1993. *The Middle Voice*. Typological Studies in Language 23. Amsterdam: John Benjamins.

Kövecses, Zoltán. 2000. *Metaphor and Emotion: Language, Culture, and Body in Human Feeling*. Cambridge: Cambridge University Press.

———. 2005. *Metaphor in Culture: Universality and Variation*. Cambridge: Cambridge University Press.

Lakoff, George. 1987. *Women, Fire, and Dangerous Things: What Categories Reveal about the Mind*. Chicago: University of Chicago Press.

———. 1990. The Invariance Hypothesis: Is Abstract Reason Based on Image-Schemas? *Cognitive Linguistics* 1:39–74.

———. 1996. Sorry, I'm Not Myself Today: The Metaphor System for Conceptualizing the Self. In Gilles Fauconnier and Eve Sweetser (eds.), *Spaces, Worlds, and Grammar*, 91–123. Chicago: University of Chicago Press.

Lakoff, George, and Mark Johnson. 1980. *Metaphors We Live By*. Chicago: University of Chicago Press.

———. 1999. *Philosophy in the Flesh: The Embodied Mind and Its Challenge to Western Thought*. New York: Basic Books.

Lakoff, George, and Rafael E. Núñez. 2000. *Where Mathematics Comes From: How the Embodied Mind Brings Mathematics into Being*. New York: Basic Books.

Lakoff, George, and Mark Turner. 1989. *More Than Cool Reason: A Field Guide to Poetic Metaphor*. Chicago: University of Chicago Press.

Lambrecht, Knud. 1994. *Information Structure and Sentence Form: Topic, Focus, and the Mental Representations of Discourse Referents*. Cambridge Studies in Linguistics 71. Cambridge: Cambridge University Press.

Langacker, Ronald W. 1968. *Language and Its Structure: Some Fundamental Linguistic Concepts*. New York: Harcourt, Brace and World.

———. 1987. *Foundations of Cognitive Grammar*, vol. 1: *Theoretical Prerequisites*. Stanford: Stanford University Press. [cited as FCG1]

———. 1990. *Concept, Image, and Symbol: The Cognitive Basis of Grammar*. Cognitive Linguistics Research 1. Berlin: Mouton de Gruyter. [cited as CIS]

———. 1991. *Foundations of Cognitive Grammar*, vol. 2: *Descriptive Application*. Stanford: Stanford University Press. [cited as FCG2]

———. 1999a. *Grammar and Conceptualization*. Cognitive Linguistics Research 14. Berlin: Mouton de Gruyter. [cited as GC]

———. 1999b. Assessing the Cognitive Linguistic Enterprise. In Theo Janssen and Gisela Redeker (eds.), *Cognitive Linguistics: Foundations, Scope, and Methodology*, 13–59. Cognitive Linguistics Research 15. Berlin: Mouton de Gruyter.

———. 2001a. The English Present Tense. *English Language and Linguistics* 5:251–271.

———. 2001b. Discourse in Cognitive Grammar. *Cognitive Linguistics* 12:143–188.

———. 2005. Construction Grammars: Cognitive, Radical, and Less So. In Francisco J. Ruiz de Mendoza Ibáñez and M. Sandra Peña Cervel (eds.), *Cognitive Linguistics: Internal Dynamics and Interdisciplinary Interaction*, 101–159. Cognitive Linguistics Research 32. Berlin: Mouton de Gruyter.

———. 2006. On the Continuous Debate about Discreteness. *Cognitive Linguistics* 17:107–151.

———. 2008. *Cognitive Grammar: A Basic Introduction*. New York: Oxford University Press. [CGBI]

———. 2009. *Investigations in Cognitive Grammar*. Cognitive Linguistics Research 42. Berlin: Mouton de Gruyter. [cited as ICG]

Levinson, Stephen C. 1997. From Outer to Inner Space: Linguistic Categories and Non-Linguistic Thinking. In Jan Nuyts and Eric Pederson (eds.), *Language and Conceptualization*, 13–45. Language, Culture and Cognition 1. Cambridge: Cambridge University Press.

MacWhinney, Brian. 1987. The Competition Model. In Brian MacWhinney (ed.), *Mechanisms of Language Acquisition*, 249–308. Hillsdale, N.J.: Erlbaum.

Newmeyer, Frederick J. 1983. *Grammatical Theory: Its Limits and Its Possibilities*. Chicago: University of Chicago Press.

Palmer, F. R. 1981. *Semantics*. 2nd ed. Cambridge: Cambridge University Press.

Reddy, Michael J. 1979. The Conduit Metaphor: A Case of Frame Conflict in Our Language about Language. In Andrew Ortony (ed.), *Metaphor and Thought*, 284–324. Cambridge: Cambridge University Press.

Regier, Terry. 1996. *The Human Semantic Potential: Spatial Language and Constrained Connectionism*. Cambridge, Mass.: MIT Press, and London: Bradford.

Riemer, Nick. 2005. *The Semantics of Polysemy: Reading Meaning in English and Warlpiri*. Cognitive Linguistics Research 30. Berlin: Mouton de Gruyter.

Rosch, Eleanor. 1978. Principles of Categorization. In Eleanor Rosch and Barbara B. Lloyd (eds.), *Cognition and Categorization*, 27–47. Hillsdale, N.J.: Erlbaum.

Ruhl, Charles. 1989. *On Monosemy: A Study in Linguistic Semantics*. Albany: State University of New York Press.

Sadock, Jerrold M. 1974. Read at Your Own Risk: Syntactic and Semantic Horrors You Can Find in Your Medicine Chest. *Papers from the Regional Meeting of the Chicago Linguistic Society* 10:599–607.

Searle, John R. 1969. *Speech Acts: An Essay in the Philosophy of Language*. London: Cambridge University Press.

Sethuraman, Nitya. 2002. The Acquisition of Verbs and Argument Structure Constructions. Ph.D. dissertation, University of California, San Diego.

Sweetser, Eve. 1999. Compositionality and Blending: Semantic Composition in a Cognitively Realistic Framework. In Theo Janssen and Gisela Redeker (eds.), *Cognitive Linguistics: Foundations, Scope, and Methodology*, 129–162. Cognitive Linguistics Research 15. Berlin: Mouton de Gruyter.

Talmy, Leonard. 1988. Force Dynamics in Language and Cognition. *Cognitive Science* 12:49–100.

———. 1991. Path to Realization: A Typology of Event Conflation. *Proceedings of the Annual Meeting of the Berkeley Linguistics Society* 17:480–519.

———. 1996. Fictive Motion in Language and "Ception." In Paul Bloom, Mary A. Peterson, Lynn Nadel, and Merrill F. Garrett (eds.), *Language and Space*, 211–276. Cambridge, Mass.: MIT Press, and London: Bradford.

———. 2000a. *Toward a Cognitive Semantics*, vol. 1: *Concept Structuring Systems*. Cambridge, Mass.: MIT Press, and London: Bradford.

———. 2000b. *Toward a Cognitive Semantics*, vol. 2: *Typology and Process in Concept Structuring*. Cambridge, Mass.: MIT Press.

Taylor, John R. 2004. *Linguistic Categorization: Prototypes in Linguistic Theory*. 3rd ed. Oxford: Oxford University Press/Clarendon.

Tomasello, Michael. 1992. *First Verbs: A Case Study of Early Grammatical Development*. Cambridge: Cambridge University Press.

———. 2003. *Constructing a Language: A Usage-Based Theory of Language Acquisition*. Cambridge, Mass.: Harvard University Press.

Traugott, Elizabeth. 1982. From Propositional to Textual and Expressive Meanings: Some Semantic-Pragmatic Aspects of Grammaticalization. In Winfred P. Lehmann and Yakov Malkiel (eds.), *Perspectives on Historical Linguistics*, 245–271. Amsterdam: John Benjamins.

———. 1988. Pragmatic Strengthening and Grammaticalization. *Proceedings of the Annual Meeting of the Berkeley Linguistics Society* 14:406–416.

Tuggy, David. 1993. Ambiguity, Polysemy, and Vagueness. *Cognitive Linguistics* 4:273–290.

———. 2003a. The Nawatl Verb *kīsa*: A Case Study in Polysemy. In Hubert Cuyckens, René Dirven, and John R. Taylor (eds.), *Cognitive Approaches to Lexical Semantics*, 323–362. Cognitive Linguistics Research 23. Berlin: Mouton de Gruyter.

———. 2003b. *Abrelatas* and *Scarecrow* Nouns: Exocentric Verb-Noun Compounds as Illustrations of Basic Principles of Cognitive Grammar. *International Journal of English Studies* 3(2):25–61.

Turner, Mark. 1987. *Death Is the Mother of Beauty: Mind, Metaphor, Criticism*. Chicago: University of Chicago Press.

Tyler, Andrea, and Vyvyan Evans. 2003. *The Semantics of English Prepositions: Spatial Scenes, Embodied Meaning and Cognition*. Cambridge: Cambridge University Press.

Vandeloise, Claude. 1991. *Spatial Prepositions: A Case Study from French*. Chicago: University of Chicago Press.

van Hoek, Karen. 1997. *Anaphora and Conceptual Structure*. Chicago: University of Chicago Press.

Vendler, Zeno. 1967. *Linguistics in Philosophy*. Ithaca, N.Y.: Cornell University Press.

Verhagen, Arie. 2005. *Constructions of Intersubjectivity: Discourse, Syntax, and Cognition*. Oxford: Oxford University Press.

Wierzbicka, Anna. 1985. Oats and Wheat: The Fallacy of Arbitrariness. In John Haiman (ed.), *Iconicity in Syntax*, 311–342. Amsterdam: John Benjamins.

———. 1988. *The Semantics of Grammar*. Studies in Language Companion Series 18. Amsterdam: John Benjamins.

———. 1995. Dictionaries vs. Encyclopaedias: How to Draw the Line. In Philip W. Davis (ed.), *Alternative Linguistics: Descriptive and Theoretical Modes*, 289–315. Current Issues in Linguistic Theory 102. Amsterdam: John Benjamins.

———. 1996. *Semantics: Primes and Universals*. Oxford: Oxford University Press.

INDEX